THE

PUNJAB ORIENTAL (SANSKRIT) SERIES

NO. XVI.

THE

Punjab Oriental (Sanskrit) Series

OR

A COLLECTION OF RARE & UNPUBLISHED

BOOKS RELATING TO ANCIENT INDIA

EDITED BY

THE WELL-KNOWN & EMINENT SCHOLARS

OF

INDIA, EUROPE and AMERICA

No. 16.

LAHORE (INDIA)

THE PUNJAB SANSKRIT BOOK DEPOT

1927.

ANCIENT INDIAN COLONIES
in the
FAR EAST.
Vol. I.
CHAMPA.

BY

Dr. R. C. Majumdar M. A., Ph. D.

Professor, Dacca University. Member of the Academic Council Greater India Society. Author of "Corporate Life in Ancient India," "Outline of Ancient Indian History and Civilisation," "Gurjara-Pratihāras," "Early History of Bengal,', etc. etc. Premchand Roychand Scholar, Griffith Prizeman, Mouat Gold Medallist etc. etc.

Greater India Society Publication.

No. I.

बृहत्तर-भारत-परिषद् ग्रंथावली ।

प्रथमः ग्रंथः ।

PUBLISHED BY

The Punjab Sanskrit Book Depot.

LAHORE.

1927.

To

The French Savants

whose labours have opened

a new and glorious chapter

Of the

ancient history and civilisation of India

this volume is dedicated

in token of

respect, admiration and gratitude

of the

author.

ABBREVIATIONS.

B. E. F.—Bulletin De L' Ecole Francaise D' Extreme-Orient.

Corpus—Collection of Sanskrit Inscriptions of Champā by A. Bergaigne published as "Notices Et Extraits des Manuscripts de la Bibliotheque Nationale etc. Tome Vingt-Septieme (1-er partie 2-e Fascicule)

J. A.—Journal Asiatiqe.

J. A. S. B. (N. S.).—Journal of the Asiatic Society of Bengal (New series)

Parm.—Parmentier.

Parm. I. C.—Inventaire Descriptif des Monuments Cams de L' Annam Par. H. Parmentier.

TRANSLITERATION.

The system followed in the Journal of the Royal Asiatic Society of Great Britain and Ireland has been adopted in this volume, with the exception, that the name of the kingdom has been written as "Champā" instead of "Campā"

As the press does not contain accents types for the notes, the notes are printed without them. Some diacritical signs for writing French words are also wanting in the press.

Table of Contents.

BOOK I.

BOOK II

Preface.

The story of Greater India is bound to be of absorbing interest, not only to every student of history, but also to all educated people in this country. The Indian colonies in the Far East must ever remain as the high-water mark of maritime and colonial enterprise of the ancient Indians. But although an extensive literature in French has grown up on this subject, hardly anything has yet been written in English. This alone accounts for the comparative apathy and ignorance in this matter which is generally noticed in this country.

No apology is therefore needed for bringing out this volume dealing with one of the many colonial kingdoms which the Indians had established in the Far East. It is intended to be the first of a series of volumes dealing with the whole subject. But when, if at all, the other volumes will see the light of day is more than I can tell. The present volume was taken in hand more than four years ago, but a variety of difficulties—the space of 1300 miles between the author and the printing press being by no means the least of them—have considerably delayed its publication. As at present planned, the second volume, dealing with Cambodge, will be published before the end of 1929, and the remaining two or three volumes, dealing with Siam, Sumatra, Java, Bali and other colonial kingdoms will not probably be delayed beyond 1931.

Champā has been selected as the subject of the first volume, partly because it is the remotest colony in the East, and partly because it is less known than Cambodge and Java on which general attention has been focussed on account of the famous monuments of Angkor Vat and Boro-budur.

The authorities on which this volume is based have been fully discussed in the Introduction. I have derived the greatest help from Maspero's "Le Royaume du Champā". This book must always remain the chief source and constant guide to anyone who tries to write a history of Champā. But the discovery of a number of new inscriptions since the publication of that book has made it obsolete and incomplete in many places. While, therefore, Maspero's work has been accepted as the chief guide, considerable deviations from it will be noticed in the present volume.

Besides, Maspero deals mainly with the political history of Champā, though in the early portion of his book he has given a brief resume of religion, administrative system, social and economic conditions, and art and architecture of Champā. An attempt has been made in the present volume to discuss all these branches of history and civilisation of Champā as adequately as is possible under the present conditions.

Similarly, Parmentier's monumental work on the art and architecture of Champā has been my chief guide in writing Chapter X of Book II. But while I have taken the data from that book, I have interpreted them in my own way, and ventured to express a different opinion on the all-important question of the origin of Cham art.

I take this opportunity of expressing my deep obligations to the authorities of "Ecole Francaise D' Extreme-Orient" for kind permission to reproduce illustrations contained in this volume.

A special feature of this volume is the collection of inscriptions discovered in Champā. Although all these inscriptions have been separately published before, this is the first complete collection of all the known inscriptions, arranged in chronological order. Although I have accepted the published readings, I have made an independent translation of all the inscriptions and have not as a rule referred to the old French renderings save in a very few instances. I am indebted to my friends and colleagues Dr. S. K. De and Pandit Nanigopal Banerji, for some valuable suggestions in this matter.

No one is more conscious than I myself of the serious shortcomings of the work. My imperfect acquaintance with Sanskrit and French has made the task of writing this volume a painful and laborious one, and I dare not hope that I have been able to avoid serious mistakes and errors. But I do hope that my indulgent readers will look kindly on this pioneer work. If this humble production arouses a general interest in this country towards this fascinating field of study, and induces others, better equipped for the task, to take up the work, I shall consider my labours amply rewarded.

RAMNA, DACCA.
3rd March, 1927.

R. C. Majumdar.

INTRODUCTION.

Although the study of Ancient Indian history has made a great deal of progress in recent years, there is one aspect of the subject which has not yet received the attention it deserves. This is the expansion of the Aryans beyond Indian frontiers towards the east and south-east. The history of Indo-Aryans usually begins with their settlement in the Punjab and ends with their expansion over the whole of India as far as Assam in the east and cape Comorin in the south. This is, however, an arbitrary line of distinction for which there does not seem to be any great justification. For the Aryans never regarded the hills or the sea by which India proper is bounded as the natural limits of their advance, and they boldly crossed over these to new regions on the other side. Their achievements in these regions are but vaguely known, but the more one thinks on this subject the more is one forced to realise that the Indianisation of these countries was probably as complete in the ancient period as we find in the Dravidian countries within the frontier of India. The study of Indian civilisation must therefore be regarded as imperfect so long as we do not take into proper account the achievements of Indians in these regions.

Until recently, however, our knowledge of this subject was limited in the extreme. Indian literature, no doubt, clearly shows that there was an intimate intercourse between India and the Far East[1] in ancient times, but it does not tell us much

---

1. Among important passages bearing upon this subject the following may be mentioned as specimens.

   (A) A passage in Ramayana referring to Yavadvipa and Suvarnadvipa, meaning the islands of Sumatra and Java.

   (B) The well-known passage in Mahavamsa referring to

regarding the activity of Indian colonists settled there. The writings of Ptolemy and Fa-Hien, also, while bearing ample testimony to the firm hold of Indian civilisation in those countries, have not preserved any detailed account of the colonial history of India. Such an account has been rendered possible only in comparatively recent times, when the colonies themselves have been made to yield up their rich antiquarian treasures, thanks to the untiring efforts of the savants of France.

The first serious attempt to study the geography, history and civilisation of the Far East was made by Christian missionaries of Europe as far back as the early seventeenth century. The most memorable scholarly work of this period was the "Dictionnaire annamite-latin-portugais" by P. Alexandre de Rhodes, published in 1651. This monumental work has served as the basis of all future research and placed it on a secure foundation. The same author published in the following year a history of Tonkin in Latin. Similar works continued to appear from time to time but it was not till two centuries later that a beginning was made of an archaeological investigation in Indo-China. In 1858 Henri Mouhot explored the valley of the Mekhong as far as the country of Laos between Korat and Luang-prabang. Although a naturalist, Mouhot was attracted by the beauties of Angkor Vat and other monuments of antiquity and his rapturous description made them known for the first time to the outside world.

---

the conquest of Ceylon by prince Vijaya.

(C) The following sentence in Milindapanha (English Translation II 269).

"As a shipowner......will be...able to traverse the high seas and go to Vanga or Takkola, or China, or Sovira, or Surat or Alexandria or the Koromandel coast or Further India........."

The enthusiasm thus created resulted in an well-organised mission of exploration in 1885 under Doudart de Lagree, an eminent archaeologist. The mission included such ardent workers as Francis Garnier and Delaporte. This mission recognised for the first time the importance of inscriptions and copied some of them.

The work of this mission was continued by individual scholars like Garnier, Delaporte and Dr. Harmand. Then came Aymonier, who began in 1882 his memorable exploration of Cambodge, Laos and Annam. and collected a vast store of materials for the history of these countries. The last important mission was that of M. Pavie, with 40 collaborators, which worked for 15 years from 1879 to 1895. One of the notable results of this mission was the preparation of a reliable map of Indo-China.

After a general knowledge of Indo-China had thus been secured, the task of special studies was taken up by special Departments. There originated in this way special Departments for the study of geography, geology and natural history of the country. The historical studies devolved upon a permanent archaeological society which soon took the name of 'Ecole Francaise d Extreme Orient'. With the foundation of this society in 1898 the historical studies and archaeological explorations have been placed on a firm foundation, and the results of these studies, regularly published in the form of Bulletins, have made accessible to the outside world a vast store of information on the history and civilisation of Indo-China.

From this very rapid and brief survey of the scholarly work in Indo-China we may now turn to a more detailed reference to the important and authoritative works with regard to the history of the ancient kingdom of Champā on which the present volume is based.

The chief sources of information regarding the history and civilisation of ancient Champā may be classified under three heads.

I Inscriptions.

II Monuments.

III Chinese texts and other foreign sources.

I. INSCRIPTIONS.[1]

The first important collection of Sanskrit inscriptions of Champā was prepared by Abel Bergaigne in 1888, and published, after his death, by Barth in 1893.[2] A large number of inscriptions written in Cham were edited by M. Aymonier in J. A. 1891 (pp 5 ff.). Since the foundation of the Ecole Francaise de Extreme Orient, a large number of new inscriptions have been published in its Bulletins, the most important being:—

(1). (A) Myson, (B) Pāṇḍuraṅga and (C) Quang Nam Inscriptions by L. Finot.

(A) B. E. F., Vol. II, pp. 185 ff; Vol. III, 206 ff; Vol. IV, pp. 917 ff.

(B) Vol. III pp. 630 ff.

(C) Vol. IV. pp. 83 ff.

(2). A collection of miscellaneous inscriptions by M. Huber (B. E. F. Vol. XI, pp. 5 ff, pp. 260 ff) and L. Finot (B. E. F. Vol. IX, pp. 205 ff; Vol. XV. No. 2 pp. 1 ff.).

1. For a detailed bibliography of the epigraphic studies in Indo-China—cf. B. E. F. Vol. XV. No. 2—pp 113 ff ; also Toung Pao 1910, pp. 126 ff.

2. Notices et Extraits des Manuscripts de la Bibliotheque Nationale et autres Bibliotheques publie par L' Institut national de France.—Tome Vingt—Septieme (1-er Partie), 2-e fascicule. Paris 1893.

Mention must be made in this connection to the very valuable list of inscriptions prepared by M. George Coedes (B. E. F. Vol VIII pp. 40 ff; Vol. XV. No. 2 pp. 173 ff).

All the inscriptions of Champā hitherto known[1] have been collected at the end of this volume, with full bibliographical notes, and hence it is not necessary to dwell on this topic any further.

II. As regards the study of archaeological monuments all previous works on this subject have been superseded by the monumental work of M. Parmentier, viz. Inventaire Descriptif des Monuments Cams vols. I and II.[2] In this book M. Parmentier has made a systematic study of all the existing monuments in Champā and fully illustrated them by pictures and plates. The descriptive catalogue of sculptures in the Touranne Museum (B. E. F. Vol. XIX. No. 3, pp. 1-114) and the archaeological notes (B. E. F. Vol. XXIII, pp 267 ff) published by the same author, may be regarded as supplements to this famous work. Reference may also be made in this connection to Ars Asiatica Vol. IV which contains a set of good illustrations of sculptures.

III. As to the Chinese texts bearing upon the history of Champā, they were first discussed by P. Gaubil[3] and Deguignes[4].

---

1. A few inscriptions have been excluded, e.g. those which are very modern and fall beyond the scope of this study, those which are too fragmentary to yield any sense and those which have been casually referred to, but the text or even a purport of which has not been pu ished.
2. Vol. I. appeared in 1909 and volume II in 1918. Both these are publications of Ecole Francaise d' Extreme orient.
3. Gaubil's 'Notice historique sur la Cochinchine' was originally published in the 18th century and later on included in "L' Histoire generale de la Chine" by P de Mailla.
4. "L' Histoire generale des Huns" Tome I, 1-er partie p. 172-173.

The more important workers in this line are Pelliot, Maspero and L. Aurousseau. Pelliot collected valuable data in his learned article "Deux Itineraires de Chine en Inde[1]" and drew up a list of Cham kings mentioned in Chinese sources.[2] Maspero made for the first time an elaborate and systematic study of all the Chinese texts bearing upon the history of Champā.[3] Last of all L. Aurousseau has considerably extended our knowledge by his learned contributions on this subject.[4]

Some valuable informations on the history of Champā are furnished by Annamite documents. In this field, again, Maspero has collected very valuable data although he was preceded by a number of writers on this subject.[5]

References to Champā are also contained in Cambodge inscriptions. Bibliographical references to them will be found in the body of the text.

---

1. B. E. F. Vol. IV. pp. 131-413.
2. Ibid pp. 382 ff.
3. The data he collected were utilised in his History of Champa (see f. n. 2 p. 7 below).
4. B. E. F. Vol. XIV. No. 9. pp. 8-43 ; Vol. XXIII pp 137-264.
5. (1) Bouillevaux—L' Annam et le Cambodge—.
   (2) Bouillevaux—Le Ciampa (Annales de Extreme Orient 1880, 1881).
   (3) P. J. B. Trn'ong Vinh Ky–Cours d Histoire Annamite; 2 vols. Saigon 1875
   (4) E. Luro–Le Pays d' Annam ; Paris 1878.
   (5) L Abbe Adr. Launay. Histoire Ancienne et Moderne de l' Annam etc. (Paris 1884).
   (6) Abel des Michels–Les Annales Imperiales de l' Annam; Paris 1889.
   (7) Camille Sainson–Memoires sur l' Annam. Peking 1896.
   (8) Legrand de la Liraye–Notices Historiques sur la Nation Annamite, Saigon, 1866.

So far about the original sources of information, and we may now turn to the modern texts dealing with the history of Champā. As early as 1888 Bergaigne published a short account of the political history of Champā, mainly on the basis of Inscriptions.[1] Five years later Aymonier read his "History of Tchampā" before the Ninth International Congress of Orientalistes held in London. Both these were superseded by the monumental work of Maspero— "Le Royaume de Champā"[2] which must remain as the standard authority on this subject for sometime to come.

Some contributions on the study of religion, manners and customs of Champā may be mentioned in this connection. The earliest publication on this subject seems to be an article by Aymonier.[3] Finot also contributed an important article on this subject.[4] A very short account of the political, social and religious history of Champā as well as a brief review of Cham art are contained in Jeanne Leuba's "Les Chams et leur art" Paris (1923) which reached my hands after the present volume had been sent to the Press. The chief interest of this book as well as of Antoine Cabaton's "Nouvelles Recherches Sur les Chams (Paris, 1901)" and Aymonier's article referred to above, seems to lie in the light which they throw on the social customs and religious practices of the modern Chams.

By a proper utilisation of all these sources, both primary and secondary, I have tried to build up a picture of the ancient

1. L' ancient royaume de Champa dans l' Indo-Chine d' apres les inscriptions—J. A. 1888 [pp. 64-70].

2. This was originally published in T'oung Pao [1910-1913] and later on as a separate book at Leyden in 1914.

3. "Les Tchames et leurs religious" in "Revue de l' histoire des religions, 1891."

4. La Religion des Chams d' apres les monuments etc. B. E. F. Vol. I, p 12.

history and civilisation of Champā, *one of the* many kingdoms founded by the Hindus in that far-off region. I propose to write the history of the other colonial kingdoms as well, in order to complete the story of Greater India. But as these might yet take a long time, I propose to discuss here very briefly two important questions of a general nature which affect the study of Indian colonisation in the Far East. These are: (I) the part or parts of India from which Indian colonists proceeded to the Far East and the route which they followed; and (II) an approximate idea of the time when these colonial enterprises were first undertaken.

I. As to the routes, the Aryans seem to have proceeded both by land and sea. Regarding the sea-route, there seems to have been emigration both from eastern as well as the western coast. From a very early period there was a regular trade intercourse between the coast of Bengal and the Far East. In the Mahājanaka Jātaka reference is made to voyages between Champā and Suvaṇṇabhūmi. Similarly passengers from distant inland cities like Patna and Benares travelled to the coast of Bengal by land or by water, and then sailed in open sea for eastern islands, Tāmralipti (modern Tamluk) being the most important sea-port.[1]

There was a similar trade-route between the Kalinga-coast and the Far East. This is referred to by Ptolemy. The ships started from Gopalpur, just a little below the mouth of the Ganjam river, and crossed the Bay of Bengal.[2]

We learn from the Periplus that there was another trade-route from three harbours on the Eastern coast near Masulipatam across the Bay of Bengal to the Eastern Peninsula.[3]

1. Cf. Mahajanaka Jataka, No. 5319, VI, 30 ff. Samudda-Vanija Jataka, No. 466. IV, 158 ff. Buddhaghosa's Introduction to Samanta-Pasadika, Vinaya Texts, Vol. III p. 3388.
2. Gerini–Researches on Ptolemy's Geography. p. 743.
3. Schoff's edition, p. 46.

We learn from the Sussondī-Jātaka that there was also a trade-route from Broach along the western coast to the Eastern Peninsula.[1]

The existence of ancient trade-routes between the eastern islands and the coasts of Bengal, Orissa, Madras and Gujarat, is thus established on good authority. It is interesting to find that it is precisely in these directions that the ancient traditions of Indian colonists in the Far East and South-East lead us to look for their original homes. To mention briefly only a few of the many traditions, there is first the story of a Bengali prince Vijaya,[2] colonising the island of Ceylon. Secondly the foundation of Ligor is ascribed by tradition to a descendant of Aśoka who fled from Magadha, embarked a vessel at Dantapura and was wrecked on the coast of the Malaya Peninsula.[3] There is also the story preserved in the chronicles of Java, that the Hindus from Kaliṅga-coast colonised the island. Similar traditions of colonists from Kling or Kaliṅga country are preserved in many other islands. Thirdly, according to traditions current among the people of Pegu, Indian colonists from the country of the lower courses of the rivers Krishna and Godavari had, at a remote time, crossed the sea, and formed settlements in the delta of the Irawadi and on the adjoining coast.[4] Lastly there is the story preserved in the chronicles of Java that the island was first colonised by a Gujarāt prince who landed there in 75 A. D.

---

1. Jataka III, 187 ff.
2. The authenticity of this story has been doubted but cf. Mr. R. Chanda in Sir Asutosh Mukherji's Silver Jubilee Volumes, Vol. III, p. 113. Also cf. J. A. S. B., 1922, p. 435.
3. Gerini, op. cit, p. 107-8. Dantapura has been identified with modern Dantan on the Kasai [Cunningham's Geography-Ed. S. N. Majumdar p. 735].
4. Phayre–History of Burma, p. 24.

The exact correspondence of colonial traditions with the evidence derived from Indian source leads to the hypothesis that generally the Indian colonists proceeding by sea to the East and South, started from the four centres mentioned above, viz Tāmralipti in the coast of Bengal, Gapālpur and ancient Kalinga, the three unidentified harbours near Masulipatam, and Broach.

In addition to the sea-route described above the Indian colonists also proceeded to the East and South-East by land-route through Eastern Bengal, Manipur and Assam. This fact, although noted long ago, has never been clearly recognised. Sir Arthur Phayre observed as early as 1883 that 'the traditions of the Burmese and the present remains and names of ancient cities, render it probable that early communication between Gangetic India and Tagaung existed, and was carried on through Eastern Bengal and Manipur, rather than through Thahtun or Pegu generally.[1] This view has received additional confirmation by the researches of Pelliot and Gerini.

Pelliot has shown[2] that from early times, at least as early as the second century B. C., there was a regular trade-route by land between Eastern India and China through Upper Burma and Yunnan. Through this route came the twenty Chinese Buddhist monks for whom Śrī Gupta built a temple, as I-tsing informs us. Later, the route was obstructed by barbarous tribes but it was re-opened again in the eighth century A. D.

Through this route the Indians came and established their colonies not only in Upper Burma but also in the mountain-

---

1. Ibid, p 15.
2. Bulletin de l' Ecole Francaise d' Extreme Orient 1904, p. 142 ff.

ous regions of the upper valleys of the Irawaddy, the Salween, the Mekong and the Red River as far as Yunnan. It is a well-known practice for colonists to name the new country after famous places in their mother land. We get a number of instances in Burma and Indo-China too well known to be repeated here. But the same spirit is also observable in the north-western regions. Yunnan was called Gāndhāra, and even as late as the 13th century A. D. Rasiduddin referred to this province by its Indian name. It may be observed that Yunnan, roughly speaking, occupied the same position in respect of Indo-China as Gāndhāra did in respect of India.

The Hindus established in Yunnan the kingdom of Nan-Chao or Tali in the upper valleys of the Mekong and the Red-River. According to local traditions, the third son of king Aśoka had nine grandsons who became the progenitors not only of the people of Nan-chao, but also of the Tibetans, the Chinese, the Annamites, the Singhalese etc. Whatever we may think of this story there cannot be any doubt about a strong Indian element in the population. Rasiduddin, writting as late as the 13th century, has remarked that the population of Yunnan originated from the Indian and the Chinese. Pelliot, too, has brought together a number of facts bearing upon the question of Hindu influence in the country. The king had the title Mahārāja and the people probably used an alphabet of Hindu origin. It was a great centre of Buddhism. According to local traditions, Avalokiteśvara came directly from Central India to convert it. There is a tradition that towards the close of the 8th century A. D. when the king of the country was inclined towards the Chinese civilisation he was abused by seven religious person of India. Buddhism had a strong hold in this region and we find the Pippala cave, the Bodhi tree, the Gṛdhrakūṭa, the Kukkuṭapādagiri, the stone mansion of Upagupta and the stūpa containing the relics of Ānanda— all appearing again in the neighbourhood of Nan-Chao. In the first half of the 9th century A. D. a Hindu Bhikṣu of Magadha named Chandragupta led a brilliant career of Thaumaturgist in Yunnan.

There were two other Hindu kingdoms between Nan-Chao and the Indian frontier. To the east of the mountain ranges that border Manipur and Assam there was the Brāhmaṇa kingdom of Ta-tsin. About 150 miles further east, beyond the Chindwin river, was another Brāhmaṇa kingdom just to the north of the town of Ngan-si. Thus we find Hindu settlements all along the hilly tracts between the frontiers of India and China, in the upper valleys of the Chindween, Irawaddy, Salween, Mekong and Red Rivers. That the Indians proceeded towards the south along these rivers is also fairly certain. The kingdoms they established in Burma at Prome, Tagaung, Lower Pugan and other places are too well-known to be described in detail. There are indications that similar Hindu kingdoms existed in the Laos country. It was formerly known as Mālava-*deśa*. Ptolemy refers to its eastern part (mod. Luang Phrah Bang) as Dasana, which, as Gerini thinks, is probably derived from the Indian name Daśārṇa. Gerini suggests that as the original Daśārṇa in India denoted the eastern part of Mālava, it was, by analogy, given in Further India to the corresponding portion of the Indo-Chinese Mālava i. e. Eastern Laos. Gerini has traced the Indian origin of many other place-names in Indo-China and has collected many traditions about the Indian colonists associated with those places. He has summed up his observations in the following sentence:—

"From the Brahmaputra and Manipur to the Tonkin gulf we can trace a continuous string of petty states ruled by those scions of the Kṣatriya race, using the Sanskrit or the

Pāli languages in official documents, after the Indū style and employing Brāhmaṇa priests for the propitiatory ceremonies connected with the Court and State. Among such Indū monarchies we may mention those of Tagong, upper Pugān, and Sen-wī, in Burma; of Muang Hāng, Chieng Rung Muang Khwān, and Daśārṇa (Luang Phrah Bang) in the Lāu country; and of Agranagara (Hanoi) and Champā in Tonkin and Annam."[1]

Although some of the conclusions of Gerini are based on mere philological grounds which are not always very reliable, the facts stated above make it quite clear that there were a good many Hindu kingdoms in the interior of Indo-China which was not easily accessible by sea, and which must therefore have been reached by the Indians through land-route. On the whole strong and conclusive evidence supports the hypothesis, advanced long ago by Sir Arthur Phayre and recently advocated by Gerini, *viz.* 'that a double stream of emigrants from India flowed into Indo-China at a very early period'—one, proceeding from the north advanced overland, through Bengal and Assam, along the valleys of the Chindween, Irawady, Salween and Mekong, while the other reached Indo-China by sea. The colonists who proceeded by sea established the famous kingdoms of Champā (mod. Annam) and Kāmboja (Cambodia) in addition to many other notable kingdoms in lower Burma, Malay Peninsula and the islands of Sumatra, Java, Borneo, Bali etc. Gerini and other scholars have held that only the Indians of the Malabar and Coromandel coasts colonised Indo-China by the sea-route. But there is nothing to support this view. As has been said above, Bengal undoubtedly played a great part in this colonisation through its well-frequented harbour Tāmralipti.

1 Gerini, op, Cit, pp. 122-123.

So far at least as the few historical evidences go, they prove a close association of Bengal with Indian colonies in south and east throughout the Hindu period.

Reference has already been made to the Buddhist stories about the voyage of merchants from Champā and Tāmralipti to Suvaṇṇabhūmi. We know from the Chinese records that the king of Fou-Nan (comprising Cambodia and Cochin-China) sent an ambassador to India about 240-245 A. D. and that the embassy reached the mouth of the Ganges at the end of a year. In the fifth century A. D. a king of Champā called Gaṅgārāja abdicated the throne and went over to India in order to spend his last days on the banks of the Ganges. It appears from the writings of Fa-Hien and I-Tsing that there was a regular maritime intercourse between the coast of Bengal and the Far East, including eastern Islands, between fifth and seventh centuries A. D. In the ninth century we find an intimate relation existing between the king of Sumatra-Java and Devapāla.[1] The Tibetan annals tell us that during Nayapāla's reign Buddhist Bhikkhus proceeded to Suvarṇa-dvīpa for education. In the thirteenth century A. D. we find a queen of Champā called Gauḍendralakṣmi (probably a princess of Gauḍa). All these evidences certainly show a far more intimate connection between Bengal and Indian colonies than has yet been recognised.

Further, most of the traditions preserved in the different colonies refer to their original home as situated in Northern India. It is true that the traditions have very little value as historical facts. But it is impossible to ignore altogether the general view-point of all these stories regarding the original home of the colonists and the methods of colonisation. Some of these stories are given below.

---

1. Nalanda copperplate of Devapala-Ep. Ind. Vol. XVII, p. 310.

According to Burmese tradition, a Śākya chief of Kapilāvastu came with an army to the country of the middle Irawaddy, long before Buddha was born. The dynasty he founded ruled for 31 generations in Burma when they were overthrown by an invasion of an eastern tribe coming apparently from China. About this time there came a second band of immigrant Kṣatriyas from Gangetic India. Their chief married the widowed queen of the last king of the previous dynasty and established a new kingdom. This was the origin of the ruling dynasty of Upper Burma.[1]

According to the traditions of Arakan the first king of the province was the son of a king of Benares who settled at Rāmāvatī a name which still exists in a corrupted form Rāmbyi or Ramri.[2] The Cambodian annals explain the origin of the kingdom of Cambodia in the following way:—

"Ādityavaṁśa, king of Indraprastha, was displeased with one of his sons and banished him from the state. He came to the country of Kok Thlok and made himself master of it by defeating the native king. One evening he was walking on a sand bank when suddenly the tide arose and obliged him to pass the night there. A Nāgi of marvellous beauty came to play on the sand and the king, overpowered by her charm, agreed to marry her. Then the Nāgarāja, the father of the betrothed girl, extended the dominions of his would be son-in-law by drinking the water which covered the country, built a capital for him and changed the name of the kingdom into that of Kāmboja."

The same tradition, in a changed form, occurs in an inscription of Champā dated 657 A. D. (No. 12). Speaking of the origin of Cambodge it says.

---

1. Phayre–History of Burma, pp. 7 ff.
2. Ibid p. 12.

"It was there that Kauṇḍinya, the foremost among Brāhmaṇas, planted the spear which he had obtained from Droṇa's son Aśvatthamā the best of Brāhmaṇas. Kauṇḍinya married the daughter of the Nāga king named Somā and from this union sprang up the royal race."

A still earlier version of the story, current as early as the first half of the third century A. D, occurs in a Chinese history compiled at the beginning of the sixth century. Referring to Fou-Nan, a kingdom comprising modern Cochin China, Cambodia and part of Siam and Laos, it says.

"Formerly the country was ruled by a queen called Lieou-ye. Then there was a man of the country of Ki called Houen-t'ien who saw in a dream that a spirit gave him a bow and asked him to take to sea in a junk. Houen-t'ien went in the morning to the temple of the Deity and found the bow at the foot of a tree. Then he got into a junk and sailed to Fou-Nan. The queen Lieou-ye saw the junk and collected her soldiers to resist him. But Houen t'ien raised his bow and shot from afar an arrow which passed through the side of a ship and struck somebody in the interior. Lieou-ye was struck with terror and submitted and Houen-t'ien married her."[1]

Now Houen-t'ien is an exact Chinese transcription of Kauṇḍinya and we know from another Chinese version of the story that he practised the Brāhmaṇic cult. This story is therefore the earliest of the different versions and it must be noticed that it is the most credible of them all. It explains, in a quite natural manner, the conquest of Fou-Nan by Indians by means of superior military power, and the social alliance between the new-comers and the old settlers. It may be added that the tradition of their origin was faithfully kept

1. Melanges Sylvain Levi, p. 203.

by the later kings who called themselves as "Śrī-Kauṇḍinya-Somaduhitṛprabhavāḥ" or as belonging to 'Soma-Kauṇḍinya Vaṁśa'. Somā, the female originator of the race, being the daughter of Soma, the dynasty was also called 'Soma-Vaṁśa.' No doubt this appellation was to a great extent inspired by the Indian tradition of the great Somavaṁśa. As a proof of this we find an attempt on the part of the rival Cambodian kings to trace their descent from Sūryavaṁśa. According to legend they were descended from Maharsi Kambu Svāyambhuva, belonging to solar race, and the Apsarā Merā. Thus Jayavarman II a king in the 9th century A. D. is called in his inscription "Śrī-Kambu-Bhūbhṛd-iṇa-vaṁśa-lalāma-goptā' or guardian of the best solar race of king Śrī-Kambu". Sūryavarman I of the eleventh century is called 'Sūryavaṁśajo' VIII and Jayavarman of the 12th century 'aṁśumāli-vaṁśodbhavo.' But this tradition about Sūryavaṁśa apparently had no strong hold on the people, for generally the kings of Cambodge adopted the tradition of Fou-Nan and called themselves descendants of Kauṇḍinya and Somā and as such belonging to Somavaṁśa[1]

II. The facts and legends quoted above unmistakably prove the Indian colonisation of the territories named at a very early date. If we now seek to find out more precisely the time when these colonies were established we find ourselves in great difficulty in the absence of any definite evidence. The utmost that we can do is to lay down a time limit before which these colonies were accomplished facts. Four different lines of evidence point out the first two centuries of the Christian era as this limit. In the first place, Ptolemy, writing about the middle of the second century A. D., has

1. Ibid pp. 205-212.

used quite a large number of geographical names of Sanskrit origin in Indo-China.

Secondly, when the Chams or the people of Annam appear in history towards the close of the second century of our era, they were already under a Hindu or Hinduised dynasty, and the inscription of Vo-chanh, written in correct Sanskrit about the second or third century A. D., shows them to have already thoroughly imbibed the Indian civilisation.

Now the royal author of the Vo-chanh inscription at Champā calls himself the descendant of Śrī **Māra**. On the other hand the Chinese refer to the foundation of the kingdom of Champā at 192 A. D. by one whose personal name was Lien and family name Kiu. It is probable that Śrī-Māra was the same person as Kiu-Lien, but whether this is true or not, we know of the definite establishment of a Hindu kingdom in Annam about second century A. D.[1]

Thirdly, the Chinese had intercourse with the Hindu kingdom of Fou-Nan in the first half of the third century A. D. At that time the throne was occupied by an usurper, and two kings had ruled before him for a period of 93 years. This takes us back to the first half of the second century A. D. as the date of the foundation of the royal dynasty.

Fourthly, an ambassador from one of the smaller Hindu kingdoms, Lang-ya-sieou (identified with Tenasserim), who visited the Chinese court in 515 A. D. is reported to have said that their kingdom was founded more than four hundred years ago.[2]

All these evidences agree in referring the beginnings of Indian colonial kingdoms to a period not later than the second century A. D.

1. See below pp. 18, 21.
2. Bulletin de l' Ecole Francaise d' Extreme Orient 1912, No. 8 pp. 3 ff.

But although this may be regarded as the lower limit of the date by which Indians had established kingdoms in these distant colonies, it should by no means be regarded as the upper limit also. The very fact that the easternmost part of these colonies, *viz.* Annam, came under the sway of the Indians not later than the second century A. D. would naturally push back by a few centuries the date of the beginnings of political activity of the Indian colonists in these regions. Further, colonisation, as distinguished from the establishment of political authority, would be pushed back still further.

About the time when the Indians gradually penetrated into Burma and countries further east these were settled by savage tribes. Those in Burma were Mongoloid in character, and akin to the present tribes of Abors and Mishmis. The people of Indo-China and of the islands of Sumatra, Java and Borneo were Malayo-Polynesian or Austro-nesian in character. "In native traditions the early inhabitants of the coast, specially near the mouth of the Salween river, are represented as savages, called in Burmese Bilu, the equivalent of Rākṣasa. They rejected all intercourse with civilised men and even Gautama himself who, it is fabled, came to the country was stoned and driven away by them.[1]" The Chinese also speak of the people of Annam in the same strain. 'They are' we are told 'so savage that they do not know cultivation and live by fishing and hunting alone. They are turbulent people who frequently rise in revolt, invade the Chinese official quarters, burn pillage and massacre wherever they go, and take refuge in their impenetrable forests whenever they are attacked by a strong army.'[2]

It was the mission of Indian colonists to bring this hete-

1. Phayre—History of Burma, p. 27.
2. T'oung Pao, 1910, p. 223.

rogeneous mass of barbarians within the pale of civilisation, a task which the Chinese, their next-door neighbours, had hitherto failed to accomplish.

As a matter of fact the political conquest of Further India and the adjacent islands was rapidly followed by a complete cultural conquest. The local people readily assimilated the new civilisation and adopted the religion, art, social manners and customs, alphabet, literature, laws and administrative system of the conquerors. This will be amply evident from the picture of civilisation in Champā contained in Book II of the present volume.

In short Indian civilisation made a thorough conquest of these lands and a new India was established in that far-off region. The Indian colonists even tried to complete the transformation by importing celebrated place-names of their motherland into their new home, and thus we find new towns and countries called Ayodhyā, Kauśāmbī, Śrīkṣetra, Dvārāvatī, Mathurā, Champā, Kaliṅga, Kāmboja and Gāndhāra springing up hundreds of miles away from their name-sakes.

The question naturally arises, what became of this splendid civilisation. The answer is not difficult. So long as the Hindu dynasties were in power the civilisation flourished. It is interesting to note that for nearly three centuries after India was conquered by the Muhammadans the banner of Hindu independence was hoisted up in those far-off lands. But like a fountain with a dried up spring these colonies decayed with the downfall of their motherland. Gradually the savage tribes from the north, like the Thais, the Laos and the Annamites, which were hitherto kept in check, overran these countries and destroyed the Hindu dynasties after they had gloriously ruled for nearly 1300 years. The result was very striking in the domain of art. As a distinguished writer has observed : 'For nearly thirteen hundred years the Indian colonists had persevered in adorning these far-off lands with edifices almost unrivalled elsewhere of their class. But at the end of that time, as happened in India, they disappear as if at the touch of a magician's wand.' The case of Java is a typical one. In the year 1479 the last Hindu dynasty was overthrown and Fergusson describes the sequel in the following words. "Then occurred what was, perhaps, the least expected event in all this strange eventful history. It is as if the masons had thrown away their tools and the chisels had dropped from the hands of the carvers. From that time forward no building was erected in Java and no image carved, that is worth even a passing notice."[1] What is true of art is also true of other elements of civilisation. From the 15th century onwards the barbarian tribes occupied Further India and destroyed the civilisation which their Hindu predecessors had built up with so much toil. But some vestiges of the old civilisation still remain to this day. The island of Bali still follows the Hindu religion and only a few years ago a great Hindu sacrifice was performed there with due pomp and ceremony. In Cambodian palace the sword of Indra is still guarded with veneration and brought out on occasions of royal consecration when a handful of Hindu priests, the last remnant of a dignified body, pour holy waters over the head of the king. The stories of Rāmāyaṇa and Mahābhārata still form the themes of their literary works and are regularly staged to the accompaniment of dances and songs. A handful of Brāhmaṇas still maintain a precarious existence in the Far East. But while all these serve as gratifying reminiscence of a glorious past, there is no longer any living connection between India and her forgotten colonial empire. Strange as it may seem, the descendants of men who founded that empire abandoned sea-voyage as something unholy and thus an impassable barrier was created between the Hindus and their brethren of the Far East. But whatever the modern Hindus might think of it, the historian now realises, that one of the most splendid, though yet unwritten, chapters of Indian history is the story of the growth of a new India in the Far East.

---

1. Fergusson–History of Indian and and Eastern Architecture Vol. II, p. 421.

BOOK I

THE POLITICAL HISTORY

Of

CHAMPĀ

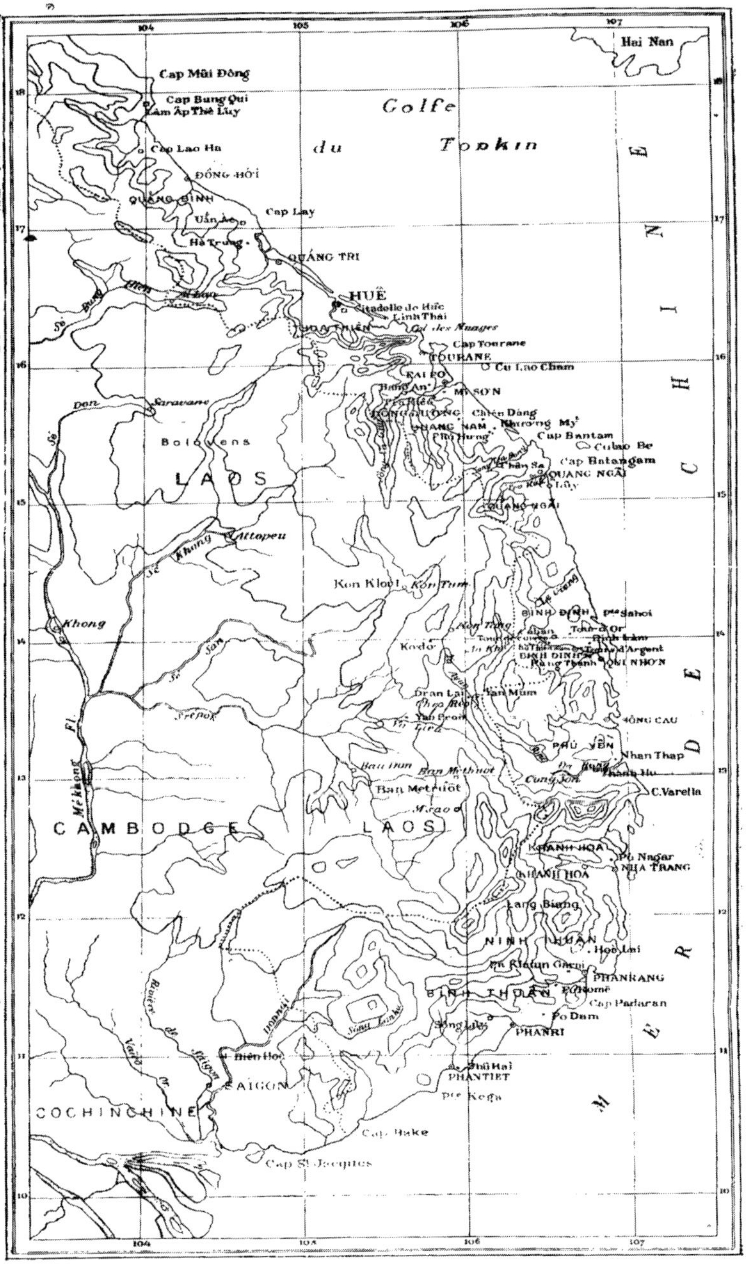

(Reproduced from the publications of Ecole Francaise D' Extreme Orient, Vol. XI, XII. Viz Inventaire descriptif des monuments Cams by H. Parmentier).

BLOCK BY THE CALCUTTA PHOTO ENGRAVING CO. 20, CORNWALLIS ST. CALCUTTA

Chapter I.

THE LAND.

§ 1. PHYSICAL FEATURES.

The ancient kingdom of Champā occupied the eastern portion of the Indo-Chinese peninsula, and roughly corresponded to the present province of Annam (excluding Tonkin and French Cochin China) with the exception of the three northern districts, Than Hoa, Nghe An and Ha Tinh. It was situated between 18° and 10° of N. Latitude. The almost uninhabited dunes which now separate Annam from French Cochin China formed its southern boundary. The eastern boundary was formed by the sea of China, while on the west a chain of hills shut it off from the valley of the Mekhong river.

This chain of hills, covered with rich forests, runs across the whole length of the country, gradually descending from north to south. Its height in the northern part is about 2750 yards, and in the southern part about 2200 yards. This mountain range has three passes which offer easy route across it to the valley of the Mekhong. Of these the southernmost one at Quinon alone seems to have been used for purposes of western expansion by the people of ancient Champā.

Champā was thus mainly a long narrow strip of territory confined between the mountains and the sea. The coast line was a bow-shaped curve, convex towards the sea. From Song Giang in Quang Binh, the northernmost district, the coast line runs due south-east up to cape Batangan. Thence it runs nearly south to Cape Padaran. From Cape Padaran it abruptly takes a south-western direction till it reaches the French Cochin China. The narrow habitable zone between the mountains and the sea varies in breadth and is intersected by innumerable spurs of hills running in various directions. Sometimes the spurs of hills extend as far as the sea coast, and the habitable zone is reduced to nothing; but nowhere does it exceed a breadth of sixty to seventy miles. A large number of rivers issuing from the mountains falls to the sea. The whole country is thus divided into a number of valleys separated by chains of hills.

In consequence of the rapid declivity of land towards the east, and the short course of these rivers, large quantities of sands and gravels are carried along with their swift currents. This has resulted in the formation of dunes and lagunes all along the coast line. These no doubt prevent the large ships from approaching near the coast, but serve as an excellent means of communication for small boats all along the coast-line. This was particularly valuable in ancient times, as journey by land was exceedingly difficult on account of the rugged mountains that traverse the country, and the savage inhabitants that lived in the interior.

The large number of river valleys in which the country abounded were rich in fertile lands, and consequently formed the centres of civilisation. But as these were practically unconnected by any land route, and could only communicate with one another by means of sea, it looks as though the whole kingdom consisted of a number of independent isolated settlements. That this was indeed the case to a very large extent is shown by the grouping of ancient monuments in different valleys without any connecting link between one another, and the constant tendency of the different parts of the kingdom to set up as independent states.

§ 2. NATURAL DIVISIONS OF THE LAND.

In view of what has just been said it is necessary to deal with the natural divisions of land in more details. The ancient kingdom of Champā may, from this point of view, be divided into five parts. Starting from the south, we may enumerate them as follows:—

I. The southernmost section comprises the district of Binh Thuan, between Cape Ba-ke, which separates Annam from French Cochin China, and Cape Padaran. The spurs of hills reach the sea at Cape Kega dominated by mount Ta-cu, about 550 yards high. The country, full of sands and dunes, is thinly peopled, the only exception being the three ports of Phantiet, Phanri and Duong, at the mouths of small rivers, and settlements in their immediate neighbourhood. The plain in the interior is now almost deserted but appears to have been rich and prosperous in the past.

II. The second section, extending from Cape Padaran to Cape Varella, comprises the district of Khan Hoa. It consists of three valleys easily accessible from one another. It is separated from the preceding section by hill ranges which abruptly descend to the sea, but the valley of Ca Na offers a passable route between the two.

The country is full of mountains but there are five valleys and bays. Three of these valleys are most important, those of Phanrang, immediately after Cape Padaran, Nha Trang, a little to the north, and lastly Ninh Hoa. Phanrang, the ancient *Panduranga* is still full of old monuments. Nha Trang, the ancient *Kauthara* was famous for the Temple of *Po Nagar* which contains a large number of inscriptions of ancient times.

III. The third section extends from Cape Varella to Sahoi Point. It contains two distinct mountain ranges with two valleys watered by the rivers Song Bā or Song Da Rang and Song Lai Giang, and the rich extensive plain of Binh Dinh between the two. Long chains of mountains separate this section from the preceding. There are only two routes, one across the peak of Da Bia (770 Yds high), and the other through an unhealthy marshy valley, both leading to the valley of Song Da Rang.

The plain of Binh Dinh is the most extensive in Annam and contains many ruins of ancient times. Not far from the present fort of Bin Dinh which was built in the 18th. century are to be found the ruins of the old fort of Caban—the old capital city of Vijaya, for a long time the capital of the ancient kingdom.

This section corresponds to the modern districts of Phu Yen and Binh Dinh.

IV. The fourth section comprises the modern districts of Quang Ngai and Quang Nam, extending from Point Sahoi to the spur of hill called 'Col des Nuages' (The cloudy Peak) on the coast. All along the coast line there are interminable dunes and equally interminable lagunes. Quang Ngai contains a rich plain watered by two rivers Song Tra Kuc and Song Tra Bong. The Song, the Great River, which takes various names, with a number of affluents water the plain of Quang Nam and fall in several channels to the sea forming a large but shallow estuary. The important port of Faifo on this estuary was once the principal port of the ancient kingdom of Champā. On one of the arms of this Great River is the Marble rock containing Buddhist caves.

The province contains innumerable vestiges of antiquity. It was the ancient kingdom of Amarāvatī. There are ruins of many famous towns of old, the most notable being Tra Kieu, the ancient Champā-nagarī, the capital of Champā, and Dong Duong, the ancient Indrapura. There are besides ruins of a group of fine temples at Myson which have yielded quite a large number of epigraphic records.

V. The fifth section extending from "Col des Nuages" to Hoan Sonh Mountains comprises the three districts of Thua Thien. Quang Tri and Quang Binh. The dunes and the lagunes along the sea-coast form its characteristic feature. Each of the three districts is watered by a large river. The river Song Gianh in Quang Binh is one of the largest in Annam, and a few miles further north is the Cape Bung Chua, the northernmost point of the ancient kingdom of Champā, the Hoan Sonh Mountains forming the frontier between it and the Annamite provinces to the north.

This region was thoroughly devastated by the long-drawn struggles between the Chams and the Annamites and by the systematic pillage of the latter when they conquered it. As a result only a few vestiges of antiquity remain on the ground. It contains the modern capital of the province viz., Hue, and near it the ruins of Kiu-Siou the old stronghold of Champā.[1]

§ 3. MODERN GEOGRAPHICAL DIVISIONS.

Annam is now divided into twelve districts. Starting from the north immediately south of Tonkin, these may be enumerated as follows :—

(1) Than Hoa
(2) Nghe An
(3) Ha Tinh
(4) Quang Binh
(5) Quang Tri
(6) Thua Thien (Quong Du'c)
(7) Quang Nam
(8) Quang Ngai
(9) Binh Dinh (Qui-nhom)
(10) Phu Yen
(11) Khan Hoa (Nha Trang)
(12) Binh Thuan

1. § 1 and § 2 are mainly based on "Inventaire Descriptif des Monuments Cams de l'Annam" by H. Parmentier, Vol. I Chapter I.

§ 4. THE CLIMATE AND POPULATION.

The climate varies according to Latitude and altitude, the heat ranging between 50° and 100° F. There are only two seasons, Summer and Monsoon. Summer commences in February or March and ends in August. The monsoon breaks out in September and continues till February. The climate is, generally speaking, unhealthy and favours diseases like fever and dysentery.

The population of the country was never very large. Judging on the basis of the present population, the kingdom of Champā, at its largest extent, may be regarded as having contained about two and a half millions of people.

§ 5. THE SOIL AND ITS PRODUCTS.[1]

Nearly throughout the country the territory between the mountains and the sea contains rich alluvial plains with clayey subsoil. On the high plateau the soil is sandy. The mountains, covered with rich forests, contain large layers of clayey, sometimes also ferrugineous, soil which is very fertile.

The most important product is rice which not only grows on low or marshy plains, but also on high grounds and even on mountains. Among other products of the soil may be mentioned the sugarcane, mulberry, pepper, betel, cotton, tobacco, maize, millet, sesame, caster-oil plant, indigo, saffron, lac, turmeric, different kinds of potatoes, sago, beans, pea, egg-plant, cucumber, hemp, fan-palm.

Among the fruit-trees, the most important are banana, cocoanut, mango, betel-nut, date-palms, jack tree and apple. Among other fruits may be mentioned mangosteen, guava, tamarind, orange, lemon, pomegranate, papaw, pine-apple and Lichi.

1. §4—§6 are mainly based on "Bouillevaux—L'Annam et le Cambodge" pp. 449 ff.

Among watery plants may be mentioned lotus, water-lily and a kind of palms whose leaves were used in making straw hats.

The forest contained a rich variety of important and valuable trees of perfume such as sandal, camphor, clove, frankincense and others. Cardamum was found with great difficulty, but valued at its weight in gold. There were ebony and other trees producing good timber, and bamboo was found in great abundance

The mountains are generally composed of granite rocks. They contain numerous minerals. The hills in Quang Nam and Thua Thien contain abundant zinc and copper, the latter being also found in Phu Yen. Silver exists in Thua Thien and Phu Yen while gold dust is found in Quang Nam and other places. Mineral oils are found nearly all over the country.

Gold was obtained in large quantities and the Chinese texts of old refer to 'Mountains of gold'. The soil abounded in precious stones of various kinds and we hear frequently of lapis-lazuli and amber being sent as presents or tributes by the king of Champā.

§ 6. THE FAUNA.

The more important domesticated animals are the elephants, the buffalo, the horse, the ox, the boar, and the goat.

Among the birds may be mentioned the duck, the pigeon, and fowls of various kinds. The goose and the rabbit are rarely found.

The mountains and forests of Annam also abound in wild animals, such as the elephants, buffalo, wild boar, ferocious bull, and another animal called Jin (midway between buffalo and bull) which is very ferocious. There are also tiger, rhinoceros, wild goats, and deer in large numbers. Besides there are monkeys and hares.

The more important aquatic birds were rose-coloured flamingo, stork, pelican, heron, crane, ibis, teal, and water-fowls.

Among other birds may be mentioned peacock, pheasant, swallow, parrots, quail, crow, small eagles, vulture, and wild-fowls.

The rivers and sea abounded in fish of various kinds and tortoises. There were besides mother-of-pearl and sea-otter.

Chapter II.

THE CHAMS AND THE FOUNDATION OF THE KINGDOM OF CHAMPA.

The country which developed later into the kingdom of Champā was originally inhabited by two classes of people, (1) the Chams, and (2) the savages. The distinction was mainly a cultural one, for ethnographically they both belonged to the same Austronesian race.[1] The Chams looked down upon the savages and called them by the general names of the Mlecchas and the Kirāṭas, in addition to various local names, such as the Vṛlas of Phanrang, Randaiy of Nha Trang, and the Mada of Binh Dinh.

The Chinese historians have left very interesting accounts of the physical features and the manners and customs of the Chams. 'They had black skin, deep sunken eyes, snub-noses, and woolly hair. Their dress consisted of a piece of cotton cloth which covered their body from waist to the feet. Neither men nor women put on any other cloth save that in winter they used a kind of thick robe. The ordinary people went bare-footed, but the nobles used shoes made of skin. Both the male and the female tied the hair into various forms of knots and perforated the ears for putting on rings or other ornaments. The people loved cleanliness. They bathed and washed several times every day and rubbed their body with camphor and musc.

(1) As usual there is a wide divergence of views in this respect, but the general consensus of opinion is in favour of the view mentioned above. The old language of the Chams, as preserved in ancient inscriptions, which by the way does not materially differ from the modern, as well as their physical features, described by the Chinese, lend support to this view. Their manners and customs also point in the same direction.

Their clothes were perfumed with the vapour of a large number of fragrant woods.'[1] Lin-yi-ki, a Chinese text composed about the close of the 5th century A. D., describes the people of Tan-eul as follows: "The people love to walk bare-footed and wear large ear-rings. Although the boys and girls have untidy naked bodies, they do not consider it a shame. In summer they cover their body with earth and expose it to the sun. Naturally their skin becomes black. For a long time this practice has been a general one and black is regarded as elegant."[2]

It appears that the population consisted of some Chinese elements, though these were ultimately absorbed by the Chams or rather the Indianised Chams. For, in the same Chinese text, Lin-yi-ki, we find the following description of the people of Kiu-sou, a fortified stronghold of Champā, about 70 miles from the capital.

"The inhabitants descended from the Chinese exiles (255-206 B. C.) have been corrupted by coming into contact with the indigenous elements, and the ancient manners and customs of Je-nan have been completely transformed."[3]

Very little is known of the early history of the Chams. The Annamites have preserved in their Annals some legends about it, but they are of little historical value. One of them runs as follows :—

(1) This description is collected by Maspero from the accounts of several Chinese authors, belonging to different periods (Toung Pao. 1910 p. 174). But as all these Chinese writers belonged to a period when the Chams had come under the influence of the Indian colonists, it is difficult to decide how for the manners and customs described by them were original or due to the Indian influence.

(2) B. E. F. vol. IV, No. 9, p. 15.

(3) Ibid, p. 13.

"In ancient times there was a kingdom, beyond the frontiers of Annam, called Dieu-nghiem. The king of this country was called the king of demons or Daśānana (having ten faces). To the north of this kingdom was the country of Ho Ton Tinh whose king was Daśaratha. The son of Daśaratha called Chung-tu had a beautiful wife. King Daśānana, being enamoured of her beauty, conquered the country of Ho Ton Tinh and brought away the princess. Prince Chung-tu, however, gathered a troop of Monkeys who bridged the ocean with mountains, and brought back his wife after defeating and killing Daśānana."

After describing the above story the Annamite Annals conclude: "The Chams are the descendants of the nation called Ho Ton Tinh." The story is, on the face of it, simply a localisation of the events of Rāmāyaṇa in Champā, and no historical conclusion can be drawn from it.

The earliest reliable information about the Chams is obtained from the Chinese sources. But in order to understand properly the relations between the two nations we must go back a little to the past history.

In the middle of the third century before Christ China was divided into a large number of small kingdoms. To the south and south-east of it, beyond the Nanling mountains, lived a large number of independent tribes who were generally designated as Yue, and who occupied not only Tonkin and the northern portion of Annam as far as Quang Nam, but also the present Chinese districts named Kouang-Si, Kouang-Tong, Fou-kien and Tcho-kiang (only the southern half).

In 221 B.C. Che-houang-ti, of the Tsin Dynasty (225 B. C.-206 B.C.) brought the whole of China under his control and established a united empire. After having properly organised the administration of his vast territories he turned his attention to the conquest of the Yue tribes. By 214 B.C.[1] the vast territories were conquered and divided for the purpose of administration into several provinces. The whole of Tonkin and northern Annam was included in the province of Siang, while the rest was divided into three other provinces. After the death of Che-houang-ti in 210 B.C. anarchy and confusion prevailed in China, taking advantage of which the governor of one of these three provinces established an independent kingdom called Nan-yue. It had its capital at Canton and comprised the modern Chinese districts of Kouang-si and Kouang-Tong. The province of Siang was soon conquered by the king of Nan-yue and was divided for administrative purposes into two provinces of Kiao-tche (Tonkin) and Kieou-tchen (the region of Than Hoa and the Chinese territory in Annam) with capitals respectively at Hanoi and Than-hoa.

In the meantime the Han Dynasty was established in China. In the year 196 B.C. the Han Emperors officially recognised the kingdom of Nan-yue and its king agreed to rule as a vassal king. In the year 183 B.C., however, he revolted and assumed the title of the Emperor of Nan-yue. He died in 137 B. C. and was succeeded by feeble rulers. The Han Emperor sent a military expedition against the kingdom in 112 B. C. and it was wholly conquered in a year.

The Han Emperors made a new arrangement of administrative units. The territories comprising Tonkin and all the southern conquests in Annam which were included in the province of Siang under the Tsin Emperors, and out of which two provinces (Kiao-tche, and Kieou-tchen) were made by the king of Nan-yue, were now divided into three pro-

(1) Maspero wrongly puts the events at 3 B. C, [T'oung Pao 1910, p. 322] probably a mistake for III B. C., but even this date is not that of the original conquest but of the later conquest by the Hans.

vinces viz., Kiao-tche, Kieou-tchen and Je-nan. In other words, Je-nan corresponded to the southern districts of Siang[1]. Je-nan was divided into five districts, the two southernmost of which had their head-quarters at Siang-lin and Si-Kuan.

The question of the exact limits of Je-Nan has long perplexed the scholars. But it may now be regarded as having been fixed with a fair degree of certainty. Pelliot has shown from a passage in Tsin Chou that the northern boundary of Je-nan was the Heng-Chan, now called Hoan-Sonh mountain, a chain which advances towards the sea between Ha Tinh and Quang Binh.[2] As to the southern boundary, M. Aurousseau has drawn attention to a passage in Heou Han Chou according to which the two provinces of Kieou-tchen and Je-nan were situated respectively at a distance of 11,580 and 13,400 li from Lo Yang. It would follow, therefore, that Je-nan was nearly 1820 li to the south of Kieou-tchen. As this latter has been definitey identified with Than-hoa, it follows that Je-nan extended at least 250 miles further south ; in other words it must have extended beyond the province of Binh Dinh in the south. This is corroborated by an Annamite Geographical text which fixes the southern boundary of Je-Nan at the mountain chain which terminates in cape Varella. Thus the ancient Je-Nan may be regarded as that part of modern Annam which lies between the Porte d' Annam and Cape Varella.[3]

(1.) This rapid survey of the relations between China and Annam is based on the admirable article of L. Aurousseau (B. E. F. Vol. XXIII, pp. 137 ff., cf. specially pp. 152 ff, 216 ff, 223 ff. 232 ff. and 263 ff)

(2) B. E. F. Vol. IV, p. 190

(3.) Ibid Vol. XIV, No 9, p. 24.

We thus find that since 214 B. C., the whole of Tonkin, and Annam as far as Cape Varella, passed under the supremacy of the Chinese. The people who lived in Tonkin and northern Annam were undoubtedly the Annamites who were destined to rise to great power in a later period and give their name to the southern part of the Chinese possessions. They belonged ethnographically to the vast Yue race that occupied the territory south of Nan-ling which was first conquered by the Tsin Emperor Che-houang-ti between 221 and 214 B.C. A large part of this Yue race was ultimately absorbed by the Chinese, but those of Tonkin and northern Annam retained their individuality, and, after centuries of Chinese subjugation, ultimately formed themselves into a powerful nation, as we shall see later on. The Annamites, however, did not as yet extend beyond the "Col de Nuages" in the district of Quang Nam. To the south of it lived the indigenous savage population. But already in the first century A. D. we find a new element, the Chams, firmly established in sufficiently large number as far north as Quang Nam. At what date the Chams pushed so far north as Quang Nam we are unable to say, but we shall not probably be far wrong, if we hold that at the time when the Han Emperor had divided the vast territories between the frontier of Kouang-Si and cape Varella into the three provinces of Kiao-tche, Kieou-tchen and Je-Nan, the first two were peopled by the Annamites and the third by the Chams. The primitive savages of Tonkin and Annam, pushed by the Annamites from the north and the Chams from the south, were gradually moving towards the high mountains as their last refuge.

To the south of cape Varella, in the districts of Khan Hoa and Binh Thuan, lived a small group of independent

Chams who constantly harassed the southern frontier of the Chinese possessions. They must have been encouraged in their incursions by the tacit sympathy of the population—their own kinsmen—who were placed under the yoke of the Chinese. As we shall see later on, the headquarters of the southernmost Chinese district were placed in Quang Nam. The Chinese control over the districts of Quang Ngai, Binh Dinh and Phu Yen were probably more nominal than real, and the country, being full of narrow valleys and thick impenetrable jungles, tempted the Chams to plunder and devastate the Chinese possessions. The Chinese historians have described these Chams as savages who were ignorant of the art of cultivation and lived upon hunting alone. They frequently invaded the residences of the Chinese officials and plunder, murder and devastation accompanied these raids. As soon, however, as the Chinese troops came to chastise them they fled and took shelter in the impenetrable forests.

The Cham incursions sometimes took a fairly serious turn. We learn from the Chinese history that in the year 137 A. D., about 10,000 Kiu-lien, a barbarous tribe from beyond the frontier of their territories, attacked their southernmost districts, destroyed the Chinese forts and ravaged the whole country. The governor Fan-Yen raised ten thousand soldiers, but they were unwilling to undertake such a distant expedition and broke into revolt. Taking advantage of this respite, the Kiu-lien pushed their conquests further north, defeated the Chinese troops that opposed them, and occupied some of the Chinese districts. The Chinese emperor was inclined to send a military expedition against the intruders, but one of his ministers pointed out the futility of such a distant expedition, and advised his royal master to rely upon diplomacy. Accordingly Tchou Leang was sent to treat with them and the Kiu-lien were induced to evacuate the conquered territory in 138 A. D. There is no doubt that the Kiu-lien denoted the Chams[1] who thus seem to have possessed great military skill and organisation, as early as the second century A. D.

But the death-blow to the Chinese authority came from within. The Cham inhabitants of Siang-lin were particularly turbulent and now and then broke into open rebellion. In 100 A. D. nearly 2000 of them revolted and attacked the Chinese possessions in the north. They killed many officials and destroyed many villages, but retraced their steps as soon as the Chinese forces arrived. In course of time they grew bolder, and, about 192 A. D., taking advantage of the troubles of the Han dynasty, a native of Siang-lin, named Lien, son of Kong tsa'o, and belonging to the family called Kiu, killed the officer in-charge of the city and proclaimed himself king in Lin-yi. As the term Lin-yi has been used by the Chinese throughout in later periods to denote the kingdom of Champā, we may trace in the successful revolt of Kiu Lien the foundation of that kingdom, at first in Siang-lin but ultimately destined to cover nearly the whole of Annam, south of Tonkin.[2]

---

1. Ibid p. 28.

2. Maspero doubtfully accepted the hypothesis that the kingdom of Kiu Lien is that of Champa, but M. Aurousseau has quoted definite evidence on this point from Chinese texts [B. E. F. vol. XIV, No 9, pp. 26-27].
As to the origin of the name Lin-yi, M. Aurousseau suggests that the Cham kingdom having been originally established in Siang-lin, the Chinese called it Lin-yi ie. capital Lin [of Siang]. "Lin-yi" which was thus the first Chinese name of the first Cham capital was ultimately extended by a natural process to denote the whole of the ancient kingdom of Champa [Ibid].

The identification of the city of Lin-yi (Siang-lin) has long baffled the scholars. But M. Aurousseau seems to have successfully demonstrated that Siang-lin is now represented by Tra-kieu, a little to the south of Quang Nam.[1] It would thus appear that the first Cham kingdom was established in Quang-Nam and this explains the presence of two such magnificent groups of temples at Myson and Dong-Duong in the neighbourhood.

We find a beautiful description of the topography of Champā in a Chinese text called Chouei King Tchou composed in 527 A. D.

'The city was about 40 li (about 6½ miles) from the sea-coast and was at a distance of 2,500 li (about 400 miles) from the *tcheou* of Kouang. At the south-west angle of the ramparts of the city were high mountains and a long chain of hills which served as a natural embankment. Quite close to the north of the hills flowed a river. To the south of the hills, at a little distance was another river which joined the former to the east of the city.

'The city was surrounded by a wall about a mile and a half in circumference. On a brick wall about 20 feet high was raised a second brick wall of half that height, pierced by square loop-holes. On the walls were placed wooden boards supporting many-storied pavillions, on the roof of which again arose towers varying in height from 40 to 70 feet. The first impression that these structures gave was that of an owl, which, with its tail turned towards the wind and touching the mountains and the clouds, was looking towards the water, but would soon, by a leisurely flight, ascend to the highest peak of the mountains. The architecture was admirable but showed lack of skill.

1. B. E. F vol. XIV. No. 9, p. 23 ff.

'There were four gates in the walls. The main gate was on the east. It opened near two islands in the river Houai. The western gate opened on a double ditch which turned to the north and reached a hill. The southern gate likewise opened on a double ditch. The northern gate opened on the river Houai but the route was closed.

'Within the walls were a small enclosure, assembly rooms and brick palaces the walls of which had no opening to the south.

'There was a palace, opening to the east, of which the loose pieces supporting the rafter looked like the tail of an owl. The gates were sculptured in open-work and painted in blue, the passages were coated with red varnish and the rafters were adorned with stone. There were other rafters, rectangular or round, all being carved in old style. On the pavillions and the palaces were columns rising to a height of 15 feet above the ramparts. The walls were besmeared with cowdung which gave them a green and brilliant look. There were eight temples of varying degrees of importance, and also temples for worshipping the spirits. The storeyed terraces and the belvederes looked like Buddhist monuments.[1]

M. Aurousseau has tried to trace from the existing ruins at Tra Kieu some features of the city as described in the above extract.[2]

---

1. Ibid pp. 21-23.
2. Ibid pp. 33-34.

Chapter III.

EARLY HINDU DYNASTIES.

The successful raids into the Chinese territory and the establishment of a powerful kingdom testify to the growth of a new spirit in the Chams towards the second century A. D. This is easily explained by epigraphic records. The Vo-Chanh Rock Inscription (No. 1) refers to the royal family of Śrī Māra, and its royal author is styled as the "delight of the family of Śrī Māra". The inscription is not dated, but may be referred, on palaeographic grounds, to the second or third century A. D. Thus a Hindu or Hinduised dynasty was founded by Śrī Māra in the second century A. D., and it was ruling over the region, later known as Kauṭhāra, about the second or third century A. D.

The coincidence in date makes it almost certain that the regeneration of the Cham power in the second century A. D. was due to the introduction of a new element in her politics, Viz. the Indian colonists.

From this time forward until the conquest of the country by the Annamites in the 15th. century A. D. the Chams, as such, never played any distinctive part in the political history of the country. They cheerfully submitted to their foreign masters and adopted their manners, customs, language and religion. They were politically merged in the Indian elements and there was a complete cultural fusion between the two races.

The Indians must have been acquainted with Champā by way of trade and commerce, long before they established their political supremacy in that region. The general question about the nature and antiquity of Indian colonisation in the Far East will be fully discussed elsewhere. Here we may confine ourselves to the traditions which the later Hindu kings of Champā preserved about their origin. The Dong

Duong (No. 31) Stelæ Inscription of Indravarman II., dated 797 Śaka, describes how Uroja, apparently the first king, was sent to the earth by Śiva himself. Three other inscriptions (Nos. 22, 29 A, and 71) refer to a king Vicitra-Sagara who flourished in the year 5911 of the Dvāpara age or about 1,779,357 B. C. Uroja is evidently a mythical conception and Vicitra-Sagara, too, belongs to the same category.

The first historical Hindu King, so far known, is, however, Śrī Māra who, as we have seen above, established a dynasty about the second century A.D. Maspero has proposed to identify this Śrī-Māra with the Kiu Lien of the Chinese history referred to above. This is probable, but there is as yet no evidence in support of it.

Nothing is known about the early Hindu kings of Champā, but the troublesome events in China which brought about the downfall of the imperial Han dynasty in 220 A. D. must have offered them a splendid opportunity to extend and consolidate their kingdom. The dismemberment of the Chinese empire into three parts (220-265 A.D.) emboldened them to cross the frontier and carry their raids far into the Chinese territory. Some time between 220 and 230 A.D. the king of Champā sent a diplomatic mission to the Governor of Kiao-Tche on the invitation of the latter; nevertheless, in 248 A.D. the Cham army made a naval attack, ravaged even the provincial capital, Kiao-tche (Hanoi) with several other towns, and defeated the fleet that was sent against them. At last a treaty was concluded by which the district of K'iu-Sou corresponding to Modern Thua-Thien was ceded to Champā[1].

1. According to M. Aurousseau the whole of Cheou-ling was ceded to Champa (Ibid p. 27), but Maspero is of opinion that only the southern part of the district, including the capital K'iu-sou was ceded to the Chams, the northern

The Chinese history has preserved the names of several kings of this period. Each of these names begins with Fan, probably corresponding to 'Varman', which was the epithet of every Cham king in later times.[1] King Fan Hiong who succeeded to the throne of Champā sometime between 270 and 280 A.D. was probably a descendant of Śrī Māra by the female line. He continued the policy of extending the Cham territory to the north at the cost of the Chinese. He allied himself with the king of Fou-Nan (in Cambodia) for this purpose, and continually ravaged the Chinese possessions in Tonkin. For ten years the struggle went on, and the Chinese were reduced to great straits. At last peace was established in 280 A.D., probably on terms unfavourable to the Chinese.

Fan-Yi, the son of Fan Hiong, succeeded him on the throne. He had a long and peaceful reign and devoted his energies to increasing the military power and strengthening the defensive works of the kingdom. He was the first Cham king to send an embassy to the Imperial court of China (284 A.D.).

Fan Yi died in 336 A.D..[2] On his death the throne was usurped by his commander-in-chief Fan Wen. Wen is said to have been originally a Chinese slave and owed his fortune to miracles.[3] It appears that he enjoyed the complete confidence of his royal master, and taking advantage of his old age

part still remaining in the hands of the Chinese; this portion of Cheou-ling together with Wou-lao were conquered by Champa in the time of Fan Wen.

B. E. F. vol. XVIII, No. 3, pp. 24-25.

1. B. E. F. vol. IV, p. 194.
2. According to some authorities, in 331 A. D., (B. E. F. vol. IV p. 382, fn (5).).
3. cf. the story as given in B. E. F. vol. XIV, No. 9, p 17.

induced him to exile one of his two sons. The other, too, forestalled his fate, and left the kingdom. Thus when the king died, the legitimate heirs were far away. But Wen found them out and had them poisoned. After thus removing all possible claimants, he ascended the throne and proclaimed himself king of Champā.

Wen was a capable ruler and soon made himself the undisputed master of the whole kingdom by defeating the savage tribes who formed independent states within the kingdom. In 340 he sent an envoy to the Chinese emperor with a request that the Hoan Sonh mountains should be recognized as the frontier between the two states.[1] This would have meant the cession of the fertile province of Nhu't-Nam (corresponding to Thua Thien, Quang Tri and Quang Binh) to Champā and naturally the Chinese emperor refused the request. But Wen decided to take by force what he could not gain by diplomacy. The people of Nhu't-Nam were mutinous on account of the exactions of the Chinese governor. Taking advantage of this situation Fan Wen led an expedition in 347 A.D., and conquered Nhu't-Nam. He killed the governor of the district and made an offering of his body in an expiatory sacrifice. The Chinese governor made great preparations against Wen, but the latter took the offensive and captured Cu'n Duc, putting to death a large number of Chinese soldiers who garrisoned it (348 A.D.). In 349 he again defeated a vast Chinese army; but he was himself wounded in the fight, and died the same year. Fan Wen thus carried his conquests to the "Porte de Annam", and the kingdom of Champā now exactly corresponded to the old Chinese province of Je-Nan, and reached its furthest limit to the north.

1. Either on this or on another occasion Fan Wen wrote a letter to the Chinese emperor in Indian characters.

Wen was succeeded by his son Fan Fo (349-80 A. D.). He wanted to emulate his father's exploits and laid siege to the chief town of the Chinese district of Cu'u-Chon. He was, however, defeated and had to accept a disgraceful treaty in 351. But within a short time he again renewed hostilities. In 353 the Chinese sent another expedition against him and reconquered Nhut-Nam. But the struggle did not end there. As soon as the Chinese returned to their country the Chams renewed their excursions. At last the Chinese inflicted a severe defeat upon Fan Fo in 358 and advanced upto the very walls of the city of Champā. In 359 a treaty was concluded by which the district of Nhut Nam, as far as the Bay of On Cang, was ceded to the Chinese. Fan Fo faithfully observed the treaty till his death in 380, and sent his ambassadors with tribute to the Chinese Emperor in 372 and again in 377.

Fan-Hou-ta, the son of Fan Fo, was very young when he ascended the throne on the death of his father in 380. But as soon as he came to age he revived the ambitious project of his father. The whole of his reign was an almost unceasing struggle against the Chinese. The times were favourable to him. The imperial Tsin dynasty was in a decadent condition, and revolts broke out throughout the Chinese empire. So Fan-Hou-ta scored some successes at first. He not only recovered Nhut Nam but carried his arms even further to the north, as far as Than Hoa. But in 413 A. D., Tou Houei-tou, the Chinese governor of Kiao-tche (Hanoi), arrived at Kieou-tchen (Than-hoa) and defeated Fan-Hou-ta in a pitched battle. Two (or one according to some version) sons of the latter fell into his hands and were beheaded. Tou-Houei-tou then laid siege to Than-hoa. He occupied the top of the hills overlooking the city and barricaded the course of the river by means of hedges of trees. Exciting attacks and counter-attacks took place almost under the ramparts of the city, and the Chinese governor retreated, after killing and wounding lots of enemies, but without apparently being able to take the city.[1]

The end of Fan-Hou-ta is not known with certainty. There is no doubt that he was a great general and increased the power and prestige of his kingdom to a very great extent, after the late reverses. One of the most important works done by him was the fortification of the city of Kiu-sou which the Chams had conquered in 248 A. D. The identification of the city of Kiu-sou had long been a difficult problem. But M. Aurousseau is probably right in his hypothesis that it occupied the site which is now covered by ruins immediately to the south-east of Hue. This city occupied a very important position from the point of view of military strategy. It was situated between two rivers which met at the foot of its ramparts, and was surrounded by high hills on three sides. Situated 400 li (about 70 miles) to the north of the capital, it commanded the route which every Chinese army had to follow in an expedition against Champā. Fan-Hou-ta fully realised the importance of the city and converted it into one of the strongest citadels in his kingdom. For obvious reasons the citadel of Kiu-sou, which was renamed by the Chams as Si-Kiuan, figures largely in the Chinese historical texts. These give a very graphic description of the fortified city. The ramparts round the city, we are told, measured more than a mile, and had thirteen gates. The plinth of these remparts was made of a brick course, 20 feet deep. Upon this was raised a brick wall 10 feet high, pierced by square loopholes. Upon the bricks rested five-storeyed wooden structures supporting high towers

1. This interesting information is furnished by Lin-yi-ki, a text composed probably towards the close of the fifth century A. D.

(B. E. F. vol. XIV No.9, p. 14).

on their roofs. The height of these towers varied between 50 and 80 feet. The outer walls of the fortified city nearly touched the mountains which were covered with thick impenetrable forest. On account of its military strength the war-materials of the kingdom of Champā were stored in this city.

Maspero has suggested the identification of Fan-Hou-ta with king Bhadravarman. This is probable but not certain. Bhadravarman is the author of two inscriptions (Nos. 2 and 4) and three other inscriptions (nos. 3, 5 and 6) also probably belong to his reign. On palæographical grounds these inscriptions have been referred to the 5th century A.D. and this agrees well with the reign-period of Fan-Hou-ta. That the latter set the fashion of engraving records on stone clearly follows from the Chinese accounts. For we are told that close to the eastern gate of his capital there was a Stelæ containing a record of his glory in barbarous character (i.e., the Indian alphabet as modified in Champā).

Whatever we might think of this identification, Bhadravarman must be regarded as one of the most important kings in ancient Champā. His full name was Dharma-mahārāja Śrī Bhadravarman. The findspots of his inscriptions show that he ruled over at least the northern and central portion of the kingdom, the provinces of Amarāvatī and Vijaya. There are, however, reasons to suppose that his kingdom also included the southern province of Pāṇḍuraṅga. But the famous work, by which he was destined to be immortal, was the erection of a temple to Śiva, under the name of Bhadreśvarasvāmī, at Myson. This temple became the national sanctuary of the Chams, and the practice he thus set on foot of calling the tutelary deity by the name of the reigning king, came to be almost universally adopted in later times. We shall have occasion to refer to this temple of Bhadreśvarasvāmī again and again in course of the history of Champā. Bhadravarman made an endowment of lands to this temple and their boundaries are given in 3 inscriptions (Nos. 4, 5 and 7) as follows: "To the east, the Sulaha mountain, to the south the Great mountain, to the west, the Kucoka mountain, and to the north, the Great River". The great river is of course the "Song-Thu-bon" and this shows that the boundaries described are not of the temple and its surroundings, as was formerly supposed, but of the lands granted to it.[1] King Bhadravarman seems to have been a scholar and it is expressly laid down in the inscription no. 4 that he was versed in the four Vedas.

According to the Chinese accounts.[2] Fan-Hou-ta was succeeded in 413 by his son Ti-Tchen. We are told that Ti-Kai, the brother of this king, fled with his mother, and the king could not induce them to come back. Grieved at heart, he abdicated the throne in favour of his nephew and himself went to India. The departure of the king was followed by anarchy and civil war in Champā. Ti Kai thereupon came back and claimed the throne from his nephew who was designated as his successor by Ti-Tchen. Wen-Ti, a brother of Ti-Kai by the same mother but a different father, and the minister Tsang Yin joined the combat. Civil war followed and led to murders and rapid successions to the throne till the dynasty was dispossessed of the kingdom of Champā after a reign of about 80 years (336-420 A.D.).

1. The northern boundary, leading to the important conclusion noted in the text, is given only in the inscription No. 5 (cf. B. E. F. vol XVIII, No. 10, p. 14). For the detailed regulations of the endowment cf. Ins. No. 4.

2. The Chinese accounts regarding the period that followed the death of Fan-Hou-ta are very conflicting cf. B. E. F. vol. IV, p. 382, fn (9).

Maspero has suggested the identification of Ti-Tchen with the king Gaṅgārāja who is mentioned in inscription No. 12 as having abdicated the throne in order to spend his last days on the Ganges. The abdication of the throne and retirement to India are certainly very striking coincidences, and the identification, although by no means certain, is undoubtedly very probable.

The civil war was brought to an end by the accession of Fan Yang Mai (420 ? A.D.). His origin is unknown but he is said to have been a son of Fan-Hou-ta, probably by a mother of inferior rank. The relations between China and Champā were not interrupted by the civil war. The Chams carried on their usual raids into the Chinese territory, attended by pillage, massacre and horrible cruelties. In the year 420 the Chinese inflicted a crushing defeat upon the Chams, and the following year Yang Mai sent an ambassador to the Imperial Court with a request that his title of king of Champā be recognised by the Chinese Emperor. Yang Mai no doubt took this step to ensure his position in the newly gained kingdom, and his example was followed by many of his successors.

Yang Mai died within a few years and was succeeded by his son Tou who assumed the name of his father. The usual frontier raids against the Chinese territory continued, and in 431 he sent more than 100 vessels to pillage the coast of Nhu't Nam and Cu'u Cho'n. This provoked the Chinese governor who sent a strong expedition both by land and sea against Champā. The Chinese army besieged K'iu-sou. Yang Mai II had gone to marry. He hurried back by way of sea and fell in with the Chinese fleet. His chief pilot was struck down by an arrow and his fleet dispersed, pursued by the Chinese. The Chinese fleet, however, could not follow up the victory on account of bad weather, and retreated. Consequently their army had also to raise the siege and fall back (431 A.D.).

Yang Mai was, however, elated with the result of the battle and his ambition knew no bounds. In 433 A. D. he sent an envoy to the Chinese emperor asking to be appointed the governor of Kiao Tcheou. This would have virtually meant the cession of the province of Tonkin and was of course refused. Irritated at the refusal, Yang Mai redoubled his efforts against Kiao Tcheou and hardly a year passed without an invasion of the district by his troops. All the while, however, he continued to pay his tribute regularly to the Chinese emperor.

The Chinese emperor now decided to bring his turbulent vassal to sense by another military expedition. The preparations took three years, and in 446 A. D. the Chinese army under T'an Ho-Tche invaded Champā. Terror now seized Yang Mai II and he proposed a humiliating peace to the Chinese emperor. The emperor accepted his offer and sent instructions to his commander to conclude a treaty, if he found Yang Mai sincere in his desire for peace. The commander accordingly sent some of his officers to Yang Mai to treat with him. In the meantime the war-party in the court, which had lost its influence on the approach of the Chinese army, regained its power and prevailed upon the king to reject the proposals of peace. Yang Mai accordingly put the Chinese envoys to prison and sent back one of them to carry the news to their commander.

The Chinese general at once advanced and laid seige to Kiu-sou[1] the principal stronghold of Champā. Yang Mai sent an army in aid of Fan Fou Long who defended the place, but although the Chams scored some successes at

1. For a description of Kiu-sou see above, pp. 26-27.

first, the Chinese ultimately captured the stronghold. The general Fan Fou Long was beheaded and all the inhabitants above the age of 15 were put to the sword. The palace halls were inundated with blood and heaps of dead bodies covered the court-yard. An immense booty of gold, silver and various other precious objects was gained by the victors.

The Chinese continued their advance and were at last met by Yang Mai himself at the head of an immense host. Yang Mai placed a large number of elephants in front of his army. This terrified the Chinese soldiers. But the ingenuity of a Chinese general saved the situation. He prepared numerous figures of lions by means of bamboos and papers, and these were thrown before the elephants. The latter took fright and fled, and in so doing threw into confusion and disorder the very army they were intended to protect. Yang Mai suffered a most terrible defeat and fled from the battlefield with his son. The victorious Chinese general T'an Ho Tche then entered the capital Champāpura in triumph and obtained a rich booty of very precious objects. The whole country was occupied, all the temples were sacked, and their statues were melted for the metals contained in them. About 100,000 pounds of pure gold were obtained from this source. The Chinese victory was complete.

After the retreat of the Chinese army Yang Mai came back to his capital. But the city was in ruins and Yang Mai died in a broken heart in 446 A.D.[1]

Fan Yang Mai II was succeeded by his son and grandson. The latter, named Fan Chen Tch'eng,[2] pursued a policy of peace and sent tributes to the Chinese emperor

1. G. Maspero puts the date wrongly as 443.
(T'oung Pao 1910, p. 499).

2. cf. T'oung Pao, 1910, p. 499 fn. (4).

on at least three different occasions, in 455, 458 and 472 A.D. The tributes were very rich and the emperor was pleased to confer high honours and titles on the ambassador.

The death of Fan Chen Tch'eng was followed by a troublesome period. Taking advantage of this a man called Fan Tang-Ken-Tch'ouen or Kieou Tch'eou Lo usurped the kingdom. He was the son of Jayavarman king of Fou-Nan. He had committed some crime in his country, and, fleeing from the wrath of his royal father, took refuge in Champā. King Jayavarman could ill brook the success of his son in the foreign land. He sent the Bhikṣu Śākya Nāgasena to the Chinese Emperor in order to complain against the usurper and ask the aid of imperial troops to punish him. The long letter which Jayavarman addressed to the Chinese emperor on this occasion, explaining the measures he proposed to adopt for driving his son out of Champā, is a very interesting reading.[1] It shows that the Chinese emperor was tacitly looked upon as the sovereign authority by all the states in the Far East, and whatever the amount of actual control possessed by him, he never ceased to exercise a political influence upon them all. Jayavarman's endeavour, however, bore no fruit. The Chinese emperor received the embassy cordially and gave a very courteous reply, but he did not agree to meddle in the affairs of Champā. On the other hand the emperor recognised the usurper as the king of Champā and gave him high sounding honorary titles[2] by an

1. The letter has been translated in full in Pelliot's "Le Fou-Nan" B. E. F., vol. III, pp. 257 ff.

2. These titles are : "General, Pacifier of the South, Commander-in-chief in all the military transactions on the Sea-coast, King of Champa.

Imperial Decree in 491 A.D. But the usurper was defeated and dethroned immediately after by Fan Tchou-Nong, great-grandson of Fan Yan Mai II. Fan Tchou-Nong was recognised by the Chinese emperor in 492 A.D., and received honorary titles like his predecessor[1], but his reign was short, and he died in 498 A.D., being drowned in the sea during a pleasure trip, or, according to some authorities, in course of a voyage to China. He sent ambassadors to the Chinese court in 492 and 495 A.D. Tchou-Nong was succeeded by his son, grandson and great-grandson, named respectively Fan Wen K'ouan or Fan Wen Ts'an, Fan T'ien K'ai (Devavarman?), and Vijayavarman. We do not know anything about them except that they sent embassies to China and received the same honorary titles from the emperor as their predecessors. The embassy of 502 A. D. was probably sent by Fan Wen K'ouan. Devavarman's embassies were dated 510, 512 and 514 A.D. Vijayavarman sent two embassies in 526 and 527 A.D.

KINGS REFERRED TO IN CHAPTER III.

1. Śrī Māra or Kiu Lien } (2nd C. A.D.)

⋮

2. Fan Hiong (c. 270-280 A.D.)
3. Fan-yi (c. 280 A.D.-336 A.D.)
   (Son of No. 2)
4. Fan Wen(336 A.D.-349 A.D.)
   (Commander-in-Chief of No. 3)

---

1. The first portion of the title was slightly changed in his case. It was "The Marshal, who maintains orders in the South".

5. **Fan Fo** (349-380 A.D.)
(Son of No. 4)

6. **Fan-Hou-Ta** (Bhadravarman ?) (380-413 A. D.)
(Son of No. 5)

7. Ti-Tchen (Gaṅgārāja) (413-c. 415 A.D.)
(Son of No. 6)
(Civil War 415-420 A.D.)

8. **Fan Yang Mai** (420-c. 425 A.D. ?)
(Son of No. 6 ?)

9. **Fan Yang Mai II** (c. 425-446 A.D.)
(Son of No. 8)

10. Son of No. 9, name unknown (446-454 ?)

11. **Fan Chen Tch'eng** (c. 454-c. 480 A.D.)
(Son of No. 10)

12. Kieou Tch'eou Lo (c. 480-491 A.D.)
(Usurper)

13. **Fan Tchou-Nong**-(491-498 A.D.)
(Great-grandson of No. 9)

14. **Fan Wen K'ouan** (c. 500-c. 508 A.D.)
(Son of No. 13)

15. **Fan T'ien K'ai** (Devavarman ?) (c. 508-c. 520 A.D.)
(Son of No. 14)

16. **Vijayavarman** (c. 520 A.D.-c. 529 A.D.)
(Son of No. 15)

Chapter IV.

THE DYNASTY OF GANGARAJA.

Vijayavarman was succeeded by Śrī Rudravarman whose genealogy is given in the Myson stelae Inscription (No. 12). The genealogy begins with a king Gaṅgārāja who abdicated the throne and retired to the banks of the Ganges. The breakage in the stone does not enable us to determine his relationship with the next king Manorathavarman. Rudravarman was the son of a Brāhmaṇa, and his mother's mother was a daughter of Manorathavarman.

Rudravarman was not, therefore, a direct descendant of Vijayavarman. But, as has been suggested above, if Gaṅgārāja is identified with Ti-Tchen, Rudravarman would belong to a collateral branch of the same family. Now Gaṅgārāja is placed at the head of the long genealogical list in No. 12, implying thereby that he was the head of a new family. This is made explicit in No. 20 wherein Prakāśadharma (or Vikrāntavarman) is said to belong to the 'family of Gaṅgeśvara,'[1] which may be taken as another form of the name Gaṅgārāja. It would then follow that the kings of this family could lay claim to the kingdom of Champā only by virtue of their relationship with Gaṅgārāja. In other words, they could not establish any legitimate claim to the throne by their relationship with any succeeding king.

The identification of Gaṅgārāja and Ti-Tchen would supply a plausible explanation of the rise of this family. As has been narrated above, the abdication of Ti-Tchen

1. We have probably another reference to Gangaraja as the founder of the family in the inscription no 7., where the isolated word "Gangesasya occurs in line l., the rest having been effaced.

was followed by a civil war between his nephew, whom he designated as his successor, and various other claimants to the throne. Manorathavarman may be regarded as the nephew, or at any rate, as deriving his claim to the throne from his nephew. But all this is at present pure conjecture.

Some important information about Rudravarman is obtained from inscription No. 7. We are told that Rudravarman belonged to the Brahma-Kṣatriya family and that during his reign the famous temple of Mahādeva, called Bhadreśvarasvāmi after its builder the king Bhadravarman, was burnt by fire. The date of this calamity is given in Śaka year, but unfortunately this portion of the inscription is badly mutilated and we can simply read "in the year four hundred and............". Rudravarman thus ruled sometime between 401 and 499 Śaka i.e., 479 and 577 A.D.

There cannot be any doubt, therefore, that he is to be identified with Kao Che lu T'o Lo Pa Mo, mentioned in the Chinese annals (the chinese name being equivalent to Ku Śrī Rudravarman) who sought for his investiture from the Chinese Emperor in 529 by payment of tribute, and renewed the tribute again in 534 A. D.

About this time the Chinese province of Kiao Tcheou had revolted and thrown off the imperial yoke under the leadership of Ly Bon. Rudravarman, probably incited by the Chinese Emperor, took advantage of the situation to conquer the province. His army was, however, defeated by the general of Ly Bon and he had to beat retreat (541 A. D.).

Rudravarman was succeeded by his son Praśastadharma who took the name Śambhuvarman at the time of his coronation. He is the author of the inscription No. 7. He re-established the temple of Bhadravarman which was burnt at the time of his father, and re-named the image as Śambhu-Bhadreśvara, thus adding his own name to that of the original founder. He also confirmed the endowments made to the temple by Bhadravarman. The two embassies sent to China in 568 and 572 A.D. probably belonged to his time.

Śambhuvarman took advantage of the weakness of the Imperial Tch'en dynasty to stop the customary tribute, but renewed it in 595 A. D. after the Souei dynasty was established on the Imperial throne. But this did not save him from a Chinese invasion. The immense booty taken from Champā by T'an Ho Tche impressed the Chinese with an idea of the fabulous wealth of the kingdom, and so when the Chinese general Lieou Fang came to quell the insurrection in Kiao Tcheou, he was ordered to advance against Champā. The Chinese advanced both by land and sea, and reached the estuary of Linh Giang (modern Song Giang) in 605. Śambhuvarman stationed his soldiers to guard the passes which separate the valley of Linh Giang from that of the Do Le (Tou Li). Lieou Fang defeated them and pitched his camp on the Do Le. He then crossed the river without difficulty and overtook the enemy a few miles to the south. A sanguinary battle ensued. The elephants on which the Chams mainly relied were dispersed by the Chinese archers, and they trampled under foot the very army they were engaged to protect. Śambhuvarman fled from the battle-field and the Chinese took about 10,000 prisoners and cut off their left ears.[1] Lieou Fang pursued his victory and occupied K'iu Sou. Near about

1. It was customary in those days to cut off the left ears of prisoners of war and send them as trophies to the Emperor. The total number of captives could also be determined thereby.

this place he inflicted several more defeats upon Śambhuvarman and reached the capital of Champā (605 A. D.). Śambhuvarman fled by sea. Lieou Fang thereupon sacked the capital city, and put into captivity all the inhabitants he could lay hands on. He further took the golden tablets of eighteen kings who had ruled over Champā before Śambhuvarman, and 1350 Buddhist works. Among his captives were included some musicians from Fou-Nan who carried to the Imperial court the musical arts of India.

Lieou Fang and his army suffered much on their return journey from a disease—Beri Beri or Elephantisis—to which the general himself fell a victim. The conquered country was divided into three divisions, each subdivided again into four 'prefectures', but owing to the distance and difficulty of communication they were never effectively occupied, and remained as part of the kingdom of Champā.

As soon as the invader had left, Śambhuvarman came back to his capital, and to avoid further difficulties, sent an ambassador to the Imperial Court for asking pardon. Later on, however, taking advantage of the dynastic quarrels in China, he stopped the payment of tribute; but when Li Yuan established the T'ang dynasty (618 A. D.) he resumed regular payment. He sent three embassies in 623, 625 and 628. Śambhuvarman was also on friendly terms with the Khmer King Mahendra-Varman who sent one of his ministers, Siṁhadeva as ambassador to the court of Champā,

Śambhuvarman was succeeded in 629 A. D. by his son Kandarpadharma (Fan T'eou Li of the Chinese). The king had a peaceful reign. He kept peace with China by regular payment of tribute. On one occasion the disrespectful conduct of his ambassador to the Chinese Emperor nearly brought the two countries on the verge of war, but the emperor pardoned the fault which was 'due to ignorance of etiquette rather than to any bad intention'. The rich tributes of Kandarpadharma so pleased the emperor that he wished to have a stone statue of the king close to his tomb. The virtues of the king are referred to in eloquent terms in verses 7 and 8 of the inscription No. 12. He is described as "Virtue Incarnate" and Kali is said to have fled away from his kingdom, knowing that he had nothing to expect from a king, who was free from passions and protected his subjects like his own sons by means of his virtues.

Kandarpadharma's son and successor Prabhāsadharma, Fan Tchen-Long of the Chinese history, had a tragic end. The events are thus summarised in the Chinese history.

"In 630, 631 A D. and the following years the king Fan T'eou Li regularly paid tributes. On his death the throne passed on to his son Fan Tchen-Long. In 645 Fan Tchen-Long was killed with all his family by his subject Mo-ho-man-to-kia-tou and the male descendants of the Fan family were extinguished with him. Then the people raised a Brāhmaṇa, a son-in-law of king Fan T'eou Li, on the throne. But he was deposed by the nobles who put the daughter of Fan T'eou Li on the throne. As she was unable to restore order, they summoned Tchou-ko Ti, son of the paternal aunt of Fan-T'eou Li. Tchou-ko Ti came back from Cambodge, where his father had fled after committing a crime, married the daughter of Fan T'eou Li and was proclaimed king. The ambassadors were sent to the Imperial court by Tchou-ko Ti in 653, by Po-kia-cho-pa-mo in 669, by Kien-to-ta-mo in 713, and by Lou-to-lo in 749."[1]

This circumstantial narrative is of great help in wading our way through the tangles of civil war and anarchy

1. B. E. F. vol. IV, pp. 901-902.

that followed the assassination of the son of Kandarpadharma.

In the first place it is quite clear that the son of Kandarpadharma was killed by his minister, for the Chinese Mo-ho-man-to-kia-tou seems to correspond exactly to Mahāmantrādhikṛta. That the murder was the result of a deliberate and well-laid plot to usher in a dynastic change is clearly proved by the fact that not only the king but also his whole family was removed. The events that follow would also make it quite clear that it was the daughter of Fan T'eou Li on whose behalf the conspiracy was laid, nor is it difficult to conclude that the kings of Cambodge were the wire-pullers from behind. But the whole situation is made quite clear by the Myson inscription of Prakāśadharma (No. 12). Here the genealogy is first of all carried down to Prabhāsadharma. Then it refers to his sister 'who was the source of welfare and prosperity of the whole world'. We are next introduced to her husband, Satyakauśikasvāmī, and their sons Bhadreśvaravarman, and his two younger brothers Anaṅgarūpa and Viśvarūpa. Next we hear of Jagaddharma,-apparently a son of Bhadreśvaravarman, though the breakage in stone does not make this point absolutely certain—who had gone to Cambodge (and here a long digression gives us a history of Cambodge from its foundation) owing to certain circumstances, and there married the daughter of king Īśānavarman. The issue of this marriage was Prakāśadharma-Vikrāntavarman, king of Champā who issued the inscription in 579 Śaka (657 A. D.).

Now the scholars have found it impossible to reconcile the Chinese annals with the data furnished by the inscriptions. Maspero's suggested emendation has proved hopelessly wrong, while Finot has to admit that the Chinese accounts are inaccurate in at least three essential elements. But there ought not to be any great difficulty in reconciling the two if the essential points are borne in mind. This may be illustrated by putting the events recorded in the two different sources in two parallel columns.

Chinese Annals.	Inscriptions.
1. Murder of Prabhāsadharma 645 A. D.	1. Prabhāsadharma, king.
2. Son-in-law of Kandarpadharma, a Brāhmaṇa, put on the throne, but deposed by the nobles.	2. Satyakauśikasvāmī, son-in-law of Kandarpadharma.
3. Daughter of Kandarpadharma reigning alone.	3. Daughter of Kandarpadharma, source of prosperity of the whole world.
4. Tchou-ko Ti returns from Cambodge, marries the daughter of Kandarpadharma and becomes king. He sends embassy in 653 A. D.	4. Bhadreśvara Varman (son of 2 and 3.)
5. King Po-kia-cho-pa-mo sends embassy in 669 A. D.	5. Jagaddharma (son of 4) who had been to Cambodge and married the daughter of the king there.
	6. Prakāśadharma (son of 5) king in 657 A. D.

The arrangement is confirmed by one important piece of external evidence. The Tra' Kieu Inscription (No. 9) tells us that the wife of Prakāśadharma's great-grandfather (Prapitāmahi) was the daughter of Kandarpadharma. The above arrangement entirely agrees with this fact.

The only point, not a very essential one, in which the Chinese annals are mistaken is their belief that the daughter of Kandarpadharma was married a second time to Tchou-ko Ti, a different husband, whereas the fact seems to be that Tchou-ko Ti (Satyakauśikasvāmī) was her first husband who had sought shelter in Cambodge after being deposed by the nobles. It appears that Tchou-ko Ti's family had some influence in the court of Cambodge, for his father had taken shelter there after committing some fault in Champā, and his grandson was married to the daughter of the king of Cambodge.

That the daughter and son-in-law of Kandarpadharma were very old when they came to the throne is established by the following genealogy of Prakāśadharma drawn up on the authority of Tra'-kieu Inscription (No. 9).

Kandarpadharma (630-640 A. D.)
|
Daughter
|
Son
|
Jagaddharma
|
Prakāśadharma (657 A. D.)

Now the way in which Prakāśadharma's prowess has been extolled in the Myson Ins. dated 657 A. D. shows that he must have then attained at least 20 years of age. Prakāśadharma's birth therefore could not have taken place later than 637 A. D. If we hold that a male must be at least twenty and a female at least sixteen before he or she can possibly have an issue, the birth of the predecessors of Prakāśadharma could not have taken place later than the dates mentioned in the following table.

Kandarpadharma (561 A. D.)
|
Daughter (581 A. D.)
|
Son (597 A. D.)
|
Jagaddharma (617 A. D.).

Kandarpadharma then must have been at least about 70 years at the time of his accession, and probably much more than that, as we have taken only the minimum number of years in the above calculation.

Now, bearing the above points in mind, we may offer the following general outline of the course of events in the light of the Chinese and epigraphic data that we possess.

In the first place the relation of the different actors in the scene may be illustrated by the following table.

Rudravarman (Lu-to-lo-pa-mo)

- Śambhuvarman (Fan Fan Tche)
  - Kandarpadharma (Fan Teou Li)
    - Prabhāsadharma (Fan Tchen Long).
    - Daughter = Satyakauśika-svāmī (Tchou-ko Ti)
- Daughter
  - Satyakauśika-svāmī (Tchou-ko Ti) = Daughter of Kandarpadharma
    - Bhadreśvaravarman.
      - Jagaddharma = Śarvvāṇī (daughter of Īśānavarman, king of Cambodge.
        - Prakāśadharma-Vikrāntavarman.
    - Anangarūpa.
    - Viśvarūpa.

The disastrous defeat inflicted by the Chinese upon Śambhuvarman must have considerably weakened the authority of the government. As usually happens, the national calamity served as an opportunity to adventurers, and in this particular instance the female line seems to have coveted the throne as against the male line. During the long reign of Śambhuvarman the interests of two such female lines were cemented by the marriage of the daughter of Kandarpadharma with the grandson (daughter's son) of Rudravarman. It is probable that an attempt was already made by this party after the death of Kandarpadharma to secure the throne, but it proved unsuccessful, and its authors had to fly to the court of Cambodge. But a few years later, the attempt was renewed, and Prabhāsadharma was killed with all the male members of the family (645 A. D.). Satyakauśikasvāmī at first occupied the throne, but was driven away by the nobles, and his wife alone ruled the state. But a female ruler was hardly likely to cope with the difficulties of the time and Satyakauśikasvāmī returned to Champā. It is extremely likely that the king of Cambodge was really pulling the wire from behind in all the successive events. The new party had all along been intimately associated with that court, for the father of Satyakauśikasvāmī had taken refuge in the court of Cambodge 'after committing some fault in Champā, as the Chinese historians put it, and Jagaddharma, the grandson of Satyakauśikasvāmī, was married to a Cambodge princess.

Satyakauśikasvāmī ruled for at least eight years from 645 to 653 A. D., with an interval. Whether his son and grandson ruled after him cannot be finally decided, but the answer is probably in the negative, for no royal title is attached to any of them in the Myson Stone Inscription. Even if they did, they must have very short reigns. For by 657 A. D. Prakāśadharma had already ascended the throne under the title of Vikrāntavarman.

Prakāśadharma-Vikrāntavarman is the author of at least eight inscriptions, Nos. 9-16. We learn from No. 12 that in the year 657 A. D. he established Śrī-Prabhāseśvara and granted lands to the gods Īśāneśvara, Śrī Śambhubhadreśvara and Śrī Prabhāseśvara. No. 14. records the erection of a temple to Kuvera, while no. 16. records the donation of a *kośa* to Īśāneśvara and a diadem to Bhadreśvara in 687, A. D. The attribution of three inscriptions nos. 17-19 is doubtful. They refer to king Vikrāntavarman, who may be either Prakāśadharma—Vikrāntavarman I, or Vikrāntavarman II. It is interesting to note that he was not only devoted to Śiva (cf. Ins No. 10 and others noted above) but also to Viṣṇu to whom he erected a temple (No. 11).

Prakāśadharma seems te have been at peace with the Imperial court of China. He first sent tributes during the period 650-656 A. D., and at least four more embassies were sent in 657, 669, 670 and 686 A. D. He must have had a long reign extending over more than 31 years (656-687).

We have no precise knowledge about the successor of Prakāśadharma—Vikrāntavarman I. The inscription No. 21 records that Prakāśadharma intended to build a *vedī* of stone, but this was actually constructed by Naravāhanavarman. The inscription then proceeds to record the glories of Vikrāntavarman. It would thus appear that Prakāśadharma was succeeded by Naravāhanavarman and the latter again by Vikrāntavarman. This conclusion is, however, not certain, as Naravāhanavarman might be another name of Vikrāntavarman, but it may be taken as a working hypothesis. The Chinese evidence in a way confirms this. We learn from the Chinese history that in the years 713 and 731 Kien Ta To

Mo, king of Champā sent tributes to the Chinese Emperor. Kien Ta To Mo may be regarded as a fairly good transcription of Vikrāntavarman. Now this Vikrāntavarman can hardly be regarded as identical with Prakāśadharma—Vikrāntavarman who sent tribute to China sometime before 656 A. D., as the interval is more than 75 years. Thus we are to presume two kings bearing the same name Vikrāntavarman. It is less likely, however, that the father and the son should bear the same name, whereas it is usual for a king to adopt the name of his grandfather. We may thus provisionally accept the following line of succession.

Prakāśadharma-Vikrāntavarman I.
|
Naravāhanavarman
|
Vikrāntavarman II.

The latest known date of Prakāśadharma is 687 A.D. and the earliest known date of Vikrāntavarman II is 713 A.D. Naravāhanavarmā's reign, therefore, falls between these dates. We hardly know anything about his reign. Vikrāntavarman II established an image of Lakṣmī in the year 731 A.D. His conventional glory is sung in lines 8-9 of the inscription No. 21. The fragmentary inscription No. 20 which belongs to his reign and is dated sometime between 708 and 717 A. D., records various donations to a number of gods. The inscriptions Nos. 17-19 may belong to his reign, but as already remarked above, this is by no means certain. Vikrāntavarman II regularly sent tributes to China. As a matter of fact at least 12 embassies[1]

1. Maspero says that Vikrantavarman sent tributes to the Chinese emperor no less than fifteen times (T'oung Pao XI, p. 524). But in the footnote he gives detailed record of only 13 such embassies. Of these the first, sent in 686, must be attributed to Prakasadharma whose last known date is 687 A. D. Of the rest, those before 713 must have been sent by one or other of the three kings Prakasadharma, Naravahanavarman, and Vikrantavarman II,

were sent to China from Champā in the years 691, 695, 699, 702, 703, 706, 707, 709, 711, 712, 713 and 731 A. D. Some of these, before 713 A. D., might have been sent by either Prakāśadharma or Naravāhanavarmā, but the majority were probably sent by Vikrāntavarman II.

Vikrāntavarman II was probably succeeded by Rudravarman II who sent tributes to China in 749 A.D. We do not know anything more about him. He died about 757 A. D. and with him probably ended the dynasty which was founded by Rudravarman I about the year 529 A. D.

The inscriptions of this dynasty are mostly found in the neighbourhood of Myson. This may be due to the sanctity of the temple and it is not proper to infer from it that their power was mainly confined to that district. The fact that one inscription (No. 8) is found in Hue and another(No. 15) in Khan Hoa province shows that their power extended very nearly over the whole of the kingdom. One of the earliest inscriptions (No. 2) of this dynasty was found at Cho Dinh in the province of Phu yen, and this also shows that from the very beginning their authority extended far beyond Myson. The epigraphical evidence undoubtedly shows that the province of Quang Nam in which Myson is situated was the chief stronghold of the dynasty from beginning to end.

KINGS REFERRED TO IN CHAPTER IV.

1. Gaṅgārāja
2. Manorathavarman
   (descended from No. 1)
3. Rudravarman (c. 529 A.D.—c. 565 A. D.)
   (Son of the daughter's daughter of No. 2.)

4. Śambhuvarman (c. 565 A.D.—629 A.D.)
   (Son of No. 3.)
5. Kandarpadharma (629 A D.—c. 640 A. D.)
   (Son of No. 4)
6. Prabhāsadharma (c 640 A. D.—645 A. D.)
   (Son of No. 5)
7. Satyakauśikasvāmī (Daughter's son of No. 3 and son-in-law of No. 5)
8. Daughter of No. 5 and wife of No. 7.
7. Satyakauśikasvāmī (a second time).
   } (645 A.D.-653 A.D.
9. Bhadreśvaravarman (?) (Son of Nos. 7 and 8)
10. Jagaddharma (?) (Son of No. 9).
   } (653 A.D.-655 A.D.
11. Prakāśadharma-Vikrāntavarman I (c. 655 A.D. — c. 690 A. D)
   (Son of No. 10)
12. Naravāhanavarman (?) (c. 690 A.D.—c. 710 A.D.)
   (Son of No. 11 ?)
13. Vikrāntavarman II (c. 710 A. D.—730 A. D. ?)
   (Son of No. 12 ?)
14. Rudravarman II (730 (?) A. D.—757 A. D.)

Chapter V.

THE DYNASTY OF PANDURANGA.

After Rudravarman II the kingdom of Champā passed on to a new dynasty. As all the inscriptions of this dynasty come from the Kauṭhāra region in the south, they probably originally belonged to that quarter. But from the very beginning they seem to have exercised suzerainty over the entire kingdom.

The founder of this dynasty is named Pṛthivīndravarman.[1] A brief reference is made to him in the Glai Lamov Inscription (No. 24), vv 2-5. We are told that he 'enjoyed the lands by having conquered all his enemies by his own power'. This seems to show that he owed the kingdom to his military genius. As we shall see, there are epigraphic references to more than one raid of Champā by the Javanese fleet within half a century of his accession. The Chinese history also contains reference to a raid as

1. Maspero attributes the title "Rudraloka" to this king on the authority of Ins. No. 24, verse 5. This verse, however, merely says 'that the king went to "Rudraloka" i.e, died, and I do not think that "Rudraloka" may be regarded as a posthumous title. (T'oung Pao. 1910, pp. 549-550). For a similar expression cf. verse 10, of the Glai Lamov Ins. (No. 24).

   Maspero further says that the throne was offered to Prthivindravarman by the nobles, but I do not find any authority for this statement' (Ibid). The verse (No. 31, B. VI) on which he relies is difficult to construe. I doubt if Prthivindravarman of that verse can be taken to refer to a king of a different dynasty who died more than 100 years ago. But even then it does not justify Maspero's assumption.

early as 767 A.D.[1] It is likely that the invasion of the Javanese fleet overthrew the last dynasty and Pṛthivīndra-varman owed the kingdom to his success against these naval marauders. But whatever may be the circumstances to which he owed his throne, the inscription tells us that 'he enjoyed the whole of Champā' (No. 24 A. V. 3). The king is said to have destroyed all the thieves. This probably means that there were disorders consequent upon the over-throw of the last dynasty and king Pṛthivīndravarman effectively checked them. He enjoyed a long reign and died sometime before 774 A.D., the earliest known date of his successor king Satyavarman. King Satyavarman was the nephew (sister's son) of king Pṛthivīndravarman. He issued the Po-Nagar stelæ inscription (No. 22) and we know a great deal about him from the Glai Lamov Inscription (No. 24) of his younger brother Indravarman, and the Po-Nagar inscription of his sister's son, king Vikrāntavarman (No. 29 A.).

The chief event in the reign of the king was the raid of the Javanese sea-men who devastated the land, and in particular destroyed a temple containing a Mukhaliṅga. There was a halo of sanctity around the temple as popular tradition ascribed its foundation to a king Vicitrasagara 'in the year 5911 of the Dvāpara Yuga' (No. 29). In the year 774 A. D. the Javanese—"vicious cannibals coming from other countries by means of ships,"—burnt this temple and carried away the image together with all the properties of the temple. King Satyavarmā pursued these marauders in his own ships and inflicted a crushing defeat upon them. But the object of the pursuit was not fully realised and king Satyavarman was very much dejected to learn that the Śivamukha, to-

1. T'oung Pao, 1910 p. 550.

gether with its property which was in the enemy ships, was thrown into water, and that the Śivaliṅga was destroyed (No. 22). The victorious king, unable to recover the old image, installed a new Śivamukhaliṅga, together with images of other deities, in the year 784 A. D. and gave rich endowments to the god. For this reason he came to be regarded as the second Vicitrasagara or an incarnation of that king.

Conventional praises are bestowed on the king in verses 6-9 of the Glai Lamov Inscription (No. 24), but no other specific event of his reign is mentioned. We are expressly told in verse 10 of the same inscription that he died without reigning for a long time, and we may therefore put the end of king Satyavarman's reign shortly after 784 A. D. King Satyavarman was succeeded by his younger brother Indravarman. He is the author of the Yang Tikuh and Glai Lamov Inscriptions (Nos. 23 and 24) in which his glory is sung in most extravagant terms. He is said to have fought with many enemies and ruled over the whole of Champa.[1] The chief event in his reign, like that of his predecessor, was a raid of Javanese sea-men. In the year 787 A. D. they burnt the temple of Bhadrādhipatīśvara, a celebrated deity of the kingdom, who was regarded as having been established there for many thousands of years (No. 23). King Indravarmā re-installed the deity under the name of Indrabhadreśvara, and endowed it with various treasures in the year 799 A. D. In addition to this, king Indravarmā endowed many other pious establishments. He at first installed Indrabhogeśvara at Vīrapura. He then installed in the excellent

1. Maspero thinks that it is by defeating the enemies that he came to rule over Champa. That does not, however, seem to be a fair deduction from the vague, general expression of his victory over enemies with which the two inscriptions abound.

house of Satyavarmā (i. e. in a temple erected by that king) the god Indraparameśvara, and endowed him with various riches in 801 A. D. Lastly, Indravarmā made a rich donation of all kinds of treasures to the god Śaṅkara-Nārāyaṇa (i. e. Śiva and Hari united in one body).

A verse in Yang Tikuh Inscription (No. 23, V. 3 and footnote) has been taken to mean that Indravarmā carried on wars in the north, north-east, east, south-east and south, and Maspero has based important conclusions upon it, locating the countries in the various directions implied in the passage. The verse does not, however, seem to bear that meaning at all.

Indravarman renewed the relations with China and sent presents of rhinoceros and buffaloes to the emperor in 793 A. D.

Indravarman was succeeded by his brother-in-law (sister's husband) Harivarman. His full name was Vīra Jaya Śrī Harivarmadeva and he assumed the proud title of 'Rājādhirāja Śrī-Champā-pura-Parameśvara', king of kings, Lord of Champā. Three inscriptions of his time are known to us (Nos. 25-27). In one of them (No. 26) he is said to have defeated the Cinas. From the Chinese history we know that in January 803, a king of Champā conquered the two chinese districts of Hoan and Ai, and renewed the expedition again in 809 A.D. But the chinese governor forced him to retreat after inflicting a crushing defeat upon him, and wreaked his vengeance upon the people of the two districts who helped the king of Champā. The king referred to in the Chinese annals is almost certainly Harivarman, though it is not easy to decide what was the extent of his success against the imperial forces.

Harivarman entrusted his son Vikrāntavarman with the government of Pāṇḍuraṅga district (modern Phanrang), but as he was too young for the responsible post, he was placed in charge of a general named Pār [1]. This general led an expedition against Cambodge on behalf of his young master, and 'ravaged the towns of the Kambujas'. Whether it was a mere border raid, or anything more serious than that, we have no means to determine. A fragmentary passage of the Po-Nagar inscription (No. 26) seems to indicate that he carried his arms into the heart of Cambodge [2]. But the fame of the general did not rest upon his victories alone. He was equally renowned for his religious establishments. A famous temple of Bhagavatī in Kauṭhāra remained empty for a long time, probably the image was carried away by the Javanese marauders. General Pār made a new stone image of the goddess, and in the year 817, erected three new temples for the *Liṅga* of Sandhaka, Śrī Vināyaka and Śrī-Malalā-kuṭhāra. He also made various other minor donations.

The known dates of Harivarman are 813 A. D. and 817 A. D. If the Chinese expeditions referred to above have been correctly attributed to him, he must have ascended the throne before 801 A. D. As the last known date of Indravarman is 799 A. D. the year 800 A. D. may be looked upon as the date of his accession.

Harivarman was succeeded by his son Vikrāntavarman III, who was the nephew (sister's son) of the two kings Satya-

1. The reading of this name is doubtful. I have adopted the reading of Finot (B. E. F. vol, III. p. 637. note 2.).

2. Maspero minimises the importance of this raid on the ground that no Cambodian document describes Jayavarman II, the contemporary king of Cambodge, as being vanquished by the Chams (T'oung Pao 1910, p. 56:) But as the inscriptions of a country very seldom refer to reverses sustained by its kings, no importance need be attached to such silence in the present case.

varmā and Indravarmā. As related above, he was entrusted with the government of Pāṇḍuaraṅga by his father and was placed in charge of general Pār. He is the author of four inscriptions found at Po-Nagar (Nos. 29 A, 29 B, 29 C, 30). Conventional praises are bestowed on him in the last, while all the four describe his religious endowments. Among others, he granted a field to Śrī Vikrānta-Rudreśvara in 854 A. D., and subsequently another to Śrī Vikrānta-devādhibhaveśvara. He also established a Mahādeva and richly endowed the god.

Vikrāntavarman III died without issue and with him ended the dynasty founded by Pṛthivīndravarman. As already remarked above the epigraphic evidence shows that the dynasty had its stronghold in the south, and it has been styled the dynasty of Pāṇḍuraṅga.

It held sway for about a century from the middle of the eighth to the middle of the ninth century A.D.

It has been suggested[1] that the capital was removed from Champā to Vīrapura during the rule of this dynasty. There does not, however, seem to be sufficient evidence for this assumption. For the only thing we know about the town is that several images of gods were established there by Indravarman. On the other hand, the fact that Harivarman is styled as lord of the city of Champā seems to indicate that Champā was still the official capital. Further, if we remember that the government of Pāṇḍuraṅga was entrusted by Harivarman to his son, we must hold that the main seat of the government was far to the north. All these, however, in no way invalidate the conclusion, stated at the beginning, that the dynasty might have originated from Pāṇḍuraṅga.

---

1. Maspero in T'oung Pao, 19 0, p. 559. Maspero says that the temple of Bhadradhipatisvara was "to the west of the town of Virapura,'. The inscription (No. 23 V. 5), however, simply refers to town and not to Virapura.

It is also a noteworthy fact that throughout this period the Chinese substituted the name Houan Wang for Lin-yi to denote the kingdom of Champā. After the downfall of this dynasty Houan Wang was replaced by Tch'eng Cheng which is undoubtedly the Chinese transcription of Champā. It is difficult to explain the meaning of the new term Houan Wang [1].

KINGS REFERRED TO IN CHAPTER V.

1. Pṛthivīndravarman (c. 758 A. D.—773 A. D).
2. Satyavarman (c. 773 A. D.—785 A. D.).
   (Sister's son of No. 1.).
3. Indravarman I (785—c. 800 A. D.).
   (Younger brother of 2).
4. Harivarman (c. 800 A. D.—c. 820 A. D.).
   (Sister's husband of No. 3).
5. Vikrāntavarman III (c. 820 A. D.—860 A. D.).
   (Sister's son of Nos. 2 and 3).

---

1. T'oung Pao, 1910, pp. 547 ff.

Chapter VI.

THE BHRGU DYNASTY.

The new dynasty that supplanted the old seems to have been founded by Indravarman II, though we are not quite certain on this point. The Dong Duong Inscription (No. 31), issued by this king in 875 A. D. gives the following account of the family.

"From the son (or family) of Parameśvara was born Uroja, the king of the world. From him was born the fortunate and intelligent Dharmarāja.

"From him was born the intelligent king Śrī Rudravarmā. The son of the latter was the far-famed king Śrī Bhadravarmā.

"The son of Śrī Bhadravarmā, known as Śrī Indravarman, has become the king of Champā through the grace of Maheśvara.

"Thus the sovereignty of the king was transmitted in its entirety from those kings (lit. sons). It was not given by the grandfather or the father.

"By the special merit of his austerities, and by virtue of his pure intelligence, he gained (the kingdom), not from his grandfather or father."

(Verses No. 31. A. 18-22)

The last verse is echoed again in a prose passage "Śrī Jaya Indravarmā Mahārājādhirāja became king of Champā by virtue of peculiar merits accruing from austerities of many previous births" (Ins. p. 87)

Now as to the genealogy of Indravarmā, it is traced from Mahādeva, and thus a divine origin is attributed to the family. Elsewhere the family is referred to as the 'Bhrgu family (No. 42, v. 8, No. 39, v. 16) evidently because of the mythology contained in No. 31, according to which Bhṛgu was sent to Champā by Mahādeva himself. The next king Uroja also belongs to the category of mythical kings, for he is elsewhere (No. 31, A. 10,) described as a god sent down to the earth by Mahādeva. As to the third king, Dharmarāja, it is doubtful whether he is a historical figure, or belongs to the category of divine or mythical beings. It may be noted that his name does not end in 'varman' which is almost the invariable custom of the kings of Champā at this period. Further, it is somewhat singular that whereas Indravarman is said to be the son of Bhadravarman, and the latter the son of Rudravarman, the last named king is simply said to have been born from Dharmarāja; similarly Dharmarāja is simply said to have been born from Uroja. Of course ordinarily such expressions indicate the relation of son and father, but here the obvious contrast in the two sets of expressions may be taken to mean that Rudravarman was merely descended from Dharmarāja and not his son.[1] In short we shall be on the safe side if we look upon the last three kings alone as historical figures viz.

Rudravarmā
|
Bhadravarmā
|
Indravarmā

Now both Rudravarmā and Bhadravarmā are explicitly referred to as kings. It would then follow that the royal dynasty to which Indravarmā belonged was founded by Rudravarmā, and the former inherited the throne of his father and grandfather. Strangely enough, this is exactly the conclusion against which we are warned by the king himself, who declares, in no uncertain voice, that he did not inherit the throne from his father or grandfather, but gained it through

1. These arguments have been elaborated by Finot. (B. E. F. vol IV. pp. 96 ff).

the grace of Maheśvara, by virtue of his meritorious acts in previous births (cf. the last four verses quoted above).

It is a very hard task to reconcile these conflicting statements. Finot supposes that the grandfather of the king (i. e. Rudravarmā) had probably usurped the throne by murdering the legitimate king, and hence Indravarman, unwilling to base his claim to the throne on this criminal act, referred to his own austerities and grace of Maheśvara as forming sufficient claims thereto.[1] This is no doubt a possible view, but a better explanation seems to be that Rudravarman and Bhadravarman were local kings, and it was Indravarman who first made himself the master of Champā. Thus although descended from a line of kings he did not owe the kingdom of Champā either to his father or to his grandfather, but only to his own meritorious acts. That kings Rudravarman and Bhadravarman were historical personages we gather from Hoa Que Inscription (No. 39 C.) and An-Thai inscription (No. 37). The last named inscription further proves that Bhadravarman actually ruled in the Quang Nam district and made donations to a Buddhist monastery. There is nothing to support Maspero's view that Vikrāntavarman III, having no children, recommended Indravarman to the principal citizens who sought him out and placed him on the throne of Champā.[2]

1. Ibid.

2. The expressions "Sandarsita" (No. 31 B, v. II) and "Mahajanavarair-anugamyamanah" (Ibid, v. 9.) have led Finot to suppose that king Indravarman was "nominated by the king" and proclaimed by the citizens" (Ibid p. 97). The passages, however, do not seem to me capable of yielding this interpretation.

Maspero's view is apparently based upon that of

In any case Indravarman II. seems to be the first notable king of this dynasty. He was originally called "Śrī Lakṣmīndra Bhumīśvara Grāmasvāmin"[1], and on gaining the sovereignty of Champā, he assumed the title 'Śrī Jaya Indravarmā Mahārājādhirāja'. He married his aunt, a niece of his grandfather Rudravarman III (Hoa Que Ins. No. 39). The Dong Duong Inscription praises him in extravagant terms, and commemorates the erection of a monastery and a temple for Svabhayada, i. e. Buddha. This is very interesting, for it shows that the king had leanings towards Buddhism. But he had of course the traditional faith in Śaivism. For the inscription not only refers to a Śivaliṅga made by him (No. 31 B. V. 3), but also contains a long invocation of the god Śambhubhadreśvara (No. 31 A. V. 10). This god is already familiar to us, and we have seen above that it was erected by Bhadravarman about 400 A. D., destroyed by fire, and re-installed by his successor Śambhuvarman. Indravarman II, however, completely ignores these historical facts and gives an altogether different story about its origin. He says in effect that the sage Bhṛgu got the *liṅga* from Mahādeva himself, while Uroja got it from Bhṛgu and installed it at Champā. Thus the two mythical names Bhṛgu and Uroja are substituted for those of Bhadravarman and Śambhuvarman. Indravarman could not possibly have

Finot, but he has transformed it a great deal. Finot apparently means that Indravarman was nominated by the king, his father, but Maspero takes this king to be Vikrantavarman, and adds two new facts viz. that Vikrantavarman had no children, and that the nobles of his court went in search of king Indravarman, nominated by him. I do not find any authority for either of these statements.

1. Dong Duong Ins. No, 31. B. v II. Cf. B. E F., vol. IV. p. 97.

been ignorant of these kings, for their inscription recording the installation of the *liṅga* were there before the temple. It was then a deliberate misrepresentation on the part of Indravarman II, actuated no doubt by a policy of ignoring kings and dynasties from whom he could not legitimately claim his succession.

Besides Dong Duong Inscription two other inscriptions (Nos. 32 and 33 [1]) belong to the reign of Indravarman II. Phu Thuan (No. 33) inscription simply records that the king exempted the temple of Śrī Bhāgyakānteśvara from taxes, and employed four priests for daily worship there. From Bo Mang inscription (No. 32) we learn that the king dedicated a field together with slaves to Śrī Mahāliṅgadeva, installed by his minister named Manicaitya in the year 889 A. D. Conventional praises are bestowed on him in An-Thai inscription (No. 37).

Indravarman II must have enjoyed a fairly long and peaceful reign between 854 A. D., the date of Vikrāntavarman III, and 898 A. D., the earliest date of his successor. His known dates are 875 and 889 A. D. [2] So far as we know he sent only a single embassy to China in 877 A. D., as he had nothing to fear from that quarter on account of its internal conditions. Indravarman II seems to have been succeeded by Jaya Siṁhavarman.[3] The relationship betwen the two is not definitely known. The Dong Duong inscription (No. 36), however, says that the mother of king Jayasiṁhavarman had a younger sister, Pov ku lyan Śrī Rājakula, also known as

1. This is doubtfully attributed to Indravarman II, cf No. 33
2. To this we may possibly add 893 A. D. (See Introduction to the Chausa Ins. No. 38).
3. This conclusion seems to follow from the Ban-lanh Inscription (No. 35), and the Chau-sa Inscripiton (No. 38).

Haradevī. Haradevī's husband was king Śrī Parama-Buddhaloka, and she installed Śrī Indraparameśvara for the sake of religious merit of her own husband. This might be taken to imply that the coronation-name of her husband was Indravarman, as the name of the gods is often formed by the addition of the name of the king. It may be held therefore that Haradevī was the queen of Indravarman II.[1] According to this view, Siṁhavarman would be the son of the elder sister of Indravarman's queen,[2] and Indravarman would have the epithet of "Parama-Buddhaloka".

We possess five inscriptions belonging to the reign of Jaya Siṁhavarman (Nos. 34-38), but they merely give a list of his pious donations and do not contain any reference to political events. Only we hear a great deal of the wealth and splendour of Indrapura which seems to have been the real capital of this dynasty, although the city of Champā is still officially recognised as such.

Out of gratitude to his maternal aunt Haradevī, to whom he owed the throne, king Jaya Siṁhavarman exempted from taxes several temples erected by her and installed the august goddess Haromā.

Other pious works of the king in the form of direct donations to gods, or protection and immunity granted to temples established by others, are referred to in Bo-Mang (No. 34), Ban-lanh (No. 35), An-Thai (No. 37), Hoa-Que (No. 39), and

1. This point has been fully discussed in the Introduction to Dong Duong Inscription No. 36.

2. Maspero concludes from a reference to Guhesvara in v. 2 of the Dong Duong Inscription, that Guhesvara was the name of Jaya 'Simhavarman's father (T'oung Pao vol. XII, p. 58). But this seems to be a far-fetched int rpretation. In any case the name should be Guhavarman and not Guhesvara.

the fragmentary Chau-sa Inscriptions (No. 38).

It is important to note that the royal patronage was not confined to Śaivism alone but Buddhism also had a fair share of it.

The queen of Jaya Siṁhavarman was named Tribhuvana-Mahādevī who is praised in extravagant terms in the Nhan-Bieu Inscription (No. 43) and whose religious donations are referred to in the Ha-Trung inscription (No. 44). The Nhan-Bieu inscription refers to her father's family as of very high standing and gives the following genealogy.

Lyaṅ Vṛddhakulā

Narendrādhipati — Son

Daughter — Tribhuvanadevī = king Jayasiṁhavarman

Pov Kluñ Piliḥ Rājadvāraḥ

The Nhan Bieu inscription furnishes a detailed account of Pov Kluñ Rājadvāraḥ, the son of the queen's cousin. He became a favourite of king Jayasiṁhavarman and was sent on a diplomatic mission to Java. The Bo-Mang inscription (No. 34) makes a vague allusion to the power of the king having spread to other lands, and this is confirmed by the diplomatic mission sent to Java which, as we shall see, was continued by his successors. King Jayasiṁhavarman was succeeded by his eldest son Śrī Jayaśaktivarman.[1] He is only referred to in the Nhan Bieu Ins. (No. 43) and probably reigned for only a short time. The earliest known date of Jayasiṁhavarman is 898 A. D. and

1. It is unnecessary to point out in detail the errors in Maspero's accounts of this period. They are due partly to the misreading of the Po-Nagar Ins. (No. 45) by Bergaigne, thereby introducing a new king Haravarman, and partly to the fact that several inscriptions throwing new light on this period were not yet discovered.

that of the successor of Jayaśaktivarman, 909 A. D. Jayasiṁhavarman, therefore, must have died sometime between 903 A. D. his last known date, and 909 A. D. His son, too, must have died before 909 A. D. The next king was Bhadravarman III. whose relationship to his predecessor is not known as yet. The way in which he is introduced in the Nhan Bieu inscription seems to indicate that he did not occupy the throne by any unfair means. For Instance, Piliḥ Rājadvāraḥ, the son of the cousin of Jaya Siṁhavarman's queen, continued to occupy a high position under Bhadravarman, as he did under his two predecessors, and was again sent on a diplomatic errand to Java. This, of course, proves nothing, but gives rise to a fair presumption that there was no violent disturbance in the internal polity of the kingdom.

We possess four inscriptions of the time of Bhadravarman III. (Nos. 39-42). Conventional praises are bestowed upon the king, and in particular his victories over enemies are referred to again and again. Whether these are mere eulogistic expressions or have any historical basis to stand upon, we have no means to determine. The Bang-An inscription (No. 42) refers to the multitude of royal ambassadors coming from different countries. The Hoa-Que Inscription (No. 39) says with reference to one of his ministers, that he was able to understand thoroughly the meaning of messages sent by kings from different countries.' The Nhan-Bieu Inscription (No. 43) states that he sent Piliḥ Rājadvāraḥ on a diplomatic mission to Java. These isolated statements, occurring in different contexts, leave no doubt that the kingdom of Champā was now recognised abroad as an important and powerful kingdom and took part in international politics. The first stages of this new departure we have already noticed in the reign of Jaya Siṁhavarman.

The Hoa-Que inscription (No 39) refers to an important

collateral branch of the royal family which supplied high officials to the kingdom. The founder of this family, Sārthavāha, was a nephew of Rudravarman III, the first king of the dynasty, and a brother of the principal queen of Indravarman II. His three sons Ājñā Mahāsāmanta, Ājñā Narendra nṛpavitra and Ājñā Jayendrapati occupied high positions in the kingdom as ministers of king Bhadravarman. These three brothers, together with a younger sister, called Ugradevī,[1] erected an image of Mahā Rudradeva, 'out of devotion to, and in imitation of the features of their father.' Other religious endowments of the members of the family are also referred to in the same inscription.

Bhadravarman erected many temples and images of gods, a list of which is given in the Hoa-Que inscription (No. 39). Other religious endowments are referred to in the Bang-an inscription (No. 42).

Bhadravarman must have a very short reign. His known dates are 909 and 910 A. D. He must have died in 910 or 911 A. D. the known date of his successor. His reign, therefore, falls between this date and 903 A. D. the last known date of Jaya Siṁhavarman. As one king intervened between the two he did not probably reign for more than a period of five years, 905 to 910 A. D.

Bhadravarman III. was succeeded by his son Indravarman

1. Huber who edited the Hoa-Que inscription remarks that Ugradevi had married a Cham king. probably Bhadravarman III, the reigning king (B. E. F. vol. XI, p. 286). This is apparently based on his interpretation of verse XXVI (c) of the inscription. But the verse does not contain any word equivalent to "queen" so far as I could see (cf the text and translation of the inscription No. 39).

III. We possess eight inscriptions of his reign (Nos. 43-50).[1] The king had a remarkable personality. His literary accomplishments are described in the Po-Nagar inscription (No. 45). He is said to have mastered the six systems of Brāhmaṇical Philosophy as well as the Buddhist Philosophy, the Grammar of Pāṇini together with its commentary Kāśikā, and the Uttarakalpa of the Śaivites. Inspite of obvious exaggerations, the king must be taken to have been a remarkable scholar in his day.

---

1. It has been usual to distinguish between Indravarman III and his successor Jaya Indravarman I, the last five inscriptions (Nos. 46-50) being attributed to the latter. But I do not see any reason for this distinction. Indravarman II, for example, is twice called Jaya Indravarman (cf. Dong Duong Ins. No. 31, B., and Bo-Mang Inscription (No. 32) and the same thing may hold good in the case of Indravarman III. Besides, the Po-Nagar inscription (No. 47) of the so-called Jaya Indravarman I refers to the re-erection of a stone image in place of the golden one formerly installed by the king himself (cf. yena in line 1 and its correlative sa in line 3). Now we know from No. 45 that Indravarman III erected a golden image of Bhagavati. The identity of the two may therefore be presumed on fairly satisfactory evidence, although it cannot be definitely proved. It may be objected that as Indravarman III ascended the throne in 910 or 911 A. D. and the last known date of Jaya Indravarman is 971 A.D. the identification of the two would lead us to presume an unusually long reign. But as the Lai-trung Inscription (No. 46) of Jaya Indravarman I is dated 918 or 921 A.D. we have in any case to presume quite a long reign. Besides, Maspero's theory that Indravarman III was succeeded by Jaya Indravarman I about 960 A.D. is proved erroneous by the Lai-trung Inscription (No. 46).

But while the king was busy with the study of Philosophy and Grammar, the kingdom was invaded by the Cambodgians. The Po-Nagar inscription (No. 47) informs us that the golden image installed by the king was carried away by the Cambodgians and the king substituted a stone image in its place in 965 A. D. This golden image is no doubt that of the goddess Bhagavatī which was installed by the king in the year 918 A. D. (cf. Po Nagar Ins. No. 45).

The date of this Cambodgian invasion is not difficult to determine. The Baksei Cankran inscription of Rājendravarman II, dated 947 A. D.,[1] states that the king was a fire of destruction to his royal enemies, commencing with that of Champā. As Rājendravarman ascended the throne in 944 A. D., his expedition against Champā must have taken place between 944 and 947 A. D.

Indravarman ultimately hurled back the forces of the Cambodgian king, but his straitened circumstances are indicated by the fact that the golden image of Bhagavatī which was carried away by the invading troops could only be replaced by a stone figure. (Po Nagar Ins. No. 47).

For a long time the kings of Champā stopped their customary presents to China, apparently because it was torn by internal dissensions after the downfall of the T'ang dynasty. The four ephemeral dynasties that succeeded the T'ang were all ignored by the Cham kings, but on the accession of Kouo Wei, who founded a new dynasty—the Heou Tcheou Indravarman sent an embassy to China with various presents (951 A. D.). The intercourse thus resumed continued uninterrupted throughout his reign. When Tchao K'ouang-Yin founded the Soung Dynasty in China (960 A. D.), Indra-

1. J. A. 1882 (2) p. 151; 1884 (1) p. 54. Aymonier, Cambodge vol. III p. 8.

varman sent an embassy to offer congratulations. Altogether seven embassies from Champā visited the Imperial court in 958, 959, 962, 966, 967, 970 and 971 A. D.[1]

Indravarman III. enjoyed a long reign of sixty years. He ascended the throne about 911 A. D. and died in 971 or 972 A. D.

KINGS REFERRED TO IN CHAPTER VI.

1. Rudravarman III.
2. Bhadravarman II.
   (Son of No. 1)
3. Indravarman II. (c. 870-c. 895 A.D.)
   (Son of No. 2)
4. Jaya Siṁhavarman (c. 895-904 A. D.)
   (Son of the elder sister of the queen of No. 3)
5. Jayaśaktivarman (c. 904-905 A. D.)
   (Son of No. 4)
6. Bhadravarman III. (c. 905-911 A. D.)
7. Indravarman III. (c. 911 A. D.-972 A. D.)
   (Son of No. 6)

---

1. T'oung Pao 1911, p. 62 ff.

Chapter VII.

The Annamite Invasions.

For nearly a century after the death of Indravarman III. the history of Champā is obscure in the extreme. Excepting one doubtful case, to be noticed later on, no epigraphic evidence comes to our help, and we are solely dependent on the Chinese and Annamite annals for guiding us in this dark period. The outstanding event of this period is the Annamite invasion, leading to internal disintegration of the kingdom of Champā, and this sufficiently explains the absence of epigraphic records bearing upon the history of the period.

Indravarman III. seems to have been succeeded by a king whose name is differently spelt in Chinese histories and may be taken to be equivalent to Parameśvaravarman. He sent embassies to China in 972, 973, 974, 976, 977, and 979 A. D. But he was soon involved in a quarrel with the Annamites which brought ruin upon himself and his kingdom.

As the Annamites began to play an increasingly predominant part in the history of Champā from this time forward till that kingdom was finally subjugated by them, it is necessary to give a brief review of the rise and growth of this new power.

It has already been related in Chapter II how a section of the widely spread Yue race had ultimately established itself in Tonkin and northern Annam, and developed a distinct nationality. It has also been pointed out that when this country passed into the hands of China (111 B. C.) during the Han period, the territory inhabited by the Annamites was comprised within the two Chinese provinces of Kiao-tche and Kieou-tchen corresponding to modern Hanoi and Thanh Hoa regions.

These two provinces were ruled by Chinese governors. The central authority in China, however, could not always keep a firm hold upon these distant provinces. Si-Kouang, the governor of Kiao-tche (in the first quarter of the first century A. D.) behaved practically as an independent king. His administration was memorable for the large measure of success which attended his efforts to introduce the Chinese civilisation in the province. But the tyranny of the Chinese, both officials and colonists, weighed heavily upon the people. In 36 A. D. To Dinh, the successor of of Si Kouang put to death the husband of Tru'ng Trac, and the exasperated people at once broke into revolt under the leadership of this spirited lady and her sister Tru'ng Nhi The Chinese governor fled in haste and Tru'ng Trac began to rule as an independent sovereign (40 A. D.). But her power was short-lived. A Chinese army under Ma Youen easily overran the country. The two sisters were taken captive and beheaded, and the Chinese authority was again established in the country.

The conqueror Ma Youen planted a column of bronze at Co-lau as a token of his victory, and also probably to mark the boundary of the province. He did not pass beyond Than Hoa in the south, but according to later legends, he passed far to the south, in the heart of Annam, planted a small Chinese colony there, and erected two copper columns to mark the southern frontier of the Chinese possessions.

The Annamites again revolted in 183 A. D., but were subjugated in 226 A. D. In 541 Ly Bon or Ly Bi, an Annamite of Chinese origin revolted against the Chinese governor and declared himself king. He and his two successors ruled for 62 years, but the Chinese general Lieou Fang reconquered the province in 603 A. D. Ly Bon ruled over the whole of Tonkin and in the south his kingdom reached the frontier of Champā. His fight with Rudravarman has been referred to in Chapter IV.

From 603 to 939 A. D. the Chinese remained the undisputed master of Tonkin. Under the T'ang dynasty a new province was created embracing all the Chinese possessions from the northern extremity of Tonkin to the borders of the kingdom of Champā. It was named Ngan-nan (pronounced by the Annamites as An Nam) meaning "pacified south". In 722 an Annamite chief, Mai Thuc Loan, made alliance with the kings of Champā and revolted against the Chinese governor. But the revolt was easily suppressed by the Chinese generals.

Towards the close of the ninth century A. D. troubles arose in the country. The political changes in China, involving frequent changes in the provincial administration, led to a state of anarchy and confusion in Tonkin. At last, unable to bear the miseries of Chinese yoke, the Annamites broke into revolt early in the 10th century A. D. The moment was very opportune. The downfall of the Imperial T'ang dynasty in 907 A. D. was followed by a period of anarchy and disintegration in China, lasting for more than half a century. The Annamites took full advantage of this situation and freed themselves from the iron yoke of the Chinese. Henceforth Annam became an independent country, nominally acknowledging the suzerainty of China at times, but quite free from Chinese control for all practical purposes. A new power thus came into existence which was ultimately destined to play an important part in the history of south-eastern Asia. [1]

---

1. The short historical account of Annam is mainly based on the following books. (1) Cordier-Histoire Generale de

The first independent royal Annamite dynasty was founded by Ngo Quyen in 939 A. D. But the supreme power did not remain with a single chief for a long time. By 965 A. D. twelve important chiefs had partitioned the country among themselves. In 968 A. D. Dinh Bo Linh defeated the twelve chiefs and proclaimed himself emperor. He ruled for 12 years but was murdered in 979 A. D. Ngo Nhut Khanh, one of the twelve chiefs defeated by the emperor, had taken refuge in the court of Champā. As soon as the news of emperor's death reached him, he planned to seize the throne and asked for the aid of Parameśvaravarman.

The latter readily consented and led a naval expedition against Tonkin in person. The Cham fleet made good progress and reached within a few miles of the capital. At night, however, a storm broke out and destroyed the whole fleet with the exception of the royal vessel which safely returned to Champā. A large number, including Nhut Khanh, was drowned and the rest fell into the hands of the Annamites (979 A. D.).

Shortly after, Le Hoan was elected by the Annamite chiefs as their emperor (980 A. D.). He successfully opposed a Chinese expedition sent by the Emperor K'ouang-Yi to reconquer the province. He sent an ambassador to Parameśvaravarman, but the latter imprisoned him against diplomatic convention of all ages and countries. Le Hoan was naturally furious, and led an expedition in person against Champā. Parameśvaravarman was defeated and killed at the first encounter, and the Annamite king marched towards the capital. Although a new king was hastily set up, he could not save the capital city which fell into the hands of the Annamites. After pillaging the city and

la Chine [Paris 1920] [2], E. Luro —Le Pays D' Annam [Paris 1878].

burning its temples Le Hoan made arrangements for governing the province and returned with an immense booty (982 A. D.). Among others, he took with him 100 ladies of the royal harem and an Indian Bhiksu.

The new king—whose name has been restored from Chinese Annals as Indravarman (IV)—took refuge in his southern territories and sent a Brāhmaṇa envoy to the Chinese court complaining against the Annamite occupation of Champā. But the emperor was not in a mood to renew the fight with the Annamites and advised the king of Champā to protect his own kingdom and live on friendly terms with his neighbours.

In the meantime the Annamite chiefs were quarrelling among themselves. The history of the internal quarrels and dissensions is but imperfectly known to us but they ultimately led to the usurpation of the throne of Champā by Lu'u-Ky-Tong, an Annamite chief, who revolted against Le Hoan. Le Hoan advanced with an army to punish him but the difficulties of the route, added to the inclemency of the weather, forced him to retreat (983 A. D.).

Lu'u-Ky-Tong was now quite secure in his dominions in northern Champā. His power was on the increase, and after the death of Indravarman IV he was officially proclaimed king of Champā. The foreign domination, however, pressed hard on the people, and they began to emigrate to the Chinese territories in large numbers. Fortunately, a national hero appeared at this time at Vijaya. Lu'u-Ky-Tong disappeared and the former was crowned king under the name of Vijaya Śrī Harivarman (II)[1] (989 A. D.). The capital was fixed at Vijaya in Binh-Dinh.

1. Maspero reads this name as Sri Indravarman [T'oung Pao 1911, p. 72] but cf. Finot's remarks in B. E. F. vol. XV, No. 2. p. 48 fn (2).

This king has left a short Cham inscription of four lines on a block of sandstone lying in the vestibule of a temple at Myson (No 51). It records the installation of the god Śrī Jaya Īśāna Bhadreśvara in the year 991 A. D., and is probably a reminiscence of the work of restoration that must have slowly followed the cruel devastation by the Annamites.

Shortly after his accession Harivarman II found his territories again ravaged by Le Hoan. He sent an embassy with rich presents to the Imperial court of China complaining about the conduct of Le Hoan, and the emperor commanded Le Hoan to keep within his own territory. Hari Varman II also wanted to conciliate the Annamite king and refused assistance to an Annamite chief who had rebelled against Le Hoan. The latter, touched by this signal mark of friendship, and probably also intimidated by the order of the Chinese emperor, not only stopped his incursions, but also released a number of Cham prisoners (992 A. D.). During the same year the Chinese emperor sent a rich present to Harivarman II, who was, glad beyond measure at such an unexpected honour, and sent in return an envoy with a rich tribute. In a letter to the emperor which he sent along with this envoy, the king poured forth his feelings of gratitude and helplessness in a pathetic manner:

"I am a chief of small renown. The foreigners always invaded and devastated my country, and my subjects, unable to defend, were scattered like straw before a storm. Then you extended your protection to me and sent me a present of magnificent horses, standards and equipments of war. Learning the Imperial favour vouchsafed to me, my neighbours no longer entertain any desire of ruining me. Now my kingdom is again enjoying peace, and the scattered people are coming back... My country has the same reverence for you as for the heaven above which covers us, and the earth below which bears us, and my gratitude is unlimited. 10,000 li of sea divides your august capital from my country, and yet your goodwill is extended towards me" The humble epistle ended with a request that three hundred of his subjects which had taken refuge in the Chinese territory might be repatriated to Champā.

Outwardly Harivarman was on equally good terms with Le Hoan, the Annamite king, and sent diplomatic missions to him. Nevertheless the soldiers of Champā ravaged the Annamite territory to the north. Once, Le Hoan rebuked the Cham envoy and refused to accept the tribute brought by him. Harivarman hastened to pacify him and sent his own grandson as hostage to his court (995 A. D.). But the Chams nevertheless continued to raid the Annamite territory. In 997 a Cham army marched upto the borders of Tonkin but returned without invading it.

Harivarman II was succeeded by a king, the first part of whose name alone has reached us in a Chinese form,[1] viz. Yaṅ Pu Ku Vijaya Śrī. He ascended the throne sometime before 999 A. D. when he sent an envoy to China. King Harivarman II, although proclaimed king at Vijaya, had re-established the Court at the ancient capital Indrapura. But that city was sacked by Le Hoan and had suffered all the horrors of foreign domination. Yaṅ Pu Ku Vijaya Śrī definitely abandoned it, and, in order to avoid the domination of the Annamites, retired to Vijaya which henceforth became the capital of Champā and remained as such till the end.

In 1004 Yaṅ Pu Ku Vijaya Śrī sent an ambassador to the Chinese Court who met there a deputation from Arab. Three years later, he sent another ambassador to the Emperor with a long letter and rich presents. Questioned by the Emperor the ambassador reported that their capital had been removed to Vijaya, 700 li to the south of the old capital.

---

1. Yang p'ou Kiu P'i t'ou yi Che li.

Yaṅ Pu Ku Vijaya Śrī was succeeded by a king, the Chinese form of whose name[1] has been doubtfully restored to Śrī Harivarmadeva III. He sent three embassies to China in 1010, 1011, and 1015, and one to Tonkin in 1011. With his envoy to China in 1011 he sent a few lions which were objects of great curiosity to the Imperial Court.

His successor, the Chinese form of whose name[2] has been doubtfully restored to Parameśvaravarman II, sent tribute to China in 1018 A. D. Early in the year 1021, the Annamites all on a sudden attacked the camp of Bo Chanh which protected the northern frontier of Champā. The Cham general opposed them, but was killed, and his army retreated in disorder. The invading army, however, also suffered great loss and did not dare to advance any further.

The next king, the Chinese form of whose name[3] has been doubtfully restored as Yaṅ Pu Ku Śrī Vikrāntavarman (IV) was on the throne in 1030 A. D. when he sent an embassy to China with tribute. His reign seems to be full of civil wars and revolutions. For twice, in 1038 and 1039 A. D., his son sought protection at the court of Tonkin, and a few months later, the entire garrison of the camp of Bo Chinh sought refuge with the Annamite Emperor. Vikrāntavarman died in 1041 A. D., and the year following, his son Jaya Siṁhavarman II asked for investiture from the Chinese court.

Jaya Siṁhavarman's indiscretion brought another terrible calamity upon the unfortunate kingdom of Champā. In 1043 his navy harassed the Annamite coast but was forced to retreat in the face of a large force sent against them. The Annamite Emperor Phat Ma now decided on an expedition on a large scale to chastise his turbulent neighbours, who had besides,

1. Che li Hia li pi ma ti.
2. Che Mei P'ai mo tie
3. Yang P'ou Kou Che-li P'i lan To Kia pau motie.

ceased to perform any act of vassalage for the last sixteen years. He constructed 100 new vessels and drilled his soldiers for both offensive and defensive war. At length, on the 12th January, 1044, he led the expedition in person against Champā. The flotilla safely reached the bank of the river Ngu Bo where Jaya Siṁhavarman was waiting with his troops. The Annamites disembarked and offered battle. The Cham army was completely routed. Jaya Siṁhavarman himself lay dead on the field which was covered by the dead bodies of 30,000 of his soldiers. Moved by pity Phat Ma at last stopped this fearful carnage and marched towards the capital city Vijaya. Vijaya was easily captured and ravaged by his army. At last the Annamite Emperor turned back with an immense quantity of booty and large number of prisoners, including all the women of the palace. It is recorded about one of these that when summoned to the royal vessel she threw herself into the sea, preferring death to dishonour in the hands of her foreign foe. The emperor admired her fidelity and gave her a posthumous title meaning 'very chaste and very sweet lady.'

KINGS REFERRED TO IN CHAPTER VII.

1. Parameśvaravarman (972—982 A. D.)
2. Indravarman IV (c. 982—983 A. D.)
3. Lu'u-Ky-Tong (Annamite usurper) (983—989 A. D.)
4. Vijaya Śrī Harivarman II (989—c. 998 A. D.)
5. Yaṅ Pu Ku Vijaya Śrī. (c. 998—c. 1008 A. D.)
6. Śrī Harivarmadeva III (c. 1008—c. 1016 A. D.)
7. Parameśvaravarman II (c. 1016—c. 1028 A. D.)
8. Vikrāntavarman IV (c. 1028—1041 A. D.)
9. Jayasiṁhavarman II (Son of No. 8) (1041—1044 A. D.)

Chapter VIII.

DECLINE OF CHAMPA.

The dynasty which came to power in 989 A. D. after the Annamite usurpation perished with Jaya Siṁhavarman II amid the disasters of the second Annamite invasion. But within six years a new dynasty was founded by Jaya Parameśvaravarmadeva Īśvaramūrti, descended from the old royal family of Champā[1]

The new king had to face a very heavy task. For nearly seventy years (980—1050 A. D.) the kingdom was a prey to foreign invasions and internal dissensions. The repeated incursions of the Annamites had brought untold miseries upon the kingdom and exhausted its resources. As the central authority became weak, provincial revolts began. The southern province of Pāṇḍuraṅga, for example, repeatedly rebelled and set up a new king on the throne.[2] The Cambodgians also probably took advantage of the weakness of their neighbour to push on their plundering raids into the kingdom.[3]

It reflects great credit on Jaya Parameśvara Varman that he bravely faced the dangers and restored peace and order in the kingdom to a considerable extent. He first turned his

---

1. Cf. Phu-Qui Ins. (No. 57). Mespero's view that "his ancestors were simple warriors, vassals of the preceding kings" rests upon a somewhat wide interpretation of the verse 2 of the Po-Nagar Ins. (No. 60). It must be added, however, that the Phu Qui Ins. was not discovered when Maspero wrote.
2. cf. Po Klaun Garai Ins. Nos. 53, 54.
3. This seems to be a legitimate inference from Po Klaun Garai Inscriptions Nos. 52, 53, 59. Otherwise we are to assume that the king of Champa made an aggressive raid on Cambodge which appears unlikely in view of the political condition of Champa.

attention towards the revolted province of Pāṇḍuraṅga. The political situation of this country, probably typical of many other provinces, is thus described.

"The people of Pāṇḍuraṅga were always stupid, of mischievous spirit, and evil-doers. For instance, on several occasions they revolted against different kings of Champā down to the time of His Majesty Śrī Parameśvaravarmadeva who gave all the Barons of the country to the God Parameśvara (probably the country of Pāṇḍuraṅga had been placed under the suzerainty of a great monastery). Nevertheless, the people of Pāṇḍuraṅga were guilty of culpable acts. They set up different individuals one after another and proclaimed them kings of the country."[1]

In order to put a stop to this chronic state of rebellion, Parameśvaravarmadeva led an well-organised expedition against the province. Three armies were sent against it, one led by the king in person and the two other by two of his nephews, the Yuvarāja Mahāsenāpati, and Devarāja Mahāsenāpati.[2] The revolted people of Pāṇḍuraṅga were completely defeated

1. Po Klaun Garai Ins. (No. 54).

2. This seems to be the only legitimate inference that may be derived by a comparison of the three inscriptions at Po Klaun Garai (Nos. 52, 53, 54,). No. 53 explicitly states that the king "sent troops in various batches". No. 52 says that Devaraja Mahasenapati came to take the town of Panduranga in 1050 A. D. on behalf of king Sri Paramesvaravarmadeva. According to No. 53. the king "ordered his nephew, the Yuvaraja Mahasenapati, to proceed with all his generals and conquer the city", and the latter installed a Linga as a mark of victory in 1050 A. D. Lastly, we learn from No. 53 that "His Majesty Sri Paramesvaravarmadeva led troops to the conquest of the country and erected a column of victory in 1050 A. D." Thus there were at least three different batches of troops taking part in the same expedition in 1050 A. D.

and came to terms (1050 A. D.). The result is thus described in one of the inscriptions:

"All the troops of Panrāṅ came to fight. He (Yuvarāja Mahāsenāpati) pursued and crushed them all and they took shelter in mountains and caverns. But the Yuvarāja, who had a powerful army, ordered his troops to pursue them in all directions. And these troops got hold of all the people of Panrāṅ with oxen, buffaloes, slaves and elephants, on behalf of king Parameśvaravarmadeva Dharmarāja."[1]

Half of the people were released in order to re-establish the city, and the other half were distributed as slaves to various religious establishments. 'Two columns were raised to commemorate the victory, one by the king himself and the other by the Yuvarāja Mahāsenāpati, and two *Liṅgas* of stone were installed by the two generals.' These were intended to impress the people with an idea of the wealth, splendour and piety of the king of Champā, and they produced the desired effect.

"And on account of his piety to Śiva, when the people of this country saw the beauty and the marks of this '*liṅga*'...... they resolved to give up their revolts against the king of Champā who was always victorious."[2]

"And when this column of victory was completed the people of Pāṇḍuraṅga, who had revolted, became, for ever, perfectly virtuous and loyal towards the king of Champā."[3]

Having brought the affairs of Pāṇḍuraṅga to a satisfactory conclusion, the king turned his attention towards his western neighbour, the Cambodgians. Here also his attempts proved completely successful. The Yuvarāja Mahāsenāpati who had played such a distinguished part in the Pāṇḍuranga war inflic-

1. Po Klaun Garai Ins No. 53.
2. Ibid.
3. Po Klaun Garai Ins. No. 54.

ted a crushing defeat upon the Cambodgians and took the town of Śambhupura. He destroyed a large number of temples there and distributed the Khmer captives among the temples of Śrīśānabhadreśvara.

King Parameśvaravarman had to devote a great deal of attention to the restoration of the religious institutions which had suffered during the troublesome period that preceded his reign. In 1050 A. D. he re-installed the image of the famous goddess of Po Nagara and endowed her with lands, slaves and various other costly articles.[1] In 1055 he restored a cave at Lai Cham[2] and erected a *vihāra* at Phu-qui, endowing the latter with men, oxen, buffaloes, grains as well as all the vessels necessary for the worship of the gods.[3] The Yuvarāja Mahāsenāpati, who had assisted his royal uncle in his military expeditions, also ably seconded his efforts in this direction. He erected or restored a number of temples and endowed them with necessary articles. He also installed many *Liṅgas* and made various gifts to temples, monasteries and *sālās* (Houses of Charity?). He devoted special attention to the temple of Śrīśānabhadreśvara in the precincts of which he erected an 'image of *Liṅga*' in 1056 A. D. (No. 59).

Jaya Parameśvaravarman cultivated friendly relations with the Emperors of China and Annam. To the former he sent ambassadors in 1050, 1053 and 1056. On the last occasion his ambassador was shipwrecked and lost all his baggages, whereupon the Chinese Emperor sent him 1000 ounces of silver. His ambassador also visited the Court of the Annamite Emperor in 1047, 1050, 1055, 1060 and also sometime between 1057 and 1059 A. D.[4]

---

1. Po-Nagar Ins. Nos. 55, 58.
2. Lai cham Ins. No. 56.
3. Phu-qui Ins. No. 57.
4. T'oung Pao 1911 p. 238. An ambassador sent from Champa

Jaya Parameśvaravarman was probably succeeded by Bhadravarman IV. This name is only known from the Po Nagar inscription (No. 60) of his younger brother Rudravarman IV, but as no royal title is attached to the name, it is doubtful whether he actually ruled. If he did so, he must have ascended the throne sometime in 1060 or 1061 A. D. In that case we may look upon him as the king of Champā who sent tribute to China in 1061.

Bhadravarman IV was succeeded by Rudravarman IV. He was born in the family of Jaya Parameśvara but the relationship between the two is not definitely known. From the very beginning he made preparations for attacking his northern neighbour. He organised his army and trained his soldiers for the purpose. He then sent an ambassador to China, in 1062 A. D., for securing assistance against the Annamites. But although the Chinese emperor was friendly and sent him some presents, he was not in a mood to send any effective aid against the Annamites. For some years, therefore, Rudravarman IV thought it politic to keep on friendly terms with the Annamite Emperor and regularly sent tributes to him in 1063, 1065 and 1068.[1] In 1064 he propitiated the goddess of Po Nagar with a variety of rich presents.[2]

But all the while Rudravarman IV continued his preparations and at last opened hostilities towards the end of 1068 A. D. The Annamite Emperor, Ly Thánh Ton, took up the challenge and moved his troops on the 16th February, 1069 A. D. He gradually arrived at the port of Śrī Banoy and there disembarked his troops. The cham army, drawn up on the

---

to Annam in 1047 was imprisoned there but it is doubtful whether he was sent by king Parameśvaravarman.

1. T'oung Pao 1911, p. 241.

2. Po Nagar Ins. No. 60.

bank of the Tu Mao offered battle to the invader. They fought furiously for a long time, but their general being killed, they lost heart and fell back in disorder, leaving a large number on the field. As soon as Rudravarman learnt the news of the defeat, he left the capital with his family. He was, however, pursued and captured within the borders of Cambodge (1069 A. D.).

The victor now took up his residence in the royal palace at Vijaya and celebrated his triumph by feasts and dances. He then gave orders to put to fire all the houses in the capital and its suburbs. This done, he gave orders for retreat. On the 17th July he made a triumphal entry into his capital. Escorted by two armies, and surrounded by his officers on horseback, he himself rode on a chariot behind which marched Rudravarman and his family accompanied by five executioners. About 50,000 Chams were taken to Tonkin as prisoners of war.

Rudravarman was not kept in captivity for long. He obtained his release by ceding three northern districts of Champā viz. Dia Ly, Ma Linh and Bo Chanh (1069 A. D.). This meant the cession of the whole of Quang Binh and the northern part of Quang Tri and brought the frontier of Champā to the mouth of the river Viet. The Chams could never reconcile themselves to this cession of important territories and it gave rise to many a battle in future.

On his return to Champā Rudravarman IV found it to be a seat of anarchy and civil war, as several persons had proclaimed themselves as kings in different parts of the kingdom. It is doubtful whether Rudravarman was able to re-establish his power to any extent. We hear of tributes being sent from Champā to Annam in 1071, 1072 and 1074 A. D. and to China in 1072, A. D., but we do not know definitely the name of the king or kings of Champā to whom these may be attributed. Amid these disorders Rudravarman IV passes from our view.[1]

KINGS REFERRED TO IN CHAPTER VIII.

1.	Jaya Parameśvaravarman	(c. 1050—c. 1060 A. D.)
2.	Bhadravarman IV	(c. 1060—1061 A. D.)
3.	Rudravarman IV (younger brother of No. 2)	(c. 1061—1069 A. D.)

---

1. Maspero infers from an Annamite record that Rudravarman took refuge in the Annamese court with his family and lived there as an exile the rest of his life.

Chapter IX.

DYNASTY OF HARIVARMAN.

Among the many aspirants to the throne of Champā during the dark days that followed the Annamite conquest and the capture of the king, one name stands in bold relief, that of Harivarman IV. We have two long inscriptions (Myson Ins. Nos. 61, 62) with interesting particulars of his life and times, and these enable us to reconstruct the history of the period to a certain extent.

The full name of the king was Śrī Harivarmadeva prince Thāṅ-yaṅ Viṣṇumūrti or Mādhavamūrti or Devatāmūrti. He was the son of Prāleyeśvara Dharmarāja of the Cocoanut clan. As his mother belonged to the Betelnut clan, he represented in his person the two chief rival families of the kingdom.[1]

Within ten years of the capture of Rudravarman, Harivarman established his authority over the greater part of the kingdom. But the civil war continued throughout his reign[2] and he had to fight with rival chiefs for the throne of Champā. To make matters worse, the Annamite king sent a new expedition in 1075,[3] and the king of Cambodge also began his plunder-

---

1. The two clans probably represented two important fiefs in the kingdom. M. Durand has located the betelnut clan in Binh Thuan (B. E. F., vol. V, pp. 368 ff)

2. cf. Po Nagar Ins. No. 64 which refers to a civil war of sixteen years ie. from 1069-1084 A. D.

3. The king of Annam sent an expedition against Champa in 1075 on the pretext of some agressive frontier raid conducted by the Chams. But the expedition proved a failure. The defeat of the Annamite king emboldened the Chinese court to send an expedition against him (1075-1076 A. D.) and the Chinese emperor ordered the kings of Champa and Cambodge to attack Annam from the south. The king of

ing raids. It reflects great credit upon Harivarman that he not only checked his internal foes but also guarded his kingdom against his powerful neighbours. No wonder, that his reign was full of military campaigns as we are told in the Myson Inscription. "He has dispersed the hostile troops in the field of battle as many as twelve times. He has cut off the heads of kings, generals, chiefs and other men in the field of battle nine times. He defeated the troops of Cambodge at Someśvara and captured the prince Śrī Nandanavarmadeva who commanded the army." (No. 62 b-d). The defeat of the Annamite forces assured the safety of the newly established power, and by dint of numerous military successes "the king of Champā became prosperous as of old." Then king Harivarman celebrated his coronation and probably assumed the title Utkṛṣṭarāja. After this he enjoyed complete happiness and tasted royal felicities.[1]

But Harivarman had another important task before him. The country had been ruined by the Annamite invasions and the Civil War and it was necessary to repair the damages as far as possible. The ruinous effect of the foreign domination

Champa obeyed and despatched a force 7,000 strong to Nghe-an. The Chinese army was, however, defeated, and so the king of Champa also had to beat retreat. The year following he sent regular tributes to the court of Annam as well as to China. Maspero supposes that the king of Champa referred to above was Harivarman, but this is at best doubtful, and hence is not incorporated in the text. The other supposition of Maspero that the Annamite raid of 1075 against Champa was undertaken with a view to restore Rudravarman to the throne is equally doubtful (T'oung Pao 1911, pp. 247-48; B. E. F. vol. XVII, No. 3 p. 44).

1. Myson Ins No. 61. The term Utkrstaraja may also be taken as an ordinary adjective rather than a special title assumed by the king.

has thus been graphically described in the Myson Inscription (No. 61.).

"The enemy had entered into the kingdom of Champā and installed themselves as masters, having taken possession of all the royal property and the wealth of the gods; having pillaged the temples, the monasteries, the *sālās*, cells, hermitages, villages and various edifices together with the horses, elephants, infantry, oxen, buffaloes and the crops; having ravaged everything in the provinces of the kingdom of Champā; having plundered the temple of Śrīaśnabhadreśvara and all that the king of past times have granted as endowments to Śrīśānabhadreśvara; having taken all the riches of the god and carried away the men belonging to the temple, the dancers, musicians ......servants, together with the various properties, of Śrīśānabhadreśvara; the temple remained empty and devoid of worship..."

The inscription proceeds: "Then his Majesty Vijaya Śrī Harivarmadeva, Yaṅ Devatāmūrti ascended the throne. He completely defeated the enemies, proceeded to the Nagara Champā and restored the temple of Śrīśānabhadreśvara." (No. 61).

Two Inscriptions at Myson (Nos. 61, 62) describe in detail the work of restoration as well as the rich endowments to the temple of Śrīśānabhadreśvara made by the king and his brother Yuvarāja Mahāsenāpati. The latter "re-erected the temples, the chapels, the gateways and the different edifices in the domain of Śrīśānabhadreśvara and made them perfectly beautiful. He re-erected the temples in the various provinces of the kingdom of Champā. He gave all the necessary articles for the worship of the god with the servants of temples, dancers, musicians......as before. He re-established the *sālās*, the cells, and the hermitages in the various provinces of the kingdom of Champā...". (No. 61).

The rich endowments of king Harivarman to Śrīśānabhadreśvara consisted of various articles of gold, silver and precious jewels, as well as of servants and various animals. The Myson Inscription informs us that "seeing Śrīśānabhadreśvara despoiled of all his possessions at the end of the war, he came to worship the god with a pious heart, and gave him all the booty taken at Someśvara (i. e. from the conquered Cambodgians) and various objects" (No. 62).

King Harivarman also turned his attention to secular buildings and "re-established the edifices and the city of Champā during the troublesome days of the war. And the city of Champā and all the edifices were enriched, as if by nature, and freshly decorated" (No. 62). The Yuvarāja also "ordered the people of Siṁhapura to construct the temples, to build the houses, to make perpetual sacrifices, to re-erect the chapels, and to reconstruct the roads, all as before." (No. 62).

King Harivarman thus successfully accomplished the two important tasks of establishing law and order and restoring material prosperity in the kingdom. With the exception of the southern district of Pāṇḍuraṅga, the whole of Champā was probably united under his sceptre, and he vigorously set himself to the task of repairing damages and reviving the old prosperity of the kingdom. Harivarman must have been endowed with exceptional qualities and the long praises bestowed upon him at the commencement of the Myson Inscription (No. 62) may have some justification.

In 1081 A. D. at the age of 41[1] Harivarman IV abdicated in favour of his eldest son, Pulyaṅ Śrī Rājadvāra, and devoted himself to spiritual exercises and worship of Śiva. He did

1. The Cham ambassador in the court of China in 1076 referred to his king as being of 36 years of age (T'oung Pao 1911, p. 250).

not however, long enjoy the rest and died within a month (1081 A. D.). It is interesting to note that 14 of his wives followed him to death in right Indian fashion.

Pu-lyaṅ Śrī Rājadvāra ascended the throne under the name of Yāṅ-po-ku Śrī Jaya Indravarmadeva. He was a boy of nine years and was obviously unfit to hold the reins of government in those troublesome days. He had hardly reigned for a month when the necessity of a stronger government impressed itself upon all and the throne was offered to Pu-lyaṅ Śrī Yuvarāja Mahāsenāpati, prince Pāñ, younger brother of Śrī Harivarmadeva. The event is thus described in the Myson Inscription (No. 65) of Jaya Indravarman himself.

"There is His Majesty Śrī Jaya Indravarmadeva, Prince Vak, son of His Majesty Śrī Harivarmadeva, prince Thāṅ...... He reigned about a month. Then as Śrī Jaya Indravarmadeva was very young, did not know what was good or bad in the government of the kingdom and made everything contrary to the rules of government, Śrī Jaya Indravarmadeva with all the generals, Brāhmaṇs, astrologers, learned men, masters of ceremonies and the wives of Śrī Harivarmadeva searched for a prince to govern the kingdom. Now they found that Pu-lyaṅ Śrī Yuvarāja Mahāsenāpati, prince Pāñ, uncle of Śrī Jaya Indravarmadeva, and younger brother of Śrī Harivarmadeva, had all the marks of a Mahārāja according to the canon of Rājacakravartin, and that he had the knowledge of the good and the bad,............Śrī Jaya Indravarmadeva, nephew of Pu-lyaṅ Śrī Yuvarāja Mahāsenāpati, with the Brāhmaṇs, Kṣatriyas, Paṇḍits, astrologers, masters of ceremonies, with all the ladies, carrying royal insignia, went to Pu-lyaṅ Śrī Yuvarāja Mahāsenāpati and made him king."

The Yuvarāja ascended the throne under the title Paramabodhisattva in 1081 A. D. "He gave bounties to the generals and to all the people of Champā, and an uninterrupted bliss reigned as before."

Paramabodhisattva quelled the disturbances in the kingdom and completed the task of his elder brother by recovering the southern district of Pāṇḍuraṅga. There a usurper had set up an independent kingdom after the Annamite expedition of 1069 A. D. and maintained his position for 16 years. Paramabodhisattva imprisoned him with all his followers. He spared their lives but confiscated their property (No. 64).

Thus after 16 years there was once more a united kingdom of Champā. The king, whose zeal for restoring the temples and palaces, during the reign of his brother, has been referred to before, now gave rich donations to the goddess of Po Nagar, the tutelary deity of the kingdom, together with his sister Garbha Lakṣmī, and his eldest son Pu lyaṅ Śrī Yuvarāja prince Vyu (No. 64). The king further installed an image of Śiva at Myson and made rich donations to the God (No. 63).

Paramabodhisattva remained at peace with the court of Annam and regularly sent tributes year after year (1081-1085). But he did not enjoy a long reign. He was succeeded in 1086 by his nephew Śrī Jaya Indravarmadeva Paramarājādhirāja who had abdicated the throne in his favour in 1081 A. D.[1] (No. 65). His known dates are 1081 and 1084 A. D. (Nos. 63-64).

1. Maspero's suggestion that Jaya Indravarman's restoration was accomplished by a bloody civil war does not commend itself to me. He remarks: "It is at least in this way that we can account for the disappearance of Paramabodhisattva, the return of Jaya Indravarman, and the passage in the Myson Ins. (No. 65) where the latter is said to have "completely reconstructed the city of Champa which was ruined and deserted." It is obvious that the first two of these events could

The full title of the new king was Śrī Jaya Indravarmadeva (V) prince Vāk yān Devatāmūrti. He is praised in extravagant terms in the Myson Ins. (No. 65) which refers to his rich donations to Śrīśānabhadreśvara and the gift of a monastery to Śrī Indralokeśvara in the district of Tranul. He also sup-

---

be easily accounted for by supposing that Paramabodhisattva had died and was succeeded by the legitimate sovereign Jaya Indravarmadeva Maspero obviously lays emphasis on the passage quoted above. He holds that if, as we are told, Harivarman and Paramabodhisattva had already reconstructed and repopulated the city of Champa, Jaya Indravarman's attempts in the same direction could only be explained by supposing that there was a fresh civil war in course of which the city was again ruined. But it is obvious that the serious damages which the Annamite hosts inflicted upon the capital city might have taken long to repair, and Jaya Indravarman probably merely supplemented the work of his father and uncle.

On the other hand, the way in which the abdication of Indravarman, coronation of his uncle and his own restoration are described in an inscription of Jaya Indravarman himself (No. 65), and particularly the favourable notice of the qualities of Paramabodhisattva contained therein discredit any idea of a civil war between the two.

Further, Maspero's view that Harivarman IV abdicated in 1080 A. D. is almost certainly wrong. The Inscription No. 62 refers to his abdication in favour of his son and also contains an account of his death in 1081. No mention is made therein of the accession of Paramabodhisattva which, as we know, took place within a month of the abdication. We are therefore bound to conclude that the abdication and death of Harivarman took place within a month some time in 1081 A. D., and Paramabodhisattva replaced his nephew on the throne almost immediately after the latter event

(cf. Maspero T'oung Pao 1911, pp. 252 ff)

plemented the work of his father and uncle in reconstructing the town of Champā.

Although Jaya Indravarman V paid his tribute to the court of Annam with fair regularity, he deplored the loss of the three districts ceded by Rudravarman. The two peoples were so much estranged over this question, that when their ambassadors, having arrived at the Chinese court at the same time, were introduced to the Emperor on the same day, they kept themselves aloof from each other. At a dinner in which they were invited they were seated at two ends of the table. At last in 1092 A. D. Indravarman stopped the payment of tribute to Annam and approached the Chinese emperor with a proposal to make a common cause against that country. The Chinese emperor, however, refused to fight with Annam. Nevertheless, Jaya Indravarman continued to withhold the tribute till a formal complaint was made by the Annamese court in 1094. Indravarman was seized with terror, and hastened to comply with the demand. The tribute was sent in 1095, 1097, 1098, 1099 and 1102 A. D.

At last in 1103 a refugee from Annam instigated king Indravarman to fight against the country. He represented that Annam was enfeebled by internal dissensions and had not the power to resist an invasion from Champā. Misled by these false statements Jaya Indravarman led an army and conquered the three ceded districts. But his triumph was short-lived. He was soon defeated and compelled to abandon those districts. To avoid further troubles he immediately sent tribute to Annam. Henceforth the two countries lived in peace and tributes were regularly sent from Champā to Annam.

Jaya Indravarman V was succeeded by his nephew Harivarman who was on the throne in 1114 A. D. (No. 68). Jaya Indravarman's reign, therefore, falls between 1086 and 1114 A. D.

Harivarman V has left us a single inscription at Myson (No. 68) from which we learn that he built two temples and a palace for Śrī Īśānabhadreśvara and bestowed various articles of gold and silver for his worship.

He was on friendly terms with the Chinese and Annamese courts. The former bestowed honorary titles on him in 1116, 1127, and 1129 A. D. The latter also treated his ambassadors with honour and distinction and invited him to the imperial palace in 1126. From 1120 to 1124 he had regularly sent tributes to the Annamese Court without any exception.

KINGS REFERRED TO IN CHAPTER IX.

1.	Harivarmā IV	(c. 1070—1081 A. D.)
2.	Śrī Jaya Indravarmadeva V (Son of No. 1)	(1081 A. D.)
3.	Paramabodhisattva (Younger brother of No. 1)	(1081—1086 A. D.)
2.	Śrī Jaya Indravarmadeva V (Second time)	(1086—1113 A. D.)
4.	Harivarman V (Nephew of No. 2)	(1113 A. D.—1126 A. D.)

Chapter X.

War with Cambodge.

Harivarman V seems to have left no heir and the next king known to us is Jaya Indravarman VI. The Myson Pillar inscription (No. 69) and Po Nagar Ins. (No. 71) give a succinct account of his life and ancestry. He was, we are told, an incarnation of Uroja, the mythical forefather of the kings of Champā, who was a descendant of Śiva himself, and is frequently referred to in the official inscriptions of that kingdom, (cf. e. g. No. 31). The theory of incarnation has been developed in an interesting way in the inscription No. 69. Uroja, after his death, was reborn as king Bhadravarman and again as king Jaya Siṁhavarman-both of whom, be it noted, are historical personages and kings of Champā. Then Uroja was again born as Jaya Indravarman himself and thus he had appeared on the earth altogether four times as king of Champā. This mythical ancestry seems to be a sure indication that Jaya Indravarman had no legitimate claim to the throne and that he wanted to legalise what he had acquired by other means, by tracing his relationship with the former kings of Champā. It is not impossible, of course, that he might have some remote relationship with Jaya Siṁhavarman II but it is not possible to decide the question one way or the other with the evidence available at present. It is equally uncertain whether he immediately succeeded Harivarman, or one or more kings intervened between the two. The latter hypothesis seems more probable.

Jaya Indravarman VI was born in the year 1106 A. D. He became Devarāja in 1129 and Yuvarāja ins 1133 A. D. Finally he ascended the throne in 1139 (No 69). This short account of his life shows that his father had also reigned before him whoever he may be.[1]

The king's religious endowments are recorded in both his inscriptions. In 1140 he erected an image (or a temple) of Śrīśānabhadreśvara, and two years later, that of a Śiva-liṅga and the Śrīśāna-Viṣṇu In 1138 while yet a Yuvarāja, he made gifts to Saddharma, apparently some god or institutions connected with Buddhism, and also to a Śiva-liṅga. With his usual propensity of looking back to the past history of Champā, he recalls, in connection with the latter, how, long ago, about 1, 780, 500 years ago, king Vicitra Sagara established the *liṅga* at Kauṭhāra.

Unfortunately, Jaya Indravarman VI was involved in a quarrel with both his powerful neighbours. Sūryavarman the bellicose king of Cambodge, ascended the throne in 1112 A. D. and began to harass the kingdom of Champā. Then in 1128 he sent an expedition, 20,000 strong, against the Annamite kingdom, and induced the king of Champā to join with him. This was probably not a difficult task, as Champā had many old scores to pay off, and was ever ready to seize any opportunity to recover the three northern districts ceded by Rudravarman. Unfortunately, the Cham army could not join the Cambodgians in time, and both armies were separately defeated. Baffled in his enterprise Sūryavarman despatched next year a navy of 700 vessels to harass the coast of Than Hoa. A similar attempt was again made in 1132 when Jaya Indravarman invaded Nghe-An in concert with the army of Cambodge, but was easily defeated by the Annamites.[2] He then settled matters with them by paying off the tribute in

1. Maspero supposes that Jaya Indravarman was adopted by Harivarman. This is a probable suggestion.

2. cf. B. E. F. vol. XVIII No. 3. p. 35.

1136 and withdrawing from the offensive alliance he had lately formed with the king of Cambodge.

But this pusillanimous conduct did not save the unfortunate king. Unsuccessful in his expedition against the Annamite king, Sūryavarman now wanted to make amends for his loss by attacking his faithless ally, the king of Champā. In 1145 he invaded the kingdom and made himself master of Vijaya. Jaya Indravarman VI was either killed in the battle, or made a prisoner. In any case we do not hear of him any more.[1]

When the kingdom of Champā lay prostrate under the victorious army of Cambodge, a scion of the old ruling family, a descendant of king Paramabodhisattva, proclaimed himself king and took refuge in the southern district of Pāṇḍuraṅga. His name was Rudravarman Parama-Brahmaloka, and he was the son of an eminent king, whose name, so far as it could be recovered, is Śrī Rudraloka...Mūrti. It is just possible that this Rudra-loka was the successor of Harivarman V. In that case Rudravarman Parama-Brahmaloka must be regarded as the legitimate owner of the throne which was successfully usurped by Jaya Indravarman VI or his father. Rudravarman Parama-Brahmaloka was formally consecrated to the throne, but he did not enjoy a long reign and died in 1147 A. D.[2]

On the death of the king, the people of Pāṇḍuraṅga invited his son Ratnabhūmivijaya to be the king of Champā, and

1. T'oung Pao, 1911, pp. 293-295.

2. Maspero's account of the events of this period is vitiated by his adopting the wrong reading of a large number of dates which have since been corrected by Finot. Maspero, for example, believed that Rudravarman did not practically rule at all, having died immediately after his coronation. But we now know that he ruled for at least two years This disposes of his argument concerning the use of the title Uroja by his son (T'oung Pao, 1911, p. 295, fn. 6.).

he ascended the throne in 1147 A. D., under the name Śrī Jaya Harivarmadeva VI, prince Śivānandana.[1]

Seven inscriptions of this king have reached us (Nos. 72-78), and they enable us to reconstruct a detailed account of his life and reign, such as we do not possess of any other king of Champā before or since. The early life of Harivarmā was far from being pleasant. "Having quitted his own country he spent a long time in foreign lands amid joys and sorrows. Then he came back to Champā".[2] This apparently refers to the period when Jaya Indravarman VI had usurped the throne and Rudravarman fled from the country with his son.

Harivarman VI ascended the throne at a very critical moment. The greater part of the kingdom was under a foreign foe who was now extending his aggressions to the south, and the Annamites as well as the Kirāṭas and other semi-barbarous tribes on its frontier took advantage of the situation to carry on plundering raids into its very heart. But Harivarman was equal to the task that faced him, and steered the vessel of state safely through these shoals, amid heavy storms, back to the harbour.

Scarcely had the king ascended the throne when the king of Cambodge commanded Śaṅkara, the foremost among his generals, to go and fight him in the plain of Rājapura. Śaṅkara was aided by a large number of troops from Vijaya i. e. the portion of Champā subject to Cambodge. Harivarman met the hostile army at Chaklyaṅ (probably the village of Chakling in the southern part of the valley of Phanrang, in the neighbourhood of the rock of Batau Tablaḥ which contains an inscription describing the battle) and gained a great victory. As the Myson inscription tells us: "Jaya Harivarman fought against the general Śaṅkara and all the other Cambodian generals with

1. Batau Tablaḥ Inscription No. 75.
2. Myson Inscription. No. 74.

their troops. They died.........in the field of battle" (No. 72). This happened in 1147 A. D. (No. 75). Next year "the king of Cambodge sent an army thousand times stronger than the previous one to fight in the plain of Vīrapura" (No. 72). Harivarman met them at the field of Kayev and completely defeated them (No. 75).

Having defeated the two armies sent against him, Harivarman now felt himself powerful enough to take the offensive. The King of Cambodge did not underrate the danger. He hastily consecrated Harideva, the younger brother of his first queen, as king of Vijaya, and "commanded various generals to lead the Cambodian troops and protect prince Harideva until he became king in the city of Vijaya." Jaya Harivarman also marched towards that city and probably re-took it before the arrival of Harideva. In any case the two hostile armies met at the plain of Mahī'a (No. 72), "to the east of the temple of Guheśvara on the river Yāmī" (No. 74), and Harideva was defeated and killed. "Jaya Harivarman destroyed the king Harideva with all his Cham and Cambodian generals and the Cham and Cambodian troops; they all perished" (No. 72). Then the victorious king, duly consecrated, ascended the throne of his forefathers with due pomp and ceremony (1149 A. D.) and reigned as supreme king from this time.[1] But the difficulties of Harivarman were far from being over yet. The king of Cambodge, thrice baffled, now hit upon a different plan. He incited the barbarous mountain tribes of Champā against their king.[2] The Rade, the Mada and other barbarous tribes,

1. The detailed account of the military campaigns is given in Myson Inscription (No. 72). The dates are supplied by the Batau Tablah Ins. (No. 75).
2. The Myson inscription (No. 72), so far as it has been deciphered, does not directly convey the impression that the king of Cambodge had incited the tribes, but that seems to be a

collectively known by the general appellation of the "Kirāṭa", now invaded the plain in the neighbourhood of Vijaya. A battle took place near the village of Slāy, and the Kirāṭas were defeated (No. 72). Unfortunately, Harivarman VI had not to fear his external enemies alone; his own relatives betrayed him. The brother of his wife called Vaṅśarāja now joined his enemies. "The Kirāṭa kings proclaimed his brother-in-law Vaṅśarāja, brother of his wife, as king in the city of Madhyamagrāma." The undaunted king bravely met this new danger. Jaya Harivarman VI led his army, defeated Vaṅśarāja, captured the Kirāṭa army, and defeated them all" (No. 72).

The Kirāṭa difficulty was over, but Vaṅśarāja remained. He took refuge in the Annamese court and asked the Emperor for military assistance in order to place him on the throne of Champā. The Annamese Emperor acceded to his request and declared him king of Champā. The inscription proceeds. "The king of Yavanas, learning that the king of Cambodge had created difficulties in the way of Jaya Harivarman, proclaimed Vaṅśarāja a citizen of Champā, as king. He gave him several Yavana generals together with hundred thousand valorous Yavana soldiers.........Then Jaya Harivarman conducted all the troops of Vijaya. The two parties were engaged in a terrible combat. Jaya Harivarman defeated Vaṅśarāja......... and large number of Yavana troops lay dead on the field." (1150 A. D.).[1]

After having thus quelled the external enemies Jaya Harivarman probably hoped to reign in peace. But that was not to be. Civil war broke out, first at Amarāvatī (1151) and

legitimate inference from the few broken sentences that have been preserved.

1. The detailed account is supplied partly by the Myson Ins. (No. 72) and partly by the Annamese documents (T'oung Pao 1911, p. 299). In the Myson Inscription the enemies are

then at Pāṇḍuraṅga (1155). Harivarman successfully put them down, but the embers of conflict were not finally extinguished till 1160 A. D. An inscription dated in that year sums up his military success as follows:

"King Śrī Jaya Harivarman, prince Śivānandana, has triumphed over all his enemies, to wit, the Cambodgians the Annamites, Vijaya, Amarāvatī, and all the countries of the north; Pāṇḍuraṅga and the countries of the south; the Rade, the Mada and other barbarous tribes in the regions of the west."[1]

Having secured the throne of Champā Jaya Harivarman had to turn his attention to the restoration of temples and the repair of damages. The inscriptions give a long list of his pious works. He installed a *Liṅga* on the Mahīśaparvata, and erected two temples there in memory of his father and mother.[2] In accordance with a former vow he restored the temple of Śrīśānabhadreśvara on the Vugvan Mount which was destroyed by the enemy, and installed several images there, including a Śivaliṅga. "The fire in the temple of Śrīśānabhadreśvara", says the king, "was extinguished by the enemies. Having killed those destroyers in battle, I have built it again." "The temple was re-established in its old beauty," and as it had been plundered by the enemy, the king gave all the necessary

---

called "Yavanas" which might ordinarily be taken to imply the people of Java. But the agreement of the epigraphic account with what we learn from Annamite documents constrains us to interpret it as Annamites. Besides, in the Batau Tablah (No. 75) and Po Nagar Inscriptions (No. 76), which contain a list of the tribes with which Jaya Harivarman was at war, mention is made of the Annamites but not of the "Yavanas".

1. Batau Tablah Ins [No. 75]; Po-Nagar Ins. [No. 76].
2. Myson Ins. No. 72.

things to the god. Elsewhere we are told that "in accordance with his former vows, he first destroyed the soldiers of Cambodge and the Yavana soldiers (i. e. Annamites), and then re-erected the temple of Śiva which they had destroyed."[1]

In the year 1157 A. D. the king installed a god, called after him Harivarmeśvara, and granted a number of fields for his worship[2]. About 1160, he made donations to the god Jaya Harilingeśvara[3] as well as to the tutelary deity of the kingdom, the goddess of Po-Nagara.[4] The king also restored a temple at Myson.[5]

Like Jaya Indravarman, king Harivarman also believed that he was an incarnation of Uroja. In order to substantiate his claim, he referred to a treatise called 'Purāṇārtha' which was apparently regarded as a holy religious text and is described as a "mine of useful information in this world" (No. 74).

"Four times I have been incarnated as Uroja; lest I be not born again, I re-install this Śiva in fulfilment of the promise I made before.

"The god of gods Śrīśānabhadreśvara, and the god of gods established on the Vugvan mountain–both will be enriched by that king who is a portion of myself longing for the glory of a Śaiva.

"Such is the Purāṇārtha, description of Uroja, which the world must know." (No. 74)

Further, it is curious to note, that like Jaya Indravarman, Harivarman also regarded himself as the fourth incarnation of Uroja; in other words, Harivarman did not admit the claim of Jaya Indravarman to be regarded as an incarnation of Uro-

1. Myson Ins. [Nos. 72, 73, 74].
2. Myson Ins. No. 74].
3. Batau Tablah Ins. [No. 75].
4. Po-Nagar Ins. [No. 76],
5. Myson Ins. [No.78].

ja, probably another evidence of the usurpation of the latter.

Harivarman kept on friendly relations with the Chinese court. He demanded from the Imperial court the same dignity which his predecessors had enjoyed, and this was accorded to him in 1155 A. D.[1] After the war with the Annamite Emperor was over (1150), he maintained friendly relations with that court also. In 1152 he sent rich presents to the Emperor, and two years later, when the relations between the two countries again became rather strained on account of the repeated incursions of the Chams against Annamite territory, he pacified the Emperor by presenting him with some women. He also sent tribute to the Annamese court in 1155 and 1160. King Harivarman died shortly after 1162,[2] and was succeeded by his son Jaya Harivarman VII. We do not know anything of his reign, not even if he actually reigned at all. He is referred to as king by his son in inscriptions Nos. 94 and 95, and might have been merely a pretender to the throne for all we know.

Certain it is, that within a year of the death of king Harivarman VI, the throne of Champā was occupied by Pu Ciy Anāk Śrī Jaya Indravarman VII, an inhabitant of Grāmapura Vijaya.[3] It does not appear that he was related in any way to Jaya Harivarman VI or VII. On the other hand we know that the latter had at least two sons who had afterwards ruled in Champā. There is, therefore, hardly any doubt that Jaya Indravarman was an usurper.

Jaya Indravarman must have ascended the throne of Champā as early as 1163 A. D., when he gave a *Kośa* to Śrīśānabhadreśvara, for which 232 golden *paṇas*, 82 precious sto-

1. T'oung Pao 1911, p, 302.

2. Ibid p. 305.

3. T'oung Pao 1911, p. 303.

nes, 67 groups of pearls, and 200 *paṇas* of silver were required.[1] Next year, as well as the year following, he made costly donations and erected an inner chamber with sandalwood, silver and gold.[2] He sent tributes to the Annamite Court in 1164 and 1165.

The ambassador whom he sent in 1166 for the same purpose performed his duties in a somewhat strange fashion. He led an army and plundered the Annamite population on the sea-coast. The Annamese court could hardly be expected to brook this insult. An Annamese force entered Champā and the leader of the expedition wrote a strong letter to the king recalling the damages done by his troops. Jaya Indravarman VII hastened to pacify him and sent a noble of his court with a large quantity of precious stones and other valuable presents. The matter was then amicably settled, and the Annamese troops retreated to their country.[3]

Jaya Indravarman was formally consecrated to the throne about 1165 A. D. Immediately after his consecration, he sent an ambassador to China asking for investiture from the Imperial court. The presents which the ambassador took to China had been plundered from Arab merchants. The amount of tribute appeared to the Chinese emperor to be so very large, that he was at first inclined to accept only one tenth of it; but when he came to know of the source from which these articles had come, by the complaints of the Arab merchants themselves, he refused to take anything at all, and ordered a letter to be written to Jaya Indravarman explaining the cause of his refusal. Moreover, the council of ministers decided that it would not be prudent to invest the king of Champā with the customary

1. Myson Ins. [Nos. 79, 81].
2. Myson Ins. No. 81.
3. T'oung pao 1911, p. 203.

honorary titles till the commotion caused by the incident had subsided.

Jaya Indravarman now turned his attention to the conquest of Cambodge. He assured the neutrality of the Annamese Emperor by payment of rich presents and sending an ambassador to pay the usual homage. Being secure in the north, he attacked the kingdom of Cambodge (1170). That kingdom was then ruled over by king Dharaṇīndravarman II.

Both the opposing forces were equally matched and the war went on for a long time without any decisive result. At this time a Chinese officer, shipwrecked on the coast of Champā, taught the king a new cavalry manoeuvre, and the art of throwing arrows from the back of a horse (1171 A. D.). Jaya Indravarman now asked the Chinese officer to buy horses for him in his own country. With the help of these horses he was enabled to secure some advantage against the enemy, and this induced him to look for more horses. In 1172 he sent a large number of men to Kiong Tcheou, in the island of Hai Nan, with the object of purchasing as many horses as possible. They were ill received there, and therefore retaliated by plundering a number of inhabitants they came across. The terrified people then allowed them to make their purchases. But the affair came to the knowledge of the Chinese Emperor, and in 1175 he issued an order prohibiting the export of horses outside the empire. Jaya Indravarman, desiring to have the horses at any cost, repatriated to Hai Nan the people captured by his soldiers in 1172, and sent an ambassador to the Imperial court, asking permission to buy horses at that island. The Emperor replied that it was forbidden to export those animals of the empire, and that the rule specially applied to the island of Hai Nan (1176 A. D.).

Jaya Indravarman now gave up the idea of invading Cambodge by land. He equipped a fleet and sent a naval expedition in 1177. Proceeding along the coast, the fleet, guided by a shipwrecked Chinese, reached the mouth of the Grand River (Mekong). Then going up the river it reached the capital city. Jaya Indravarman plundered the capital and then retired, carrying an immense booty with him.[1]

The glorious victory of Jaya Indravarman VII indicates the revival of the old prosperous days of Champā. This was further shown by the rich donations of the king to various temples. We have already referred to his rich donations to Śrīśānabhadreśvara in 1163 A. D. The Myson inscription (No. 81) describes in detail how he continued these rich endowments, year after year, in 1167, 1168, and 1170 A. D. Further, he "installed Buddha Lokeśvara, Jaya Indra Lokeśvara and Bhagavatī Śrī Jaya Indreśvarī in the district of Buddha, and Bhagavatī Śrī Indra Gaurīśvarī in that of Śrī Vināyaka."[2]

The king also made rich donations to the goddess Bhagavatī Kauṭhāreśvarī of Po Nagar temple. "Part of these was made when the king went to conquer Cambodge". The gift was jointly made by the king, the queens Parameśvarī and Rayā, princess Bhāgyavatī, princess Sumitrā, princess Sudaksiṇā and Māń s'i Ai Grāmapura Vijaya (the prince?).[3]

---

1. T'oung Pao 1911, pp. 305—308.

   There is some difficulty in fixing the date of Jaya Indravarman's invasion of Cambodge. Maspero, apparently on Chinese and Annamese authority, fixes it at 1170 A. D. But the Po Nagar Inscription [No. 80] which refers to the king's campaign against Cambodge is dated 1167 A D. (This date was formerly read as 1105 Saka but Finot has corrected it to 1089 Saka). In that case the campaign against Cambodge must have begun 3 years earlier.

2. Myson Ins. [No. 81].
3. Po Nagar Inscription [No. 80].

An inscription at An Thuan (No. 82) has preserved relics of something like a military feudalism that prevailed at the time. Three dignitaries of the kingdom named Taval Vīra Siṁha oṅ Vayāk, Taval Śurādhika varmma, and Taval Vikrānta Siṁha oṅ Dhuṅ took an oath of allegiance to the king which contained, among other promises, an undertaking to the effect that they and their children will fight for their lord in case of war as long as they live.

The last known date of Jaya Indravarman VII is 1177 A. D.[1] How long he lived after that, and whether he could leave the kingdom he had usurped to his legitimate successors, are yet unknown.[2]

KINGS REFERRED TO IN CHAPTER X

1. Jaya Indravarman VI	(1139—1145 A. D.)
2. Rudravarman Parama-Brahmaloka	(1145—1147 A. D.)
3. Jaya Harivarmadeva VI (Son of No. 2)	(1147—1162 A. D.)
4. Jaya Harivarman VII (Son of No. 3)	(1162—1163 A. D.)?
5. Jaya Indravarman VII	(1163-c.1180 A.D.)

---

1. cf. the Chinese account of the king's expedition against Cambodge. The last known date from epigraphic records is 1170 A. D. (Myson Ins. No. 81).

2. Maspero's account of this period is now proved to be hopelessly wrong in the light of new inscriptions or new interpretation of old inscriptions. I have not made any attempt to point out the difference between his version and mine as the two are almost radically different.

CHAPTER XI.

The Cambodian, Mongol and Annamite invasions.

After Jaya Indravarman VII we find a new king at Champā named Jaya Indravarman VIII oṅ Vatuv. Whether there was any relationship between the two is yet unknown.[1] But the latter continued the "forward" policy of his predecessor, and carried on an agressive campaign against Cambodge. In 1190 A. D. the king of Cambodge, Jayavarman VII, son and successor of Dharaṇīndravarman II, sent an expedition against Jaya Indravarman oṅ Vatuv.

The leader of this expedition, who was ultimately destined to play an important part in history, was Śrī Sūryavarmadeva, prince Śrī Vidyānandana of Tuṁprauk-Vijaya. He was apparently an inhabitant of Champā, but betook himself early in life to Cambodge (1182 A. D.). The king of Cambodge welcomed him and employed his services on various occasions. Thus we read: "During his stay at Cambodge, a dependent town of Cambodge called Malyaṅ, inhabited by a multitude of bad men, revolted against the king of Cambodge. The latter seeing the prince well-versed in arms ordered him to lead the Cambodgian troops and take the town of Malyaṅ. He did all that the king of Cambodge desired."[2]

The king of Cambodge, pleased at his valour, conferred on him the dignity of Yuvarāja, and when war broke out with

1. Maspero identifies the two kings (T'oung Pao 1911, p. 304, fn. 2). But this does not seem probable (cf. Finot's remarks B. E. F. vol, XV, No. 2. p. 50. fn. 2).

2. Myson Ins No. 84. The account of Suryavarmadeva—Vidyanandana that follows, is entirely based on this inscription.

Champā, as related above, he "sent the prince at the head of Cambodgian troops in order to take Vijaya, and defeat the king Jaya Indravarman oṅ Vatuv"[1] Śrī Sūryavarmadeva obtained a complete victory. He captured the king and had him conducted to Cambodge by the Cambodgian troops.[2]

The king of Cambodge now divided Champā into two portions. He placed his own brother-in-law Sūrya Jayavarmadeva prince In, as king of the northern part, with Vijaya as capital, while Sūryavarmadeva, prince Śrī Vidyānandana, the victorious general, became king of the southern portion with his capital at Rājapura in Panrāṅ.

Sūryavarmadeva prince Śrī Vidyānandana defeated a number of 'thieves or pirates', apparently the adherents of the late regime that had revolted against him, and reigned in peace at Rājapura. The northern kingdom, however, was soon lost to Cambodge. Within two years, Prince Raṣupati, apparently a local chief, led a revolt against the Cambodgian usurper, Śrī Sūrya Jayavarman prince In. The latter was defeated, and returned to Cambodge, while Raṣupati ascended the throne under the name of Śrī Jaya Indravarmadeva.

The king of Cambodge now sent an expedition against Vijaya (1192 A. D.). With a view, probably, to conciliate the national sentiments by placing the captured king of Champā Śrī Jaya Indravarman oṅ Vatuv on the throne, as a dependent of Cambodge, he sent him along with this expedition. The Cambodgian troops first went to Rājapura. There the king Sūryavarmadeva prince Śrī Vidyānandana put himself

---

1. Ibid.

2. Ibid. cf also the Ta Prohm Inscription of Jaya-varman VII, where the king is said to have captured and then released the king of Champa. B. E. F. vol. VI. p. 44.

at their head, and marched against Vijaya. He captured Vijaya and defeated and killed Jaya Indravarman cei Rasupati.

The victorious king of Rājapura now ascended the throne of Vijaya and the whole of Champā was again re-united under him. Jaya Indravarman oṅ Vatuv, who was thus deprived of the throne, fled to Amarāvatī. There he collected a large number of troops and advanced against Vijaya. "The king defeated him, compelled him to fall back on Traik, and there captured him and put him to death." Henceforth Sūryavarmadeva Vidyānandana ruled over the whole of Champā without opposition (1192 A. D.).

But he had shortly to reckon with the king of Cambodge whom he had so basely betrayed. In 1193 an expedition was sent against him, but he gained an easy victory. Next year the expedition was repeated on a larger scale.

"In Śaka 1116 (1194 A. D.) the king of Cambodge sent a large number of Cambodgian generals with all sorts of arms. They came to fight with the prince. The latter fought at Jai Ramya-Vijaya, and vanquished the generals of the Cambodgian army."[1]

This was the crowning triumph of Śrī Sūryavarmadeva, prince Śrī Vidyānandana of Tumprauk-Vijaya, who began his life as an exile, but after a romantic career gained the undisputed supremacy over the whole of Champā.

Immediately after his victory the king sent an ambassador to the Annamese court (1194 A. D.). Four years later, he was formally consecrated to the throne with all due rites, and asked for formal investiture from the Chinese Emperor. This was granted to him in 1199 A. D.[2]

1. Ibid.

2. T'oung Pao. 1911, p. 311.

After the Cambodgian war was over, the king, we are told, "marched to Amarāvatī and re-erected all the houses."[1] In other words, he set himself to the task of restoration, which was badly needed after the late troublesome period of civil war and foreign domination. As usual, he made rich gifts to Śrīśānabhadreśvara.[2] He also erected a house called Śrī Herukaharmya. But the king was not destined to enjoy his sovereignty for a long time. He was defeated in 1203 A. D. by his paternal uncle, called Yuvarāja (or son of Yuvarāja) Mnagahna oṅ Dhanapati or Yuvarāja oṅ Dhanapatigrāma,[3] who was sent by the king of Cambodge against him.

The career of this Yuvarāja was analogous in many respects to that of king Sūryavarmā himself. He, too, lived as an exile in the Court of Cambodge and obtained the favours of the king by successfully suppressing the revolt of Malyaṅ. It is just possible that these two Cham chiefs, uncle and nephew, both went together to Cambodge and the Malyaṅ revolt, which both claim to have subdued, was the self-same

1. Myson Ins. (No. 89).
2. Ibid.
3. The account of Dhanapatigrama is based on the concluding portion of two inscriptions at Myson, Nos, 62 and 84. The identity of Dhanapatigrama, mentioned in No 62, with Mnagahna on Dhanapati (No 84) is not certain but very probable. It is to be noted that the portion of No. 62 containing the account of Dhanapatigrama begins with Svasti, which is generally used at the commencement of a new Inscription. It was probably added at a later date. The account is partly corroborated by Annamite documents (T'oung Pao 1911. p. 311 fn 6), The difficulty in the identification, noted by Finot. does not really exist; cf the text.

military expedition in which both of them took part. But the nephew soon surpassed the uncle, and, as we have seen above, ultimately became the king of Champā.

The king of Cambodge, twice baffled in his attempt to defeat him, at last sent the uncle against the nephew. In 1203 A. D. king Sūryavarman was defeated and the Yuvarāja oṅ Dhanapati ruled over champā.

Sūryavarman now sought protection at the court of Annam. Accompanied by 200 vessels and a number of his faithful soldiers he went with his family to the port of Co La and asked for shelter. The Annamites, however, suspected his intention, and Pham Gieng, the governor of Nghe An, wanted to get rid of him. Forewarned of this, the king invited Pham Gieng aboard his ship. That officer went with a number of vessels, with a quantity of arms concealed therein, and asked his men to examine the vessels of the Cham king with the light of their torches. But at night, while the watchmen of the Annamite vessels fell asleep the Chams threw torches at them. The Annamites started up out of their sleep, and being seized with panic threw themselves into the sea. A large number of Annamites was thus drowned. Sūryavarman again took to sea and what became of him is not known.[1]

The Yuvarāja Dhanapatigrāma, who now ruled over Champā, had a hard time before him. Rebellion broke out in various parts of the kingdom. The most formidable was one led by Putau Ājñā Ku, but it was put down by the Yuvarāja. "Then Putau Ājñā Ku revolted. He conquered from Amarāvatī as far as Pidhyaṅ. The king of Cambodge commanded the Yuvarāja to lead the troops of Cambodge and capture Putau Ājñā Po Ku. He captured him and

1. Toung Pao 1911, pp. 311—312.

sent him to Cambodge according to the desire of the king" (No. 62).

The king of Cambodge, pleased at his valour, conferred high dignities on him, and apparently formally appointed him as the ruler of Champā in 1207 A. D. (cf. No. 86).

While the Yuvarāja was ruling in Champā, a new figure appeared on the scene. This was Jaya Parameśvaravarmadeve On Anśarāja of Turai-Vijaya,[1] son of Jaya Harivarman VII. He was the legitimate owner of the throne of Champā of which his father had been wrongly dispossessed by Jaya Indravarman VII Grāmapura Vijaya. During the period of usurpation by that monarch, and the disastrous Cambodge war that followed, On Anśarāja lived as an exile and at last took refuge in the court of Cambodge.

In 1201 A. D. the king of Cambodge conferred upon him the title of "Pu Poń pulyań Śrī Yuvarāja", and afterwards gave him permission to live in Champā with the Governor Yuvarāja Dhanapatigrāma.[2] It must have been with a mixed feeling of joy and sorrow that the exile returned to his native land, only to find the throne of his forefathers occupied by an usurper. Why he was sent to Champā, and what he did here tfor the next twenty years are yet unknown. It appears, however, that Champā was at this time very hard pressed by the Annamites. The Cho Dinh Inscription tells us: "Then (sometime after 1207 A. D.) the Siamese and the Pukam (Paganese) came from Cambodge and a battle took place with the Annamites. The Cambo-

1. The account of On Ansaraja of Turai-Vijaya who ascended the throne under the name of Jaya Paramesvaravarman is based on nine inscriptions (Nos. 85-92).

2. T'oung Pao 1911. p 313

dgian generals led the troops which opposed the Annamites and the loss on both sides was very great."[1] The Annamite documents inform us that the Chams aided by the Cambodgians attacked Nghe-An in 1216 and 1218, but the governor of the Province dispersed them.[2]

It would thus appear that since about 1207 A. D. a long series of battles followed, in which victory more often inclined to the Annamites.

These long-drawn battles must have exhausted the Cambodgians. As a matter of fact, the series of warfares in which they were involved ever since 1190 A. D., when they conquered Champā, must have proved too great a burden for the people of Cambodge, and, to make matters worse, the Siamese at this time began to press them hard from the west. At last in 1220 A. D, the Cambodgians evacuated Champā, and a formal peace was probably concluded with Oṅ Aṅśarājā of Turai-Vijaya in 1222 A. D. In any case the latter ascended the throne of his ancestors under the name of Jaya Parameśvaravarman IV, and was formally consecrated to the throne in 1226 A. D. Henceforth the king reigned in peace. He restored order in the different parts of his kingdom and set himself to the task of repairing damages caused by the "Cambodge war of 32 years" (1190—1222 A. D.)[3].

The king, as usual, made rich donations to Śrī Īśānabhadreśvara[4] and the goddess Po Nagara.[5] He installed the

1. Cho-dinh Ins. (No. 86).

2. T'oung Pao 1911, pp. 313-14; cf. also B. E. F. vol. XVIII, No. 3 p. 35.

3. Cho-dinh Ins (No. 86).

4. Myson Ins (No. 87).

5. Po Nagar Temple Ins. (No. 88).

image of the god Svayam-Utpanna[1] and endowed him richly.[2] He re-installed all the *liṅgas* of the south, viz. those of Yān Pu Nagara and the *liṅgas* of the north, viz. those of Śrīśāna-bhadreśvara, and made donations to the god Campeśvara,[3] as well as to a number of Buddhist divinities [4]

The last known date of the king is 1234 A. D. and the earliest date of his successor, 1243 A. D. The death of the king must, therefore, have taken place sometime between these dates.

Jaya Parameśvaravarman IV was succeeded by his brother Jaya Indravarman X prince Harideva of Sakaṅ-Vijaya. About this time a powerful dynasty was established on the throne of Annam. The new king of Annam made remonstrances to the court of Champā against the conduct of Cham pirates who pillaged the Annamite population on the sea-shore. The king of Champā demanded in reply the restitution of the three northern districts of Champā conquered by Annam. This irritated the emperor of Annam who led in person an expedition against Champā. The campaign was long and arduous, but did not lead to any decisive result. The Emperor returned with a number of prisoners, including a queen and a number of nobles and concubines of the king of Champā.[5]

After this Jaya Indravarman X lived at peace with his northern neighbour and devoted his time to pious works. He made rich donations to Śrīśānabhadreśvara [6] His daughter Pu-lyaṅ Ratnāvalī, princess Sūryadevī, and her husband, a nobleman

1. Cho-dinh Ins. (No. 89).
2. Lomngoeu Ins. (No. 91). Phanrang Ins. (No. 92).
3. Lomngoeu Ins (No. 91).
4. Kim Choua Ins. (No. 93).
5. T'oung Pao 1911, p. 452.
6 Myson Ins. (No. 94).

called Oṅ Raṣu Nandana made rich presents to the Po Nagar temple, and installed there the images of goddess Mātṛliṅgeśvarī and goddess Kauṭhāreśvarī.[1]

In the year 1257 A. D. the king was murdered by his nephew, sister's son, named Pulyaṅ Śrī Yuvarāja Vlom. The regicide then ascended the throne under the name of Śrī Jaya Siṁhavarman III (1257 A. D.). There seemed to have been some disturbances in the kingdom. An inscription at Po Nagar, dated 1257 A. D., records the donation of the king Śakrānta belonging to Mandavijaya. Apparently a local chief had set himself up as king at the place named. But nothing more is heard of him. Most probably Jaya Siṁhavarman defeated him. Jaya Siṁhavarman further cut off the two thumbs of his only surviving maternal uncle, the younger brother of king Jaya Indravarman X, so as to remove all possibilities of danger in that direction. Having thus secured his position against all possible enemies, Jaya Siṁhavarman was formally consecrated to the throne in 1266 A. D. under the name Indravarman (XI).[2]

The new king wanted to remain at peace. So immediately after his coronation he sent an ambassador with tributes to the court of Annam (1266) and renewed it again in 1267, 1269, and 1270.

The pious endowments of the king are recorded in several inscriptions. In 1274 A. D. he presented the god Svayamutpanna with a large elephant and 6 slaves (No. 106). Four

1. Po Nagar Ins. (Nos. 97, 98, 105).

2. Batau Tablah Ins. No. 104. It may be concluded from this inscription that during the period 1257-1266 A, D. Jaya Simhavarman was king of the southern region only and in 1266 he became the king of the whole country. It is possible that Sakranta was the king of the northern regions during that period but convincing proof is lacking.

years later, his noble queen Sūryalaksmī installed the statue of the god Bhūmivijaya.[1] In the Po Nagar temple the king installed Śrī Indravarma-Śivaliṅgeśvara, and dedicated three infants to the god. He also installed there Śiva-liṅga and the god Śrī-Īśānabhadreśvara and endowed the goddess Kauṭhāreśvarī with lands (Nos. 108 and 109).

But the reign of king Indravarman XI was destined to involve Champā into one of the greatest calamities that ever befell her. She had just passed through Cambodgian incursions lasting 32 years; now she was to suffer the unspeakable horrors of a Mongol invasion.

The Mongols had suddenly risen as a great power in Asia towards the close of the twelfth century A. D. Their great leader Chenghiz Khan (1162—1227 A. D.) had conquered large territories in Asia and eastern Europe, and planned the conquest of China when he died. At his death his empire extended beyond the Caspian sea and the Black sea on the west, as far as Bulgaria, Servia, Hungary and Russia. To the east it included Korea and reached the Pacific ocean, and on the south it was bounded by India, Tibet and the ruins of the splendid empire of Khwarezm, Ogotai, the son and successor of Chenghiz Khan, conquered that portion of China over which the Kin dynasty ruled, and was aided in this task by the Soung dynasty who ruled over the rest. But the turn of the Soung dynasty was soon to come. Ogotai's son and successor Kou youk having died in 1248, the Mongol empire passed on to Mangkou (1248—1259), a grandson of Chenghiz Khan, and then to his brother the famous K'oublai Khan (1260). K'oublai had conquered Yun Nan (1253) during his brother's reign, and after his accession to the throne, he looked forward to the conquest of the whole of the Chinese Empire by putt-

1. Yang Kur Ins. (No. 107).

ing an end to the Soung dynasty. But even while he was carrying on the struggle with the Imperial dynasty, K'oublai Khan sought to exact the oath of allegiance from all foreign states that had hitherto accepted the Chinese Emperor as their suzerain. So an invitation was sent to the kings of Annam and Champā to come and pay their homage as vassals to the Great Khan. In 1278 Sagatou, a high official of the Khan, reported that king Indravarman of Champā was willing to submit. On hearing this K'oublai gave the title of "Prince of second rank" to the king and gave rich presents to the Cham ambassadors who presented themselves to the court in 1279. But K'oublai Khan wished his feudal kings to come in person to the court in order to perform the act of vassalage, and so early in 1280 sent an embassy to Champā, inviting king Indravarman to come in person to the court. The latter was unwilling to do so, and in the month of May sent an embassy offering submission. This, however, did not satisfy the Khan who on 1st July renewed his command to the king to present himself to the court. In reply the Cham king sent on the 5th September some nobles of his court with a few elephants as presents, whereupon the great Khan sent 'an ambassador extraordinary' to king Indravarman, asking him to send to the Imperial court a few nobles of his court together with one of his younger sons. Indravarman then sent two embassies, one on the 13th August, 1281, and the other, two months later, so that K'oublai at last decided to confer on him the insignia of "Prince Imperial of the second rank."

K'oublai now treated Champā as part of his empire. He appointed Sagatou and Lieou Cheng as viceroys to administer Champā in the name of the king. The old and feeble king submitted to this humiliation, but his proud son, the prince Harijit, could not bring himself to yield to it. He fanned the popular discontent which ultimately became so serious that the viceroys of the Khan, no longer feeling their position secure, went to their country.

K'oublai now decided on an expedition against Champā. He made extensive preparations and entrusted it to Sagatou. But before this expedition could start, Champā gave another provocation to the great Khan, by arresting and imprisoning his ambassadors to Siam and Malabar. Nevertheless, the Khan, who was a thorough diplomat, called a Cham ambassador who was present in his court, gave him some clothes, and asked him to tell the old king, that he had nothing to fear, that his guilty son alone will be punished, and none else need be afraid at all. At last in 1282 Sagatou, invested with the title of "the governor of the province of Champā," embarked his troops on thousand vessels–the land route through Tonkin being refused by the Annamite King—and landed his army unopposed on the coast of Champā. The Cham army guarded the citadel of Mou Tcheng and was led by prince Harijit in person. Sagatou tried the method of conciliation, but failed. At last the battle took place in January, 1283. The Chams, 10,000 strong, fought obstinately for six hours, but then beat retreat. The Mongols entered the citadel and killed about a thousand persons. King Indravarman XI put his magazine to fire and then retired with his troops to the mountains.

The Mongol army now made preparations to conquer the metropolitan province. On the third day, however, an envoy came from king Indravarman, tendering submission on the part of his master. Next day Sagatou, who had already reached the south-eastern limit of the province, dismissed the ambassador, and charged him to tell his master, that he was pardoned, but must come in person and present himself before him. On the following day Sagatou entered into the province when an envoy from Indravarman announced that the king would presently arrive, whereupon Sagatou camped outside the capital city.

But the king never really intended to present himself before the Mongol Chief he merely wanted to temporise. But still fearing the wrath of the Great Khan he sent on the following day his maternal uncle Pao-t'o-t'ou-houo (Bhadradeva?) for presenting tribute of submission. He represented that the king wished to come in person but was prevented by a malady, and that his son wants three days' time to present himself. Sagatou became furious and Pao-t'o-t'ou-houo went back to Indravarman to narrate what had happened.

The heir-apparent, prince Harijit, had no more desire than his father to present himself before the Mongol commander. He sent, instead, two of his brothers to the Mongol camp. They told Sagatou that their elder brother had died of the wounds he had received in battle, and that their father, the king, was struck by an arrow in his chin, and although gradually improving, was not yet in a condition to present himself. Sagatou saw through the trick and would not listen to any excuse. He even doubted whether the envoys were really sons of king Indravarman. But he sent them back and transmitted through them the order to the king to come and pay respect in person.

Shortly, the Chinese spies brought news that king Indravarman had entrenched himself on mount Ya Heou, with 20,000 men, and that he had sent ambassadors to Annam, Cambodge and Java, asking for military assistance. Sagatou then sent a detachment of his army against the king. Although successful at first, the Mongol troops were harassed by the enemy in the unknown mountain forests, and regained the camp with great difficulty and after heavy losses. But Sagatou being re-inforced from China, himself took the offensive on the 14th June, 1283, and inflicted great loss on the Cham army. King Indravarman again retired to the mountains and the great Mongol general had again to fall back on the old expedient, viz. writing letters to king Indravarman to come and tender his submission in person.

Thus inspite of all his victories Sagatou could not secure any substantial result. The king of Champā was as inaccessible as before, and his own position, in an enemy's country, was ever precarious. Besides, he was unpopular in the army, and there were heavy desertions both among soldiers and officers.

The Cham campaign had already cost K'oublai Khan heavily in men and money. Nevertheless, in 1284, he arranged to send another supporting army of 15,000 soldiers. The number of vessels being insufficient, only a part of the army could immediately start. But disaster dogged their footstep and the first division of the navy, carrying the first batches of soldiers, completely disappeared, within sight of the Chon Mei Lein canal, and no one knew what became of her.

The rest of the troops safely reached the coast of Champā under the leadership of Wan Hou Lieou Kiun K'ing. But having arrived at Śrī Banoy, Wan Hou learnt to his great surprise that Sagatou had burnt his camp and started on his return journey a few days before. He then advanced alone and sent an ambassador to Indravarman asking him to come in person with his son. But the king was in no mood to listen to this after the departure of the main Mongol force. He merely sent a reply saying that the army of Sagatou had put the country to fire and sword, without leaving anything that could be offered as present, and that next year he would send his own son with presents. He then decided to send his grandson to the Emperor to renew the oaths ef allegiance (1284). Three months later, he sent to K'oublai a map of his kingdom and the following month he sent an embassy of 18 persons with a prayer for the withdrawal of troops on condition of regular payment of tribute. Three months later still, the same ambassadors again presented themselves to the court of the great Mongol with rich presents.

But inspite of all these embassies and assurances of submission, things continued as before. The king stationed himself in the mountains, re-forming his army as soon as it was dispersed by the Mongols, while the latter, unable to secure any solid advantage, suffered from heat, diseases and want of provisions. So, in order to bring the campaign to a successful end at any cost, the great Khan resolved to send by land an army sufficiently strong for the final conquest of Champā.

In order to reach Champā it was necessary to pass through Annamite territory. The king of that country, like Indravarman, had obstinately refused to pay homage in person. His son and successor Nho'n-Ton resolved to follow the same policy, and when invited to present himself at the court, sent his uncle Tran-di-Ai. K'oublai, furious at this obstinacy, declared Nho'n—Ton to have forfeited the throne, and appointed Tran-di-Ai as king in his place. He also appointed Tch'en Tch'ouen as "Ambassador Extraordinary and Generallissimo of Annam", and asked him to go and install Tran-di-Ai on the throne.

They were, however, unable to enter into Annam, and Nho'n–Ton also refused passage to the troops of Sagatou. Next year Sagatou asked him for men and provisions, but he refused. He stated that Champā was a small country long since subject to his government, that his father had lived on good terms with it, and that he also followed the same policy. Moreover, for thirty years there was no war between the two countries, and he, therefore, excused himself from supplying provisions. Four months later, in 1284, he gave a similar reply to a fresh demand for provisions. At the same time he protested against the accusation that he had helped Champā with 20,000 men and 500 vessels.

It was undoubtedly an enlightened view of his own interest, rather than any sympathy for Champā, that made Nho'n Ton so obstinate in refusing a passage through his country. He knew he was secure from an invasion by the Mongols so long as they were busy with Champā, and that the moment his neighbour would submit, his own turn would come. So when he at last received a peremptory order to give passage to the troops bound for Champā, he opposed their advance into his territory.

The Mongol troops were commanded by Togan the son of K'oublai. Failing to win over the Annamite king by diplomacy, he at last invaded the passes leading to that country and carried them one after another. Then winning victory after victory, he crossed the Red river and entered the capital of Annam as victor. At the same time Sagatou advanced from the south and defeated the enemy at Nghe-An and Than Hoa. At last the Annamite Emperor took the offensive. He defeated Togan in the north and drove back his army beyond the Red river. Sagatou, unaware of this defeat, was still advancing into the enemy's country, when he was surprised and completely defeated. He was killed in the action and his head was presented to Nho'n Ton.

Thus Champā was at last delivered from the scourge of Mongol invasion. In order to prevent a repetition of the catastrophe Indravarman hastened to send an ambassador with rich presents to K'oublai (1285). The great Khan had now renounced all hopes of conquering Champā and released the prisoners.[1]

1. The account of the Mongol expedition to Champa is based on T'oung Pao 1911 (pp. 456-475).

King Indravarman XI, who had heroically sustained the arduous struggle against his powerful foe, probably did not long survive this happy deliverance. It appears from the account of Marco Polo who visited Champā about 1288 A. D. that king Indravarman was already dead.[1]

He was succeeded by his brave son prince Harijit, born of the queen Gaudendralakṣmī, who had bravely stood by his father in his hours of trial, and now ascended the throne under the name of Jaya Siṁhavarman IV. He restored peace in the kingdom which it badly needed after the long and arduous campaign.

The proud king dispensed with all marks of vassalage in respect of the great K'oublai Khan. When the Mongol fleet passed by the coast of Champā in course of an expedition to Java, the king mobilised his forces, and held himself in readines to prevent any attempt at landing. Fortunately no untoward events took place.

He also stopped the payment of usual tribute to Annam. There King Nho'n Ton had abdicated the throne in favour of his son Anh-Ton and retired to hermitage. After spending a secluded life for some time, Nho'n-Ton desired to visit the holy places of different countries, and in 1301 A. D. came to Champā. He lived there for 9 months and was so hospitably treated by Jaya Siṁhavarman that before his departure he promised the king the hand of one of his daughters.

The court of Annam coldly received the proposal. But Jaya Siṁhavarman, who had already married a princess of Java (or Malaya Peninsula) named Tāpasi, was eager for this new alliance. Negotiations continued as late as 1305, but Jaya

1. Different dates are proposed for Marco Polo's visit to Champa, but 1288 is generally accepted. (Yule—Marco Polo vol. II. p. 271). T'oung Pao, 1911 p. 476 fn. 2. p. 474. fn. 3.

Siṁhavarman, impatient at the delay, sent an ambassador with nuptial presents and promised to cede to Annam, on the day of marriage, the two northern provinces of his realm, corresponding to Thua Thien, the southern portion of Quang Tri and the northern part of Quang Nam. It is an irony of fate that the man who fought so valiantly for his country even at the risk of his own life, did not scruple to part with two of the most valuable provinces of his kingdom, including the famous stronghold of Kiu S'ou, for a mere hobby. Thus was Champā dismembered a second time (cf. p. 82 above). The Annamite council made a last attempt to prevent the alliance which they considered as humiliating for the daughter of an Emperor, but Anh-Ton, more practical than his ministers, was ready to sacrifice his sense of prestige and brotherly sentiments for the good of the country. He accepted the provinces and sent the princess to Jaya Siṁhavarman. All along the way, popular ballads, composed on the occasion, were sung by the young and the old alike, jeering "at the Emperor of the Hans who had given away his daughter to the king of the Huns"[1] (1306). Aymonier supposes that this daughter is probably referred to as Paramośvarī, daughter of king Devādidova, in the Posah Ins. (No. 110), for the Annamite kings were known as the kings of gods among the Cambodgians.[2] But king Jaya Siṁhavarman IV did not live long after this marriage, and died in 1307 A. D. He had established a Mukhaliṅga called Jaya Siṁhavarmaliṅgeśvara at Tali and made many other religious endowments.[3]

1. The allusion is to two political marriages between Han princesses and the Hun chiefs that took place long ago.
2 Bulletin de la commission archeologique del'.Indochine, 1911, p. 17.
3. Po Klong Gorai Inscriptions (Nos. 111-115), and Tali Ins. No. 116.

As soon as the king of Annam heard of Jaya Siṁhavarman's death he sent a high official to bring back his sister. It was a delicate task, for according to the custom of Champā the queen had to be burnt alive on the funeral pyre of her husband. After a great deal of difficulty, however, the queen was brought back to Annam.

Jaya Siṁhavarman was succeeded by his son prince Harijitātmaja, born of the queen Bhāskaradevī. He was born in 1274 A. D. and was therefore 33 years old at the time of his accession. His early career is known to us from one of his records.[1] In 1298 A. D. he had received the title Taval Śurā Adhikavarman. Two years later he was appointed to govern a district extending from the river Vauk as far as Bhūmanā Vijaya. In 1301 his father gave him the name Pulyaṅ Uddhṛta Siṁhavarman. In 1306 he got the name Mahendravarman.

He at first kept friendly relations with the court of Annam. But this attitude was not preserved for long and he often turned rebellious. The fact was that he regretted the cession of two provinces by his father which brought the northern boundary of Champā far to the south, and the people of the two provinces also chafed at the foreign domination. The result was rebellions and frequent incursions into those provinces, so much so that the Annamite colonists installed in the two provinces found it impossible to live there. So at the beginning of 1312, the Annamite emperor Anh Hoang decided to lead an expedition against Champā. Just at this moment an ambassador from Siṁhavarman presented himself with tribute. The ambassador was prevailed upon to go back and induce his master to submit to Annam.

The Emperor himself led the expedition and king Siṁha-

1. Po sah Ins No. 110.

varman was induced to submit without any fight. The king with his whole family went by sea and presented themselves before the Annamite Emperor. His soldiers, however, were enraged at this humiliation, and attacked the camp of the Emperor. They were, however, soon defeated and took to flight. Thereupon Siṁhavarman was made prisoner, and his brother Che-Da-a-ba-niem was entrusted with the government of Champā with the title "Feudatory prince of the second rank." The campaign was over in six months and Anh Hoang came back to his capital with his royal prisoner. He gave him high honours but that was a poor consolation to the captive who died at the beginning of 1313. His body was burnt and the ashes were buried in the ground according to the custom of Champā.[1]

The kingdom of Champā had now practically become an Annamite province. The Chinese Emperor, however, could ill brook it. He pretended that Champā was still his own vassal-state and ordered its king to send him rhinoceros and elephants. Anh Hoang, however, paid no heed to these demands, and looked upon himself as the sole king of Champā. At the same time he accepted the responsibility of the position, for, when in 1313 A. D. bands of Siamese invaded Champā and committed pillage and destruction, Anh Hoang sent one of his officials against them and they were driven away.

Che-Da-a-ba-niem, who had been placed on the throne by the Annamites, assumed the name of Che Nang after coronation (1312 A. D.). Two years later, Anh Hoang abdicated the throne in favour of his son Ninh Hoang. Che Nang took advantage of this change of master in throwing off his yoke to

1. T'oung Pao 1911, p. 590-594. The history of Champa for the next hundred years is almost solely known from Annamite documents, the next Cham Inscription being dated 1401 A, D. The account in the text that follows is almost solely based on Maspero's account in T'oung Pao 1911 pp. 595 ff.

Annam. He had some successes at first but was soon defeated and took to flight. Afraid of meeting with his brother's fate he fled the country and took refuge in Java (c. 1318 A. D.). With him ended the dynasty founded by Rudravarman Parama-Brahmaloka in 1145 A. D.

KINGS REFERRED TO IN CHAPTER XI.

1. Jaya Indravarman VIII oṅ vatuv	(1180—1190 A. D.).
2. Sūrya Jayavarmadeva prince In (Cambodian usurper)	(1190—1191 A. D.).
3. Jaya Indravarman IX cei Rasupati	(1191—1192 A. D.).
4. Sūryavarmadeva prince Śrī Vidyānandana	(1192—1203 A. D.).
5. Oṅ Dhanapatigrāma	(1203—1222 A. D.).
6. Jaya Parameśvaravarmadeva (Son of Jaya Harivarman VII; cf chap. X).	(1222-c. 1240 A. D.)
7. Jaya Indravarman X (Younger brother of No. 6)	(c. 1240-1257 A. D.)
8. Jaya Siṁhavarman III or Indravarman XI (Nephew, sister's son, of No. 7)	(1257-c. 1287 A. D.)
[9- Śakrānta ! (usurper ?)	1257 A. D.]
10. Jaya Siṁhavarman IV also called Harijit (Son of No. 8)	(c. 1287-1307 A. D.)
11. Harijitātmaja-Mahendravarman (Son of No. 10)	(1307—1312 A. D.)
12. Che Nang (brother of No. 11)	(1312-c. 1318 A. D.)

Chapter XII.

The Annamite conquest of Champa.

The kingdom of Champā was now without a king and there was probably no legitimate heir to the throne. On the recommendation of the victorious Annamite general, the Emperor appointed a military chief called A-Nan as his viceroy in Champā (1318 A. D.).

A-Nan behaved exactly like his predecessor. As soon as he felt himself powerful enough he tried to shake off the Annamite yoke. For this purpose he commenced negotiations with the Mongols who had never ceased to demand contributions from Champā. In 1321 A-Nan received the order to send some domesticated elephants, and sent an ambassador with the tribute in 1322. Next year he sent his brother to the Chinese Emperor asking for assistance against his powerful neighbour in the north. The Emperor Jen Tsong agreed to this and sent ambassadors to Ninh Hoàng asking him to respect the integrity of Champā (1324). Ninh Hoàng replied to this message by sending an expedition against Champā in 1326. But it led to disasters. A-Nan defeated his army and henceforth ceased to consider himself as his vassal.

On the other hand A-Nan continued his relations with the Mongols, and sent ambassadors to the Chinese court in 1327, 1328 and 1330. Then he ceased to send them and reigned as an independent sovereign. Neither Annam nor China was in a position to make an effective protest against this. In the case of the former, the practice, which had hardened into a custom, for the emperors of the Tran dynasty to abdicate the throne in favour of a boy made it impossible to assert its rights, while the discord between the Mongols and the native inhabitants in China enfeebled the central authority there. Thus

A-Nan reigned during the last eleven years as an independent king and brought back peace and tranquility to the kingdom which had not known it for a long time.

A-Nan had a son-in-law Trà Hoà Bo De and placed more confidence in him than in his own son Che Mo. Bo De, while outwardly showing great affection for Che Mo, excited popular sentiment against him, and ingratiated himself into the favour of the military chiefs. Thus when A-Nan died, Bo De had no difficulty in removing Che Mo and making himself king in his place (June, 1342).

Che Mo did not take this act of usurpation lying down. He collected the loyal people and fought with Bo De for the throne. Being defeated he sought protection in the court of Annam. The king of Annam took advantage of this to demand tribute of Bo De and the latter hastened to send an ambassador; but his presents were considered insufficient.

At the same time although Che Mo was well received, and his presents accepted with thanks, no preparation was made for sending an expedition to Champā in his favour. At last, tired of waiting, one day he addressed the king of Annam: "My lord, in old days a king of Champā was very fond of a monkey and announced a reward of 10,000 gold coins for anyone who could train it to speak. At last a man offered to do it in three years, on condition of receiving 100 gold coins every month. "Within these three years" said he, "either the king or the monkey or I shall die." The king of Annam understood the import of the parable, and sent an expedition (1353), but as the army did not meet with the navy at the appointed place, it came back. Che Mo, who returned with the army, died shortly afterwards.

Bo De, elated beyond measure at the retreat of the Annamite troops, now took the offensive in order to reconquer the northern districts, but he was defeated in his first attack (1353 A. D.) and gave up the enterprise.

Bo De was succeeded by Che Bong Nga. The date of his accession and his relationship with Bo De are alike unknown. But it is probable that he came to the throne sometime about 1360 A. D.

The reign of Che Bong Nga was remarkable for a series of victorious campaigns against Annam. In 1361 he suddenly raided the port of Da Li (Li-Hoa in Botrach). Having put to flight the soldiers who defended it, he pillaged the town and its neighbourhood, massacred the population and returned by sea with an immense booty. Next year he plundered the chief town of Hoa Chau. In 1365 the Chams carried away the boys and girls of Hoa Chau who gathered to celebrate a festival according to local custom.

At last in 1368 Du Hoang, the king of Annam, sent a powerful army against Champā, but Che Bong Nga lay in ambush, surprised them completely, and put them to a precipitate retreat.

In the meantime Tchou Youen-Tchang had driven away the last Mongol emperor from China and ascended the throne under the name of Houng Wou (1368). He founded the Imperial Ming dynasty and installed his court at Nanking. His first care was to re-establish the unity of the empire, and with this view he ordered all his vassal states to pay allegiance to the Emperor. Che Bong Nga had already sent tributes to the new emperor, and the latter was pleased to send presents to him and confer upon him the title of "King of Champā." The Cham king sent another ambassador in 1370, and continued to pay the homage regularly year after year. Houng Wou sent one of his officers to Champā to offer propitiatory sacrifices to the spirit of the mountains and rivers and to institute an examination for the students. At the same time he enjoined upon both Annam and Champā to cease their quarrels and live on good terms with each other.

Du Hoang, the king of Annam, died in June, 1369. One of his younger sons was placed on the throne by the intrigues of the queen-mother. But Phu, the brother of the deceased king, revolted against him, put him into prison and ascended the throne under the name of Nghia-Hoang (1370 A. D.). The queen-mother Du'o'ng Khu'o'ng then fled to Champā and enlisted the help of Che Bong Nga. In 1371 the latter sailed with a fleet and marched unopposed to the capital. He pillaged the city, burnt the royal palace and returned with a rich booty (1371).

Next year, Che Bong Nga, with impudent effrontery, wrote a long letter to the Chinese Emperor, complaining that the Annamite troops had invaded his territory and were harassing his people. "I beg your Majesty," the letter concluded, "to send me some military equipments, instruments of music and some musicians. Then Annam will see that the kingdom of Champā is tributary to your Majesty, and will not dare to molest it". This direct perversion of truth was apparently intended to forestall the complaints of Annam, and assure the neutrality of China. The Chinese Emperor fell into the trap. He did not send the things asked for, but sent a long letter in reply, observing, among others, "that from this day forth Annam must take back his army, and Champā should make peace with her, so that the two countries might be content with their own legitimate dominions." Further, Che Bong Nga pleased the Emperor beyond measure by presenting to him the rich booty which he had taken from the pirates subdued by him (1373).

In the meantime Nghia-Hoang had abdicated the throne of Annam in favour of Kham Hoang (1372). The new King resolved to avenge the insult that Champā had inflicted upon his dynasty, and made preparations on a large scale. As soon as Che Bong Nga came to know of this, he hastened to communicate to the Chinese Emperor that he was attacked by the Annamites. The latter, tired of these reciprocal complaints, justly observed that if this year Champā complained of Annamite aggression, last year it was Annam who demanded aid against the aggression of the Chams, and that consequently it was impossible to know who was in the wrong. He again advised both of them to suspend their war-like activities and live on good terms with each other.

After a great deal of delay, Kham Hoang at last marched at the head of more than 1,20,000 men in January 1377, and arrived unopposed before the town of Vijaya which was surrounded by a palisade. There a Cham reported to Kham Hoang that the town was deserted, that the king had taken to flight, and that by a quick march he could yet overtake the king. Heedless of the prudent counsels of his generals, Kham Hoang marched with his army which advanced pell mell without any order or organisation. When they had proceeded some distance the Chams suddenly fell upon them and intercepted their passage. This produced such a panic in the Annamite army that it was completely routed. The Emperor with his two commanders-in-chief and several other nobles lay dead on the field.

Immediately after this great victory Che Bong Nga sailed with a fleet towards the capital of Annam. Gian Hoang who was hastily proclaimed king made arrangements for defending it, but Che Bong Nga entered into the town and pillaged it for a whole day. He returned with an immense booty which was sent as tribute to the Chinese

Emperor. Next year he again marched towards Annam. Having conquered Nghe-An, and appointed there his own governor, he plundered the capital and returned with an immense booty. A part of this was sent as tribute to the Chinese Emperor.

Henceforth the people of Annam lived in constant terror of the Chams. The Emperor Gian Hoang removed his treasures to the mountains of Thien Kien and the caves of Kha lang for saving them from the cupidity of the Chams (1379). And it was well indeed that he had done so. For inspite of the injunctions of the Chinese Emperor to leave the Annamites in peace Che Bong Nga led a new expedition against them in 1380. The old king of Annam made preparations for defending the country both by land and sea and at last succeeded in inflicting a defeat upon Che Bong Nga who took to flight.

Inspite of this defeat Che Bong Nga remained master of Thuan Hoa, Tan-Binh and Nghe-An, and his constant incursions against Than Hoa reduced the Annamite authority over that province almost to a shadow. In 1382 he invaded Than Hoa, but this time also he met with disaster ; a part of his navy was burnt and his army retreated with great loss (1382).

Nothing undaunted, Che Bong Nga formed a daring plan. As he was unsuccessful at sea, and the defiles between Than Hoa and Ninh Binh were well guarded by the Annamites, he marched with his commander-in-chief La-khai over the high ranges, across mountains and forests, and descended at a point north of the Annamite capital (1383). After inflicting a heavy loss upon the enemy he returned to his kingdom in 1384.

Five years later, Che Bong Nga led another victorious expedition. By a ruse he completely defeated the Annamite army and advanced towards the capital. He reached the river Hai Trieu and there was nothing to prevent him from occupying the whole country. The situation appeared so desperate that the younger brother of the Annamite Emperor passed over to the camp of Che Bong Nga, expecting no doubt to be appointed to the government of Annam after its conquest.

But at this moment the treachery of a Cham military officer changed the whole complexion of things. As Che Bong Nga advanced with about 100 vessels to reconnoitre the forces of the enemy, one of his officers, who was reprimanded and afraid of his life, passed over to the enemy and told them that the king's vessel was easily recognisable by its green colour. On learning this the Annamite commander made for the Cham navy and asked his men to concentrate the fury of their attack on the royal vessel. Suddenly a volley of musketry was fired at Che Bong Nga and he fell dead. The Chams lost heart at the sudden death of their chief and beat a precipitate retreat to rejoin the main army which was stationed at the river Hoang under the command of the general La Khai (February, 1390). La Khai immediately led back the army by forced marches day and night. The enemy overtook him but was easily defeated. As soon as he reached Champā he proclaimed himself king of the country. The two sons of Che Bong Nga, deprived of their legitimate rights, sought protection in the Annamite court. But although received there with honours and distinction they could not secure any support to regain their throne.

La Khai, who thus established a new dynasty, is almost certainly to be identified with Śrī Jaya Siṁhavarmadeva V Śrī Harijātti Vīrasiṁha Champa-pura, the founder of the Bṛsu family of kings.[1]

1. Binh Dinh Ins. (No. 117). The identity was first established by Finot (B. E. F. vol. XV, No. 2, p. 14). Maspero

One of the first acts of Jaya Siṁhavarmadeva was to send tributes to the Chinese Emperor Tái Tsou. But the Emperor, who had himself usurped the throne by driving away his master, refused to accept the tribute from the usurper (1391). Jaya Siṁhavarman did not insist, but he again sent the tribute in 1397, and it was accepted. The tribute was renewed in 1399.

Immediately after the death of Che Bong Nga, the two provinces Tan Binh and Thuan Hoa, which he had annexed, made submission to Annam. It is probable that other parts of Champā, too, did not acknowledge the authority of Jaya Siṁhavarmadeva. We hear indeed of a Cham general seeking protection in Annam in 1397 with his family. Everything indicates an unsettled time, but unfortunately we know very little of the reign of Jaya Siṁhavarmadeva. He ruled for twelve years (1390-1401), and was succeeded by Śrī Vṛsu Viṣṇujātti Vīra Bhadravarmadeva.[1] The king was formerly called prince Nauk Glauṅ Vijaya[2] and after a reign of 32 years he was consecrated and took the name Śrī Bṛṣu Indravarman..[3]

The Annamites had never given up their intention of conquering Champā and led an expedition against it in 1401. Vīra Bhadravarman, who had just ascended the throne, opposed the enemy vigorously and forced them to retreat. It was with considerable difficulties that the Annamite forces could regain their own territory.

In 1402, the Annamite army again invaded Champā. Bhadravarman sent his general to oppose them, but he was

identifies Jaya Siṁhavarman with the successor of La khai (T'oung Pao 1913. p. 156.)

1. Binh Dinh Ins. (No. 117).
2. Bien Hoa Ins [No. 121].
3 Nui Ben-Lang Ins. [No. 122].

killed in a fight with the vanguards of the enemy. The king was now terribly afraid for his life and throne, and sent his maternal uncle with rich presents to treat with the enemy. He offered the rich province of Indrapura on condition of cessation of hostilities and the retreat of the Annamite troops. The Annamites demanded Quang Nghia in addition, and thus the whole of Quang-Nam and Quang-Ngai, the ancient Amarāvatī, was ceded to the enemy. It was a terrible blow to the power and prestige of Champā. The ancient capital of Indrapura was full of accumulated riches and trophies and was associated with the glorious days of the past. The province of Amarāvatī was also one of the richest and the most fertile. By this humiliating treaty the kingdom of Champā was reduced to half its size; it lost its rich fertile regions in the northern plain, and was confined to poor mountainous regions in the south.

The Chams of the ceded provinces could ill brook the Annamite domination. Although a son of Che Bong Nga was appointed as their governor, they emigrated in large numbers. King Bhadravarman also repented of his act. He sent a pathetic appeal to the Chinese Emperor (1403), and the latter sent two plenipotentiaries to the Annamite court, asking it to leave its neighbour in peace. The Annamites replied by sending a force, 200,000 strong, against Champā both by way of land and sea.

Bhadravarman had been assured by the Chinese Emperor that Annam would leave him in peace. He, therefore, hastened to inform that Emperor of the new expedition. On the 5th September, 1404, his ambassador arrived at the Imperial court with a rich present consisting of a rhinoceros and other indigenous products, and delivered his message to the emperor. It ran as follows;

" In a recent report I have informed your Majesty that

Annam had violated our territories and killed and carried away men and animals, and at my request your Majesty was pleased to order the king of Annam to withdraw his army. But the latter has not complied with the order of your Majesty In the fourth month of the year (between 9th May and 8th June 1404) he again ravaged the frontiers of my country and caused sufferings to my people. Recently, during the return journey of my ambassador who had gone to pay the tribute to the Imperial court, all the presents sent to me by your Majesty were forcibly taken by the Annamites. Moreover, in order to indicate my vassalage to him, the king of Annam has forced me to use his crown, dress and seal. Besides, he has seized upon Cha-li-ya and other places in my kingdom. Still, even now he does not cease to attack and molest my territories. I fear I have not the power to protect myself and I therefore place my kingdom at the feet of your Majesty and request you to have it administered by your officials."[1]

The Chinese Emperor became furious and asked his minister to send an ambassador. He also sent battleships in aid of Bhadravarman. These met the Annamite fleet which retreated before it without fighting. The Annamite army which besieged Vijaya also raised the siege and turned back, because their provisions ran short and the town was well defended.

Tch'eng Tsou then sent presents to Bhadravarman and wrote to Han Thu'o'ng, the Annamite emperor, condemning his action (1404). The latter was unwilling to provoke the wrath of his powerful neighbour. He, therefore, returned to him the two elephants which the king of Champā had sent to China, but which he intercepted and kept with him, believing, said he "that they were presented to him by the Cham king for delaying the despatch of troops."

1. The letter is quoted in the Chinese text "Ngan-nan ki cheou pen-mo", composed between 1404-1432 A. D. It is thus a contemporary record. cf. B. E. F. vol. XIV, No. 9, p. 42.

But Tch'eng Tsou was now inclined to fight with his turbulent neighbour, and the king of Champā excited him to this action. Although Han Thùo'ng tried to avoid war, he was forced to it, and it was fatal to himself and to his dynasty. In July, 1407, he fell into the hands of the Chinese with his father and son, and they all died in exile.

Vīra Bhadravarman, gratified beyond all measure at this defeat of his implacable enemy, sent a sumptuous tribute to the Emperor, and received in return a still more sumptuous present. He then sent an expedition to recover the ceded provinces. The Annamite forces who defended it were easily defeated, the son of Che Bong Nga who still governed the provinces on behalf of the Annamites lay dead on the field, and the two provinces, ceded in 1402, passed again into the hands of Champā.

In the meantime, after a long struggle, the Chinese general Tchang Fou became the undisputed master of the whole of Annamite territory which was reduced to the position of a Chinese province. The Chinese general now coveted the two Cham provinces which were ceded to Annam in 1402, but were reconquered by Vīra Bhadravarman as stated above. The Chinese general even solicited the permission of the Emperor to lead an expedition against Champā. The Emperor was not, however, willing to go so far, but he ordered the king of Champā to restore the two provinces. The latter offered excuses and sent regular tributes, but did not give up the provinces.

Soon the whole situation was changed. In 1428 the Chinese were finally driven out of Annam by Le Lo'i who proclaimed himself emperor. Vīra Bhadravarman hastened to make friends with him, and sent an ambassador who came back with rich presents. But six years later, when Le Lo'i died and was succeeded by a boy of 11 years, Bhadravarman regarded it as a suitable opportunity for renewing the attacks against Annam. In 1434 he sent an expedition by both land and sea. Two of his men were taken prisoners by the Annamites. They were made to review the Annamite army and then sent back. Bhadravarman, having learnt from them the military strength of the enemy, wished for peace. The plenipotentiaries were exchanged and the pacific relations were established between the two countries in 1434.

Free from troubles in the north by the Chinese victory over the Annamites in 1407, Bhadravarman had invaded Cambodge, and made himself master of it. The king of that country Chau Ponha Yat complained to the Chinese Emperor in 1408, and again in 1414, and asked for his assistance. The Chinese Emperor addressed a letter to Vīra Bhadravarman asking him to withdraw his troops from Cambodge and leave it in peace. What came out of it we do not know, but in an inscription dated 1421 A. D. 'the king is said to have vanquished the Annamites and taken possession of a kingdom called Braḥ Kānda. He gained innumerable victories, erected an image of Viṣṇu called Tribhuvanākrānta, and appropriated the booty he had taken from the Khmers to the service of the god.'[1] The king, besides, made various rich gifts to Śrīśāna (Śrīśānabhadreśvara ?)

It was during his reign that Nicolo de Conti visited Champā. He went west from the island of Java " towards a maritime city named Ciampa rich in Aloe wood, camphor and gold." Vīra Bhadravarman was the last king who has left inscriptions in the Cham language. After him Champā knew peace no longer. It remained a scene of civil war and foreign invasion till its downfall at no distant date.

1. Bien Hoa Ins. (No. 121)

Vīra Bhadravarman died in 1441 A. D. and was succeeded by his nephew Mahā Vijaya. In a letter to the Ming Emperor he declared himself to have been nominated to the succession by his uncle himself; but his nephew and successor Mahā Qui Lai later on advanced a similar claim, and announced that as he was too young, he had abdicated the throne in favour of his uncle. The probability seems to be that the death of Bhadravarman was followed by a civil war for succession and his nephew Mahā Vijaya came out successful at first.

Immediately after his accession Mahā Vijaya sent an ambassador to the Chinese Emperor and asked for investiture, representing that his uncle had left the throne to him by a formal testament. The Emperor nominated him king of Champā and sent presents for the king and the queen.

Having thus been assured of friendship or at least the neutrality of China, Mahā Vijaya commenced the old tactics of harassing the Annamite frontier. He sent expedition against the border province of Hoa Chau in 1444, and again in 1445. The second one was disastrous, for the army was suddenly caught during an inundation at the citadel of An Dung, and suffered severe losses.

The Annamite court, tired of these border campaigns, resolved to carry the fight into the heart of Champā. They tried to secure the neutrality of China, and represented, that taking advantage of the young age of their Emperor, Mahā Vijaya made plundering raids into the province of Hoa Chau and inflicted considerable damages upon the country. The Chinese Emperor rebuked the king of Champā and asked him to fix the limits of the two countries and forswear all war in future. " You must" concluded he " issue strict commands to the officers of your frontier posts not to lead any incursion against the Annamites." At the same time he asked the Annamites to refrain from commencing a war of vengeance against their neighbour. But the Annamites had already assembled their troops and collected the munitions of war. Their army entered into Champā, defeated the enemy troops and besieged the capital city Vijaya (1446 A. D.). Mahā Vijaya shut himself up into the city with all his troops, and hoped to be able to defy the enemy. But he was betrayed by his nephew Mahā Qui-Lai. On condition of being recognised as king of Champā he delivered up the city to the Annamites. Mahā Vijaya was made prisoner with his wives and concubines and the enemy returned to their country with an immense booty. Amid pompous ceremonies, the captive king 'was presented to the ancestors' of the Annamite Emperor. Most of the Cham prisoners were then released but the king was not allowed to return, although the Chinese Emperor sent an order to that effect. Nevertheless he was well treated. He was allowed to put on his royal costume and invited to the feast offered to the ambassadors of his country (1447).

Mahā Qui-Lai asked for formal investiture from both the Annamite and Chinese courts, and his request was granted by both. The Chinese Emperor repeated to him his advice to be on friendly terms with the Annamite Court. He listened to this counsel and sent tributes to Annam (1447). But he could not long enjoy the sovereignty which he had purchased by betraying his king and his country. He was dethroned by his younger brother Qui-Do who threw him into prison and declared himself king (1449).

The Annamite Emperor Nho'n Ton was very angry and refused the homage of the new king. "A subject" said he "who assassinates his king, and a younger brother who kills his elder, merits an exemplary punishment according to all laws, both ancient and modern. I categorically refuse all your presents and return them." He further sent an officer to Champā to obtain first-hand information about the recent happenings in that country. Apprehensive of the results of this inquiry Qui-Do sent another ambassador to the Annamite court. But he did not fare better than his predecessor. When questioned about the crime of his royal master he could not give any reply but simply made the most humble obeisance. Nho'n Ton not only dismissed him but recalled all the Annamites settled in Champā, and wrote a strong letter to Qui-Do. "In a kingdom" said he "there must be a king and his subjects ; this is an eternal principle. You Chams, you dare transgress this eternal law. When the old king had died, you elected Bi-Cai (Mahā Vijaya) to the throne, instead of the son of the late king. He refused to respect our authority and created troubles for us. He was punished for his crime and fell in our hands. You then demanded investiture for Qui-Lai and again abandoned him for placing Qui-Do on the throne Are you then devoid of all principles and fidelity ? Do you regard the king as merely a piece on a chess-board ?"

The Cham king could very well retort by pointing out the support which the Annamite court had extended to the traitor and regicide whom he had displaced. But it was the logic of the strong towards the weak. Qui-Do sent back about 70 Annamites (1449) and did not make any further attempt to establish friendly relations with the Annamite court.

Some time elapsed before Qui-Do asked for investiture from China. In 1449 the Chinese Emperor Ying Tsong was made prisoner by the Mongols and his brother King had ascended the throne. The delay of Qui-Do in asking for investiture was probably due to these events. But in 1453 he sent ambassadors to the Emperor King. They reported the death of Mahā Qui-Lai and requested that his brother Mahā Qui-Do might be recognised as king. Their prayer was granted. When the Emperor Ying Tsong recovered the throne, Qui-Do took oath of allegiance again in 1457.

Towards the close of 1457 or the beginning of the next year Qui-Do was assassinated by the son of a nurse at the instance of Mahā Bàn-La Trà-Nguyet. The latter then ascended the throne. He was a nobleman and had married a daughter as well as a niece of Mahā Vijaya. The new king was recognised by China but he did not pay any homage to the Annamite Emperor. The result was the renewal of hostility between the two countries, and once the Cham king lodged a formal complaint to the Chinese Emperor against the incursions of the Annamites. The king did not reign long, having abdicated the throne in 1460 in favour of his younger brother, Bàn-La Trà-Toàn.

The new king inherited the enmity of Annam which his predecessor's action had provoked. The Annamite Emperor Thành Ton pretended that Champā was a feudatory state of his and demanded some white elephants of the king. Trà Toàn who had already been recognised by China, now requested the Chinese Emperor to send an official to fix a definite frontier between the two countries. The new Emperor Hien Tsong was dissuaded by his advisers from trying to establish peace between two countries which had been enemies for such a long time, and he simply asked the king of Champā to maintain peace.

Trà-Toàn, unable to defy Annam without the help of China, sent tributes to Thành Ton in 1467. But the latter persisted in his contention of being treated by Champā exactly on the same footing as the Chinese Emperor, and demanded a supplementary tribute consisting of rhinoceros, elephants and many precious objects. The Cham ambassador represented that he was unable to concede the additional demand without a reference to his master, and asked Thánh Ton to send an envoy to Champā to settle this question. Trà-Toàn, however, refused this new demand and informed Hien Tsong of it (1469). He resolved to maintain the independence of his country at any cost and decided to risk a war.

He first sent a naval expedition against Hoa Chau (1469) and next year invaded the province at the head of an army 100,000 strong. He had a strong cavalry and a number of war elephants with him. The Annamite general, unable to oppose this vast army, shut himself up in his stronghold, and informed Thành Ton of his precarious situation.

The Emperor was waiting for this very opportunity. He at once made extensive preparations for the compaign. Then, with a view to avoid hostility with China, he sent an ambassador to Hien Tsong informing him of the war in which he suddenly found himself involved. He also explained the cause of the war, and particularly emphasised the repeated Cham incursions against the frontier of Hoa Chau. Lastly, he issued a long proclamation addressed to the Chams. "In a month", said he, "peace will reign again............your last hour is near at hand". He reproached them for the accusations they made to the Chinese Emperor against himself, for the way in which they treated his ambassadors, for the assassination of their king, and for raising Trà-Toán to the throne. He exposed the tyranny of the usurper in the following words: "Boys and girls are forced to the corvee, and widows are ill-treated. You have to pay most excessive taxes and it must be a great trial for you to see the people of Śrī Vini[1] raised to high offices and honours." The proclamation conti-

1. This was the birth-place of the king.

nued: "you have imprisoned men and women of my country and given shelter to the fugitives whom we want.........When I am at peace, you assemble a band of men and attack my country. But as soon as I take the field you wag your tail like a dog, and ask for pardon. I have now, by the order of God, brought a magnificent army and brave soldiers for chastising you and showing you my majesty. I have resolved to conquer your kingdom and thus to wipe away the disgrace inflicted upon the preceding emperors."

After issuing this proclamation the Emperor offered solemn prayers for victory before the altar of his ancestors. He had already despatched a magnificent fleet containing 100,000 men, and now started in person with 150, 000 soldiers. The huge army reached the soil of Champā in safety (1471). Trà-Toàn sent his younger brother with 5,000 men on elephants to surprise the enemy camp. But the small force was hemmed round in all sides and practically cut off by the enemy.

Trà-Toàn was very much alarmed at the news of this disaster and sent a member of his family to the emperor to offer submission. But the latter continued to advance, seized Śrī Vini, and at last invested the capital city Vijaya. The city was taken by assault without much difficulty. 60,000 Chams were put to the sword, and 30,000 made prisoners. Fifty members of the royal family fell into the hands of the conqueror. Trà-Toàn was led before the Emperor. "Art thou the Lord of Champā?" asked he; "Yes my Lord" was the reply. "Who do you think am I?" "One glance at your face is enough to tell me that you are the Emperor." "How many children have you?" "More than ten."

Thánh Ton constructed a shed outside the palace to guard the prisoners. As his officers were jostling against Trà-Toàn he asked them to treat that king with more respect. "He was the lord of this country", said he, "it is not right to treat him thus." But Trà-Toàn did not long survive the disgrace.

Abandoned by all, even by the Chinese emperor, who for fear of provoking the hostility of Annam did not even dare to ask for his release, deprived of his wives[1] and attendants, he fell ill and died in a ship on his way to Annam. His body was burnt and the ashes cast into the winds, but the head was fastened to the forepart of the imperial vessel with a white flag on which the following words were inscribed; "This is the head of the very wicked Trá-Toàn of the kingdom of Champā."

Meanwhile a Cham general Bo Trì Trì collected the remnants of the army and took refuge in Pāṇḍuraṅga. There he proclaimed himself king and sent an ambassador to offer the oath of allegiance and tribute to Thánh Ton who accepted them. The mountains which separate the present provinces of Phu Yen and Khan Hoa and terminate in cape Varella henceforth formed the boundary between Annam and Champā. A boundary stone marked the limit.

Thus not only the whole of Amarāvatī which was once ceded in 1402, but retaken by the Chams again in 1407, but also the whole of the province of Vijaya passed into the hands of the Annamites. The kingdom of Champā, which now consisted only of Kauṭhāra and Pāṇḍuraṅga, was thus reduced to nearly one-fifth of what it was even in the days of Che Bong Nga. Even the small territory that remained (viz; the modern districts of Khan Hoa and Binh Thuan) was absolutely at the mercy of the powerful Annamites.

But old prestige dies hard. The petty Cham chiefs of the south still bore the proud name of the king of Champā, and the Chinese emperor not only invested them as such, but even called upon the Annamites to restore the provinces of Vijaya and Amarāvatī to them. Three kings received formal investi-

1. Only two were allowed to accompany him.

ture in this way from the Chinese court. The first, Tchai-Ya-Ma-Fou-Ngan, said to be the nephew of a former king, died In 1478. He was probably killed by his brother Kou Lai who succeeded him and ruled from 1478 to 1505 A. D. His son and successor Cha-Kou-Pou-Lo received formal investiture from the Chinese court in 1509 A. D. and sent an ambassador to China in 1543 A. D. This was the last embassy from the king of Champā to the Chinese court.

The king had a tragic end. Taking advantage of some troubles among the Annamites he made a last desperate effort to free himself from the Annamite yoke. But he was defeated and confined in an iron cage where he died. The Annamites on this occasion annexed the Cham territory up to the river of Phanrang. The seat of the kingdom of Champā was then removed to Bal Chanar at Phanri. There in 1720 the officers of the SS. Galathee saw the king of Champā seated on a throne and have left us an interesting account of the palace.[1] In course of the seventeenth and eighteenth centuries the Chams were dispossessed of Khan Hoa and Phan Rang. In 1822, Po Chong, the last king, unable to bear the oppressions of the Annamites, passed over to Cambodge with a colony of exiles, leaving princess Po Bia to guard over the so-called "Royal treasures of Cham" at Bal Chanar. She died a few years ago, mourned by her faithful subjects who looked upon her as the last emblem of their independence.

Thus closes a brilliant chapter in the history of Indian colonisation. Brave sons of India, who planted her banner in far off lands and maintained its honour and dignity for more than 1500 years, at last vanished into the limbo of oblivion. But the torch of civilisation which they carried dispelled the darkness of ages and still throws its lurid light over the pages of history.

1. B E. F, vol V, pp. 385—6.

KINGS REFERRED TO IN CHAPTER XII.

1.	A-Nan	(1318—1342 A. D.)
2.	Bo De (Son-in-law of No. 1)	(1342—c. 1360 A. D.)
3.	Che Bong Nga	(c. 1360-1390 A. D.)
4.	La Khai or Jaya Siṁhavarman V	(1390—1401 A. D.)
5.	Bhadravarman V or Indravarman XII (Son of No. 4)	(1401—1441 A. D.)
6.	Mahā Vijaya (Nephew of No. 5)	(1441—1446 A. D.)
7.	Mahā Qui Lai (Nephew of No. 6)	(1446—1449 A. D.)
8.	Mahā Qui-Do (Younger brother of No. 7)	(1449-c. 1457 A. D.)
9.	Mahā Ban-La-Tra-Nguyet (Son-in-law of No. 6)	(1457—1460 A. D.)
10.	Bàn-La Trà-Toàn (Younger brother of No. 9)	(1460—1471 A. D.)
11.	Bo Tri Tri	(acc. 1471 A. D. ?)
12.	Tchai-Ya-Ma-Fou-Ngan	(died in 1478 A. D.)
13.	Kou-Lai (Brother of No. 12)	(1478—1505 A. D.)
14.	Cha-Kọu-Pou-Lọ	(1505—c. 1543 A. D.)

Chapter XIII.

Administrative System.

Having concluded the political history of Champā we may now proceed to give a short sketch of the system of administration prevailing in the kingdom. The materials for this study are very scanty as we have to depend mainly upon the indirect allusions and references contained in the inscriptions. It is not possible to trace the gradual evolution of the political system and we must remain content, for the present at least, with only a general outline of the essential features of administrative system.

Monarchy was the form of government in Champā from beginning to end. The king administered the whole state with almost absolute authority. The central administration might be broadly divided into three classes, civil, military and religious. At the head of the civil administration were two chief ministers with three grades of officials under them.[1] The Captain of Guards and Senāpati[2] were the chief military officers, while the religious establishment consisted of a High Priest the Brāhmaṇas, Astrologers, Paṇḍits and Masters of ceremonies.[3]

The ministers naturally occupied a very high position and some inscriptions throw interesting light on their status.[4] Sometimes the ministers seem to have been chosen from the same family and the post acquired almost a hereditary character.[5]

The kingdom was divided into three provinces.

(1) Amarāvatī, the northern part, corresponded to Quang Nam. Here were the two famous capital cities Champāpura

1. T'oung Pao 1910, p. 194, fn 6. 2. cf. Ins. Nos 26, 35. 3. cf. Ins. No. 65. 4 cf. Nos. 32. 39. 5. cf. No. 39.

and Indrapura. The latter occupied the site of Dong Duong.

(2) Vijaya, the central portion of the kingdom, corresponded to Binh Dinh. Its chief city, Vijaya, served for sometime as the capital of the whole kingdom. It contained the famous port Śrī Vinaya.

(3) Pāṇḍuraṅga, the southern part corresponded to the valleys of Phan-ranh and Binh Thuan. Its chief town Vīrapura, also called Rājapura, once served as the capital of the whole kingdom.

The region called Kauṭhāra, corresponding to Khan Hoa, was usually included in this division, but sometimes formed an independent province.

These provinces were divided into districts, the total number of which, according to a Chinese authority, was thirty-eight in the reign of Harivarman III (1080 A. D.). Each district contained a number of towns and villages which were the lowest territorial units. The population of any of these hardly ever exceeded 700 families, and there were more than hundred which contained three to five hundred families each. The population of the provincial capitals was of course considerably larger. According to the census taken by Li Than Tonh in 1069 there were 2,560 families in Vijaya.

It would appear that two high functionaries, a "governor" and a "senāpati", were placed at the head of each provincial administration. Thus king Harivarmadeva appointed his own son Vikrāntavarmā as the governor of Pāṇḍuraṅga, and at the same time deputed Senāpati Paṁr to guard the prince (No. 26). The selection of the heir-apparent as the governor was probably due to the importance of the province. We have already seen how the province frequently rebelled against the central authority and sometimes maintained its independence for a fairly long period (pp. 78-89).

The provincial governors had under them nearly fifty officials of different grades for general administration and collection of revenue. None of these officials was paid in cash, but got something like a *jāgir* or maintained themselves at the cost of the people under them. The people were bound to provide for these officials, and the system of *corvee* or forced labour was in vogue.

The principal source of revenue seems to be the land-tax which consisted usually of one-sixth the produce, though some times reduced to one-tenth.[1] The kings sometimes made a gift of this royal share to a temple for its maintenance. In addition, the king often exempted the lands belonging to a temple from taxes.[2]

Taxes were also imposed on all industrial products and articles of merchandise. The royal officers boarded the foreign merchant vessel after its arrival at the port and took a fifth of the goods as royal revenue. The king even took a share of the products of the forest, such as timber and animals collected by the toils of the people.

Justice was administered apparently in accordance with the Hindu principles, for we are told that Jaya Indravarmadeva V "followed the eighteen titles of law prescribed by Manu" (Ins. No. 65). Harivarmadeva IV also did the same (No. 62). King Jaya Indravarmadeva VII is said to have been versed in the Dharmaśāstra- notably the Nāradīya and Bhārggavīya (No. 81).

We gather a few details from epigraphic records and Chinese texts. Certain crimes were punished by confiscation of goods and loss of personal freedom. Slavery was also a punishment for debts. Crimes were ordinarily punished by flogging. The criminal was stretched on the ground while

1. cf. Ins. No. 4. 2. cf. Ins. Nos. 33, 36. 37.

two men on the right and two on the left alternately struck him as many as 50, 60 or even 100 times according to the gravity of the offence. Theft and robbery were punished by the mutilation of fingers, while adultery involved capital punishment for both the accomplices [1]

The capital sentence was inflicted in many ways. Ordinarily the condemned person was fastened to a tree; then his neck was pierced through by means of a sharp spear and afterwards his head was cut off. For cold-blooded murder, or murder accompanied by robbery, the criminal was either delivered up to the people who throttled him to death, or trampled under the feet of an elephant. The rebel was tied to a post in a lonely place and was not released till he submitted. Lastly certain crimes were punished by deportation.

It appears that "the Divine Judgment" was resorted to in certain extraordinary cases. If a man were devoured by a tiger or a crocodile his family complained about it to the king. The king ordered the High Priest to invoke the divine judgment. The latter offered prayers and conjurations at the very place where the man met his death, and it was believed that the tiger and crocodile would be obliged thereby to return to the same place to take punishments. If the complaint appeared to be false, the priest, in order to ascertain the truth, asked the man to go to the riverside. If he were guilty of telling lies he would be devoured by a crocodile. If he were innocent the crocodile would take to flight.[2]

In view of the constant wars in which the kingdom was involved the military organisation was a thing of the highest

---

1. It appears that sometimes the adulterers escaped by paying the price of a bull.

2. This account of administration of justice is based upon T'oung Pao 1910 pp 202-203 Maspero laments the absence of any legal code of ancient Champa, but fails to note the reference to Manu Samhita and its adoption by the kings as legal code.

importance. A large regular army was maintained by the state. At the time of Fan Wen the army was nearly forty to fifty thousand strong. It must have been considerably increased in later times. At the time of Che Bong Nga, the royal guard alone numbered 5000 The armament of the soldiers consisted of a shield, javelin, halberd, bow and cross-bow The arrows were not feathered but their tips were poisoned. The soldiers marched with their standards at the sound of drums and conchshells. They were arranged into groups of five who were responsible for one another. If any one of them fled, the other four were liable to death.

According to Maspero the Cham army consisted merely of infantry and elephants till 1171 A D. when they learnt the use of cavalry from the Chinese. This is not, however, quite correct. What the Chams learnt from the Chinese in 1171 was the art of throwing arrows from the back of horses, a somewhat difficult operation inasmuch as both hands of the rider had to be kept free. But cavalry was a part of their army long before that. This is proved by the following vivid description of a battle-field contained in an inscription dated 909 A. D. "Which (the battle-field) is grey with the dust raised by the swift-moving sharp hoofs of horses galloping high; whose surface has been dyed red with drops of blood, like Aśoka flowers, shed by means of various weapons; and in the four regions of which the sounds of war-drums were drowned by the roars of gigantic beautiful elephants" (Ins. No. 39, v. 17).

The elephants formed an important part of the army and we have already seen how the Chinese army was perplexed by this new element in warfare which was no doubt introduced by the Indian colonists. The number of war elephants maintained in Champā was nearly one thousand. Odoric de

Pordenone says that at the time of his visit to Champā (c. 1323 A D.) the king had 14,000 tame elephants.[1]

The navy consisted of large turret-ships as well as light junks. The total number of vessels was fairly large and we have several references to squadrons of more than 100 vessels supporting the movement of an army on land.

The king often entrusted his brothers or other members of the royal family with the chief command of the army. The generals had the title of Mahāsenāpati and Senāpati, and there were several grades of officers under them. They all took an oath to the king to fight for him till their death. Their pay consisted of subsidies in kind, and they were exempt from taxation. The ordinary soldiers received two bushels of rice per month and three to five dresses for winter and summer.

The Chams had a fair knowledge of the art of fortification. They protected their towns by brick walls flanked by watchtowers made of stone. These citadels and a stronghold named Kiu-sou specially fortified for the purpose served as the depot for their war materials. A detailed account of the fortification of Kiu-sou has been given above (p-26). Lastly the Chams constructed entrenched camps by means of palisades and turrets. They painted the outer gates of their citadels with the ashes of an animal. They believed that these were thereby made impregnable.

While the Chams assiduously cultivated the arts of war, they did not neglect the arts of peace. The kings maintained diplomatic relations with neighbouring countries. Constant embassies to the courts of China and Annam have already been referred to in the preceding pages. The Nhan-Bieu Inscription (No.43) records the career of a nobleman named Rājadvārah who was twice despatched by the king to Yavadvīpa on a diplomatic mission. The Bāng-An Ins. (No 42) refers to a multitude of royal ambassadors coming to

1. Marco Polo. Edited by Yule—Vol. II p. 352.

Champā from different countries The Hoa Que Ins. (No 39) relates, among other qualifications of the minister Ājñā Jayendrapati, that "by hard exertion he was able to understand thoroughly the meaning of messages sent by kings from different countries." All these references, taken together, leave no doubt that the kingdom of Champā maintained extensive diplomatic relations with her neighbouring countries.

The art of diplomacy, as practised in India, was fairly understood. The neighbouring states were classified as friends, enemies or neutrals, and the relation with these powers was guided by the four expedients of *sāma* (conciliation), *dāna* (gifts), *bheda* (discord) and *daṇḍa* (chastisement) (Nos. 9 and 62). Sometimes *daṇḍa* is replaced by *upapradāna* (bribery) (No. 65). What is more important still is the reference to "*sāḍguṇya*" which is undoubtedly identical with the "*sāḍguṇya*" of Kauṭilya, meaning the sixfold measures of royal policy.[1] Kāmandakīya Nītisāra, a treatise on politics based upon Kauṭilīya Arthaśāstra, deals extensively with the four expedients and the sixfold measures of royal policy. It is possible that political science was studied in Champā from books of this kind.[2] It is to be remembered, however, that Manusaṁhitā, which we know from other sources to have been used in Champā, also deals with both these topics, *viz.* the four expedients and the sixfold measures of royal policy, but its discussion on these subjects is neither full nor accurate, the author having evidently borrowed his materials from books on political science which he did not clearly understand. But howsoever that may be, there is no doubt that the statesmen in Champā were thoroughly imbued with the ideas of Indian Political Science and it formed the basis of polity in that kingdom.

1. Kautiliya-Arthasastra Bk. VII ch I
2. Dr. R. Mitra pointed out in the Introduction to his edition of Kamandakiya Nitisara that the book was imported into Bali island by its Hindu inhabitants as early as the fourth century A.D.

Chapter XIV.

The King.

The king of Champā was not only the head but also the centre of administration, and it is therefore necessary to discuss his position and status at some length. Fortunately, our materials for the study of this subject are fuller and more reliable than those for the administrative system.

In theory the king was regarded as of divine origin, the colonists following in this respect the view of the orthodox Brahmanical schools of India. Indeed the whole conception of the status and position of the king seems to be dominated by the Brahmanical views such as those propounded in Manusaṁhitā.

Reference to the divine nature of kings is found in Po Nagar Ins. (No.29A., v.2). In Dong Duong Ins. (No.31A, v.8) kings are referred to as "the gods dwelling upon earth". Lastly he is said to have the *vigraha* or body of Chandra, Indra, Agni, Yama and Kuvera (No.23, v.3). Now no body can possibly ignore the striking resemblance between these views and those propounded at the beginning of Chapter VII in Manusaṁhitā. We read there that the king "is a great deity in human form" (v.8) and that the Lord created him "taking for that purpose eternal particles of Indra, of the Wind, of Yama, of the Sun, of Fire, of Varuṇa, of the Moon, and of the Lord of Wealth (Kubera)".[1]

To what extent this theory of divine origin modified the status of king in practice it is not possible to say. In one respect, however, it was carried to its logical conclusion, in a manner which would have been regarded as horribly scandalous in India. In Po Nagar Ins. (No.30) we read that king's feet were worshipped, even by Brāhmaṇas and

1. Laws of Manu' Transl. by Buhler, pp 216-217.

priests. This would be quite in keeping with the divine origin of kings, but in India the Brāhmaṇas were careful enough to safeguard their own position, and thus the first and foremost duty of the "divine kings" was to worship the Brāhmaṇas.[1] The kings in Champā were not apparently dominated by the influence of the Brāhmaṇas, at least to the same extent as in India.

But although theoretically the king appears to be vested with absolute authority, there might have been limitations to his power in actual practice. Unfortunately our knowledge in this matter is very vague. The Vo-Chanh inscription (No. 1) refers to an "assembly", but we do not know any thing about its power and functions.

Maspero supposes that the crown-prince could not ascend the throne without the approval of the nobility. He admits that this rule was violated when the king was powerful enough, but holds that it was the normal rule. Unfortunately the evidence in support of his view is slender in the extreme. The modern practice of Cambodge to which he refers can hardly be taken as a sure guide for practice in ancient Champā. The passages of Dong Duong Ins.[2] on which he relies, as translated by me, do not support the contention in any way. On the other hand such boasting expression as is used by Indravarman viz. that he "gained the kingdom by the special merit of his austerities, and by virtue of his pure intelligence, and not from his grand-father or father" seems to indicate that hereditary succession was the normal rule. It is quite true that in troublesome times, or probably for some special reasons such as the absence of a legal or suitable heir, the king was sometimes elected by the people. Thus when Jaya Rudravarman died at Pāṇḍuraṅga in 1147 A. D.

1. cf. Manusamhita, Ch. VII, vv, 37 ff
2. No. 31 B vv. VI, IX and XI

the people of that town invited his son Harivarmā to be the king of Champā (Ins. No. 75). According to Myson Ins.=(No. 12) the kingdom was bestowed on Prakāśadharma by holy men. When Harivarman abdicated, the people offered the authority to his son (No. 62).

In connection with the hereditary succession it is necessary to note the importance of the females. Kings are succeeded not only by their sister's son, but also by their sister's husband and even wife's sister's son.[1] This has been attributed to the system of matriarchy supposed to be prevalent in those parts of the country.

After his accession to the throne the new king performed his coronation ceremony with great pomp and splendour. Sometimes a long interval elapsed between the accession of a king and his coronation. Thus Harivarman ascended the throne in 1147 A. D., but was "consecrated to the throne with due ceremonials" only in 1149 A. D. King Vīra Bhadravarmadeva was consecrated 32 years after his accession.

There seems also to have been a fairly general practice among kings of Champā to take a new name called *Abhisekanāma* (No. 7) at the time of the coronation. Thus Praśastadharma, son of Rudravarman, took the name Śrī Śambhuvarman at the time of his coronation (No. 7). Several other instances of this kind are shown in a tabular form below.

	Ordinary Name.	Coronation Name.
1.	Prakāśadharma.	Śrī Vikrāntavarman (No. 12)
2.	Pu lyaṇ Śrī Rājadvāra.	Śrī Jaya Indravarmadeva (No. 62)
3.	Prince Nauk Glauṇ	

1. Cf. the genealogy of kings referred to in Ch. V and also the case of Jaya Simhavarmadeva (No. 36).

Vijaya or Vīra Bhadra-varma-deva — Śrī Bṛsu Indravarman.

Whether the assumption of new names at the time of coronation was a universal practice we cannot say, but there is no doubt that it was a fairly common practice.

After his accession to the throne the new king was confronted with a heavy list of duties. Numerous references to personal qualities of the king enable us to form a general idea of what the kings were expected to be, if not what they actually were. A general picture of these ideal qualities of a king would throw light not only on the ideal of kingship in those days, but also, to a certain extent, on the ideals of human life at Champā. An analysis of these ideal qualities as culled from different inscriptions[1] is given below.

I. Physical charm.

The king "had all the marks of a Mahārāja, according to the canon of Rājacakravartin" (No. 65). He had the 32 signs (33 according to No 94) as well as grace and beauty, youth and ability (Nos. 62, 65.). His beauty was like that of Cupid and yet his appearance was terrible like that of Garuḍa (No. 24).

II. Strength and Valour.

The king was skilled in all the weapons and was heroic and energetic (62, 65.). He was possessed of innate courage and of great strength. He took part in numerous battles and cut off the heads of kings, generals and other men of the hostile party (62,65,72,81).

III. Administrative capacity.

The king knew and practised the four expedients viz. *sāma*, *dāna*, *bheda* and *daṇḍa* (or upapradāna) (62,65.). He

1. The figures within brackets in the succeeding paragraphs refer to the number of inscriptions.

maintained the eighteen titles of law laid down by Manu, and the uniformity of procedure (Nos. 62,65). He knew the true import of the sixfold measures of royal policy. He was strictly impartial in discharging his duties (65), and never transgressed the eternal rules of conduct (12). He dutifully protected his subjects (No. 12) and destroyed all the thieves (24). He was constantly devoted to his duty and faithful to law like Dharmarâja (24). Embraced by the goddess of sovereignty he was "without equal in respect of royal glory, knowledge, wisdom, splendour, fame, sacred learning, polity, renown and conduct" (31).

IV. Learning and culture.

The king had the knowledge of 64 *Kalās* (arts) (62,72). He was wise, eloquent, and profoundly intelligent. (65,74). He was versed in all the different branches of knowledge[1] (32,94).

V. Moral qualities.

The king had the knowledge of the good and the bad (62 65) and possessed a sense of duty, patience, forbearance, calm of heart, liberality, truthfulness and compassion towards all beings (65,41). He impartially pursued the three objects—wealth, virtue and pleasure—without showing preference to any (65). He controlled the six passions viz. *kāma* (sensual passion), *krodha* (anger), *lobha* (covetousness), *moha* (infatuation), *mada* (pride) and *mātsarya* (malice) (65).

1. King Bhadravarman was versed in the four Vedas (No. 4). King Indravarman knew the six systems of Philosophy, including Mimamsa and Buddhist Philosophy, the grammar of Panini with Kasika commentary, and the Akhyana and the Uttarakalpa of the Saivas (No. 45). King Sri Jaya Indravarmadeva was versed in Grammar, Astrology, Philosophical doctrines like Mahayana and Dharmasutras, notably the Naradiya and the Bhargaviya (No. 81).

VI. Religious qualities.

The king knew the supreme truth and the absolute reality without egotism (65). He installed gods and temples and endowed them liberally[1] (94,110). Realising that the body and its pleasures are ephemeral, he performed *yoga*, *dhyāna* and *samādhi* and practised virtue constantly and thoroughly (65). He was the fore-most among those who regarded sacrifices as their principal treasures (23). He made pious works such as digging tanks, building roads, making religious endowments (110) and gave gifts day and night (62), particularly to *munis*, ascetics and learned Brāhmaṇas (24).

The king was not only of a religious temperament but was also, in a manner, the defender of faith and protector of religion. It was his duty to maintain intact the castes and Āśramas in society, and we also hear of his zeal in protecting Dharma (No. 23). In this respect he followed the traditional role of kings in India.

We also get some account of the royal life in Champā from the Chinese accounts and epigraphic evidences. The following description of King Harivarman by his ambassador to the Imperial Court (1076 A. D.) is recorded in a Chinese Text.

"The King is 36 years of age. He is dressed in rich embroidered silks,[2] and a long tunic held by seven chains of gold. He wears a golden crown[3] adorned by seven kinds of precious gems, and puts on sandals of copper. When he goes

1. For a detailed account, see later.
2. Sometimes the silk was of black or green colour with flowers in gold embroidered upon it.
3. The crown was of elegant design and very richly decorated. We can have a fair idea of it from actual specimens included among the "royal treasures of Champa" (B. E. F. Vol, V. P. 40 ff).

out he is attended by fifty men and ten women, who carry betel and nuts on golden plates and play on musical instruments".

The Po Nagar Ins. (30) says with reference to king Vikrāntavarman, that a big white umbrella was raised over his head and his "body was decorated with diadem, waistband, necklace, and earrings made of gold, ruby and other jewels." The Glai Lomov Ins. (No. 24) says of Indravarman that his hands and breast were made white by the application of an abundance of perfumed sandal and musk.

We possess other incidental allusions to the royal dress and habits. The undergarment of the king was made of very fine white cotton, probably muslin, bordered by lace or furnished with golden fringe. He put on this dress alone, even in court, except on ceremonial occasions, when he wore the silk tunic as noted before and put on, round his waist, a rich belt of gold decorated with pearls and jewels. Even his shoes were decorated with precious stones.[1]

Attired in his gorgeous robe the king entered the Hall of Audience where he held his court. The immediate entourage of the king consisted, among others, of nobles, eminent Brāhmaṇas, Purohita, Paṇḍits, astrologers and masters of ceremonies.

Strangely enough, the sons, brothers, and more important officials of the king had no immediate access to his person. This was apparently due to fear of being assassinated by them. The daily life of the king was regulated by a fixed routine. Every day at midday he gave audience to his people in an open *Durbar*. The king sat cross-legged on a high throne. Those who were presented to him saluted him in Indian fashion, bowing down their heads very low, while

1. T'oung Pao, 1910, pp. 193—94.

placing the arms across their breast. This was again repeated when the audience was finished.

On leaving the *Durbar*, the king mounted an elephant, to the accompaniment of the sounds of drums and conchshells, and a cotton umbrella was raised over his head. Close behind him marched an official with a plate of betelnut. Then followed the royal guard of more than 1000 soldiers, armed with spear, sword, shield, bow and arrow. On less formal occasions the king went in a chariot, escorted by 30 women carrying betels and a shield. Sometimes the king went in a palanquin carried by four men.

After the arduous toils and anxieties of administrative work the king sought for relaxation in his very big harem. There were a large number of queens of various ranks, concubines, dancing girls and a large retinue of servants. According to Marco Polo, "no woman in the kingdom of Champā was allowed to marry until the king had seen her. If the woman pleased him then he took her to wife; if not, he gave her a dowry to get a husband." When Marco Polo visited Champā, about 1285 A. D., "the king had, between sons and daughters, 326 children, of whom at least 150 were men fit to carry arms."

Odoric de Pordenone who visited Champā about 40 years later also remarks that the king of the country had about 200 children, for he had many wives and a large number of concubines.[1]

On the death of a king, the more favourite among his women, particularly the queens, burnt themselves on the funeral pyre according to the "Satī rite" prevalent in India. The rest remained faithful to their dead lord, and passed their lives in good deeds and religious ceremonies; unless, as

1. Marco Polo-Ed. Yule, Vol II, pp. 249-250 and the footnotes.

it happened in some cases, they entered into the harem of the next king, either willingly or under compulsion.[1]

It would be unfair to conclude, however, that the kings of Champā were as a rule devoted to luxury and sensual pleasures. Some of them were of religious bent of mind. We even hear of some kings abdicating the throne in order to spend the last days of their lives in religious practices. The cases of Gaṅgārāja and Harivarman may be cited as examples. In this respect, too, the colonists followed some of the best traditions of India.

1. Fan Wen starved to death those women of Fan Yi who refused to obey him.

BOOK II

THE CULTURE and CIVILISATION OF CHAMPA

CHAPTER I.

Religious Evolution in Champa

Religion has been one of the most important factors in the building up of Indian civilisation. It is no wonder, therefore, that the Indian colonists who founded a new kingdom in Champā transplanted to their land of adoption the religious ideas with which they were imbued at home. Indeed, it is a matter of common knowledge that no other feature of Indian civilisation left such a profound impress upon these colonial kingdoms, and even now, when the political supremacy of the Indians in those far-off lands is merely a dream of the past, they contain unmistakable traces of the Indian religion and its handmaid, art and architecture.

Several circumstances make the study of Indian religion, as developed in these countries, one of profound interest. In the first place, although it is a familiar story how Buddhism made extensive conquests in foreign lands, Hinduism had never been known to make its influence felt outside the boundaries of India. Yet it is precisely the conservative form of Brāhmaṇical religion that became predominant in the new colony, and dominated the entire development of Hindu civilisation. Secondly, the religious ideas of India were confronted there by a system of primitive beliefs and superstitions, and we find here a repetition, on a smaller scale, of what took place in Northern India, when the Aryans swept away the whole country and imposed their own religion upon the primitive people.

Thirdly, the study of Indian religion in ancient Champā not only affords an interesting insight into the vigour and vitality of the Brahmaṇical religion, but also shows the completeness with which the foreigners had absorbed the Hindu civilisation. Nothing demonstrates more strikingly the absolute hold which the Indian civilisation had over the native mind.

It is not only a story of a great triumph, but of a triumph against enormous odds. It has been already related in the previous pages that the political power of the Indian colonists in Champā was never very secure. Threatened by the Chinese, the Annamites and the Cambodians they had always to lead an insecure life. Repeated incursions of these powers almost destroyed the solidarity of their political fabric. Yet, amid all these vicissitudes of political fortune, Hinduism never ceased to make headway and inspire its million devotees to place their wealth and energy at its service. The triumph was all the greater because Hinduism had to reckon in this distant land with the all-powerful civilisation of China. As a matter of fact China was first in the field, and was already master of the greater part of the country when the Indian colonists made their influence felt. Further, throughout the course of history the Chinese empire which reached the borders of the new Indian colony exercised political influence of both direct and indirect character. The Hindu kings of Champā had often to acknowledge the nominal suzerainty of the Chinese emperor and send him regular tributes and presents; now and then the Chinese army even occupied and devastated the whole country. Yet, inspite of all these natural advantages, the Chinese civilisation had to give way before the onward march of the Indian in a distant land practically cut off from the mainland of India.

The superiority of the Indian civilisation was once more demonstrated, and it was apparent that Brāhmaṇical religion was not probably much behind Buddhism in respect of missionary zeal and proselytising activity.

The Brāhmaṇical religion that flourished in Champā was not the Vedic religion of old but the neo-Brāhmaṇical religion that was evolved in India almost at the same time as Buddhism and Jainism. The essential characteristic of this new religion was its sectarian character, the chief God being recognised as either Brahmā, Viṣṇu or Śiva. The belief in a multiplicity of gods which prevailed in Vedic times was replaced by absolute faith and devotion to one supreme God. Gradually the new faith inspired a new literature, the Purāṇas, and ushered in elaborate rituals and ceremonies. We find an echo of the pomp and grandeur of Buddhism in the magnificent temples erected to Viṣṇu, Śiva and the hosts of gods associated with them. These gods formed the centre of new philosophical speculations and hosts of myths and legends, and on them was lavished the wealth and luxury of an opulent people.

In course of time the sectarian Brāhmaṇical religion triumphed over Buddhism which had hitherto played a dominant part in India. But although worsted in the struggle Buddhism maintained its existence for centuries to come. Thus the religious history of India during the first thousand years of the Christian era presented a new spectacle, the gradual rise of the new sects and the corresponding decline of the once triumphant Buddhist religion.

All these characteristic features can be traced in minute detail in the religious history of Champā. Fortunately, materials for the study of this history are abundantly supplied by the large number of inscriptions and images of deities that are still to be found in that far-off land.

Of the two Brāhmaṇical sects that flourished in Champā, Śaivism was by far the more influential and exercised a profound influence on the whole course of religious development. The hold of the Viṣṇuites and the Buddhists was poor in comparison. But there is no trace of any religious struggle. On the other hand we have abundant traces of mutual good will and attempts at reconciliation between the different sects.

CHAPTER II.

The conception of Siva.

Of the three members of the Hindu Trinity Śiva occupied an unquestioned position of supremacy in the Hindu colony of Champā. The causes as well as the process of gradual elevation of one of the gods above his rivals are but imperfectly known to us, but there can be no doubt about the fact. Of the 130 inscriptions discovered in Champā and published in this volume, about 21 do not refer to any religious sect in particular. Of the rest, 92 refer to Śiva and the gods associated with him, 3 to Viṣṇu, 5 to Brahmā under the name Svayamutpanna and 7 to Buddha, while two refer to both Śiva and Viṣṇu.[1] This analysis of the known inscriptions is an eloquent testimony to the predominance of the god Śiva. The same conclusion is forced upon us when we remember that the two principal groups of temples in ancient Champā, Viz. those of Myson, and Po-Nagar are dedicated to Śivaite gods. Further, the preeminence of Śiva is clearly indicated by the fact that the god was regarded as the tutelary deity of both the city and the kingdom of Champā. Thus according to the Ins. No. 41, the city was created by the rays issuing from the pair of feet of Śrīśānabhadreśa', while in the Ins. No. 94, the same god is referred to as 'the origin of the kingdom of Champā. These brief allusions are fully explained in the Ins. No. 31 which describes how Uroja, sent to the earth by Śiva, established the kingdom of Champā, having at first placed a *liṅga* of that God as the protector of the city. In the Ins. No. 42 we are told that the god Śrī Īśāneśvara 'lives here triumphantly together with his

---

1. In this calculation, account has been taken only of the principal God mentioned in the inscriptions. In several cases, although Siva is the principal God, Viṣṇu and other gods have been mentioned as subsidiary gods.

multitude of servants for the sake of the prosperity of Champā'.

The god Śiva was known by various names. These may be roughly classified as follows :—

(a) Names denoting his position of supremacy over other gods[1] :—

Maheśvara (4)
Mahādeva (6)
Mahādeveśvara (29)
Amareśa (10)
Adhīśa (31)
Devadeva (34)
Īśvaradevatā (59)
Īśvaradevādideva (32)
Vṛddheśvara (35)
Parameśvara (36)

(b) Names denoting general greatness, mastery etc :—
Īśāna (20) Īśānadeva (21) Īśāneśvara (12) Īśānanātha (16) Īśāneśvaranātha (17).

(c) Names denoting the beneficent nature of the god :—
Śambhu (22) Śaṅkara (28) Śaṅkareśa (38) Bhāgyakānteśvara (33) Dharmeśvara (39).

(d) Names denoting the destructive or fierce character of the god :—
Śarva (79) Bhima (17) Ugra (24) Rudra (24) Rudramadhyeśvara (35) Rudrakoṭīśvara (39) Mahārudradeva (39).

(e) Names arising out of mythological attributes or characteristics :—

1. Figures within brackets after each name indicate the serial number of the Inscription where it occurs. Although one reference only is given to each, sometimes a name occurs in several inscriptions.

Śūlī (7), Bhava (17), Paśupati (17), Vāmeśvara (19), Vāmabhūteśvara (20), Yogīśvara (59), Guheśvara (74), Jayaguheśvara (35), Vijayasiṁheśvara (61), Bhūmivijaya (107), Indralokeśvara (65), Suvarṇākṣa (18), Ṣaṇḍhaka (26).

(f) Names connected with *liṅga*.

Devaliṅgeśvara (43)
Mahāliṅgadeva (32)
Śivaliṅgeśvara (35)
Śivaliṅgadeva (35)
Mahāśivaliṅgeśvara (39)
Dharmaliṅgeśvara (41)

The various names attributed to Śiva would convey a fair idea of the conception of the god in the mind of his devotees at Champā. Fortunately we are not dependent upon such a slender means alone for our knowledge in this respect. The inscriptions contain hymns and praises addressed to Śiva, as well as a large number of incidental allusions, and these enable us to enter more fully into this subject.

Śiva is expressly referred to as 'the chief of the Trinity' and the 'supreme god of gods' in quite a large number of inscriptions. Thus Śiva is said to have 'obtained the position of the head of the gods by means of his extraordinary power and fame' (No. 31 A. v. 15). He is the preceptor of gods (No. 39, v. 13), He is the supreme deity extolled and revered by all the gods beginning with Brahmā or Indra (No. 16, v. 1; No. 21, v. 1; No. 32, v. 1; No. 46, v. 1) The gods as a class, derive their strength from Śiva (No. 31, v. 13). Brahmā and Viṣṇu bow down to Him, saying 'Thou great god, of gods; please grant a boon to us' (No. 39, v. 10). Lastly, the brilliant picture of the assembly of gods, drawn in No. 42, sets the final seal of supremacy to the god Śiva. 'With Indra in front, Brahmā to the right, the Moon and the Sun at the back, and the god Nārāyaṇa to the left,

Śiva sits in the middle, glowing with splendid rays, while those and other gods bow down before him and sing a chorus of praise and thanksgiving beginning with' om' and ending with 'Svadhā-svāhā'.[1]

Quite in keeping with this position of unique supremacy among the gods, Śiva is endowed with a number of the highest divine attributes. He controls the creation, maintenance and dissolution of this world, while he himself has neither beginning nor end.' He is not only the creator but also the preceptor of the three worlds, *bhūḥ*, *bhuvaḥ* and *svaḥ*; he is the knower of all things and the fixed cause of the universe (No. 7). He is 'the primaeval being' (No. 32, v. 1), calm, pure supreme and sublime (No. 16, v. 1). He is possessed of *aṇimā* and other divine faculties (No. 17); he cannot be cut or pierced (No. 16, v. 10); he is without cause (No. 17, v, 6) and without atoms (No. 21 v. 1); his body is imperceptible (No. 95. v. 1); he permeates everything (No. 73, v. 1), penetrates everywhere (No. 46 v. 1), and embodies the entire world in himself (No.73, v. 1). There is none in the world who knows Śiva in his true aspects, for his true nature is beyond the domain of thought and speech (No. 17, v. 1).[2] He is the supreme energy (No. 23, v. 1) and the source of the supreme end of life (No. 17). His image, identical with the universe, is manifested by his forms,–earth, water, fire, air, sky, sun, moon and sacrificer. He is constantly devoted to the welfare of all beings (No. 12, v. 28). He is the one lord of the world and grants supremacy to gods and men (No. 17). From him are born all creatures and to him they ultimately resort (No. 23, V. 1).

---

1. For a similar presentation of Mahadeva, cf Mahabharata Anusasanaparvan Ch. X I V.

2. Also cf the prose portion on p. 35.

Śiva has dual aspects. He is the destroyer (No. 73, v. 1), and burnt all forms including gods (No. 7). On the other hand, he removes the sin of the world (No. 7) and delivers men from the ocean of existence by destroying the seeds of *karma* which lead to successive re-births (No. 12).

He is the object of meditation of the ascetics (No. 32, v. 1) and even thoughts of him alone are capable of yielding infinite bliss (No. 12, v. 30).

But Śiva is not conceived in the abstract alone. He appears as a concrete divine figure with familiar myths and legends clustering round him. The old popular god of Indian masses reappears in a foreign land with his well-known features. He has matted hair (No. 24), three eyes (No. 24), five (No. 79) or six (No. 84) faces, and holds the trident in his hand (12). He originated from the nether world (No. 23) and is a resident of heaven. But sometimes he lives in the Himālaya (No. 24) or Malaya mountains (No. 31 B, v. 2), and sometimes sports in the Mānasa lake with his Śaktis (No. 95 v. 1). Besmearing his body with ashes (No. 23) he rides on a bull (No. 17) and dances in cemetery (No. 12, v. 28). He married Gaurī, the daughter of Himālaya, (No. 17) but maintains the Ganges on his head (No. 23). He is not, however, a frivolous god. He is learned (No. 62 v. 3) and intelligent. (No. 74, v. 13). He practises austerities without desiring any reward therefrom (No. 17). Indeed, he has no desire of his own ! (No. 12, v. 30). His body is purified by means of miracles, *yoga*, *japa*, *huṅkāra* etc. (No. 24b). He is attended and worshipped by men and gods as well as the semi-divine beings like *siddhas*, *cāraṇas*, *yakṣas* etc.

Some of the great achievements of Indian Śiva were quite familiar in Champā. The famous episode of burning the Cupid to ashes is again and again referred to. (Nos. 17, 21, 24, 36, 41, 74). Being struck with the arrow named *Saṁmohana* by

Cupid (No. 41, v. 2), he reduced the latter to ashes by means of burning fire proceeding from his eyes (No. 17), but later on again restored him to life (No. 36, v. 1). This well-known allegorical myth, depicting Śiva's absolute control over sensual passions, is a favourite theme of Sanskrit poets, and has been immortalised by Kālidāsa in his famous poem Kumāra-Sambhava. Apparently this aspect of Śiva's character made a deep impression upon his devotees at Champā.

The second memorable achievement of Śiva, stressed in the inscriptions of Champā, is the destruction of the demon Tripura (Nos. 17, 24, 32) and his three cities in the sky. As has already been noted, the details of this event agree closely with those given in the Mahābhārata.[1]

The third mythological incident about Śiva is the story of Upamanyu (No. 17). This has been narrated at great length in the Anuśāsanaparvan of Mahābhārata (Ch. XIV) which agrees with the inscriptions of Champā in extolling Mahādeva in the most extravagant terms and placing him above all other gods including Brahmā and Viṣṇu.

Liṅgapurāṇa, an extremist Śaiva book of the same type, is probably the source of another story in the inscription of Champā (No. 39). It is said that on one occasion there was a contest for supremacy between Brahmā and Viṣṇu when a luminous *Liṅga* appeared before them. The two combatants agreed to trace the source of the *Liṅga*. Brahmā took the form of a swan and went upwards, while Viṣṇu in the form of a boar went downwards. For a thousand years they tried but could not reach the end of the *Liṅga* one way or the other. Mahādeva then appeared before the discomfited gods and received homage from them, and they promised eternal devotion for him.[2]

1. Cf. Ins. No. 17 V. 4 and the footnote.
2 For the story cf. Lingapurana I, 17, 5-52. Vayupurana, ch. 55.

The Hoa-Que Inscription from which we learn the above story contains an elaborate praise of the *Liṅga* form which virtually credits the *Liṅga* with the same attributes as those given to Śiva himself. The *Liṅga* is primaeval, having no beginning or end, and revered by gods and men. The *Liṅga* assumes various forms for the sake of prosperity of this world, and those who even once bow down to these *Liṅgas* realise their desires.

Chapter III.

The Worship of Siva.

In Champā, Śiva was represented both as a human figure as well as in his *liṅga* form. The latter occurs more frequently, as in India, than the image of Śiva.

The ordinary *liṅgas* are placed on a pedestal (*Snāna-droṇī*) which is usually square and sometimes richly ornamented with human figures or other decorative designs. In a few instances the pedestal is round and the *Yoni* is represented therein. Very often several *liṅgas*, sometimes as many as seven, are found on the same pedestal.

The *liṅgas* are of the usual cylindrical shape. Sometimes a head is sculptured on this *liṅga*. This is undoubtedly the *Mukhaliṅga* so frequently mentioned in the inscriptions of Champā. M. Finot supposes that this head represents that of the king who founded the *liṅga* and identified himself with Śiva. But M. Aymonier seems to be right in his view that the head represents Śiva himself. For, according to the Ins. No. 39, after Brahmā and Viṣṇu had bowed down before the *liṅga* of Śiva, the latter "showed them his face, issued from the middle part of the *liṅga*." But it is quite probable that the face was deliberately made to resemble that of the king. In support of this view we can quote the Ins. No. 39 in which we are told that three brothers erected images of Śrī Mahā-Rudradeva and Bhagavatī out of devotion to, and in imitation of the features of their father and mother. In India we meet with similar Mukhaliṅgas, sometimes with four faces.

As a human figure Śiva is represented in a variety of forms.

I. Ordinary human figure with two hands.

Two mutilated early Śiva figures of this type found at Tra-kieu are given in Ars Asiatica Vol. IV. Pl. XXII. The god is represented as a strongly built figure standing in a defiant attitude.

The head is covered with rich curls of matted hair magnificently arranged in conical shape. A richly decorated diadem surrounds it at the base, while a brilliant *mukuṭa* (crown) covers the upper part. Stray locks of hairs fall on the breast.

The *nāgas* or serpents serve as the ornaments of the ears and also take the place of the sacred thread. This last is attached to the lower of the two necklaces around the neck. Belts of pearls etc, surround the waist and the upper part of the abdomen. The upper part of a dagger is seen from above the belt.

The figures being mutilated, the position of hands and feet cannot be ascertained. One arm shows trace of a bracelet made of serpents. In the face, the eyebrows and moustache are very prominent. There are crosses and circles in the diadem which might represent the sun and the moon but the third eye is not represented on the forehead.

The images of Śiva found at Myson are less decorated and much simpler in design.[1] The god is represented as standing. The upper part of the body is nude, while two garments fixed by a belt round the waist cover the lower part. The lower garment reaches almost upto the ankle, but the upper one stops at the knee. There is a rosary round the wrist of the right hand while the left hand holds a vase. The hair is arranged in three stages on the head. The god has a smiling face with fine moustache and the third eye is represented on the forehead.

Very often Śiva is represented as seated, in an attitude of meditation.[2] Sometimes there is a beautifully decorated halo behind the head.[3]

1. Parm. I. C., vol. I Fig 78, p. 362 and Fig. 79, p. 363.
2. Ibid vol. II, Figs. 108, 109, pp. 404—5.
3. Ibid Fig. 71. p. 290.

In a few instances even the normal human figure of Śiva has got an uncanny appearance. The Śiva found at Yañ Mum[1] may be cited as an instance. The god is represented as seated, with a trident in one hand and an elephant's goad in the other. He has three eyes and the sacred thread. But he is attired like a king and the expression of his face is almost ghostly. Sometimes, as at Drañ Lai, Śiva is represented as seated on Nandin, very much in the same style as one sits in a chair[2].

2. Śiva is sometimes represented as a human figure with extra hands in various attitudes. The following varieties may be noted.

(i) Standing,—six arms, the two upper joined behind the head, others holding a Triśūla, lotus, sword and a cup (?).

(ii) Standing on Nandin, in an attitude of attack; holding a lance in two hands;—has 24 or 28 arms; attributes:—Aṅkuśa (Elephant-goad), nāgī, bell, pitcher, bag and bow.

(iii) Dancing the Tāṇḍava—sometimes surrounded by Nāgīs playing on harp and drum.

(iv) Seated—holding a rosary in one hand and trident in another.

3. In decorative designs, specially on the Tympanum, Śiva is represented as *dvārapāla* (gate-keeper of temples). In these cases he has mostly a terrible appearance with projecting eyes and long teeth. He is armed with a club, and wears a crown, ear-drops of skulls, upavīta and bracelets of serpents.

Sometimes the *dvārapāla* is represented as standing on a bull

1. Ibid, Fig 77, p. 309
2. Ibid, Fig. 105, p. 401

and brandishing a sort of wedge-shaped iron instrument, while a small figure on the head of the animal and turned towards the main figure holds a sword in the right and a buckler in the left hand.

The images of Śiva at Champā are too numerous to be treated in minute details. The following summary of Parmentier would give a fair idea of the general position.

"As an idol, Śiva is more frequently represented as a *liṅga* which, on the other hand, seldom figures in decorative designs. As to the figure of Śiva, it is more often represented as a normal human being, rather than of monstrous appearance. The figure is usually seated, but, in rare cases, standing. In the earlier period he is represented with a corpulent body; in the later period, as an ascetic. It is only in the form of *dvārapāla* that he takes a terrible appearance. But this form of sculpture gradually disappeared. It is in the decoration of tympanum again in the earlier period, that the god is represented as fighting or victorious. It is specially in these cases that the god has monstrous forms. This is only partly caused by the multiplication of hands which vary from four to thirty. It is only in exceptional cases again that the god is represented with a multiplicity of heads. On the other hand he has very often the third eye on the fore-head. His usual vāhana (vehicle) is Nandin, and he has the Brāhmaṇical sacred thread as his distinctive sign. He is sometimes covered by serpents in the shape of ornaments. The usual attributes of the god are the sword, the rosary, the lotus-stem, the triśūla, and the vajra. Among other attributes, less generally found, may be mentioned discus, lance, bow, arrow, pen, purse, wallet, comb, cup, bowl, horn, bell, and elephant-goad. Sometimes the Oṁkāra is marked on the head-dress"[1]

1. Ibid, pp. 411-12

One of the oldest *liṅgas* of Śiva came to be regarded as the national deity and maintained this position throughout the course of history. The *liṅga* was established by king Bhadravarman towards the close of the fourth or the beginning of the fifth century A. D. and was named Bhadreśvara, for it was customary to designate the god by a term composed of the first part of the donor's name and the word Īśvara. This *liṅga* named Bhadreśvara or Bhadreśvarasvāmī was placed in a temple at Myson which soon became a national sanctuary and the centre of a group of magnificent temples. The king endowed the temple with lands whose boundaries are described in three inscriptions (Nos. 4, 5, and 7). This temple was burnt sometime between 478 and 578 A. D. but restored by king Śambhuvarman who confirmed the endowments previously given by Bhadravarman. Following the custom set on foot by the latter he associated his own name with that of the god, and called him Śambhu-Bhadreśvara. Successive kings, such as Prakāśadharma (No. 17) and Indravarman II (No. 31) and many others vied with one another in richly endowing this 'god of gods', and composing hymns of praise in his honours[1]. In course of time a mythical origin was attributed to the *Liṅga*. It is said in an inscription, dated 875 A. D., that Śiva himself gave it to Bhṛgu, and Uroja having got it from the latter established it in Champā. We are told that Śambhu-Bhadreśvara, the greatest of gods, and the only one fit to be worshipped, was the guardian deity of Champā, all the kings of which have become famous in the world through his grace and favour.

From the middle of the eleventh century A. D. Śrīśāna-Bhadreśvara came to occupy the position of national god. It appears extremely likely that we find here the old god Śambhu-Bhadreśvara under a new name, for the god Śrīśāna-

1. cf Ins. No. 17, p. 35.

Bhadreśvara is also said to be installed by Uroja (No. 73, v. 3). Henceforth king after king declares himself to be an incarnation of Uroja, and restores or endows the temple of Śrīśānabhadreśvara which Uroja had formerly established on the Vugvan mountain (cf. pp. 93, 99 ff above). The temple suffered much in the hands of the enemies, particularly the Cambodgians, and was therefore repaired and endowed by a succession of kings,[1] sometimes with the booty taken from the Cambodgians themselves. An idea of the wealth and grandeur of the god and its surroundings may be formed from the numerous lists of articles granted to the god by the kings of Champā in perpetual endowments. In 1088 A. D. Śrī Jaya Indravarman gave him a "golden *Kośa* of six faces ornamented with serpents and decorated with coloured jewels fixed at sharp points in the diadem". The *Kośa*, which was a frequent gift to *Śiva liṅgas* in Champā, appears to be an outer covering for the same. The one given by Jaya Indravarman V had six faces, and also an *Ūrddhvakośa* or the *Ādhāra Ūrddhva-mukha*.

As the weights of the Kośa and of these last two items are all given separately, it appears that both the faces and the *Ūrddhvakośa* were detachable elements fixed on to the *Kośa*. This *Kośa* of Jaya Indravarman, when complete, contained a large number of costly gems and gold weighing about 43lbs *Troy*. About eighty years later, another king of the same name, Jaya Indravarman VII, gave still richer endowments to the same god (1163-1170 A. D.). He gave a golden *Kośa*, decorated with costly jewels, constructed an *antargṛha* (inner chamber) of sandalwood with silver and gold decorations, and offered vessels, pitchers and various other objects of gold and silver. He also decorated the temple of Śrīśānabhadreśvara with silver and coated all the pinnacles of the temple with gold.

1. cf. Ins. Nos. 59 61, 62, 68—73, 79, 81, 84 87, 94, 101, 109, 117.

The total amount of gold required for the above purposes was nearly 75 lbs. Troy in weight, and the amount of silver nearly 35,000 lbs. Troy.[1] Besides, the king gave large elephants, male and female slaves etc. Among the various objects which we find dedicated to the god by a succession of pious kings may be mentioned, diadem decorated with jewel, necklaces and other ornaments, pitchers and other utensils of gold and silver, variety of articles made of gold, silver and sandalwood, the exact nature of which cannot be ascertained, male and female servants, and other women including dancers and musicians, fields, grain stores, oxen, buffaloes, and elephants. (cf. also the lists of articles in Nos 23, 24, 29.).

It is thus absolutely clear that Śambhubhadreśvara or Śrīśānabhadreśvara was regarded as the national deity of Champā from beginning to end, and most elaborate arrangements compatible with the wealth and resources of the kingdom were made for his worship. There were apparently the system of 'Devadāsīs',—'female dancers', who dedicated their lives to the service of the god—which forms so characteristic a feature of Indian temples even to-day. The enormous wealth of the temples of Champā would also remind one of the temples of India, the wealth and grandeur of which have been so vividly described by Sultan Mahmud and the writers of his time.

In addition to the Śiva-*liṅga* which attained the position of the national deity there were many others though of less importance. The most remarkable among these was a *Mukha-liṅga* of Śambhu in Po-Nagar. We learn from an inscription of the 8th century A. D. (No. 22) that this *Mukha-liṅga* was established by a king named Vicitrasagara Two inscriptions (Nos, 29, 71) even profess to give the exact date of this event. It was established, we are told, in the year 5911 of

1. According to the Measures of weight given by Maspero (T'oung Pao, 1910, p. 210).

the Dvāpara Yuga, about 1, 780, 500 years ago. How this date was arrived at, it is impossible to say, the main idea, no doubt, being to refer it to a hoary antiquity. This *linga* was destroyed in 774 A. D. by savage races coming by way of sea, but king Satyavarman (see pp : 50 ff) restored it and called it Satyamukhalinga. We find reference to this *linga* as late as the 12th century A. D. but it never acquired the status of a national deity like Śambhu-Bhadreśvara or Śrīśāna-Bhadreśvara.

The kings of Champā seem to have regarded it as a pious duty not only to maintain and endow the famous *lingas* of olden times but also to establish new ones. In such cases the almost universal practice was to associate his own name with the new image. Below is given a list of kings and the names of gods established by them.

NAMES OF KINGS.	NAMES OF GODS.	NUMBER OF INS.
1. Bhadravarman	Bhadreśvara.	2
2. Śambhuvarman	Śambhu-Bhadreśvara.	7
3 Indravarman.	Indra-Bhadreśvara.	23
Do.	Indra-Bhogeśvara Indra-Parameśvara.	24
4 Vikrānta-Varman	Vikrānta-Rudra.	30
Do.	Śrī Vikrānta-Rudreśvara.	Do.
Do.	Śrī Vikrāntadevādhibhaveśvara.	Do.
5. Jayasiṁhavarmadeva	Jaya Guheśvara.	39
6. Bhadravarmadeva.	Prakāśa-Bhadreśvara Bhadra-Malayeśvara Bhadra-Champeśvara Bhadra-Maṇḍaleśvara Bhadra-Pureśvara	39

7. Indravarman.	Indra-Kānteśa.	44
8. Harivarman.	Harivarmeśvara.	74
9. Jaya Harivarman.	Jaya-Hariliṅgeśvara.	75
10. Jaya Indravarman.	Jaya-Indra-Lokeśvara. Śrī-Jaya-Indreśvara Śrī-Indra-Gaurīśvarī	81
11. Indravarman	Indravarman Śivaliṅgeśvara.	108
12. Jayasiṁhavarmadeva	Jayasiṁhavarmaliṅgeśvara.	112 116

In addition to these instances where the kings associated their own names with the gods established by themselves, there are other cases on record where kings and nobles associated the names of their beloved relations with the gods founded by them. Thus king Jayasiṁhavarmadeva installed the goddess Horomā for increasing the religious merit of his mother's younger sister, queen Haradevī. The latter installed Indra-Parameśvara for the sake of religious merit of her husband Indravarman (No. 36.). She also installed Rudra-Parameśvara and Rudromā for increasing the religious merit of her father and mother. These names are also probably to be explained in the same way, though nothing definite can be laid down as we are ignorant of the names of her parents. The Ins. No. 38 records the consecration of a *liṅga*, called Indradeva, in honour of king Indravarman, by a dignitary of the realm. Again, Īśvaradeva, brother of a minister, installed the god Īśvaradevādideva (No. 32). The Ins. No. 12 mentions two gods Īśāneśvara and Prabhāseśvara, and it is extremely likely that these two gods are associated with the kings named Īśānavarman, and Prabhāsadharma referred to in that inscription. There are similarly other cases, where the names of gods are apparently derived from some kings, though we are unable either to identify the king or to decide whether the king himself founded the image or somebody else installed it in his honour. Two conclusions however stand out prominently from the above analysis. In the first place, the kings of Champā vied with one another in installing images of Śiva as it was regarded pious to do so, and secondly, they identified or associated themselves with the gods by adding their name to that of the god, and also at times by making the image of the god resemble their own.

The practice of associating the name of the king with that of the god founded by him was certainly not unknown to India. Thus the Chandella king Pṛthvīdeva installed an image of Śiva named Pṛthvīdeveśvara[1]. Two queens of the Cālukya king Vikramāditya II, named Lokamahādevī and Trailokyamahādevī installed two images of Śiva called respectively Lokeśvara and Trailokyeśvara.[2] The Rājataraṅgiṇī furnishes numerous examples from the history of Kashmir. Thus we are told "that Śūra founded the temple of Viṣṇu Śūravarmasvāmin. Two sons of a younger brother of Śūra called Dhīra and Vinnapa built under their own names temples.........

"Mahoday, who was the chief door-keeper of Śūra, consecrated the (shrine of Viṣṇu) Mahodayasvāmin.......

" The illustrious Prabhākaravarman, the king's minister, built a temple of Viṣṇu called Prabhākarasvāmin."[3]

---

1. Ep. Ind., Vol. I, p. 38.
2. Bom. Gaz. Vol. I, Part II, p. 190.
3. Rajatrangini, Bk. V, vv. 23 ff.

CHAPTER IV.

Saiva Gods.

A number of deities came to be associated with Śiva. The most prominent among them was of course the 'Śakti' of Śiva, known variously as Umā (Nos, 4, 22), Gaurī (26), Bhagavatī (26, 80), Mahābhagavatī (26), Devī (39) and Mahādevī (32). She was also called Mātṛliṅgeśvarī (97) and Bhūmīśvarī (50). She was the daughter of Himālaya and the incomparable and loving spouse of Śiva, worthy of being adored with joy by that god (13).

The cult of Śakti worship seems to have been most prevalent in the southern region known as Kauṭhāra. Here was established the goddess Yǎpu Nagara or Bhagavatī Kauṭhāreśvarī, in the temple of Po-Nagara which became a national sanctuary of the Chams comparable to that of Śambhu-Bhadreśvara or Śrīśānabhadreśvara.

We learn from an inscription of king Harivarman (No. 26) that 'an old image of Bhagavatī in Kauṭhāra, famous all over the world, remained empty for a long time'. In other words the image was carried away by savage tribes or destroyed by enemy troops, and the temple remained empty for a long time. Then in 817 A. D. king Harivarman made a new stone image of the goddess, adorned with a variety of ornaments, and offered her gold, silver, jewels, clothes of variegated colour and other articles. He further dedicated to the goddess fields in the Kauṭhāra country together with male and female slaves, buffaloes etc. Within half a century the stone image was coated over with a plate of gold, and ornaments with costly jewels were added to the head and ears of the image. (No. 29). In the year 918 A. D. king Indravarman established a golden image of the goddess (No. 45). This was unfortunately carried away by the Cambodians sometime between 944 and 947 A. D.

The war apparently taxed the resources of the king to the utmost, for in 965 A. D. he replaced the golden image that was lost by a stone one (No. 47). About a century later, in 1050 A. D. king Parameśvaravarman made rich gifts to the goddess, viz. vase inlaid with gold, a diadem, waistband, silver vase, an umbrella decorated with peacock feathers, a vast silver canopy and several golden pitchers and vases (No. 55). In 1084. king Paramabodhisatva, together with his sister and eldest son, gave to the goddess, among other things, elephants, a golden crown, a necklace decorated with jewels, and various other ornaments and utensils of gold and silver (No. 64). In 1160 A. D., king Harivarman, after having triumphed over all his enemies, both foreign and internal, 'first of all honoured the goddess called Yāpu Nagara by giving her great riches' (No. 76). Again, in 1167 A. D., king Jaya Indravarman VI, together with his queens and daughters, made rich donations to Bhagavatī Kauṭhāreśvarī (No. 80). In 1233 A. D. king Jaya Parameśvaravarman granted land and slaves to the goddess Pu-Nagara. The slaves belonged to both the sexes and to various nationalities such as the Khmer, Cham, Chinese and Siamese (No. 88). Probably the image of the goddess was destroyed soon after. For we learn from two inscriptions (Nos. 97-98) that princess Sūryadevī, daughter of king Jaya Indravarmadeva gave a sum of money for making a statue of the goddess Bhagavatī Kauṭhāreśvarī. She also gave various ornaments of gold and silver to the goddess and prescribed regulations for the dancing girls employed in the service of the goddess (1256 A. D.). Later kings of Champā also continued the donations to the goddess (cf. Nos. 99, 105, 109).

The general conception of Śakti is beautifully illustrated by the long hymn with which the Ins. No. 55 begins. Her power is conceived to be equal to that of god Śiva. 'She is in her very essence at one with whatever is in the world of God during its creation as well as in its dissolution. She is the primordial energy of the existent and the non-existent'. But, as we have seen above, these are exactly the attributes of Śiva himself. Hence the Śakti and Śiva are conceived as essentially one and the same: 'Thou hast as body, half of that which has moon as its diadem i.e. Mahādeva; thou art of beautiful appearance and form part of the body of the lord of embodied beings'.

Here we have evidently the conception of 'Ardhanārī'. Bergaigne concludes from it that the image of Bhagavati Kauṭhāreśvarī, also named goddess Yāpu Nagara, was that of an Ardhanārī i. e. an idol which represents Śiva and Durgā in the same body, prominence being given to the female part under Tantric ideas. This may or may not be true, for the epithets in question might refer to the general conception of Śakti and not to the particular image.

It is true that an image of *Ardhanārī* has been actually found at Dong Phuc. The female side in this statue is emphasised by the dress and developed breasts while the male part is indicated by fine moustache. The identity of 'ardhanārī' is revealed by the third eye on the forehead.[1]

But the image of the goddess of Po Nagar at Nha Trang is of a quite different character. It is a beautiful statue of black stone. The goddess, seated cross-legged, has developed breasts, and the folds on her belly indicate her maternity. She has ten hands. Two of these are placed on the two knees with palm upwards.[2] The eight other hands behind the two

1. Parm. I. C., Vol. II, pp. 413-14, Fig, 79, p. 312.
2. Parmentier thinks that these indicate the two Mudras of dana (gift) and abhaya (assurance). The published

carry dagger, lance, bow, arrow, elephant-goad, shield, discus and conch-shell. The goddess, adorned with bracelets and necklaces has a rather sombre expression. This statue of the goddess has been supposed by Aymonier to be the one erected by Indravarman in 965 A. D. More likely it is the statue erected by princess Sūryadevi about 1256 A. D. (See ante).

Sometimes, in bas-relief, the goddess is represented as standing on Nandin. In a bas-relief at Myson the goddess is represented as dancing, holding different attributes in her ten hands. These attributes are generally speaking the same as those of Śiva. Another bas-relief at Chien Dang represents the goddess in a fighting attitude. She has six arms and holds a bow and an arrow.

The number of images of Bhagavatī, so far discovered, does not correspond to the importance which the inscriptions attribute to that goddess. But in one respect the monuments corroborate the epigraphic records. It appears equally from both that Umā or Bhagavatī was more regarded as a female counterpart of Śiva than as a separate goddess. She has got the same attitudes, attributes and characteristics as those of Śiva. She has a third eye on the forehead, a large number of arms varying from four to ten, and even the same Vāhana viz. the Nandin. Only, unlike Śiva, she does not wear the sacred thread which is peculiar to the male sex.

The second deity associated with the Śiva-cult is Gaṇeśa, also called Vināyaka (No. 26). We know from Ins. No. 26 that a separate temple was dedicated to that god at Po Nagar. He had, besides, two temples at Myson. Very often the image of Gaṇeśa is found in other Śaiva temples, sometimes along with those of Bhagavatī and Kārtikeya, his mother and brother. The extant images of Gaṇeśa at Champā are indeed so

---

figures, however, do not make this quite clear.
Parm. I. C. Vol. II p. 412. B. E. F., Vol. I. p. 15, Fig. 1.

numerous that his cult seems to have been at one time even more popular than that of Umā, his mother.

The god is usually represented as seated on a pedestal, with a corpulent body and the head of an elephant. The end of the trunk is usually put in a bowl which the god has in his left hand, while his right hand holds a small object which may be a *liṅga* or the missing tusk. In at least three figures a garland is substituted for this object. The god wears a sacred thread. Sometimes he has two of the attributes of Śiva—a third eye on the forehead, and ornaments of serpents.

There is only one figure, at Myson, in which the god is represented as standing. He has four arms, with one of which he holds the bowl with the end of the trunk in it, while the three others have a garland, a pen and a rosary. The figure is richly attired, the dress on the lower part of his body being covered by a tiger skin.

In the temples of Dong Duong and Myson the figures of Gaṇeśa appear in the decorations of tympanum. These resemble the separate images of the god described above.[1]

The third Śaiva deity, Kārttika (No. 24), known also as Kumāra (No. 9), seems to have enjoyed a great popularity in Champā. He is referred to in four inscriptions (Nos. 9, 24, 36 and 39), from one of which we learn that an image of the god was placed with those of Gaṇeśa and Umā in a Śaiva temple. He is conceived as a great hero who repelled all his enemies (No. 9), and this no doubt refers to the part he played as commander-in-chief of the gods in their wars against the Asuras. In the Ins. No. 36, Śiva, here called Guheśvara, is said to have brought about peace, victory and happiness to Kumāra.

1. Cf. Parm. I. C Vol. II, pp. 415-417. Figs. 117-120. B. E. F., Vol. I. P. 17. fig. 2.

Four or perhaps five images of the god have been discovered so far.[1] In two of these the god has his usual *Vāhana* the pea-cock. In two others, however. the god rides on rhinoceros, a conception unknown in India though familiar in Cambodge. In one instance the god is represented as standing on the peacock with the peacock's train at his back. In other cases the god is represented as squatting on his *Vāhana*. The *Vajra* and sword are his principal attributes. The hair of his head is beautifully arranged in four parts, a fashion peculiar to this god. Sometimes the god is adorned with necklaces and bracelets. In one instant only the god figures in the tympanum of a temple in the train of Śiva.

Lastly, a word must be said about Nandin, the *Vāhana* of Śiva and Umā. Separate images of Nandin are found in large number in the vestibules of temples. The figure is that of a recumbent humped bull, looking towards the god in the temple. Sometimes the pedestal of the image was richly decorated and a number of bells was tied round the neck of the bull in the form of a necklace.[2]

1. Cf. Parm. I. C. vol. II pp. 417-18. Figs. 121-122.
2. Parm. I. C. Vol. II, p. 419, Figs. 123, 136. B. E. F. Vol, I, P. 17, Fig 3.

CHAPTER V.

Vaisnavism.

Although not so prominent as Śaivism, Vaiṣṇavism also played an important part in Champā. The number of inscriptions which are distinctly Vaiṣṇavite in character are indeed small (Nos. 11, 27, 121) but numerous incidental references to the gods associated with that religion leave no doubt of its strong hold in the country.

Viṣṇu was known by various names, such as Purusottama (11), Nārāyaṇa (24), Hari (23), Govinda (39), Mādhava (62), Vikrama (23) and Tribhuvanākrānta (121).

He was given high attributes: Viṣṇu is the preceptor of the whole world and without beginning or end (11). He is revered by the gods, Asuras and munis (No. 24). He is valorous in battle (62) and protects the whole world (24).

Some mythological feats of Viṣṇu are referred to. He churned the ocean by means of the Mandara mountain (95) and raised the world by his two hands (23). He defeated the Asuras (24), Madhu and Kaiṭabha for example (24), and crushed other enemies (23).

But as in India, the incarnations of Viṣṇu probably claimed greater homage than the god himself. Two of these, Rāma and Kṛṣṇa, are again and again referred to. Viṣṇu is said to have divided his essence under the form of four Rāmas viz. Rāma and his three younger brothers (No. 74), and we have already seen how the events of Rāmāyaṇa were localised in Champā (p. 13). Prominence is given to the heroic feats performed by Viṣṇu in his incarnation as Kṛṣṇa. He held aloft mount Govardhana, and destroyed Kaṁsa, Keśī, Cāṇūra, Ariṣṭa and Pralamba.[1] Again, the Cupid is referred

1 According to the Visnu Purana, Pralamba was killed by Balarama at the command of Krsna (Part V, Section IX).

to as the son of Viṣṇu (No. 74), apparently in the incarnation of Kṛṣṇa, for, according to the Purāṇas, Kāma is the son of Kṛṣṇa and Rohiṇī.

Kings of Champā took delight in comparing themselves to Viṣṇu, and sometimes even regarded themselves as his incarnation. Thus Jaya Rudravarman was regarded as incarnation of Viṣṇu (75) and his son, king Śrī Jaya Harivarmadeva, Śivānandana regarded himself as a unique Viṣṇu whose glories surpassed those of Rāma and Kṛṣṇa, firmly established in all directions (74).

The concrete conception of Viṣṇu is that of a god with four arms. His *Vāhana* is Garuḍa, but he sometimes lies down on the fathomless bed of the ocean of milk, served by Vāsuki, the serpent king, with infinite hood.

The epigraphic record is in this respect fully corroborated by the actual images of Viṣṇu discovered at Champā. The one erected by prince Nauk Glauṅ Vijaya (No. 121) and found at Bien Hoa[1] is seated cross-legged in Indian fashion and richly decorated. He has four arms. Two of them hold two clubs, while the other two hold a discus and a conchshell. He wears a sacred thread, a unique feature as it is absent from the other images of Viṣṇu in Champā, about 7 or 8 in number, which have so far been discovered. The chief attributes in the hands of these images, other than those nentioned above, are lotus, sceptre, and military weapons such as sword, club, axe and bow. In very rare cases Viṣṇu has only two hands, but he has generally four, and never more than that. He is usually represented as seated.

In some decorative panels Viṣṇu is represented as riding on Garuḍa or seated cross-legged on its back.[2] There are also

---

1. For the image see Parm. I. C. Vol, I, p. 554, fig. 1.7 and B. E. F. Vol. I. P. 19. fig, 4.

2. Parm I. C. Vol II, p 422 fig 124.

images of the *Anantaśayana* of Visnu. The god is lying at ease on the coils of serpent Vāsuki, whose seven hoods guard his head. From the navel of the god rises a lotus on the petals of which is seated Brahmā in an attitude of meditation. That the scene is laid on the bed of the ocean is indicated by wavy lines with fishes.[1]

We find also an image of Kṛṣṇa in the act of protecting the cows and cowherds by holding aloft the mountain Govardhana over their heads.[2]

Lakṣmī:—Lakṣmī the Śakti of Viṣṇu, also referred to as Padmā and Śrī, was a well-known goddess of Champā. She is frequently referred to in inscriptions (Nos. 12, 21, 43), and emphasis is laid on her proverbial inconstancy (No, 43). She is the ideal housewife (No. 43) and faithfully follows Viṣṇu (No. 12). The favourite Indian convention of regarding Lakṣmī as the symbol of sovereignty was also not unknown (No. 12). She is said to have been born in the Kailāsa mountain (No. 21), though the Indian tradition regards her as arising from the ocean of milk on the occasion of the churning of the ocean.[3]

The Ins. No. 21 gives the long history of an image of Lakṣmī, originally installed by King Śambhuvarman, and re-installed by king Vikrāntavarman in 731 A. D. The altar of this goddess, we are told, was made of gold and silver.

Three images of Lakṣmī have been so far discovered.[4] But the goddess figures largely in the decorative panels. A

1. Ibid-p. 423, fig. 125.
2. Parm. I. C. Vol. I, p. 259, fig. 48
3. cf. Visnupurana Bk. I Chap. VIII ff. But the Indian tradition also seems to have been known in Champa. cf. e.g. ll. 6–7 of Ins. No. 22
4. Parm. I. C. Vol. II pp. 421-22, For another figure doubtfully identified with Laksmi cf. B E. F. Vol. I p. 20. fig. 6

tympanum at Dong Duong represents the goddess with two hands as seated between two elephants, who are pouring water upon her head from a vase held aloft by their upraised trunks. In another tympanum the goddess is represented as seated on a coil of serpents, the thirteen heads of which surround her on all sides. She has four arms: three of them carry conch, discus and a club, while the fourth points to something by the extended fore-finger. The goddess is frequently represented as having only two arms, and holding stems of lotus plant.[1]

Garuḍa. Like Nandin, the *Vāhana* of Śiva, Garuḍa, the *Vāhana* of Viṣṇu, was also a familiar object in Champā. It not only figures in connection with Viṣṇu as its *Vāhana*, but a large number of separate images of it occur in decorative panels in various parts of temples.

According to Hindu legends, Garuḍa is the king of birds and the great enemy of snakes. He is represented in Champā with the head of a bird, but with the rest of the body very often like that of a lion. He has beak, tails and wings of a bird; as a king he is crowned with *mukuṭa* and richly decorated with jewels; and being divine in nature he wears the sacred thread. Sometimes Garuḍa is represented as if on the point of taking his flight, and his legs are in different planes. Sometimes the legs are in the same plane and hold a number of snakes. The snakes are often represented as forming a dais for Garuḍa, and are treated more as companions of the latter than his victims.

The head of the Garuḍa is not always a faithful reproduction of that of a bird. Sometimes it looks like that of a monkey, and sometimes it is almost human. Sometimes Garuḍa is represented with the head of a monster crushing a large number of snakes with his teeth.[2]

---

1. Parm. I. C. Vol. II pp. 421-427, figs 127, 128. B. E. F. Vol. I pp. 18-20, figs. 5, 6.
2. Parm. I. C. Vol. II pp. 262 (f. n. 7), 272 ff; 4 5. Fig. 62. B. E. F. vol. I p 20.

CHAPTER VI.

Brahma and the Hindu Trinity.

Brahmā, the third god of the Hindu Trinity, is referred to as creator in several inscriptions (No. 12, v. 24; No. 62, v. 3), but does not seem to have held a very prominent position in Champā. He is also called Caturānana, having four faces (No. 12), and in several inscriptions of the 13th century A. D. he is referred to as Svayamutpanna or self-created (Nos. 89, 91, 92, 96, 106). In Ins. No. 21 he is said to have made the golden peak of mount Meru. King Jaya Parameśvaravarman installed an image of Svayamutpanna at Phanrang in 1233 A. D. (No. 89) and rich endowments were made to the god by the king himself (Nos. 89, 91, 92), his heir apparent Nandabhadra (No. 92), his Commander-in-Chief Abhimanyudeva (No. 96) and by king Indravarman (No. 106). The evidence of iconography is in full accord with that of epigraphic records in respect of the inferior position of Brahmā. Only two small images of Brahmā have been discovered in Myson. These were originally placed in temples A and B as secondary gods. Brahmā also figures in bas-relief decorations of temples, but, mostly as a subsidiary god.

The characteristic features of the image of Brahmā are his four faces—of course only three being visible in most cases—and his *Vāhana*, the goose. His common attributes are rosary and lotus—stems. In a bas-relief in the Touranne Museum he is represented as standing, with four heads and eight arms holding a sceptre in one of them.

The scene figuring the birth of Brahmā has been referred to in connection with Viṣṇu. Here Brahmā wears a sacred thread, and holds a discus and a long-necked bottle in his hands.

Brahmā is usually seated on lotus though in one case the serpents form his bed.

The real importance of Brahmā lies in the fact that he is regarded as a member of the Trinity. We meet with the conception of the Trinity of Hindu gods in one of the earliest records of Champā. The Myson Ins. of Bhadravarman dating from 5th century A. D. begins with a reverence to Umā and Maheśvara, as well as to Brahmā and Viṣṇu. This decided leaning towards Śiva is further developed in Ins. No. 39. Here Śiva is represented as the supreme god, and the two others pay homage to him; finally the three gods stand together, Śiva in the middle with Brahmā on the right and Hari on the left.

The same idea is conveyed by iconographic representations on decorative panels. The Tympanum at Trach Pho[1] has a Mukhaliṅga in the middle with Brahmā seated on a serpent to the proper right, and Viṣṇu, seated on a boar, to the proper left. Both these gods are turned towards Śiva with joined hands, and two attributes of Viṣṇu viz. a discus and a club are shown in the background. In the tympanum at U'u Diem,[2] Śiva and Umā riding on a single bull occupy the centre; Brahmā and Viṣṇu, with joined hands, and seated respectively on a lotus and a Garuḍa, are in the upper right and upper left corners, while two other figures, an armed soldier and Kārttika (?), occupy positions just below these figures. At Thuy Trieu, however, Viṣṇu occupies the central position with Brahmā on the left and Śiva on the right. Śiva rides on a boar, and both the gods have their hands joined in an attitude of prayer.

Thus Viṣṇu and Śiva were both claimed to be the chief

1. Parm, I. C. Vol. II, p. 411. fig. 115.
2. Ibid Vol. I. p. 518 fig. 120.

of the Trinity by their respective followers.[1] An attempt at compromise resulted in the conception of a new god Śaṅkara-Nārāyaṇa. Here the two gods are placed on the same level in theory, and this is expressed by a concrete image, half of which is Śiva, and half Viṣṇu. Such an image is clearly referred to in Ins. No. 24;[2] but unfortunately no actual remains of such a figure have yet been discovered.

The idea of association of the chief gods also probably led to the practice of decorating the temple, dedicated to one god, with figures of the other group. Thus the temple of Phong Le dedicated to Śiva has its front decorated with images of Viṣṇu. Similarly figures of Lakṣmī and Brahmā appear on the tympanums of Śaiva temples. The principal tympanum in a temple, however, usually figures the god or gods to whom the temple is dedicated, though a Śaiva temple in Myson has the scene of the birth of Brahmā, and a temple at Phanrang, dedicated to Brahmā, shows the Trinity with Viṣṇu as the chief god.

---

1 M. Parmentier observes as follows :—A close study of the evidences furnished by epigraphy and iconography seems to indicate that from the 12th century A. D. a silent religious revolution in favour of Vaisnavism was taking place in Champa. The references to Vaisnava cult or Vaisnava temples before this period are few and far between. But from this period onwards we find an increasing number of them. Again. whereas the figures of Visnu and Laksmi hold but a minor place in the decoration of temples of the earlier period they gradually occupy an increasingly preponderant position in the later period. Lastly Siva is clearly subordinated to Visnu in the image of the Trinity under discussion.

M. Parmentier thinks that the position of Siva as the supreme god was lowered in the eyes of the Chams on account of the constant reverses sustained by them in the hands of the Annamites and other enemies. They naturally discarded Siva who was unable to afford them the necessary protection, and turned to other gods in the hope that they might succeed where Siva had failed. This might also account for the rise of Brahma into importance at the cost of Siva (Parm I. C. vol. 11. pp. 432-433)

2 The god "Srisana Visnu", mentioned in No. 71, may also, refer to such an image,

CHAPTER VII.

The minor deities of the Hindu pantheon.

Although the great gods of the Hindu Trinity, *viz*. Brahmā, Viṣṇu and Śiva almost monopolised the homage and worship of the people, the lesser gods of the Hindu pantheon were not altogether forgotten. Thus the Ins. No. 24 begins with "a reverence to all the gods", and the Ins. No. 31 frankly recognises their importance in the following words:—

"In some places Indra, Brahmā and Viṣṇu, in some places Vāsuki, in some places Śaṅkara, in some places ascetics, Sun, Moon, Agni, Varuṇa, and in some places image of Abhayada (Buddha) appeared for the deliverance of creatures."

While the list of gods in the above passage is by no means exhaustive, it is worthy of note that deities like Indra, Vāsuki, Sun, Moon, Agni and Varuṇa are placed on the same level as the great gods, and regarded as deliverer of human beings. It shows that side by side with the pompous worship of Śiva and Viṣṇu there were popular cults of various gods and goddesses.

This view is corroborated by the opening lines of Myson Ins. (No. 4) of Bhadravarman. The inscription begins with "reverence to Umā, Maheśvara, Brahmā and Viṣṇu", and this is immediately followed by "reverence to the Earth, Wind, Sky, Water and Fire" i.e. the five elements of nature. Apparently these were regarded as divine in nature. Ins. No. 17 refers to these five together with Sun, Moon and Sacrificer as the eight forms of Śiva.

The epigraphic records introduce us to a number of these gods. A short account of them is given below.

1. *Indra.*

Indra is referred to in a large number of inscriptions (Nos. 12, 16, 17, 22, 23, 24, 42, 62, etc.).

He is referred to as the chief or king of the gods (No. 16) who killed Vṛtra (17) and other Asuras (24), and worked the miracle of creating the three worlds (17). He is said to have performed severe austerities and a large number of great sacrifices (Yajña) in previous births. Having gained the kingdom of heaven by virtue thereof (23), he protected it according to rules of Dharma (31). His son is also extolled for the prowess of his unconquered arms. The popularity of the god is indicated both by the large number of references in Inscriptions as well as by the fact that no less than twelve kings assumed the name Indravarman. Many kings of Champā are also referred to as Indra personified (No. 30) or Indra fallen from heaven to earth in order to rule over the country.

Two images of Indra have so far been discovered in Champā, one at Tra Kieu and the other at Myson. These are two small human figures and only identified with Indra by the figure of elephant, the *Vāhana* of Indra, before the pedestal. In one of them Indra has probably the Vajra (thunderbolt) in his hand [1]

2. *Yama.*

Yama, the god of death, is conceived as a terrible figure, but he faithfully maintains the law in his kingdom (Nos. 22-24). He is referred to as Dharma (No. 12) and Dharmarāja (24)

3. *Candra.*

Candra is referred to as god and the victim of Rāhu (Nos. 23, 74).

4. *Sūrya.*

The Sun-god is often coupled with the Moon. They both form part of the grand assembly of gods described in Ins. No. 42. Two small images of Sūrya have been discovered at

1. Parm. I. C. Vol. II p. 430

Myson. They are identified by means of the figure of horse, the *Vāhana* of Sūrya. The god holds the sword in his hands.[1]

5. *Kuvera*

Kuvera is described as a friend of Maheśvara and a mine of wealth (No. 12). He is also called Dhanada and is praised for his liberality (No. 23). He is called "Ekākṣa piṅgala", apparently in allusion to a story described fully in the Rāmāyaṇa (Uttarakāṇḍa ch. XIII). A temple of Kuvera was erected in the seventh century A. D. by king Prakāśadharma (No. 14). This god was worshipped by the people for increasing the wealth and guarding against evils (No. 14). The god referred to as Artheśvara in No. 92 may be the same as Kuvera. Yakṣas, the mythical attendants of Kuvera, are also frequently mentioned (No. 23, 31 etc.).

6-7. Agni and Vāsuki are mentioned in the passage quoted above in Ins. No. 31.

8. Sarasvatī is mentioned in Ins. No. 12 v. 26; but whether she is conceived as a goddess or merely regarded as a symbolical expression for knowledge and learning cannot be determined.

9. A god called Vanāntareśvara seems to have been worshipped in the later period, but its identity is at present unknown (Nos. 129, 130).

10-11. Two gods Mandara and Praṇaveśvara are referred to in No. 28 but their identity is unknown.

In addition to these gods, there were other beings of the nature of demi-gods who are frequently referred to in the inscriptions of Champā. Chief among these are the divine sages (Ṛṣis) (Nos. 23, 46 etc.) who are placed on the same level as the gods in the passage quoted above from Ins. No. 31. Among them Bṛhaspati, the preceptor of the gods, and

1. Parm. I. C. vol. II, p 430

Kāśyapa, the preceptor of the gods and demons (23), are mentioned by name. The former is extolled for his eloquence (No. 74) and knowledge of Śāstras (No. 62).

Next to the divine sages mention may be made of the Siddhas (Nos. 24, 35, 46), Vidyādharas (23), Cāraṇas (24), Yakṣas (23, 31), Kinnaras (24), Gandharvas and Apsaras or celestial nymphs (24, 46).

A number of evil spirits also figure prominently in the mythical conceptions of the people. Prominent among them are the Daityas and Asuras who are the eternal enemies of the gods in heaven (Nos. 12, 22, 31, 42, 46 etc.). There were also the Uragas (23), Rākṣasas (23), Pretas (22) and Piśācas (42).

Images of Apsarās are found in decorative panels. They wear rich *mukuṭas* and are represented as flying figures with lotus stem in their hands.[1]

The Rakṣas are represented by demoniacal figures, with clinched teeth and a multiplicity of heads and arms.[2]

Figures of Nāgīs are also to be seen in the decorative panels. They resemble the Indian figures, having the body of a serpent with a female bust.[3]

In order to complete the sketch of religion in Champā we must briefly allude to certain general conceptions.

In the first place, the abstract conception of a supreme God was not altogether superseded by the images of Śiva, Viṣṇu etc. We find reference to Him in Inscription No. 12. He is referred to as the Creator whose ways are incomprehensible to men.

Secondly, emphasis is laid upon the performance of sacrifices. Merits of sacrifices are extolled again and again (12, 23). Sacrifices are regarded as the principal treasure of good

1. Parm. I. C. Vol. II. p. 431.
2. Ibid
3. Ibid.

men (23), and they beget not only material prosperity but also supernatural powers (12). The actual sacrifices before a kindled fire are referred to in Ins. Nos. 2 and 3. In the latter case we have probably an instance of human sacrifice. That this was not unknown in Champā is proved by the fact that king Fan Wen, after having defeated the Chinese governor of Nhut Nam, offered his body in an expiatory sacrifice (see p. 24). Aśvamedha sacrifice is referred to in Ins. No. 12 but we do not know of any instance of its actual performance.

The pessimistic current of Indian thought seems to have made a deep impression upon the Chams. Again and again we read in the inscriptions how the kings and nobles, 'recognising the unsubstantial nature of wealth and worldly gain[1] and thinking that this body is as impermanent as the foam floating on waters,' performed "meritorious works", to atone for all evil deeds as well as for the sake of salvation, or, as is often expressed in a more concrete form, for gaining the heaven of Śiva. These meritorious works took various shapes. It might be the installation of gods or perpetual endowments to religious institutions, for "gifts made to gods are a mode of purification" (59). But sometimes we hear not only of the worship of Śiva, but also of *Dhyāna* (meditation) *Yoga* (spiritual exercises) and *samādhi* (concentration) (Nos. 46, 62, 65). Sometimes kings abdicated their throne in order to pass the remaining days of their life in these religious practices. (No 62). Pilgrimage was also regarded as a meritorious work and an old king abdicated the throne and went over to India to enjoy the bliss of spending his days on the banks of the Ganges (No. 12).

The Myson Ins. No. 59 claims the highest results from these pious practices. The author of this inscription, "knowing

1. Cf. Ins. 43 (c) v. 18

that the body and its pleasures are vain and transient", installed *liṅgas* and made gifts to the gods "who were present in their symbols." He embellished and enriched Śrī Īśānabhadreśvara and increased the riches and the land of the god. The thought of Īśvaradevatā, otherwise known as Yogīśvara, was always present in his mind. By the force of effort and concentration of mind he at last saw Īśvaradevatā, who became entirely visible (*pratyakṣa*) to him (No. 59). This may be taken as a sketch of the ideal of religious life in Champā.

A characteristic feature of the religious development in Champā is the spirit of toleration that marked it from beginning to end. Although sectarianism prevailed, and two or three predominant Brāhmaṇical sects flourished side by side with Buddhism, we hear of no animosity in the field of religion. On the other hand, we find a liberal and catholic spirit paying reverence to all religious sects. This is proved by the passage in Ins. No. 31 quoted above on p. 200. The kings, too, often practically demonstrated their eclecticism. Thus king Prakāśadharma installed Śiva *liṅgas* (Nos. 10, 12) and at the same time erected a temple of Viṣṇu (No. 11). King Indravarman, too, shows equal zeal towards Śaivism and Buddhism (No. 31). Such instances can be multiplied to almost any extent. The people, too, followed the example of the kings (28). In this respect the Indian colonists maintained the best traditions of their motherland.

This brief sketch of the religious life may be concluded by a short account of some striking popular beliefs and superstitions.

The Indian theory of transmigration and "Karmaphala" (effects of deeds done in one life passing to the next) seems to have been the basis of religious life (No. 4). Thus king Prakāśadharma established a god "with a view to destroy the seeds (of Karma) which have the power of leading to births in quick succession" (No. 12). King Jaya Indravarman believed that "he became king of Champā by virtue of peculiar merits accruing from austerities of many previous births" (No. 31). The very interesting fact that several kings believed themselves to be inacrnations of Uroja, who was born four times in this earth, have been already referred to. King Satyavarman was also regarded as an incarnation of Vicitrasagara (29)

We find also a belief in the influence of stars and planets and their power of guiding the destinies of man. Thus king Jaya Indravarman's glory and wisdom is said to be due to the protection of Mercury, Mars, Jupiter, the Moon, the Sun, Venus and Saturn (No. 31).

The belief in heaven and hell of course played a predominant part. In general, heaven is looked upon as the abode of gods and abounds in pleasures of all kinds. Hell is on the other hand the place for sorrows and torments of all kinds. We hear of heaven associated with a particular god, such as Rudraloka, Īśvaraloka (24) Buddhapada (31. c. 8.). On the other hand, hells, too, were many in number. The conventional number of hells is given as eight (31). In particular reference is made to Raudra, Mahāraurava (31) and Avīci (33).

The question of heaven and hell is frequently raised in connection with perpetual endowments. Imprecations in right Indian fashion are added at the end of inscriptions containing record of perpetual endowments. Any one maintaining these is promised salvation, heaven, or *nirvāṇa* along with his friends and relations, while those who destroy them are threatened with the direst consequences, such as living in hell for aeons with their relations and ancestors. In one case it is threatened that even the mother of the man, who destroys the goods of temples, would be haunted by multitude of dogs (32).

Lastly, there was the belief in the Yugas. Three of them are mentioned by name viz. Kṛta, Dvāpara and Kali. The Kṛta age is the ideal or golden age (74), as in India, when Dharma prevailed in its entirety (12). The Dvāpara which immediately preceded Kali, is brought within historical range by the mention of king Vicitrasagara who is said to have flourished in that age (29). The Chams even professed to know the exact date when Dvāpara Yuga began. For we are told that in the year 5911 of the Dvāpara Yuga king Vicitrasagara established a *Mukhaliṅga* in Kauṭhāra (No. 29). Again the same event is placed 1, 780, 500 years before 1065 Śaka (No. 71). Thus the Dvāpara Yuga commenced in 1, 785, 268 B. C. It would be interesting to know the basis on which this calculation was made.

The Kali Yuga is, of course, full of evils (Nos. 26, 29). It always tries to "lead people to error and pride" (No.65) and kings have always to be on their guard in order to withstand its evil effects. It is antagonistic to the prosperity of kings (35, 62, 74) who are consequently obliged to wage an eternal war against it. The only way of fighting it is to follow the path of virtue and righteousness. This is beautifully expressed in the following passage.

"I have nothing to expect from a king who, free from passion, dutifully protects his subjects like his own sons'–with this melancholy reflection, Kali, chased by the splendour of the king, sadly moved away, nobody knows where, even as the army of darkness flies before the Sun leaving its unbearable rays behind." (No. 12, v, 8)

CHAPTER VIII.

Buddhism.

Buddhism had also a fairly strong hold on the people of Champā. At least eight inscriptions specifically refer to that religion (Nos. 28, 31, 37, 43, 93, 103, 123, 126.) and interesting information about it is supplied by them.

Buddha is known by various names such as Jina (28), Lokanātha (37), Lokeśvara (31), Sugata (37), Dāmareśvara (123), Svabhayada (31), Abhayada (31), Śākyamuni, Amitābha, Vajrapāṇi, Vairocana (37), Saddharma[1] (?) (69, 71), and Pramuditalokeśvara (37).

Buddha is regarded as born from a succession of Buddhas (31). He is omnipresent in this world (37) and his essential characteristics are conceived to be kindness and an anxiety to deliver all creatures from misery. "The essence of his soul is pity and his intelligence is wide awake in saving creatures. He is always full of kindness and his patience is incomparable. Men overpowered by sorrows and the dwellers in hell long to see him day and night; as thirsty men, overpowered by sun's heat long for cool water in summer, so they, suffering from many sorrows, wish to have a view of Buddha" (31).

Utmost emphasis is laid upon the doctrines of Karma and transmigration as propounded by Buddha.. Deeds done in this life must have their effect, and evil deeds lead people to the clutches of Māra, the Buddhist Satan. The Buddha alone can grant salvation and release people from the terrible hosts of Māra in hell. These ideas are beautifully expressed in the two following verses, the first of which is unfortunately mutilated.

---

1 Saddharma really means Buddhism, but it seems to be used also for Buddha.

"Hail! constant reverence to that merciful one........... Those whose happiness was over, and who were being struck by iron rods...got the highest salvation by thinking of Lokeśvara.

"Sinful men attached to their works in former lives, and without any hope of deliverance, were eternally surrounded by the terrible hosts of Māra, and overpowered by hunger and thirst on account of their want of liberality and aversion to Sugata (i. e Buddha) in former times. But being rescued by Vajrapāṇi from the hell, they secured the way to salvation pointed out by the Buddha". (No. 37, vv, 1-2)

This salvation is defined as the "attainment of the Buddhist Nirvāṇa to which there is no parallel" (No. 31). It is also evident from the Dong Duong Ins. (No. 31, c-8) that there was a popular conception of a Buddhist heaven, where virtuous people might enjoy pleasures along with their servants.

Buddhism seems to have obtained a great deal of royal favour, and statues and temples of Buddha were erected by kings and people alike. There was also a powerful community of Buddhist monks and we hear of erection of monasteries in different parts of the kingdom.

We learn from the inscription of Sthavira Buddhanirvāṇa dated 829 A. D. (No 28), that his father erected a Buddhist temple and a Buddhist monastery and granted lands to the latter, apparently for defraying the expenses of the monks living therein. The famous Dong Duong Ins. (No. 31) informs us that king Śrī Jaya Indravarman, also known as "Lakṣmīndra, Grāmasvāmī, installed an image of "Lokeśvara", called after him "Lakṣmīndra-Lokeśvara, in 875 A. D. He also founded a monastery for the perpetual enjoyment of the Bhikṣu-saṅgha or the community of monks, and placed therein all the necessaries of life. He also endowed the monastery with a large number of fields. He did all these for the sake of Dharma, for the propagation of Buddhism and not for his own enjoyment or increment of royal revenues. Usual benedictions and imprecations for those who maintain or destroy the gifts are added at the end. Indravarman, who was thus a devoted follower of Buddhism, got the posthumous title of Parama-Buddhaloka (No. 36). The An-Thai Ins. (No. 37) dated 902 A. D. records the erection of temples and monasteries by kings Bhadravarman and Indravarman, apparently at the request of, and out of respect for a monk called Nāgapuṣpa. Again, the Nhan-Bieu Ins. (No. 43), dated 911 A. D., records that a dignitary of Champā erected a temple of Avalokiteśvara and a monastery, called Vṛddhalokeśvara, apparently after his grandmother, princess Lyaṅ Vṛddhakula.

Referring to the condition of Buddhism in Lin-i or Champā, I-tsing remarks that "the Buddhists generally belong to the Āryasammiti-nikāya and there are also a few followers of the Sarvāstivādanikāya". This would mean the prevalence of Hīnayāna sects.[1] But, according to the inscriptions, the later Mahāyāna form of Buddhism was most predominant in Champā. This clearly follows from the reference to Avalokiteśvara, Amitābha etc. as well as from the conceptions of Vajradhātu, Padmadhātu and Cakradhātu (No. 37). Hence it is that a large number of Buddhist gods and goddesses received the homage of the people. Some of these divinities are named in Kim Choua Ins. (No. 93) viz Śrī Jina Parameśvara, Śrī Jinalokeśvara, Śrī Saugatadeveśvara Śrī Jina Vṛddheśvarī and Śrī Jinadevadevī

It is a notable fact that sanctuaries of Śiva and Buddha and monasteries of these two sects were often erected side by side by the same donor (cf. Nos. 28, 31, 43). The reciprocal

1. I-tsing by Takakusu p. 12.

influence of these two religious sects is also indicated by the fact that Buddha was called Ḍāmareśvara (No. 123), the lord of Ḍāmaras or *bhūtas*, an epithet originally belonging to Śiva. It is also a note-worthy fact that figures of Śiva decorated the famous Buddhist temples of Dong Duong.[1]

It may be observed in conclusion that the famous Buddhist formula "ye dharmāḥ hetuprabhavāḥ" etc. is also found in Champā (No. 126).

The archaeological remains have corroborated the evidence of inscriptions in regard to the importance of Buddhism. The Dong Duong Ins. of Indravarman Parama-Buddhaloka refers, as we have seen above, to the erection of a Buddhist temple and a monastery Now, the excavations at that place have unearthed the remains of a Buddhist temple, far greater in dimensions than the largest Brāhmaṇical temple in Champā. Several images of Buddha have also been discovered amid the ruins. On the whole Dong Duong appears to have been an important stronghold of Buddhism.

An image of Buddha found at Dong Duong is nearly 5 ft. in height. It is seated in European fashion with the hands on the knees and has Ūrṇā and Ūṣṇīṣa. The god is seated on a large pedestal and around him are a series of figures paying homage to him. A fine standing image of Buddha in bronze has also been found at Dong Duong. It is regarded as the most artistic representation of Buddha so far discovered in Champā.

There is a peculiar Buddha figure at Trung Tin. Buddha is seated cross-legged on the body of a serpent, which has been arranged in the form of a rectangular pillar, and is protected by its seven hoods. Sometimes, as at Khan Tho Dong, Buddha figures are seated between two *stūpas*. A

1. Parm I. C. II. p. 434.

terracotta figure discovered at Phuoc Tinh also represents Buddha as protected by a Nāga and seated between two stūpas.

A number of small but interesting terracotta seals containing Buddhist figures have been discovered in the cave of Phong-nha in Quang-Binh. They represent (1) a dāgaba, (2-3) two images, probably of Avalokiteśvara and (4) a female deity, probably Tārā, and (5-6) two Buddha figures, one in Bhūmisparśa and the other in Dharmacakrapravartana-mudrā. It appears that the cave was a sanctuary of the Mahāyāna Buddhists who frequented it in large numbers and purchased these seals probably to preserve them as amulets.

The influence of the Mahāyāna form of Buddhism is further indicated by a bronze statue of Bodhisattva found in the neighbourhood of Binh Dinh. The god is seated cross-legged on the coils of a Nāga, and his head is protected by its seven hoods. He is decorated by a rich headdress, rich ornaments hanging from the ear, necklaces and bracelets. His dress is transparent like that of the Buddhist figures of the Gupta period, and not marked by waving lines as we find in the Gāndhāra images and in the Buddha figure described above. It passes under his right armpit and covers the left shoulder. The soles of his feet are marked by *cakra* or the figure of a wheel. The two hands rest on the lap, while the palm of his right hand, placed on that of the left, shows the sign of a lotus flower.

There is also a standing image of Bodhisattva in stone, found at Phuoc Tinh. Two other figures discovered at Binh Dinh have been doubtfully identified as Buddha or' Bodhisattva [1]

1. Parm I. C. Vol. II, pp. 433 ff. B. E. F. Vol. I, pp. 22 ff Figs. 7-12.

The evidence of inscriptions and sculptures thus leads to the conclusion that although not so predominant as Śaivism, Mahāyāna form of Buddhism had a great hold on the country.

King Śrī Jaya Indravarmadeva VII was evidently a great patron of this sect. We are told that he was learned in the doctrines of Mahāyāna and installed several Mahāyāna deities (No. 81)

It is rather remarkable that remains of stūpas, a structure almost invariably associated with Buddhism, are almost conspicuous by absence. But the existence of *stūpas* in Champā in ancient times is proved by references in Chinese books.[1] It may be safely held that the ruins of these structures proved useful quarries in later times, as in India, and the stūpas nearly vanished from the surface of the earth.

---

1. T'oung Pao—1910, p. 497.

CHAPTER IX.

Society.

The Indian colonists in Champā tried to build up a society of the orthodox Hindu type, but it had to be modified in some essential aspects by the pre-existing traditions, manners and customs.

The people were theoretically divided into four castes, Brāhmaṇa, Kṣatriya, Vaiśya and Śūdra.[1] But this division hardly existed in practical life except with regard to Brāhmaṇas and Kṣatriyas. The terms Vaiśya and Śūdra are only referred to in a solitary inscription, whereas references to Brāhmaṇa and Kṣatriya are numerous. Even when a general enumeration of castes is intended, the terms Vaiśya and Śūdra are conspicuous by their absence. Thus we read in the imprecatory verses: "Those who take away those goods—Kṣatriyas, Kings or Brāhmaṇas—fall every day into the doleful hell along with their father and mother." Again: "Those kings, Kṣatriyas, Brāhmaṇas, ministers...merchants who take away or destroy these etc."[2]

It is evident, therefore, that the fourfold division of society in accordance with the injunction of the Hindu Śāstras was merely theoretical. The Indian colonists belonged mainly to the ranks of Kṣatriyas and Brāhmaṇas, while there was probably no very sharp distinction between the other classes of society. The merchants, on account of their wealth, probably occupied a high position in society as indicated by the passages quoted above, but beyond this there were probably no social divisions among the common rank of people, whether Indian or Chams. There is no clear indication in the inscriptions that the conquered Chams were specially marked out for the servile position.

---

1 Ins No. 65. 2. No. 31.

The distinction between Brāhmaṇas and Kṣatriyas seems more akin to that of classes rather than that of castes. For one thing, it is evident that intermarriage between the two was in vogue. Thus, according to the Ins. No. 12. King Rudravarman was the "son of an eminent Brāhmaṇa", and the "son of the daughter's daughter" of glorious Manorathavarman". Manorathavarman, as is apparent from his title Varman, must have been a Kṣatriya, and thus Rudravarman had a Brāhmaṇa father and Kṣatriya mother. This conclusion is corroborated by the fact that in Ins. No. 7 he is called the "ornament of the Brahma-Kṣatriya family (or families). Again, the sister of king Prabhāsadharma married Satyakauśikasvāmī. The latter was undoubtedly a Brāhmaṇa (see p. 39ff. above) and the issue of this marriage, Bhadreśvaravarman, is said to have "shed lustre on both the Kṣatriya and Brāhmaṇa families" (Ins. No. 12, vv. 12-13). That such marriages were pretty frequent seems to follow from Ins. No. 75, where the king, Śrī Jaya Harivarmadeva, is said to belong "to Kṣatriya family on both the father's and mother's side". Such qualifying phrases would have been absolutely uncalled for if marriage usually took place between members of the same caste.

It is probably the marriage relation between Kṣatriyas and Brāhmaṇas that gave rise to a new clan, the Brahma-Kṣatriyas,[1] to which frequent reference is made in inscriptions. The word literally means "partaking of the character of both Brāhmaṇa and Kṣatriya." Two kings viz. Rudravarman (Ins. No. 7) and Indravarman (No. 23) are said to be the head of the Brahma-Ksatra clan. The Brahma-Kṣatra is a well-known caste in India. The Sena kings of Bengal be-

1. On the meaning and origin of the term Brahma-Ksatra, See Prof. Bhandarkar's article in J. A. S. B (N. S.) Vol. V. 1909, pp. 167-87.

longed to this caste and it exists till to this day in many parts of India. In Champā, however, the Brahma-Kṣatriyas do not seem to have formed a separate caste or class, but were merely a subdivision of the Kṣatriyas. This is conclusively proved by a comparison of the two inscriptions, Nos. 72, and 75. In the former, the king, Śrī Jaya Harivarmadeva, is said to belong to "Brahma-Kṣatriya caste", but in the latter inscription he is expressly said to belong to "Kṣatriya family on both his father's and mother's side". Thus Brahma-Kṣatra can only be regarded as a sub-class under the Kṣatriyas, and in any case there could not possibly be any rigid distinction between the two.

The Brāhmaṇas occupied a high position in society. As has already been observed,[1] they did not dominate over the king and the state to the same extent as in India. But otherwise they occupied a position of great dignity. The Brāhmaṇas are regarded as gods among men. and the murder of a Brāhmaṇa is regarded as a very heinous crime (No. 12). According to the same inscription even kings are said to be devoted to them (No. 12). It is doubtful, however, whether they ranked above the Kṣatriyas. It is true that in the only instance where the traditional four castes are enumerated, the Brāhmaṇas occupy the conventional position of supremacy; but in a good many instances where only the two classes are mentioned, the Kṣatriyas are placed before the Brāhmaṇas,[2] as we find in Buddhist and Jaina books, according to which the Brāhmaṇas are inferior to the Kṣatriyas. On the whole, the available materials seem to show that the distinction between the Brāhmaṇas and the Kṣatriyas was not a very rigid one, and they cannot be said to have formed two castes in the strict sense of the term.

---

1 cf. p. 156 above

2 cf. Ins, No. 12, v. 13 ; Ins. No. 31, C v. 7, and D.

The constant mention of the Brāhmaṇas and the Kṣatriyas seem to show that these were really distinguished from the rest of the population. But whether this distinction led to any restriction about food and marriage such as prevails in India between two castes, we are unable to determine. Taking everything into consideration it would seem quite safe to conclude that the society was really divided into two broad classes, the higher one composed of Brāhmaṇas and Ksatriyas, and the lower one consisting of the remaining people.

But there was another important distinction in society viz. that between the aristocracy and commonalty. These two divisions were certainly overlapping to a great extent. In other words, the members of the aristocracy most often belonged to the Brāhmaṇa and Ksatriya classes but it almost certainly comprised other people, who gained this high rank by virtue of wealth or services rendered to the state.

The external symbols of aristocracy are described in detail in the inscription No. 39. We are told that these privileges "difficult to be attained by others in this world" were granted to the minister Ājñā Mahāsāmanta by the king as reward for faithful services.

The privileges consist of:—

(1) Articles of dress and ornaments.

(2) Right to use special conveyances, such as palanquins and elephants, to the accompaniment of music etc.

(3) Claim to be seated near the king.

Among the articles of dress are mentioned : "The honour of putting a garland on his head, the distinction of being marked by an excellent *tilaka* (mark on the forehead), a complete ornament for the ears, best ear-ring, a pair of robes, decoration by golden girdle-string, an axcellent dagger with a golden sheath, a vessel and a *cirāṇḍa* white as silver. To these are added "an umbrella made of the feathers of peacock and a multitude of pitchers and vases, and a palanquin with silver staff" Similar honours were conferred by the king a brother of the minister named Ājñā Jayendrapati as a mark of appreciation of his poetical merits. We are told that in nine different temples of the realm Ājñā Jayendrapati composed poetical inscriptions engraved on stones, and as a reward, obtained from the king various distinctions such as palanquin, parasol decorated with peacock feathers etc. (Ins. No. 39, b)

In both these respects the Indian colonists kept up the tradition of their motherland. In ancient India people laid a great stress upon the special privileges of wearing particular dresses and using particular conveyances, and these distinctions were granted by the king upon poets and other great personages in recognition of their loyal and faithful services. Traces of these customs still persist in the Native States of India, particularly among the Rajput States.

The family to which the two ministers belonged may be regarded as a typical aristocratic family. Of the three brothers, two, as we have seen above distinguished themselves in court by administrative ability and poetic talents. The third brother, Ājñā Narendra Nṛpavitra was no less famous. He was "versed in all sacrificial ceremonies and in all treatises dealing with the Śaiva religion". Besides, he was a linguist, and by hard exertion mastered the languages of neighbouring countries. We are told that he "was able to understand thoroughly the meaning of messages sent by kings from different countries, after looking over them only for an instant". Whether he was a Brāhmaṇa or Kṣatriya by caste we do not know, but the case of the three brothers certainly shows that so far at least as occupation went there was no very hard and fast line between the Brāhmaṇas and the Kṣatriyas.

In addition to the distinctions mentioned above the king also granted titles to the members of the aristocracy. We have got reference to several high officials who were rewarded in this manner. Thus king Jayasiṁhavarman gave three titles to his favourite Captain of Guards viz. Īśvarakalpa, Śivakalpa and Śrīkalpa (Ins. No. 35). Again Pov Kluñ Piliḥ Rājadvāraḥ "obtained the title of Akālādhipati as a reward for the zeal with which he served the king" (Ins. No. 43). But Rājadvāraḥ obtained something more substantial for his services, viz. a grant of lands. It appears that such grants almost always accompanied the other distinctions in order to enable the recipients to maintain their dignity, and this laid the foundation of a hereditary landed aristocracy. Unfortunately there are not enough details to pursue the subject any further.

A general idea of the manners and customs of the aristocracy may be formed from what has been said above regarding the king (pp. 161 ff). But history, as properly understood, should concern itself more with the life of common people than with big events connected with kings and nobles. Unfortunately, however, it is difficult and well-nigh impossible to make this the guiding principle when one has to discuss the history of any ancient civilisation. For the written materials on which we are to base our accounts are mostly concerned with the higher classes of people, and it is only in an indirect way that we can glean some informations from them about common people. It is only when we are fortunate enough in coming across a highly developed national art that we may entertain some hopes of reconstructing the life of the people at large. For true art is a fair index of common life, more so when it is rich in phonetic value.

The art of Champā was fairly developed and its phonetic value, although not very high, is not altogether negligible. It is possible therefore to get some valuable information from a careful study of this art. But one note of warning has to be sounded before we proceed to this task. As will be demonstrated in the next chapter, the art of Champā was derived from that of India and not of indigenous growth. Its spirit was also Indian. It is difficult to judge therefore the extent to which it reflects the national life of Champā as against merely handing down the traditions of the parent art. With this reservation, and subject to the risk of being led astray at times, we may cull a few valuable informations regarding the dress and ornaments of common people in ancient Champā.

First as to the dress. It is indeed very striking that the sculptures represent the dress of the people as very scanty. Only the portion below the waist is covered; the rest of the body, even in cases of females, is nude. The evidence of art in this respect is in full agreement with the Chinese accounts (cf. p. 11 above). It is possible that in course of time a garment for the upper part of the body was introduced, but this is not reflected in the artistic representations, till a very late period.

As to the dress which covered the lower part of the body it may be broadly divided into two classes, the long and the short. The long one extends down to the ankle while the short one never reaches beyond the knee, and sometimes even stops short much above it There were of course great varieties in both. Sometimes the cloth was quite plain, but often it contained rich and varied designs in variegated colours, and was plaited in fancy patterns. In most cases we find a loose scarf over the dress hanging between the legs. At a later period this was replaced by either aprons, or richly

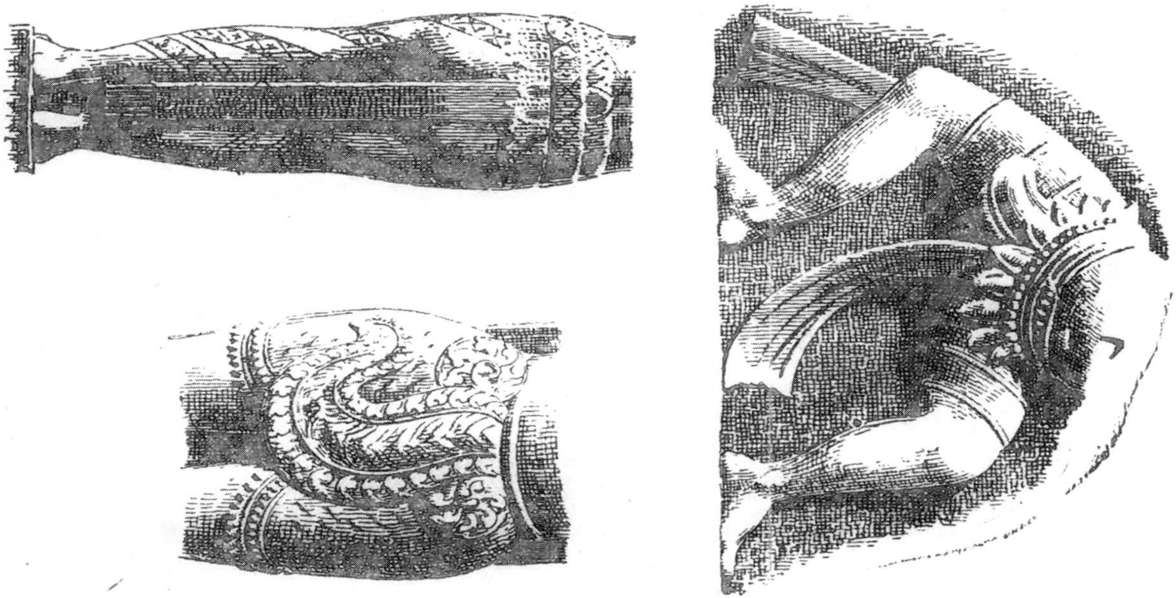

Pl. I. Dress, as illustrated in Sculptures. (cf. p. 220.)

(*Reproduced from the publications of Ecole Francaise D' Extreme-Orient, Vols XI, XII viz. Inventaire descriptif des monuments Cams by H. Parmentier, Planches CLXXV, CLXXVI.*)

1

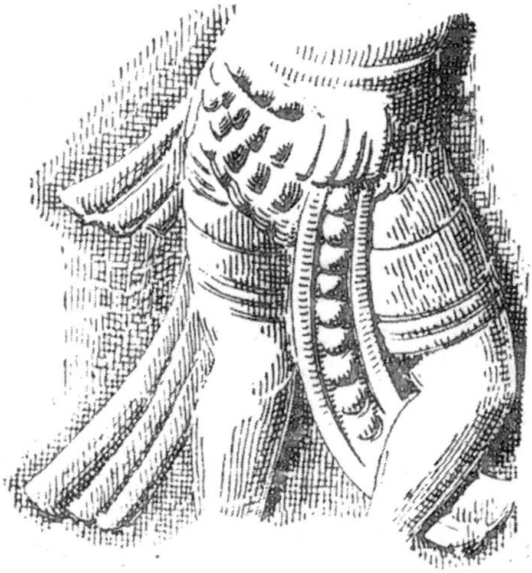

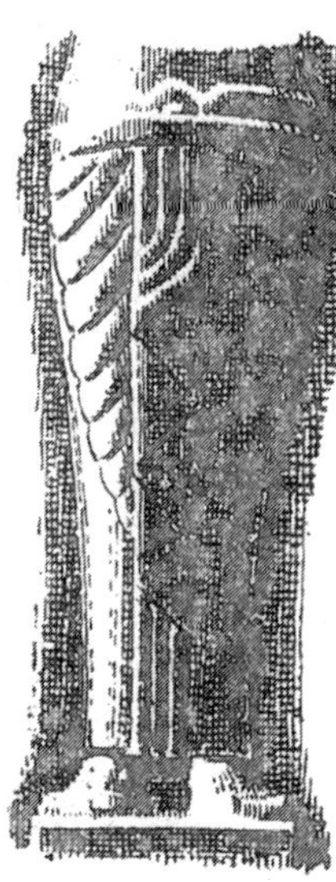

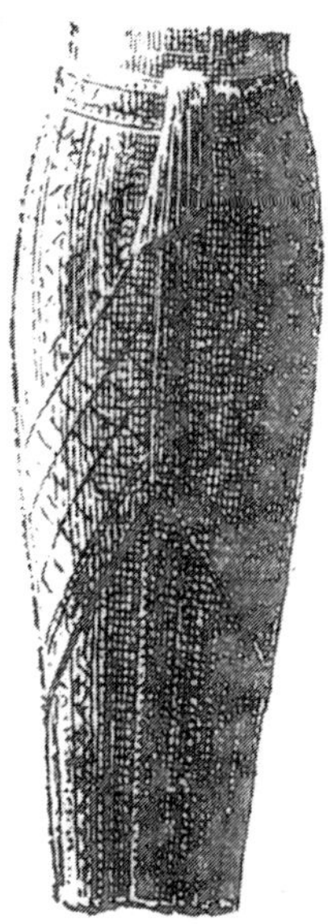

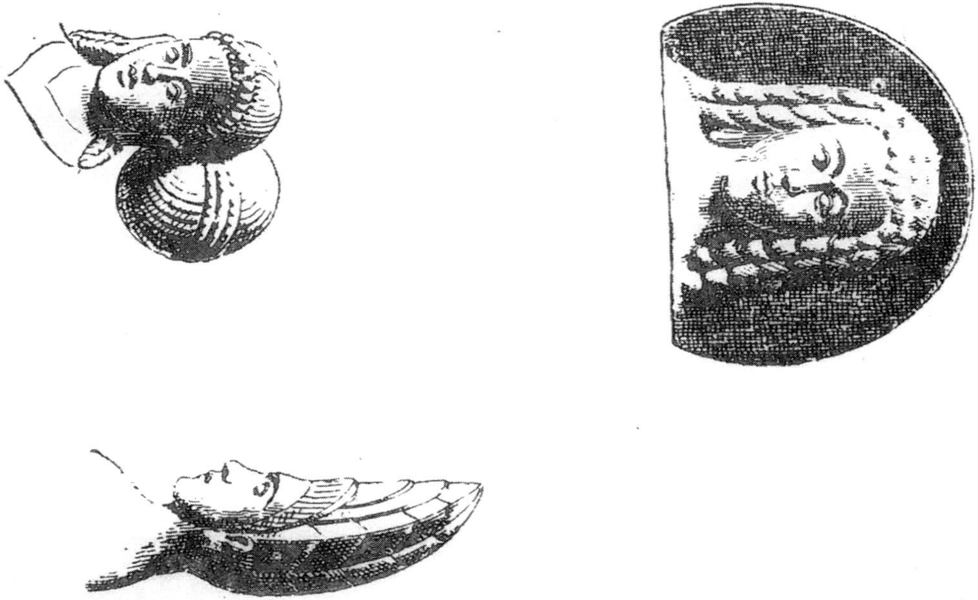

Pl. II. Head-dress, as illustrated in Sculptures. (cf. p. 221.)

(Reproduced from the publications of Ecole Francaise D' Extreme-Orient, Vols. XI, XII viz. Inventaire descriptif des monuments Cams by H. Parmentier, Planches CLXXVIII-CLXXIX.)

2

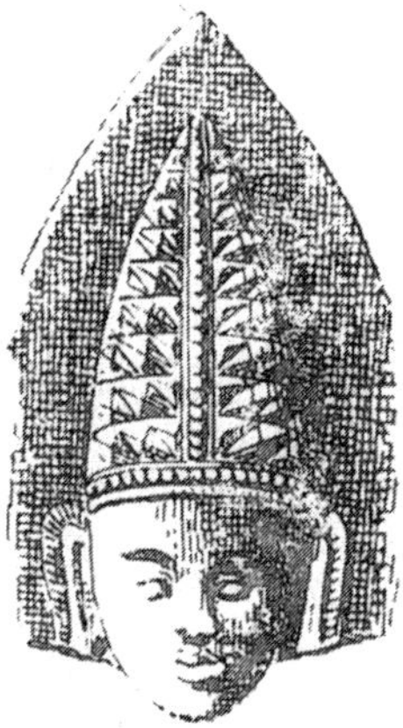

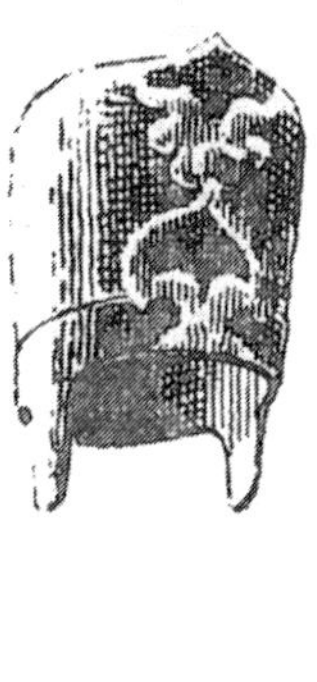

plaited folds, of cloth. The long dress resembles a modern petticoat, while the short one looks like drawers. As a rule women put on the former and the men the latter. Both were tied to the waist by a belt which was sometimes richly decorated with jewels.[1]

The ascetics and the servants are often figured as dressed in an Indian *languti*, a narrow strip of cloth passing round the hip and between the legs.

As to the colour of these dresses the sculptures teach us nothing. One Chinese authority says that the colours chiefly used were black, yellow, red and purple, whereas the use of white was punishable by death.

The Chams paid some attention to hair-dressing. The sculptures have preserved a number of specimens, showing the curious ways in which they tied their hair in various fanciful patterns. They also used head-coverings of various types. It appears on a careful examination of the sculptures that during the early period the hair was either tied in round and high chignon or allowed to fall loosely over the neck and soulders. Sometimes a diadem was used either by itself or just to keep the chignon in its place. Later on caps (*mukuṭas*) of various shapes were introduced, most of these being either conical or cylindrical. Sometimes they showed rich designs and a high degree of workmanship.[2]

As regards foot-wear the Chinese evidence is in full accord with the evidence of sculptures. According to an authority quoted by Ma Touan-lin, only the upper classes used shoes made of skin, while the common people walked barefooted. Another authority belonging to the 15th century reports that "only the king wears shoes, the courtiers are

1. Parm, I. C. Pl. CLXXV—CLXXVI.

2. Parm. I. C Pl. CLXXVIII, CLXXIX.

barefooted", and the officers of S. S. Galathee have noted the same state of things. But the last two observations can only refer to the well-known oriental custom according to which the courtiers must leave their shoes before appearing in king's presence. Even to-day nobody can appear before a ruling prince in the Native States of India with shoes on; but this does not prove that they are in the habit of walking barefooted even outside the court. We can, therefore, accept the statement of Ma Touan-lin, viz. that the practice of wearing shoes was limited to upper classes alone. This is corroborated by the fact that shoes are very rarely represented in the sculptures. The few specimens that we come across are all of the type of sandals tied to the foot by means of a strap. Sometimes is decorated with jewellery (cf. above p. 161. 1. 18).

The ornaments of the ear are many and varied in character. There is first the disc set in the ear-lobe. It is either circular or oval and sometimes of the shape of a flower. It has a knob in the centre which is also variously designed. Then come the rings, sometimes quite large in number, which are set round the ear. Lastly the pendants, which are often fairly heavy.

Next to the ear-ornaments may be mentioned the bracelets round the wrist as well as round the upper part of the arm near the shoulder. Similar ornaments are also put round the ankles.

Among other ornaments noticeable in the sculptures may be mentioned necklaces and girdles both of which show a rich variety of designs.

Lastly, it appears that the sacred thread *(upavīta)* lost its religious character in Champā and came to be used as an ornament among the people.

It is evident from a general study of art in ancient Champā that the people led a life of ease, if not always of opulence and luxury. The few data we possess regarding their economic conditions also corroborate the same view.

Agriculture was no doubt the principal occupation of the people. Although the quantity of fertile lands was rather small they made good the defect by a system of irrigation, traces of which exist even to this day. The chief products have been already referred to (p. 8) and the cultivation of these must have afforded maintenance to the great majority of people. But trade and industry was also fairly developed and we have many references in Chinese literature to the manufactures, and arts and crafts of Champā.

A few of these may be noted below :—

A. AGRICULTURAL.

1. (a) They cultivated the mulberry-tree for the production of silk-worms, as well as the cotton-tree. They made cloths of silk and cotton of various kinds and hues, and these formed an important industry of the people. Sometimes embroidery of gold, silver, pearls and jewels was added to cloths, and the Chams made great progress in this art.

(b) Manufacture of perfumes from sandalwood and similar other trees.

2. Manufacture of alcohol from the juice of betel-nut.

3. Straw hats were made from a kind of palms grown in water.

4. Mats were made from fan-palm.

5. Ropes and fine basket work made out of a variety of plants and herbs.

B. MINERAL.

1. The different metals gold, silver, copper, iron and tin were extracted from soil and manufactured in the shape of utensils and ornaments of various kinds.

2. Large number of precious stones developed the art of jwellery.

3. There was also a brisk trade in corals of all sorts and pearls of great value.

4. China vases were also manufactured to a very large extent.

C. ANIMAL PRODUCT.

1. Ivory work was a very important industry.

2. The horn of rhinoceros was regarded as very valuable on account of its medical property, and formed an important article of commerce.

In addition to the above there were also the important arts of carpentry, stone-cutting, brickmaking and masonry.

Last, but not of the least importance among the industries was that of ship-building. By their very geographical position the Chams were dependent for their safety upon a keen martitime activity, and the Chinese evidence makes it quite clear that they had a powerful navy. The Chams were hardy fearless mariners and boldly plied the ocean for the purposes of trade and war. There were mercantile vessels as well as ships of war. We often hear of Cham fleet harassing the coasts of Annam and Cambodge and pillaging the sea-coast towns and ports. They also visited China, Java and other neighbouring countries.

An infamous activity of the Cham mariners was the systematic piracy in which they were engaged. Not only did they piliage defenceless towns and ports on the sea-coast by a sudden raid but they also captured and plundered vessels which passed along their coast. The vessels going to or coming from China which had of necessity to sail close to the shores of Annam, were their special victims, and for some time the Annamese waters came to be regarded with terror by the trading people of the east.

An indirect consequence of this nefarious activity of the Chams was the influx of slaves among them. Regular slave-trade was carried on by the Cham merchants, and slaves formed a prominent element of the population in addition to aristocracy and commonalty. We get frequent references to slaves in the inscriptions and it became a normal practice for all who endowed a temple to assign to it both male and female slaves for carrying on menial work. These inscriptions refer to slaves of both the sexes belonging to all nationalities such as Khmer, Cham, Chinese, Siamese etc. The prisoners of war were also sometimes condemned to slavery, and the same lot often awaited the rebellious subjects. As we have seen above (p. 79), when the rebellion of Pāṇḍuraṅga was crushed by King Parameśvaravarmadeva Dharmarāja, half of the population were distributed as slaves to various establishments.

The only other element of Cham population which deserves special notice is the woman folk. Some scholars are of opinion that the matriarchal system prevailed in Champā before it was colonised by the Hindus. This may be regarded as probable though little traces of it remained in historical times. Maspero refers as an example to the practice observed in matters of succession to the throne, viz that the son of a queen of the first rank had preference over even elder sons born of a queen of second rank. This practice was, however, observed even in India and can be explained without assuming the existence of matriarchy. Of far greater interest in this connection, however, are a series of successions through female lines in historical times. Thus king Pṛthivīndravarman was succeeded by two sons of his sister, Satyavarman and Indravarman, and the latter was again succeeded by his sister's husband, and sister's son. Again Indravarman II was succeeded by his wife's sister's son. These instances might be attributed to matriarchal principles, but as we do not know whether there were any direct male descendants in any of these cases we are unable to form any definite conclusion. A Chinese author, of course, remarks: "among the Chams it is the female who counts, the male is of no importance". Several coustoms of the modern Chams in Annam have also been regarded as bearing traces of matriarchal principles, which, besides, are the general characteristics of Malayo-Polynesian or Austronesian race to which they belonged. But whatever that might be the custom, if it prevailed at all, must have been thoroughly modified by the Hindu colonists. So far at least as the extant evidence goes, the position of women in Champā seems to be on all fours with that in India.

Marriage was regarded as a sacred ceremony which laid the foundations of a family life. As in India, the marriage was confined to one's own clan corresponding to *gotra*. We have reference to two important clans—those of *nārikela* (cocoanut) and *Kramuka* (betelnut). These names were derived from a mythical story according to which the founder of each of these clans was discovered, while infant, in a cocoanut (or betelnut) tree by the king who reared him up and ultimately gave him his own daughter together with his kingdom. There were possibly other clans of this type, and the clannish sentiments, although based on mythical legends, superseded all other barriers of society. Thus we are told that a lady belonging to a noble family would marry even a man of no substance if he belonged to the same clan, and that marriage relations were determined by considerations of clan rather than those of caste. In other words, a man would marry a woman belonging to the same clan but to a different caste.[1]

The details of marriage ceremony such as are recorded in the Chinese texts immediately recall those of India to which they bear a close resemblance. The inevitable matchmaker, usually a Brāhmaṇa, as in India, settles the prelimi-

1. Maspero, T'oung Pao, 1910, pp. 184 ff.

naries. He arrives at the bride's house with some presents, such as a quantity of gold, silver, and jewels, two pitchers of wine, and fish. After the proposal is agreed to on both sides he settles an auspicious day for the ceremony, for, as in India, the ceremony could take place only on certain *tithis*. On the fixed day friends and relations of both the bride-groom and bride gather at their respective houses and indulge in joyous festivities amid dance and music. Then the bride-groom goes to the house of the bride who is attired in a splendid dress suitable to the occasion. A priest after introducing the bride-groom to the bride joins their hands together and pronounces the sacred *mantras*. This finishes the ceremony which is again followed by dance, music and other festivities.

Like the marriage ceremony the relation of husband and wife, too, probably resembled that of India. At least we have undoubted evidence of some of the most important characteristics of that relation. Thus when the husband died, the wife—at least one belonging to a high family—followed him in the funeral pyre, according to the well-known *satī* rite in India. Some inscriptions even record a number of queens burning themselves on the funeral pyre of a king. The case of the Annamese queen of Jaya Siṁhavarman IV shows how difficult it was even for an unwilling victim to avoid this tragic fate (see above, p. 124). The traveller Odoric de Pordenone remarks with reference to Champā:—

"When a man dies in this country, his wife is burnt along with him, because they say that it is only right and proper that the wife should live with the husband in the other world"[1]

Those who did not die along with their husbands mostly lived like Hindu widows the rest of their lives.[2] They led retired

1. T'oung Pao, 1911, pp. 600-601.
2. B. E. F. Vol. XIV, No. 9, p. 14.

lives and did not dress their hair. It is possible that in exceptional cases, the widows were remarried. All these are exactly analogous to what we find in India. On the same analogy we should expect the prevalence of polygamy and this is confirmed by the examples of kings (see. p. 162 above) who had numerous wives and concubines.

The sacred ties of marriage, however, sometimes sat loosely upon the lower classes of people, if we are to believe in an account preserved in the Chinese Text called Tao-yi-tche-lio. We are told that when a vessel stopped at a coast-town for some days, the sailors married the women of the locality. The men and women lived as husband and wife during the short residence of the former, and when the time of parting came they took leave of one another amid tears and lamentations. Next year the women again married the new batch of sailors, and so on. We are told that if perchance any one of these sailors returned to the same country after a long time, he was warmly received by his former wife and offered food and drink, but the old ties of husband and wife being once dissolved, could not be automatically revived.[1]

Nevertheless there was a high ideal of womanhood, and feminine virtues are frequently referred to. The good qualities of Pu lyaṅ Rājakula enumerated in Ins No. 36 (vv. 8 ff) may be regarded as those of an ideal woman. The women were, as a general rule, very religious, and many inscriptions record their religious gifts and pious endowments. The heroic example of a lady determined to save her honour even at the cost of her life has been referred to on p. 76. above.

Some of the popular customs and ceremonies of Champā have been recorded by Chinese historians. These were held on fixed dates in accordance with the Hindu calendar which was in vogue in Champā. The year began with the month of

1. Ibid p. 37. Similar forms of short-term marriage are said to be prevalent even now among the mariners of Hue.

Caitra, and months ended in Amāvasyā or New-moon. Many of the Hindu festivals were observed there. A few peculiar ceremonies are recorded below.

On the New Year's day an elephant was taken out of the town and let loose; for they believed that they would thereby get rid of the evil spirits for the year. In the month of Āṣāḍha they held grand boat-races in which even the fishing boats took part. At the feast of the winter-solstice, which took place on the full-moon day of the 11th month, the people presented the king with samples of their agricultural and industrial products. Lastly, on the 15th day of the month of Caitra, a wooden tower was constructed outside the walls of the capital city; the king and people of all ranks placed there clothes and perfumes which were then burnt as sacrifice to God.

Maspero has regarded all these customs as of indigenous origin, but this may be doubted. The practice of letting loose an elephant, particularly when there is no heir to a king occurs in many old stories of India. The annual boat races are held even to this day on the Dussera festival in various parts of Bengal. The practice of presenting the "first fruits" to kings, landlords or great men is a well-known custom in this country, and the last festival mentioned above has its counterpart in the modern Dolayātrā festival. The festivals in Champā recorded above may thus be regarded, like many others, as ultimately derived from India, although modified by local ideas.

There were many popular festivals connected with harvest, as we find in India. Even the king took part in them and was to give the signal for harvest by himself cutting a handful of rice.

Some of the customs and ceremonies were horrible and barbarous. Thus every year on the 15th day of the first month and the 15th day of the 12th month, the people were authorised to procure the galls of living persons and sell them to officials. These galls were mixed with an intoxicating drink and taken by the official with his family. They believed that they would thereby be feared by other persons and be safe from infectious diseases.[1]

The funeral ceremony was analogous to that of India. The usual practice was to burn the body on a pyre. The cremation took place the very next day, in the case of the ordinary people, and three or seven days after death, in the case, respectively, of nobles and kings. The dead body was soaked in beer and placed on a hearse. It was then taken to the burning place to the accompaniment of music. All the members of the family, both male and female, with shaved heads, accompanied the procession uttering loud shouts of lamentations all the while, until they arrived at the river-bank. There they burnt the body on a pyre, and having collected the ashes in an earthen pot and thrown it into the river, returned to their house in profound silence. If the deceased belonged to any noble family, or had performed any high functions in the state, the burning ceremony had to be performed near the mouth of a river, and the ashes were placed in a copper pot. In the case of the king this pot must be of gold and it had to be thrown into the sea. Thus the distinction of ranks was carefully preserved even after death.

For a period of two months the members of the family came to the pyre at the end of each week with incense and perfume, and uttered wails and lamentations over the remains of the departed. On the hundredth day, and again in the third year, some ceremony had to be performed in honour of the dead.

1. B. E. F. Vol. XIV. No. 9, p. 37.

Although cremation was the usual rule, the practice of exposing the dead body was not unknown. In accordance with the custom prevalent among the Parsis, and among several peoples in ancient India, the dead body was left in an open field and devoured by the "sacred vultures". After a few days the family of the deceased collected his bones, burnt them to ashes and threw them into water.[1]

It is difficult to form an idea as to the general tone of morality prevalent among the people. According to some Chinese authorities the people did not use any fermented drink, whereas others say that they made alcohol by extracting the juice of betelnuts.

The Chams were very fond of dance and music. Inscriptions frequently refer to dancers and musicians and the bas-reliefs depict many dancing and musical parties together with a variety of Indian musical instruments. There were probably also some dramatic performances in which men and women both took part, and some heroic ballads were sung to the accompaniment of suitable musical instruments.

A few words must be said in conclusion regarding the study of Indian literature in Champā. It is evident from the published inscriptions that at least upto the tenth century A. D. the Classical Sanskrit Literature, particularly the Kāvya, was thoroughly studied, probably even to the exclusion of the native literature, if there were any. Sanskrit became the language of the learned and the indigenous tongue suffered a cold neglect. Not only were Indian books imported and studied but even new books were written in Sanskrit, and the name of at least one such book and an extract from it has reached us (No. 74).

The kings seem to have taken a leading part in the culti-

1. B. E. F. Vol. XIV. No. 9, p. 16.

vation of Sanskrit language and literature. Thus as noted before' king Bhadravarman (5th century A. D.) is said to have been versed in the four Vedas (No 4). King Indravarman III is said to have been versed in the well-known six systems of Philosophy, as well as in the Buddhist Philosophy. In addition, he knew Pāṇini's Grammar with Kāśikā, and the Ākhyāna and Uttarakalpa of the Śaivas (No. 45). King Śrī Jaya Indravarmadeva VII was versed in Grammar, Astrology, the Mahāyāna Philosophy and the Dharmaśāstras, notably the Nāradīya and Bhārggavīya (Ins. No. 81). Whether these kings were as learned as their court-poets woud have us believe may be doubted, but that these different branches of Sanskrit literature formed familiar subjects of study in Champā may be regarded as fairly certain.

To the list of subjects thus obtained others may be added on the strength of epigraphic records.

1. The Epics.

That the two epics, the Rāmāyana and the Mahābhārata, were quite familiar in Champā is evident from a number of allusions to the chief characters or episodes described in them. Thus reference is made to Yudhisṭhira, Duryodhana and Yuyutsu in No. 41, to the glories of Rāma and Krṣṇa in No. 74, to Rāma, son of Daśaratha in No. 12, to the irrepressible valour of Dhanañjaya in No. 23, and to the son of Pāṇḍu in No. 39 Besides, the story of the destruction of the Tripura-Asuras as contained in No. 18, bears a very close resemblance to what we find in the Anuśāsanaparva of Mahābhārata. The allusion to the epithet "Ekākṣapiṅgala" of Kuvera, occurring in No. 14, is also evidently based on the Uttarakāṇḍa of Rāmāyaṇa. All these point to a very intimate knowledge of the epics on the part of the people of Champā.

2. The religious literature, particularly the literature of the Śaiva and Vaiṣṇava sects, must have been thoroughly stu-

died. The familiarity of the people with the numerous epithets and legends of Śiva, Viṣṇu and other gods, as discussed in Book II Chaps. II and V above, cannot be explained except on this assumption. We have also some specific references to it in inscriptions. Thus the minister Ājñā Narendra Nṛpavitra is said to have been versed in "all treatises dealing with the Śaiva religion" (No. 39). The minister of King Indravarman III "was versed in sacred scriptures" (No. 46).

3. The Smṛti literature, specially the Mānavadharmaśāstra or Manu Smṛti, must have been regarded as a standard and authoritative treatise. Specific reference to it is found in No. 65, and the Bhārggavīya Dharmaśāstra, mentioned in No. 81, may also refer to the same.[1] The latter inscription also refers to Nārada Smṛti.

4. The great influence of Classical Sanskrit literature, including Kāvya and Prose romances, is met with in all the Sanskrit inscriptions that have reached us. The writers of these inscriptions show great familiarity with different metres and styles of poetry and prose-writing. Even the extremely artificial style, consisting mainly of ślesas and anuprāsas such as is met with in Kādambarī, Naiṣadha-Carita and Śiśupālavadha are not wanting in our Inscriptions. No. 55 may be cited as an instance of alliterations. Artificial Prose style, chiefly characterised by placing two apparently contradictory statements side by side is illustrated by No. 17.

5. The Chams had evidently a knowledge of the Purāṇas. We have reference to a book called Artha-Purāṇaśāstra in Ins. No. 72, and Purāṇārtha in No. 74, both apparently mean-

1. According to Manusamhita, Chap. I, v. 60, the entire text was narrated by Bhrgu, who originally learnt it from Manu. This is corroborated by Chap. V, vv 1-3 and Chap. XII, v. 2. Thus the text may also be called Bharggaviya, in the sense that it was narrated by Bhrgu.

ing the same thing. From the little knowledge that we have of its contents, it appears to have dealt, among other things, with past and future kings. Now this is exactly in conformity with the treatises called the Purāṇas. The Purāṇārtha or Artha-Purāṇaśāstra thus seems to have been a commentary to or a Cham edition of an Indian Purāṇa.

On the basis of what has been said above we may draw up the following list of the branches of Sanskrit Literature which were studied in Champā.

I. The Four Vedas.
II. The Six systems of Indian Philosophy.
III. The Epics.
IV. Buddhist Philosophy, including the Mahāyāna system.
V. The religious literature of the Vaiṣṇava and Śaiva sects.
VI. Grammar, notably that of Pāṇini, together with its commentary, the Kāśikā.
VII. Astrology.
VIII. The Dharmaśāstras, specially those of Manu and Nārada.
IX. The Purāṇas.
X. Classical Sanskrit literature including Kāvya and Prose Romances.

CHAPTER X.

Architecture and Sculpture.

§ 1. *Plan and Scope.*

The study of the civilisation of Champā would remain incomplete without a brief reference to the architecture and sculpture of the country. Although Champā cannot boast of such splendid edifices as we find at Cambodge and Java, and her monuments, mainly built of bricks, have mostly disappeared, yet the remains, such as still exist, indicate a fairly developed artistic sense and manual skill of her people. As in India, the art in Champā was mostly the handmaid of religion, and the people lavished their skill and resources mainly on religious edifices and images of gods and goddesses. It will be well, therefore, to begin with a description of her temples. The few existing remains of civil or military structures of olden times are almost insignificant in character and will be briefly noticed at the end.

The temples which are in a good state of preservation, or the ruins of which enable us to form a fairly accurate idea of their forms and characteristics are quite large in number. It will be impossible to describe them in detail, nor will this serve any useful purpose to a general reader. I shall therefore begin with a general description of the Cham temples and then proceed to give some details of the three important groups viz. those of Myson, Dong Duong and Po Nagar. This will be followed by a very brief reference to some other important groups or detached temples which show important and characteristic features of a somewhat novel type. Finally, an attempt will be made to make a chronological classification of the different styles and to trace their origin. Those who want to study the subject in greater details may consult the monumental work of Parmentier—"Inventaire Descriptif des Monuments Chams De l 'Annam"[1] from which the following account has been summarised.

§ 2. *General characteristics of the temples in Champā.*

All the temples in Champā belong essentially to one characteristic type, though varying a great deal in detail. They generally face the east and are situated on an eminence, in order, no doubt, to make them visible from a great distance.

The sanctuary or the cella, containing the image of god, occupies the centre. It is a small room with a square base and a pyramidal roof. The Chams call it *Kalan*. It generally faces the east and has sometimes in front of it another building of similar shape running from east to west which serves as the porch or *Nāṭamandir*.

This building has two rooms with a communicating door. Only the western room has a door, opening towards the north: otherwise the rooms are lighted only by the windows. Sometimes we find two subsidiary sanctuaries built in the same line from north to south as the principal sanctuary. These are often later additions. In rare cases this central group of shrines is accompanied by subsidiary temples. Sometimes these are very small and attached to the wall of enclosure. These structures are all built in brick and generally covered by pyramidal arches.

All these buildings are enclosed by a wall and the only access to this sacred enclosure is through a Gate-Tower towards the east. It has the shape of the principal sanctuary, and its two doorways, opposite each other, are approached by two flights of stairs on the east and the west. Be-

1. In the footnotes that follow, chapter, page, figure, and plate, unless otherwise stated, shall be taken to refer to this book.

yond this is often found a Big Hall with tiled roofs, supported by thin walls or merely pillars. There are also other structures close by, which served as record rooms, store rooms etc. In most cases, however, no traces of the wall of enclosure have been found. In these cases either the wall was not built at all, or built of very light materials which have perished.

The interior of the sanctuary is a square chamber. Its vertical walls are plain but polished. Above, the roof consists of one conical vault formed by a succession of rings which rise in gradually diminished proportions as far as the top. At about mid-height between the floor and the summit a stone slab is fixed at each corner with a hole pierced at the end. It was probably a device to put an awning or a canopy above the divine image. The cella usually has only one door towards the east; on the other sides there are niches in the walls which probably served the purpose of lamp-stand.

The idol is placed in the centre of the room on a platform ending in a *Snāna-droṇī*. It has a long narrow projection which serves to carry away water used for bathing the idol. Sometimes there was a *Soma-Sūtra*, either along the ground, or suspended high up in the air, for removing the water outside the room. The sanctuary opens into a vaulted passage which leads to an elaborate doorway with threshold, lintel and frames, all made of stone, and above the lintel is a frame of brick or stone called *tympanum*. The tympanum often contains sculptures which are sometimes of an elaborate character. This massive doorway opens into another vaulted passage which leads to an antechamber or vestibule. This antechamber, which looks like the sanctuary in miniature, is not, however, always present. In such cases the vaulted passage is extended upto the Gate-Tower. The entire building, both sanctuary and the vestibule, is placed on a common foundation which follows in the main the entire outline of the buildings themselves. Only in front of the entrance gateway it is intersected by a staircase.

Externally, the sanctuary consists of a square tower with a *Śikhara*. There are at least three distinct types of Śikharas, but those of the normal type consist of a series of four storeys, one above the other, diminishing as they rise, and crowned by a curvilinear pyramidal stone slab.

The square tower, which may also be regarded as the lowest of these stories, is of course formed by the walls of the sanctuary. Each wall has one elaborate moulding at the base, and another at the top, which may be designated respectively as the Base and the Cornice. The body of the wall is intersected by a number of bold vertical projections with broad flat surfaces between them. These have been termed Pilasters and Inter-pilasters. Sometimes these were decorated by carvings of various patterns.

The Pilasters are usually five in number, but the central one is hidden behind the false doorway which covers the centre of each of the three walls other than that which contains the real doorway. These false doorways are a characteristic feature of Cham temples and will be described in detail in connection with individual temples.

The Base and the Cornice are often decorated with richly carved figures and other ornamental designs, notably, in the case of Cornice, by the frieze of garlands. A peculiar characteristic of the Cham temples is an attempt to strengthen the junction of two Cornices by slabs of stone which are often elegantly carved into beautiful forms of *Makaras* and *Apsaras*.

At the four angles of the Cornice, on the roof of the central tower, are four small towers. Each of these Corner-towers is a miniature representation of the sanctuary itself.

In the vacant space between them but leaving a margin, sometimes broad and sometimes very narrow, rises the first storey of the Śikhara. This storey as well as the next higher one are diminutive forms of the sanctuary itself and possess all its essential parts,—only false niches are substituted for the false doorways, and the number of Pilasters on the walls is gradually reduced to 4 and 3. The 'Base' is also wanting in these upper storeys, but they have, in addition, sculptured stone slabs fixed on the Inter-pilasters. The third storey has usually two, but sometimes no Pilasters. It differs from the two lower stories in one important respect alone viz. the absence of Corner-towers. From the roof of it springs the crowning ornament of the whole building, a slab of stone, square or polygonal at the base and curvilinear and pyramidal in shape.

In addition to the normal type of Śikhara described above, two other distinct types may be noted. The first of these consists of two storeys, the upper one having the shape of an elongated arched vault with ogival ends at two sides and a slightly concave curve at the top. This type will be briefly referred to as 'ridge-shaped with ogival ends.' The third type of *Śikhara* consists of a curvilinear pyramidal dome springing directly from the walls of the sanctuary, and surmounted by a massive circular member of corrugated form, resembling what is called the Āmalaka in the Śikharas of North Indian temples.

The temples in Champā are made of brick though stone slabs are used to add strength or for decorative purposes. Thus the door-frame, lintel, angular pieces etc. are frequently made of stone.[1]

---

1. Vol. I, pp. 17-25.

§ *3. Myson Group.*[1]

The Myson group of temples is situated in a valley formed by the chains of Deo Le, about 21 miles, as the crow flies, south-south-east of Touranne. The valley is almost circular and measures about a mile from the top of one ridge to another. It has only one opening to the north through which a small river drains its waters to the Song Thu Bon.

The temples at Myson may be divided into several distinct groups which cover the valley as well as the low peaks of neighbouring hills.[2] The groups A and A' are on the right side of the river and face the groups B-C-D directly on the opposite bank. A little lower down the river on its right bank is the Group G on a low peak. It towers over the preceding groups as well as on Groups E-F, still further down on the same bank. At about 440 yards from the last, on the same bank of the river, is the Gate-Tower K. On the left bank, lower down the river than the groups B-C-D is the Group H, while a little further up from the former is a small chamber L about the mid-height of a peak. There are also remains of other structures which have almost wholly disappeared.

GROUP A.

The most ancient temples in the Myson group are A-1 and its six subsidiary temples A-2—A-7, three on each side.[3] All these temples are built on one terrace, situated in a large quadrangular courtyard surrounded by brick walls. A Gate-Tower A-8, with two doorways and double flight of stairs, standing on the same line as A-1 cuts this wall

1. Vol. I, Chap. VII, pp. 327-438; B. E. F. Vol. IV., pp. 805-977.
2. Pl. LXVII.
3. Pl LXVIII-LXXII.

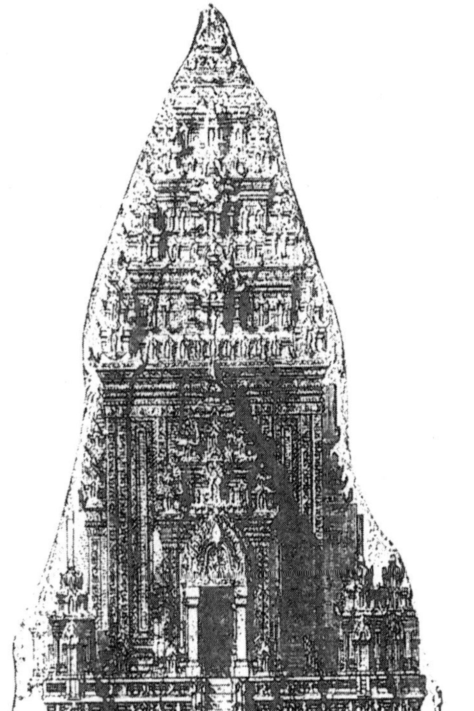

Pl. III. Myson Temple A-1 (cf. p. 241)

(Reproduced from the publications of Ecole Francaise D' Extreme-Orient, Vols, XI, XII viz. Inventaire descriptif des monuments cams by H. Parmentier, Planche LXXII)

3

on the west and forms the main entrance. A Big Hall A 9, which is almost completely ruined, stands in front of A 8, just outside the boundary wall. Within the enclosure are four other subsidiary temples of different styles and of later date. These are A 10, just to the north of the main group, and A 11, A 12 and A 13 bordering the southern and eastern wall.

The temple A-7 opens both towards the east as well as towards the west. It belongs to the normal type of temples described above and is profusely decorated with very elegant carvings. The inner chamber is square and very lofty. The walls begin to bend at about 4-5ths of their height and form an arch. There are six niches in the walls. The idol, a *liṅga*, is now broken, and its *Snānadroṇi* corresponds to the *Soma-Sūtra* in the false doorway to the north. It is impossible to say whether the *liṅga* was turned to the east or to the west.

The two doors of A-1 are connected by two arched passages with two vestibules. The roofs of the vestibules are high and pyramidal in shape.

The vast basement or the terrace of the temples A 1 and A 2-7 presents a cruciform plan and consists of two main stages or stories. These are decorated with fine mouldings, figures of animals and various other fantastic and pleasing motives. The terrace is about 6½ ft. high above the ground level and is reached on the west by a staircase.

Externally, each wall of the temple is divided by vertical projections *viz.* Pilasters and Inter-pilasters, and these are decorated with luxuriant foliage pattern of various designs. The frieze is ornamented by garlands and busts of *Apsaras*.

The false doorways at the sides are also treated as projections. That on the southern side consists of two parts. The upper part is a replica of the temple itself with three niches at the base containing images. The lower one, double in plan, imitates a doorway with side pilasters sculptured with foliage pattern.

In the first stage of the pyramidal roof, each side contains three Pilasters, that of the middle being larger than the other two. The front is ornamented by the head of a monster and foliage terminating in *Makaras.* The false doorways are represented by niches divided into two parts.

The second and third stages are repetitions of the first though on a smaller scale. No data are available for forming an accurate idea of the fourth stage, but it appears that the terminal stone was a conical and curvilinear octagon in shape.

The vestibules were treated as miniature temples. Of the doorways only a few fragments remain.

The temples 2-7.[1]

Around the central shrine there are, as already remarked, six small temples on the same platform. All of them have a separate basement and, with the exception of A 6, resemble the main temple in form. A 6 has no storied pyramidal roofs but its eastern and western walls end in a curved gable. Its faces are ornamented with pilasters.

The other buildings (A 8—A 13) do not call for any particular notice.

GROUP A'.

To the south of group A is found the front of four temples A' 1-4, all open to the east. It is just possible that there was a fifth temple which is now completely gone.

All these temples are now in ruins and they all seem to belong to the normal type.[2]

GROUP B.

This group is the southern-most of all, and is bounded

---

1. Pl. LXXIII—LXXV.
2. Pl. LXXVI—LXXVII.

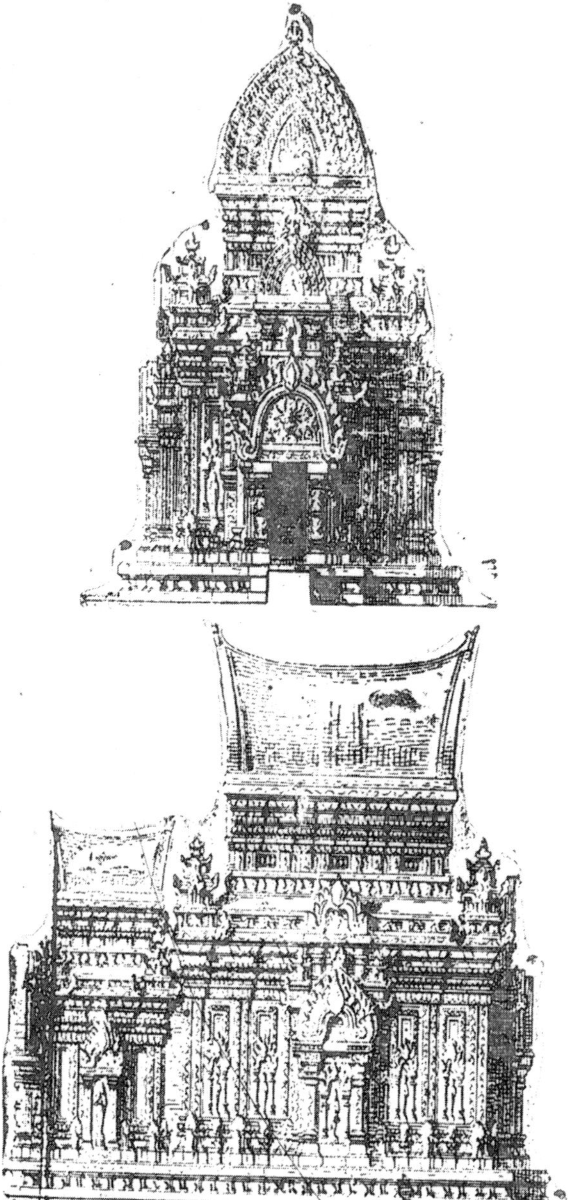

Pl. IV. Myson Temple C—1. (cf. P. 243)

(Reproduced from the publications of Ecole Francaise D' Extreme-Orient, Vols. XI, XII viz. Inventaire descriptif des monuments Cams by H. Parmentier, Planche LXXXII.)

4

by a wall which is nearly a square. In the centre of the enclosure is the principal temple B-1 made mostly of stone but badly constructed. A hall with double doors gives access to the court from the east. Two subsidiary chambers B 5 and B 6 occupy respectively the south-eastern and north-eastern angle. There are two other temples within the enclosure, B 3 in the south-west angle, and B 4 in front of it. There are besides, seven miniature temples B 7-B 13 attached to the enclosing wall.[1]

Lastly, there is a colonnade in front of B 1. The columns seem to have been removed from their original positions, but they are very elegant. The octagonal shaft is fluted and ornamented at both ends. The base and capital are both executed with rare perfection. The abacus is decorated with the busts of 4 figures brandishing a sword of a peculiar kind. The topmost member is a beautiful lotus.[2]

The temple B 5 is of peculiar construction. It has only two storeys and the roof of the upper one is ridge-shaped with ogival ends. It is very ancient and probably of the same age as A 1. B 6 resembles B 5 but is of smaller dimensions.[3]

GROUP C.

This group is enclosed by a wall parallel to that of B, but the principal sanctury C 1 has got a different orientation from B 1. The Gate-Tower C 2 and five other edifices, three temples C 3, C 4, and C 5 and two subsidiary halls C 6, C 7, have all the same orientation as B 1.[4]

The temple C 1[5] is not of normal type. Externally, it resembles B 5 with a vestibule of the same shape. Besides,

1. LXXVIII—LXXIX.
2. Fig 82. p. 377.
3. Pl. LXXX—LXXXI.
4. Pl. LXXVIII.
5. Pl. LXXXII.

the temple looks like two different buildings, the sanctuary and the vestibule being separated by an open space. Internally, the arched vault is not of a regular pyramidal character, but rises straight to a certain distance.

The Gate-Tower C 2, as well as the buildings C 3, C 4 and C 5 all have the same external forms as B 5 and B-7[1]. C 7, C 6 and C 5 are placed close together in the same line from left to right. It appears that C 6 was added at a later period in the vacant space between C 7 and C 5. Both C 7 and C 6 belong to the normal type of temples.[2]

GROUP D.

The two groups B and C contain only the principal parts of two temples. Their Big Halls, which are necessary complements to a temple, are placed together in a common court D. All the three groups are enclosed by a continuous wall which forms a circuit round the northern, southern and western walls of B and C.

The two edifices D 1, and D 2, connected respectively with B 2 and C 2 are both large halls, illumined on each side by three windows. Each is divided into three parts by the pillars attached to the walls, and opens at the two ends by two doorways with the usual passage and porch.

There are two other subsidiary temples D 3 and D 4, and two minor buildings D 5 and D 6 within the same enclosure. Of these D 4 and D 6 appear to belong to the same age as A-7 and the two others are later.[3]

GROUP E.[4]

E 1, the main temple and the central building of this group, differs from the normal type of temples represented by

1. Pl. LXXXIII.
2. Pl. LXXXIV.
3. Pl. LXXXV—LXXXVI.
4. Pl. LXXXVII-XCI.

A 1. It is not covered by a vault of brick, but its comparatively thin walls could only carry a tiled roof, the remains of which now completely cover the building. The inner chamber is square in plan, and has four wooden columns at the four angles. It opens by a doorway to the west, and has in the centre a richly sculptured pedestal carrying an enormous *liṅga*.

There were originally two subsidiary temples E 5 and E 6 to the south and south-west, and a third E 4 was added to the north at a later date. There are two other edifices E 7 and E 8, and a small foundation E 9, no doubt designed for a building which was never finished. Besides, there are a number of pillars in front of E 4 belonging to a building of peculiar shape, the foundation of which has, however, completely disappeared.

All these buildings are enclosed by a wall with a Gate-Tower E 2 in the middle of the southern wall, providing access to the interior. This is preceded by a Big Hall E 3.

Of these temples, E 5 alone faces the east, while all the others face towards the west. It may be noted that Gaṇesa was the deity of E 5. E 7 has a ridge-shaped roof with ogival ends.[1]

GROUP F[2]

This group consists of a central temple F 1. and another, F 3, built to its south at a later date. The whole is enclosed by a wall, the access to the interior being provided by the Gate-Tower F 2. Both F 1 and F 3 seem to have had a tiled roof.

GROUP G.[3]

The principal sanctuary G 1, facing west, occupies the centre of the courtyard enclosed by a wall which is opened by a

1. Pl. XCII.
2. Pl. LXXXVII, XCIII, XCIV.
3. Pl. XCV—XCVI.

Gate-Tower G 2. In front of the latter is the usual Big Hall G 3, and to the north-east of it, outside the enclosure, is a temple G 5, with four entrances on the four sides. Within the enclosure is a residential chamber G 4 at the south-eastern extremity of the court.

The temple G 1, though belonging to the normal type, has certain peculiarities. Its vestibule has three entrances and its foundation has got special decorations. Terra-cotta has been largely used instead of stone, and the false door-ways on the walls are comparatively narrow.

GROUP H.[1]

The principal sanctuary H 1 faces east. In front of it is the Big Hall H 2, preceded by a small doorway H 3, the substitute of the Gate-Tower. This door cuts the enclosing wall in the east and provides access to the interior which contains, besides, a subsidiary building H 4 at the south-eastern angle. It is to be noted that the Big Hall, facing the gate, which is usually situated outside the boundary wall, is here placed within the enclosure itself between the entrance doorway and the temple.

GROUP K.

The group has got only the Gate-Tower giving access to a courtyard enclosed by brick walls. The temples within the enclosure have wholly disappeared.[2]

THE HALL L.

This building erected at the mid-height of a small peak overlooking the groups B.–C.–D. on the south, consists merely of a long chamber without decoration. It has two doorways at the two ends. These are made of bricks and appear to have never been closed.[3]

1. Pl. XCV, XCVII.
2. Pl. XCVII.
3. Pl. XCVII.

GENERAL NATURE AND ANTIQUITY OF MYSON TEMPLES.

The Myson group of temples belonged to the Śaiva cult. This is evident from the *Snānadronī* found in A1 and other temples, and enormous *liṅgas* in A 10 and E 1. *Liṅgas* have also been found in A' 1, [illegible] 4, F 1, F 3, and A' 4, B 1 and probably also C 1 contained imag[illegible] of Śiva. Among other divinities may be mentioned Ganesa (B 3, E 5) and Skanda (in front of B 3).

The subsidiary temples contained the images of other gods. Among the ruins of Group A have been found small figures of Brahmā, Sūryya and other gods and goddesses, and these probably occupied the small temples A 2–A 7. Similarly, the temples B 7-B 13 contained Brahmā, Sūryya, Indra and other deities.

Sculptures on the tympanum and other parts of the buildings represent various Brāhmaṇical gods to which reference has already been made.

A large number of inscriptions have been discovered among the ruins of Myson temples. These are arranged below according to their findspots.

Group A—(On the basement) Inscriptions Nos. 4, 7, 13, 21.
(Near A 10) Nos. 14, 18.
(Near A1) No. 78.

Group B—B 1-Nos. 20, 51, 68, 69, 73, 79, 87, 90, 94, 95, 128.
B 6-No. 16.

Group D—Nos. 62, 65, 70, 81, 84.

Group E—E 6-No. 12, No. 19.
E 10-Nos. 59, 61, 63.

Group F—F 3-No. 17.

Group G—G 1-No. 72,
G 5-No. 74.

It is difficult to fix the precise date of the various temples at Myson. But with the help of the data furnished by the inscriptions and the style of the buildings themselves, they may be arranged in four distinct chronological periods [1]

I. Style of Śambhuvarman (6th-7th century A. D.)

The temples A 1, A 2-7, B 3, B 5, B 7-9, B 11-13, C 1-5, D 1, D 4, D 6, E 1.

II. Style of Prakāśadharma-Vikrāntavarman (7th-10th century A. D.)

(a) Earlier-A 8-13, A' 1, B 4, F 1,

(b) Later-C7, A'2, C 6, E 7, F 3.

III. Style of Harivarman (11th century A. D.) D 2, E 4, E8.

IV. Style of Jaya Harivarman (12th century A. D.) B 1, B 2, D 5, and G, H, K, L,

§4. DONG DUONG GROUP[2]

The ruins of Dong Duong cover a rectangular area of 328 yds. by 164 yds. It is enclosed by a low brick wall which has only one opening to the east.[3]

The rectangle is divided lengthwise in three long narrow blocks of slightly unequal dimensions running east to west. At the western end of the central block is situated the principal sanctuary, A. It is surrounded by four sanctuaries A 1-A 4 built on the same terrace. An imposing building B, with four bays, stands in front of A and there are two other temples C and D and two residential blocks E and F. The whole is surrounded by a wall, forming the first courtyard. Along the sides of this wall, within the courtyard, are seven small temples. A porch in the eastern side of the wall serves as the only entrance to this courtyard. In front of the porch stand

1. Cf. B. E. F. Vol IV, p. 898. Some mistaken views in this article have been corrected in the light of Parm. I. C. Vol. I, pp. 439-505.

2. Vol. I, Chap. VIII, pp. 337-438.

3. Pl. XCVIII-Pl. CV.

two columns, more than 11 yds. high, on two sides of the entrance.

To the east of Court I stands the Court II. It contains a long chamber and is likewise opened at the east end by a second porch preceded by two columns.

To the east of Court II stands Court III. It contains an imposing Hall opening to the east into a third porch preceded by two columns. There are also two side-entrances to the Hall, one in the north and and another in the south.

Then follow a number of long narrow courts, at present full of jungles, till one comes to the fourth porch, which serves as the main entrance to the enclosure and is preceded by two columns.

The first Court is flanked by two others on the north and south. The northern one contains the ruins of three temples, and the southern, those of a square chamber. These two side-courts, together with Court I, are surrounded by a wall, the vacant space within being probably utilised for gardens or temporary sheds which have disappeared. Similarly Court II is also surrounded by a wall of enclosure of nearly the same dimensions.

The south-eastern corner of the rectangular area is covered by ruins of brick buildings and the north-eastern corner by a hollow basin.

It may be noted that the walls of Courts II and III are decorated only on the inner side, and this shows that the long narrow passage which connects the main gate (porch IV) with the principal temple in Court I was the only portion really meant for the public.

The different buildings were possibly constructed in different ages extending the whole group gradually towards the east. It is just possible, however, that all these buildings were part of the original plan and at first made of wood, being replaced at a later date by more durable materials.

The temple is completed by a rectangular enclosure 328 yds. by 270 yds. at a distance of about 850 yards from the main entrance. According to popular tradition it was a reservoir and this view may be correct.

The principal temple in Court " belongs to the normal type—but there are large niches in the interior and big projections in front of the false doorways on the exterior of the walls The buildings have thus the appearance of a cross. In addition to the staircase in front of the main doorway to the east, there is another before the false doorway on the western side. Both are nicely carved and decorated with elegant figures. The false doorways are decorated with richly ornamented pilasters and beautiful statues. The walls of the Court also are decorated with pilasters and figures. In front of them are a series of ornamented brick columns, cylindrical in plan and conical in section. They have a circular base placed on a square block, and are adorned by a series of rings.

The walls of the other two Courts are also similar in design.

It appears from Ins. No. 31 that the ruins at Dong Duong are those of a Buddhist temple and monastery, built by king Jaya Indravarman in 875 A. D. From Ins. No. 36 we further come to learn that the temple was situated within the town of Indrapura which was at that time the capital of Champā, and that the widowed queen of Indravarman, named Haradevī Rājakula installed many gods and goddesses within the temple area. The actual discovery of Buddhist images among the ruins of the temple also demonstrate the Buddhist character of the building.

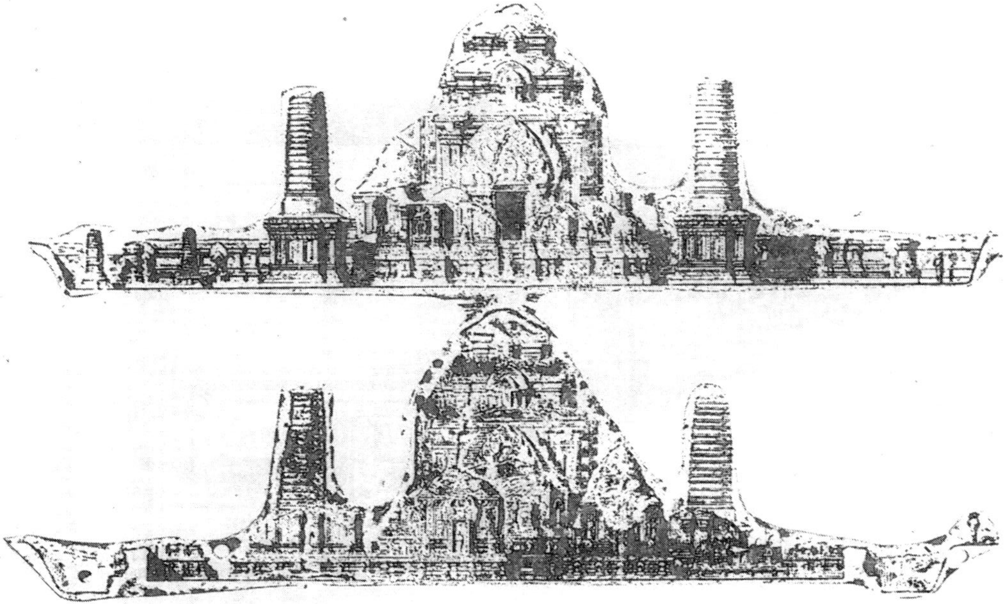

Pl. V. Principal Shrine of Dong Duong Front and Back view. (cf. p. 250)

(Reproduced from the publications of Ecole Francaise D' Extreme-Orient, Vols. XI, XII viz. Inventaire descriptif des monuments Cams by H. Parmentier, Planche CIII).

5

Pl. VI. Po Nagar Temple A. (side-view). (cf. p. 251)

(Reproduced from the publications of Ecole Francaise D' Extreme-Orient, Vols. XI, XII viz. Inventaire descriptif des monuments Cams by H. Parmentier, Planche XXII)

6

§ 5. PO NAGAR GROUP[1]

The temple of Po-Nagar or Yāṅ Po-Nagar, the goddess of the city, is situated close to Nha Trang, at the village of Cu Lao in the district of Khanh Hoa,

The group facing east is situated on the eastern end of a small hillock at the entrance of a valley. It commands a good view of the lagune at the foot of the hillock and of the sea close by.

The temples are arranged in two lines, running north to south, on the top of the hillock. In the front line are three temples, the principal temple A, and two others B and C to its south. In the line behind were also three temples in the same order, F, E, D. In front of A stands a rectangular building of inferior construction, G. All these buildings were enclosed by a wall traces of which still remain to the south and west.

A steep staircase in front of G leads to a lower terrace containing an imposing Hall, M, with a colonnade.

Lastly, there seems to have been a Gate-Tower on the ground level.[2]

The Principal temple A-It belongs to the normal type, but being very well preserved in all its parts, serves as a good specimen of the temples of Champā.[3]

In the interior, the only noteworthy point is a curious system of air-hole. The interior of the roof is a pyramidal vault ending in a long chimney to which are attached, at the height of the third stage of the roof, two cross pipes which extend over the entire summit of the building. The same arrangement exists also in the vestibule. A beautiful figure of Umā is placed in the centre of the sanctuary. There is

1 Vol. I, pp. 111-132.

2 Pl. XX.

3 Pl. XXII.

the usual *Somasūtra* throwing out water across the northern wall.

Externally, the false doorway is of much plainer design than usual. The superstructure consists of a small member of ogival shape super-imposed upon a bigger one of the same shape. Each of these stands upon two pilasters, between which, at the bottom, is a human figure decorated with a *mukuṭa* and with hands joined near the breast.

The roof consists of four stages. On each of these stages, on the two sides of the central niche corresponding to the false doorway, are figures of birds and animals, such as geese, deers and elephants.

The vestibule is a copy of the main building in all its essential features. But the figures of the birds and animals on the roof and the human figure between the pilasters of the false doorway are wanting.

The other buildings. The temple B is of somewhat peculiar design. The false doorway is more complicated, its superstructure consisting of a series of ogee-shaped members of gradually diminished proportions super-imposed upon one another. But the most characteristic feature of the temple is the roof which does not consist of several storeys but of a single curvilinear pyramidal dome of elegant shape. The finials of this dome consist of two bulb-shaped stones with one of *liṅga* form at the top. It may be added that internally the sanctuary shows the same pyramidal arch as in temple A, though a little more curvilinear than usual. The roof of the vestibule also consists of a single arch, the longitudinal section of which would correspond to the shape of the curvilinear superstructure of the prolongation of the upper part of the doorway.[1]

The temple F has got many peculiar characteristics.

1. Pl. XXIII-XXIV.

There are no false doorways, their place being taken by sculptures. The roof is ridge-shaped with ogival ends.[1]

Of the building M we can trace at present only four rows of pillars. According to M. Parmentier's hypothetic reconstruction, its interior was like that of an apsidal Buddhist *Caitya*, having a central nave and two aisles.[2]

A large number of inscriptions have been discovered in the ruins of Po Nagar. These are arranged below according to the findspot.

1. In front of the principal temple A.—Nos. 22, 29a, 29b, 29c, 45, 47.
2. Principal Temple A.
   Interior of the temple, Nos. 30, 50, 109.
   Doorway—Nos. 26, 55, 58, 60, 64, 66, 76, 80, 85, 88. 97, 98, 105.
   Vestibule—48, 49.
3. Temple F.—No. 25.
4. Temple B.—Nos, 71, 108.
5. Under the ground within the enclosure containing temples A, B, C, D, E, F.—No. 99.

Some of these inscriptions refer to the erection of various temples at Po Nagar. The original wooden temple containing a *Mukhaliṅga* must have been built in very early times, so that in the eighth century A. D. it came to be associated with the mythical king Vicitrasagara. This temple was burnt by pirates in 774 A. D. Ten years later, king Satyavarmā built a new temple and installed therein a new *Mukhaliṅga* together with images of other gods and goddesses.[3] In 817 A. D. Senāpati Par erected three temples with maṇḍapas and gates and installed gods and goddesses.[4]

1 Pl. XXV.

2 Pl. XXI, and fig 27, Vol, I, p. 127.

3 Ins. No. 22.

4 Ins. No. 26.

It is difficult to identify the temples mentioned in the above inscriptions with those existing to-day either intact or in ruins. The date, terminus ad quem, of some of the modern temples, however, may be ascertained with a fair degree of certainty from these inscriptions. Thus the main temple A must have been completed by 817 A. D., as the Ins. No. 26, dated in that year, is engraved on its doorway. For similar reasons, the temple F containing the inscription No. 25 must be placed before 813 A. D., and the temple B, containing No. 71, before 1143 A. D.

§ 6. MINOR GROUPS OF TEMPLES

A. *Pho Hai Group*[1]—This group of temples is situated on the top of a hillock near the village of Thien Chanh not far from Phantiet. It consists of three temples in two different levels of the rock. The principal temple, on the higher level, together with another building in ruins to the north-east, is enclosed by a plain stone wall. A little lower down to the north is a third temple, probably contemporary to the principal one. All the temples face the east.

The principal temple differs from the normal type in certain details, such as the absence of Corner-Towers and slabs of stone at the junction of the Cornices, and shows striking affinity to the Cambodgian type. The doorway, particularly, shows a great resemblance.

The absence of Corner-Towers brings out very prominently the resemblance of this type of temples with the storied stūpas of India, from which it seems to have been ultimately derived.[2]

1 Vol. I, pp. 29ff. Pl. I-III

2 Cf. e g. Pl. III With the Dhamek Stupa (Fergusson-History of Indian and Eastern Architecture, Vol. I, p. 72. fig. 16).

Pl. VII. Pho Hai Temples (cf. p. 254.).

(Reproduced from the publications of Ecole Francaise D' Extreme-Orient, Vols. XI. XII viz. Inventaire descriptif des monuments Came by H. Parmentier, Planche III.)

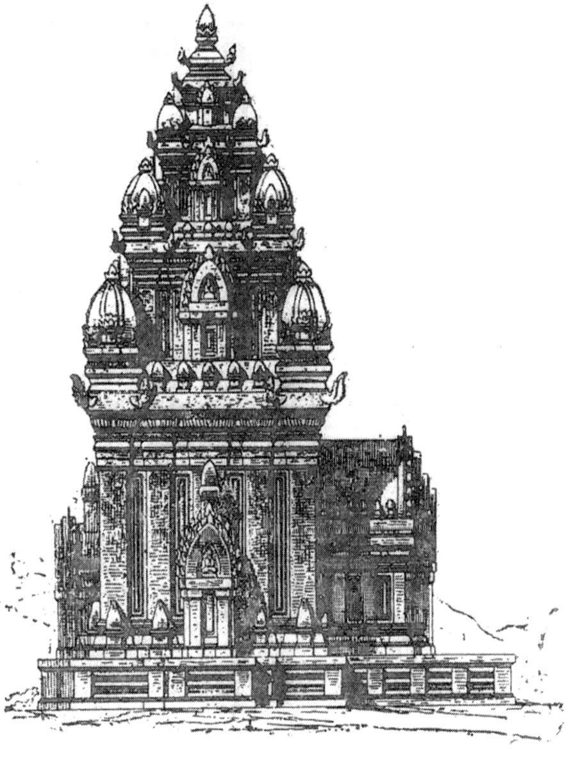

Pl. VIII. Po Klong Garai Temple (Side-view, showing the false doorway on the south (cf. p. 255)

(Reproduced from the publications of Ecole Francaise D' Extreme-Orient, Vols. XI, XII viz. Inventaire descriptif des monuments Cams by H. Parmentier, Planche XIII.)

8

B. *Po Dam Group*[1]—This group of six temples is situated on a hill about two miles north of the village of Phu Dien near the town of Phanri.

The temples are divided into two groups of three each and face towards the south. The principal temple is richly decorated. The upper storeys of one of the smaller temples have curved roofs and show a great resemblance to the small Javanese temples figured at Borobudur.[2]

C. *Po Rome Group*[3]—This group consisting of the principal temple and another building to the south, is situated on a rocky elevation near the village of Hau Sanh in the district of Binh Thuan. The temple which is in a good state of preservation is of very plain design. The only thing of interest is the curvilinear pyramidal shape of the Corner Towers. The southern building preserves decorations in painting, the only extant specimen of that art in Champā.

The presence of very late inscriptions on the door-pillars of this temple seem to confirm the tradition that it was built in the 17th century.

D. *Po Klong Garai Group*[4]—This group of six buildings is situated on a peak which commands a fine view of the plain of Phanrang. The principal sanctuary is very well preserved and enablest us to understand properly the construction of the different parts of temples, even of those which are in a state of decay. Among the peculiarities of the temple may be noted, its high foundation, the prominent cha-

---

I merely throw out a suggestion here as to the ultimate origin of temples in India from which those of Champa are derived (see post). The scope of the present work, however, is not compatible with a detailed discussion of the subject which I reserve for separate treatment in future.

1 Vol. I, pp 50ff. Pl. VI-VII.

2 Vol. I, p. 51. fig 9; Pl. VII-fig 4, 4'.

3 Vol. I, pp. 63ff. Bl. VIII-X; Vol. II, p. 16.

4 Vol. I pp. 81 ff. Pl. XI-XIV.

racter of its false doorways which are almost completely detatched from the wall, and curvilinear pyramidal shape of the Corner-Towers.

The roof of one of the buildings is ridge-shaped with ogival ends.

It appears from Ins. Nos. 111-115 that the principal sanctuary has to be referred to the reign of Jayasiṁha Varman IV (c. 1287-1307 A. D.)

E. *Ho Lai Group*[1]—This group of three temples is situated in the village of Nhon Son, at the end of the long plain which stretches to the north of Phanrang. The temples show high architectural skill. The vestibule, although a mere prolongation of the arched doorway, contains false doorways. The upper part of the false doorways of the temples is of peculiarly elegant design. The walls of the temples are not vertical but inclined outwardly from the base, so that the decorations on the base, although projecting out of it, are on the same vertical level as the top of the wall. The temples are mostly in ruins.

F. *Hu'ng Thanh Group*[2]—This group is situated at the foot of a hill. close to the road which goes from Binh Dinh to Qui Nhon, and about two miles from this last town. There were originally four or five buildings within an enclosure, but at present the ruins of only two buildings can be discerned.

The chief characteristic of these temples is the peculiar shape of the roof, a curvilinear pyramid divided into a large number of parallel stages, very slightly diminishing as they rise.

G. *Duong Long*[3]—This group of three temples is part of a larger group of which only a few traces are visible. It is

1 Vol I, pp. 98ff. Pl. XV-XIX.

2 Vol. I, pp. 146 ff. Pl. XXX-XXXI.

3 Vol. I. pp. 185 ff. Pl. XLII-XLVII.

Pl. IX. Hung Than Temple. (cf. p. 256)

(Reproduced from the publications of Ecole Francaise D' Extreme-Orient, Vols. XI, XII viz. Inventaire descriptif des monuments Cams by H. Parmentier, Planche XXXI.)

9

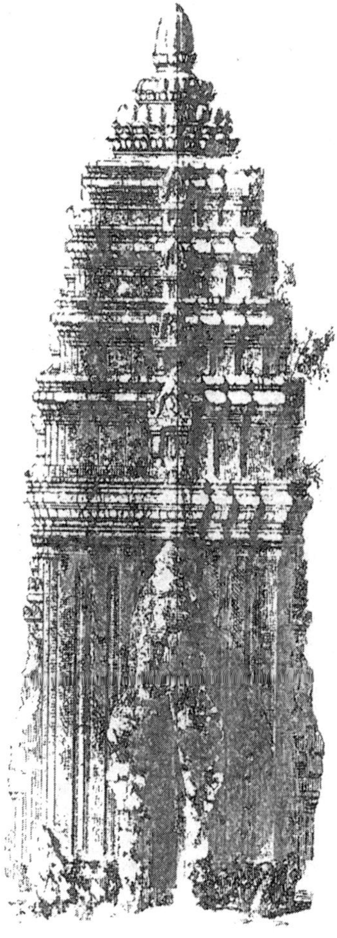

Pl. X. Temple of Duong Long (cf. p. 256)

(Reproduced from the publications of Ecole Francaise D' Extreme-Orient, Vols, XI, XII viz. Inventaire descriptif des monuments Cams by H. Parmentier, Planche XLV.)

10

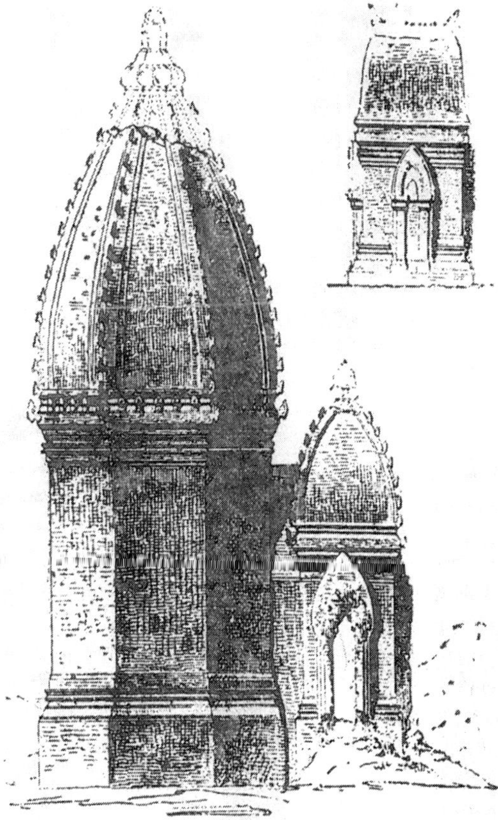

Pl. XI. Bang An Temple (showing in right upper corner a subsidiary temple in S. W.) (cf. p. 257)

(Reproduced from the publications of Ecole Francaise D' Extreme-Orient, Vols, XI, XII viz. Inventaire descriptif des monuments Cams by H. Parmentier, Planche LXV.)

11

Pl. XII. Specimens of Pillars.

(Reproduced from the publications of Ecole Francaise D' Extreme-Orient, Vols. XI, XII viz. Inventaire descriptif des monuments Cams by H. Parmentier, Planche CLI.)

12

situated on a low eminence in the village of Van Tu'ong. These three large temples have some peculiar characteristics. The upper part of the false doorways is elaborately carved. The roofs of stories have no Corner Towers and the uppermost stage is designed like an inverted lotus. The crowning member thus looks like the pericarp of a lotus. It is just possible that its general forms, as noticed in other temples, may also have been derived from this original idea.

H. Other Temples.

Among other peculiar characteristics of Cham temples calling for special notice may be mentioned:

(1) The richly decorated false doorways of the temple of Binh Lam.[1]

(2) The peculiar T shaped inner cell of the southern temple of Khuong My.[2]

(3) The octagonal temple of Bang An with a curvilinear pyramidal roof, belonging probably to the tenth century.[3]

The roof of Yaṅ Proṅ temple which has no stages but consists of a single mass of the shape of a curvilinear pyramid, with horizontal circular ribs, ending in an inverted lotus[4]

§ 7. CHRONOLOGICAL CLASSIFICATION OF THE TEMPLES.

M. Parmentier who has made a special study of Cham architecture has tentatively adopted the following chronological classification of the different styles in Champā, on the basis of temples whose dates can be fixed with a tolerable degree of certainty.[5]

1. Vol. I, p. 169-Fig. 31, Pl. XXXIX.
2. Vol. I, p, 248, Fig. 46., Pl. LVI.
3. Vol. I, p. 311 Fig. 68, Pl. LXV. ; Vol. II, p. 13.
4. Vol. I, p. 557, Pl. CVII.
5. Vol. II, pp. 19 ff.

I. *The primitive art* (7th-10th century), which shows a real inspiration and freshness of artistic idea [1] is represented by the Myson temple A-1 (beginning of 7th century A. D.) and the Po Nagar temples F and A (813 and 317 A. D.).

II. *The cubic Art* (7th-9th century), so called from the low massive roof of the shape of a cube such as that of Hoa Lai Temple, is represented by Myson temple F, (beginning of the 8th century), Po Nagar E (third quarter of the 9th century) and the most ancient part of Dong Duong (875 A. D.).

III. *The Mixed Art* (10th century), which shows the proportions of Primitive Art together with decoration proper to the Cubic Art, is represented by Dong Duong A.

IV. *The Classic Art* (11th Century), so called from its strict adherence to architectural formula, is represented only by Myson E 4 (middle of 11th century A D.).

V. *The Pyramidal form* (10th-14th Century), so called from the pyramidal termination, is represented by the Bang An Temple (c. 900 A. D.), Po. Nagar temple B (1145 A. D.), and Yañ Proñ temple (beginning of 14th century).

VI. *The derived Art* (12th-17th century), so called from its departure from recognised canons, is represented by Myson B-1 (1114 A. D.), Myson G (1157), Po Klaun Garai (beginning of 14th century) and Po Rome (second quarter of the 17th century).

M. Parmentier styles the first three as *Primary*, and the last three, *Secondary*. His ideas of the relation between these classes may be illustrated in the following tabular form.

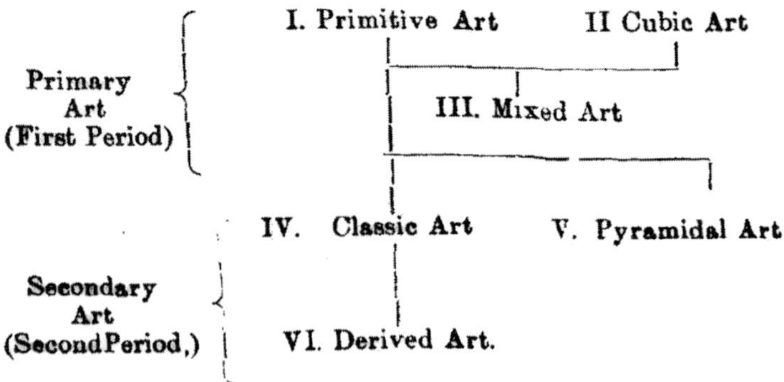

§ 8. THE CAVES.

The cave architecture did not make very great progress in Champā. About five of them are known, all of very simple design, though one or two have massive proportions.

1. Phu Duoc (near Bong Son).

This cave is nearly oval in plan. The inner chamber has a vaulted roof, and two cells radiate from it. One of these is circular and the other rectangular. The cave is entered by a narrow passage opening in the east. A little to the south of this passage on the outer side of the rock is a small cell. The cave is about 4 yds by 2 yds, and the height, a little over 1 yard. It is popularly supposed to be the residence of a hermit.[1]

2. The Marble mountains near Hoa Que contain several caves round a central Hall which is however open to the sky. One of these caves has its entrance guarded by a sculptured balustrade.[2]

3. The caves of Phong Nha (near Bo Trach) are of massive proportions. An opening in the rack about 20 yards long gives access to a circular chamber of the same diameter. Its arched roof is decorated by bunches of stalactites. A low narrow passage about 20 yards long leads to a second vaulted chamber. From this again issues out a very long arched passage, about 20 yards broad and 15 to 18 yards high, whose walls still retain in many places traces of high polish. At the end of this passage, which is more than 1300 yards from the entrance, is found a narrow tunnell more than 325 yards long. The whole of this underground passage, nearly a mile in length, is covered upto a certain height by a clear sheet of water and can be traversed by small boats. The cave contains some sculptures, and the discovery of an image of Buddha

1. Vol. I, p. 218. Fig. 41.
2. Vol. I, p. 317. fig. 69.

and of the word 'Śāriputra' among the almost illegible inscriptions, indicates that it was a Buddhist sanctuary in the origin.[1] Altogether 97 inscriptions have been traced in this cave, but they are mostly illegible.[2]

4. A very small cave named Chua Hang, containing a small statue of Buddha, is situated in the village of Bo Khe near Bo Trach.[3]

5. Some caves, close to the village of Lac Son, were transformed into Buddhist sanctuaries by the Chams. On the side of a mountain washed by a river, an ogival opening, 8 yards by 10 yards, leads to an inner chamber. The side rocks of this chamber have been divided into a number of pillars by the corroding action of water, and the whole thing therefore looks like a peristyle. This peristyle opens into a passage about 90 yards long. Its roof is ogival and about 15 yards from the ground. From the apsidal end of this passage issues another very narrow passage, through which one could crawl into a circular chamber with a diameter of about 4 yards.

From the two opposite sides of this chamber, again, issue two other passages. That on the left or the east is about 12 yards long and has a funnel shaped end. The opposite passage bends round and runs parallel to the long passage in the direction of north to south, till it ends in two very narrow passages.

About thirty-six inscriptions have been discovered in these caves but they have not yet been deciphered.[4]

---

1. Cf. Supra p. 212 of the text.
2. Vol. I, pp. 542 ff.
3. Vol. I, p. 546.
4. Vol. I, pp. 548 ff.

§ 9. CIVIL ARCHITECTURE.

Very little remains of secular buildings have been traced so far in Champā. Of palaces of kings we may form some idea from the accounts of Chinese writers. They were high and of large proportions. The roof was made of ornamented tiles and the whole building was surrounded by an earthen wall. This was plastered with lime and its wooden doors were sculptured with beautiful animal figures. Beyond the wall were vast courtyards for the accommodation of horses, chariots and elephants.

More details are known about another kind of secular architecture viz the fortifications. We have already quoted the Chinese description of the strongholds of Kiu-Sou (pp. 26-27) and Champā (pp. 19-20) which may serve as a type of the rest. Although ruins of several other citadels have come to light, their existing remains in most cases do not enable us to form a clear idea either of their topography or of their principle of construction. But they make it quite clear that the Chams fully utilised the natural means of defence, such as are afforded by hills and rivers, in building their fortifications. A few of these are noted below.

1. The Citadel of Śrī Banoy or Bal Canar, situated on the right bank of the river Song Luy, had the shape of an irregular quadrilateral. Its northern face was washed by the river, and on all other sides it was surrounded by walls. The ramparts of the fortress are represented to-day by mounds, composed of earth and pebbles, about 9 or 10 yards high. The abundance of limonites in the ground shows that this material was used in the process of revetment.

This citadel shows greater knowledge in the art of fortification than any other. We find here an attempt towards 'flanking' and also the protection of the gates. Three salients advance from the three sides not protected by the river, in such a way that one had to pass along one or other of them in order to enter the citadel. There were probably two or three gates, of which one alone now exists in the south-western corner. This together with the south-western salient are the best preserved in the whole group.

Near the centre, but closer to the river side, is a raised platform, the exact nature and object of which is not apparent. It probably served as a reduit.[1]

2. *Thanh Ho.*—This citadel is situated about 10 miles from the mouth of the river Song Da Rang. It is enclosed between a mountain and the left side of the river, and the open face is protected by a wall. It covered an area, nearly 750 yards square, and was protected by a ditch nearly 32 yards wide. It was also protected by reduits and towers, and had several gates. Bricks of enormous size were used in building this fortification.[2]

3. At *Cabau*, the ancient capital-town of *Vijaya*, about eight miles from the citadel of Binh Dinh, are found extensive ruins of what appears to be a first class military fortification of ancient Champa. They cover a rectangular area of over 1500 yards from north to south and of 1200 yards from east to west. It was protected by an arm of the Binh Dinh river on the north and a strong wall, without any flanking, on other sides. The wall was built of earth with revetment of limonite, and was pierced through by tunnels for the ingress and egress of a small brook. There are a number of high mounds on all sides which probably conceal some towers or gates. At present the ruins of one gate only are found but

1. Vol. I, pp. 36 ff. Pl. IV.
2. Vol. I. p. 137, Pl. XXVII.

according to an old plan of the 15th or 16th century it had four gates. The citadel containes a large number of beautiful sculptures.[1]

4. The Citadel of *Chausa* (*Conton* Lin Chau, *Huyen* Binh Sonh).

The ruins of this citadel cover a square area, each side measuring nearly 430 yds. The surrounding walls made of brick have a ditch in front There was probably a gate on each side.[2]

5. The Citadel of *Co Luy* seems to have served as an advanced protection of that at Chausa (No. 4). It defended the access to the Song Tra Kuk river which passed close by the latter. Its sides measured about 163 yds. each, and it was protected by two hillocks one on the west and the other on the south-east[3].

§ 10. SCULPTURES.

The art of sculptor in ancient Champā may be studied under the following heads:—

A Human Figures.

B. Animal Figures.

C. Ornamental Decorations.

A. *Human Figures.*

Human figures in the art of Champā are either detached images or part of decorative elements in the temples. The images, again, are mostly either of gods and goddesses or of kings and queens.

---

1. Vol. I, pp. 198 ff. Pl. XLIX.
2. Vol. I, pp. 235 ff. Pl. LV.
3. Vol. I., p. 235.

1. The Images.

The images of gods and goddesses have been described before. It is needless to say that they form the best specimen of the artistic activity of Champā. It is, of course, idle to expect that all the idols would show a high degree of artistic skill, but some of them at any rate indicate the height of skill to which the sculptors of Champā had attained in this line of activity. The following may be selected as fair specimens.

1-2, Two standing images of Śiva in Myson A 4 and Myson C.[1] The images resemble each other to a great extent. The features, at least of the upper part of the body, are well-proportioned and the expression of face is pleasing. The main defect of Indian Sculptures, viz. the lack of accuracy in physical details, is also manifest in the art of Champā.

3. Even more beautiful than the preceding is an image of Skanda standing on his peacock. By the clever handling of the artist, the body of the peacock has been made the pedestal and its variegated train, a nicely decorated background, for the image of the youthful god. The pose and the expression of the god are really charming.[2]

4. The seated image of a deity in Myson B shows good proportions, but unfortunately the head is missing.[3]

5. The figure of seated Buddha in Dong Duong III, although not very good, reproduces in a striking manner all the features of an Indian Buddha viz. the fold of dress, the Urṇā, the Uṣṇīsa and the arrangement of hair in schematic curls.[4]

Like Indian art, again, the images of gods in later periods became more and more deformed till they assumed some-

1. Vol. I, pp. 362-3. Figs. 78-79.
2. Vol. I, p. 379, Fig. 84.
3. Vol. I, p. 378. Fig. 83.
4. Vol. p. 503, Fig. 117.

Pl. XIII. Statue of Śiva (from Myson Temple A'—4) (cf. p. 264).

(Reproduced from the publications of Ecole Francaise D' Extreme-Orient, Vols. XI, XII viz. Inventaire descriptif des monuments Cams by H. Parmentier, vol. I, p. 362, Fig. 78.

13

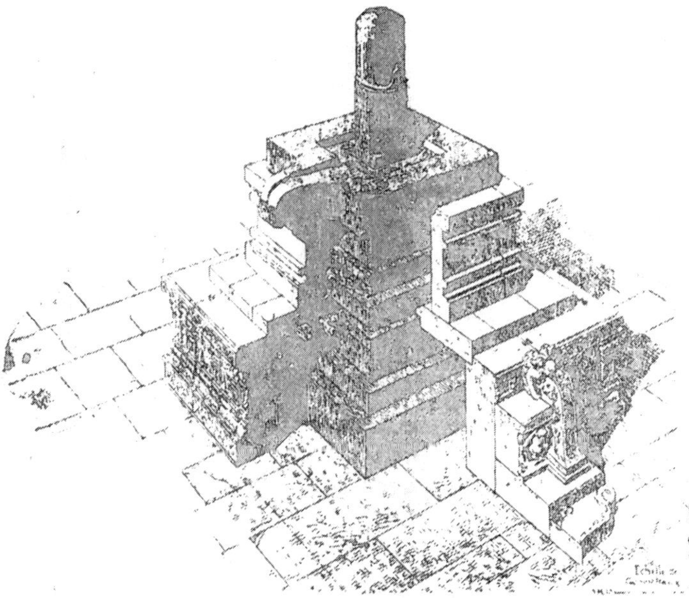

Pl. XIV. Śiva-liṅga (Myson Temple E-1) (cf. p. 177)

(Reproduced from the publications of Ecole Francaise D' Extreme-Orient, Vols, XI, XII viz. Inventaire descriptif des monuments Cams by H. Parmentier, Planche CXX.)

14

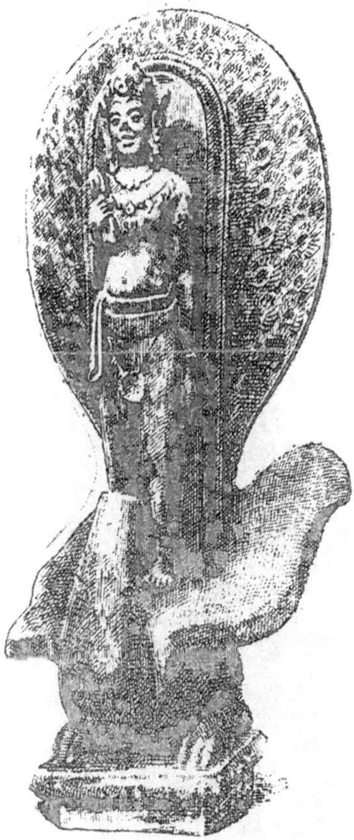

Pl. XV. Statue of Skanda (Myson B—3)
(cf. p. 264).

(Reproduced from the publications of Ecole Francaise D' Extreme-Orient, Vols, XI, XII viz. Inventaire descriptif des monuments Cams by H. Parmentier, vol. I, p. 379, Fig. 84.

15

Pl. XVI. The Statue of Buddha (Dong Duong court III) (cf. p. 264).

Reproduced from the publications of Ecole Francaise D' Extreme-Orient, Vols. XI, XII viz. Inventaire descriptif monuments Cams by H. Parmentier, vol. I, p. 502, Fig. 117.

16

Pl. XVII. Two musicians. (Pedestal of Myson E—1) (cf. p. 265).

(Reproduced from the publications of Ecole Francaise D' Extreme-Orient, Vols, XI, XII viz. Inventaire descriptif des monuments Cams by H. Parmentier, vol. I, p. 410, Fig. 90.

17

Pl. XVIII. Tympanum of Myson C—1
(for description, see pp. 265—6).

(Reproduced from the publications of Ecole Francaise D' Extreme-Orient, Vols. XI, XII viz. Inventaire descriptif des monuments Cams by H. Parmentier, vol. I, p. 391, Fig. 86.

18

times a monostrous appearance. This is best seen in the figures of Dvārapālas which adorned many temples.[1]

There are several statues of kings and queens, mostly of very late date. Artistically, they cannot be pronounced to be successful. Two figures, alone, may be referred to as having reached a fair level of success. These are the figures of king Po Narup and queen Śucih.[2]

2. HUMAN FIGURES IN DECORATIONS.

The human figure forms the most distinguishing trait of decoration in the Primitive art of Champā. It occurs almost in every part of the temple, in various forms and shapes, such as praying figures, persons mounted on *gajasiṁha*, *apsaras*, demons etc. Some of the figures show good proportions and are really charming. Compare, for example, the exquisite figures of two musicians in Myson E, one playing upon a lyre and the other upon a flute.[3]

The Cubic art employs human figures more sparsely. But some of them, the figure of *dvārapāla*, for example, in the false doorway of Hoa Lai, are fairly good.[4]

The most interesting sculptures in temples occur on the tympanums of outer doors which are mostly in stone. In the earlier period they were engraved with composite scenes in bas-relief. As a general rule the principal figure occupied the centre, while the subsidiary figures were ranged on all sides. Two good examples may be noted below.

1. TYMPANUM OF MYSON C.[5]

In the centre, a pedestal, with Nandin sculptured in front, bears the image of dancing Śiva. The upper part of

1. Vol. I, p. 430-431, Figs. 111-112.
2. Vol. I., p. 48. Fig. 8 ; p. 68, Fig. 14.
3. Vol. I, p. 410, Fig. 90.
4. Vol. II, p. 284, Fig. 69.
5. Vol. I, p. 391, Fig. 86.

the image is unfortunately broken, but enough remains to show that the god had a necklace and several hands. There are three figures on each side of the central image. Of those to his proper right, the one nearest to him is dancing, while two others are playing on musical instruments viz. flute and a kind of drum. (*Tabalā*). Of the three figures on the other side, a figure with joined hands probably stands for the king or the donor, while the other two, a female figure and an infant, probably represent Durgā and Skanda. Two trees on two sides, with a parrot on one of them, show that the scene is laid in an open ground. The upper part of the sculpture represents gods or *apsaras* flying through clouds. The whole composition is graceful and charming and reflects great credit on the artists of Champā.

2. TYMPANUM OF KHUONG MY TEMPLE.

It represents Kṛṣṇa as holding aloft mount Govardhana in order to afford protection to the cows and cowherds. The mount Govardhana is indicated by a number of boulders with trees, deers and anchorites moving in them. The cows are shown below in several rows in their true perspective[1]

Another good specimen is the lintel of Chanh Lo which represents a king surrounded by his entourage.[2]

In some cases the tympanum contains a large group of figures, without making any distinction between principal and subsidiary ones. The tympanum of the principal temple of Dong Duong offers an example. It contains about 40 seated figures divided into four or five panels—but they are too imperfectly engraved to give any clear idea.[3]

1. Vol I, p. 259, Fig. 48. Parmentier has here wrongly identified the scene, but cf. Vol. II, p. 425.
2. Vol. II, p. 354, Fig. 90.
3. Vol. I, p. 467, Fig 103.

Pl. XIX. Pedestal of Dong Duong Temple (cf. p. 267).

Reproduced from the publications of Ecole Francaise D' Extreme-Orient, Vols. XI, XII viz. Inventaire descriptif monuments Cams by H. Parmentier, vol. I, p. 470, Fig. 104.

Sometime the tympanum contains one prominent figure only and this is usually the case in later periods. These images are as a rule of inferior type. Two good examples are furnished by the image of Umā in Chanh Lo[1] and an image of Śiva in Po Klaun Garai[2]

Bas-reliefs depicting composite scenes are also found in the pedestals of the First Period. The most remarkable specimens are furnished by those of Tra Kieu and Myson E-1. Both seem to represent some stories which have not yet been identified. Each of the first three faces of the former contains rows of men and women standing in various attitudes and carrying different articles. The fourth face contains eleven dancing women in various postures, probably indicating various forms of dance.[3] The Myson pedestals are each divided into several small panels by decorated pilaster designs. Each panel contains two or three figures in various postures. In several cases two men are engaged in animated conversation while in others they are found playing on musical instruments like flute, drum, guitar etc[4].

The bas-reliefs on these pedestals are of high phonetic value and they may be compared with those at Java. The pedestals at Dong Duong are even richer in composition though of less artistic merit. They depict various scenes of war, procession etc. and deal with quite a large number of human beings of different degrees of status[5].

During the Second Period this art of composing bas-reliefs underwent a rapid degradation and the few composite

1. Vol. I., p. 230, Fig. 43.
2. Vol. II. p. 307. Fig. 76
3. Vol. I, pp. 294-295, Figs. 61-64.
4. Vol. I, pp. 412-413, Figs. 91-92.
5. Vol. I., pp. 470-471, Figs. 104-105, pp. 476-7, Figs. 106-7.

scenes we possess show neither the richness of composition nor the skill of execution such as are noticed in the earlier period.

B. *Animal Figures*—As we have seen above, animals are figured as *Vāhanas* of gods, and they also occur in bas-relief scenes.

Animal figures also formed an important part in decoration in Primitive Art. We meet with a large variety of animals such as rhinoceros, lion, elephant, *Gajasimha*, *Makara*, *Nāga*, *Garuḍa*, bull, horse, hare, deer, goose, peacock and monkey. These are all made with a fair degree of success. Although conventional to a certain extent, the figures are not very far removed from nature. Special reference may be made to a monkey in the Myson Temple D and the head of a lion in Myson K[1].

Later on, in Cubic Art for example, decorations by animal figures were reduced in quantity, being replaced in large measure by floral decorations. But even the few representations of animals in buildings indicate clearly that the Cham artists had not lost their high skill. Some new species appear in this period viz. wild boar, dog and butterfly. In Mixed Art, the representations of animals are almost wholly absent.

During the Second Period the animal sculptures cease to play any important part in the decorations of buildings. Only we find the friezes decorated by long rows of animals. Moreover, the representations of animals become gradually unnatural, conventional, and ultimately hardly recognisable. It may be pointed out here that although the figures of lions are executed with great skill and form an important element in the decorations of temples this animal was unknown in Indo China[2] There can be hardly any doubt that

1. Vol. II, p. 252, Figs. 51, 52.

2. This is the general view But 'lion' is referred to in a single

Pl. XX. Decorative Designs (cf. p. 269)

(Reproduced from the publications of Ecole Francaise D' Extreme-Orient, Vols. XI, XII viz. Inventaire descriptif des monuments Cams by H. Parmentier, Pl. CLXV.

20

Pl. XXI. Pilasters and Inter-Pilaster (with floral decorations) (cf. p. 233, p. 269).

(Reproduced from the publications of Ecole Francaise D' Extreme-Orient, Vols, XI, XII viz. Inventaire descriptif des monuments Cams by H. Parmentier, I, p. Fl. CXXXV.

21

its occurrence in decorations is due to the influence of Indian traditions. The same indeed may also be said of the mythical animals such as *Makara*, *Nāga*, *Garuḍa* etc. The *gajasiṁha* is, however, a peculiar creation of the Chams. It is composed of the body of a lion with the head of an elephant.

The bull appears more as a *Vāhana* of Śiva than a pure decoration, and, as in India, detached images of this animal are often met with in temples.

Certain birds and animals appear only once or twice in bas-relief scenes and do not otherwise play any important part in the art of Champā. Among these may be mentioned squirrel, tiger, parrot, fish and tortoise.

C. ORNAMENTAL DECORATIONS.

The Cham artists excelled in floral decorations. Although they treated foliage in a conventional manner, they added an element of grace and beauty which made it highly charming. This is particularly the case in the Primary Art. The number of specimens collected by Parmentier in Pl. CLXV, shows the high degree of excellence that the Chams had attained in this direction. The style is purely Indian and we find here the same "undulating stem of a creeper with large curling and intertwining leaves.[1] Most of the foliage patterns occur on pillars and pilasters, and are in the shape of scrolls; sometimes, as in India, "the whole scroll is deeply sunk and very clearly and carefully carved". Sometimes the foliage is of an intricate and complex design, but the Cham artists show high skill in handling

Chinese Text. This may be due to faulty reading, or the Chinese author might have made a confusion between a tiger and a lion.

1. Cunningham's description of Gharwa Temple, Arch. Surv. Rep. Vol. III—quoted in V. A. Smith's Fine Art in India and Ceylon p. 166.

it. But here, as in other instances, the history of the art of Champā, like that of India, is written in decay. We miss the vigour and refinement of the early patterns in those of succeeding ages which gradually become lifeless and mechanical in the extreme. In the Second Period when the art of floral decoration was at low ebb and the pilasters were mostly plain, we meet, instead, with geometrical patterns which although lacking the grace and Charm of old, are not altogether devoid of aesthetic elements. A number of fair specimens may be seen in Parmentier's Plate CLXVIII. In one respect, however, the efforts of Cham artists to imitate the Indian models have not proved a great success. The lotus design which forms such a beautiful element in Indian art also figures largely in the art of Champā. But any one conversant with the very elegant and charming lotus flowers depicted. in early Indian art, such as in the railings of Bhârhut and Amarâvatī stūpas, cannot but be conscious of the striking inferiority of the same design in Champā. There are one or two specimens which have attained moderate success, but by far the great majority are but poor productions. A fair idea of this *motif* in the Cham art during the First and the Second Periods may be obtained respectively from Parmentier's plates CLXIX and CLXX.

One characteristic feature of the Cham art in connection with the foliage decoration must be mentioned. The corner pieces of buildings were often made of a highly conventionalised foliage design. Here the stem forms a curved line in the centre and the leaves radiate on both sides in regular schematic curls of gradually reduced proportions. The sharp edges of these curls form indentations on both sides at almost regular intervals, and in many cases the whole thing looks like a curved saw. There are of course variations in their shapes and sometimes figures take the place of the central stem.[1]

Among other decorative *motifs* may be mentioned the rosettes and beads. The rosettes in simple form are found in Myson[2] and with four petals at Chien Dang[3] Alternate courses of beads and petals are found in Myson E-1.[4]

Of the art of painting in Champā we have got only one very late specimen in Po Rome. The *motifs* are similar to those met with in sculpture, and the whole thing has got a pleasing effect.[5]

§ 11. THE ORIGIN OF CHAM ART.

A few words must be said in conclusion regarding the origin of the peculiar style of architecture prevalent in Champā. M Parmentier has discussed this question at great length, and come to the conclusion that the Cham art is not derived from any other known art. He holds that the art is of indigenous growth and derives it from a wooden origin evolved on the soil itself.

It is with great diffidence that we venture to differ from the opinion of one who has probably gone more deeply into the subject than any other living scholar. But the derivation of Cham art from Indian seems to us to be such an obvious fact that it appears impossible to accept the conclusions of M. Parmentier without demur.

It may be stated at the very outset that we are in full agreement with the general principles laid down by Parmentier for guiding a fruitful inquiry into the relations between

1. Pl. CXLVIII.
2. Pl. CLXVI, Figs. E, I.
3. Pl. C. LXVIII-Fig. L.
4. Pl. CLXVI-Fig. V.
5. Vol. II. Fig. 50.

two different systems of art. These may be briefly summarised in his own words as follows:—

"In order to infer the relationship between two arts, it is sufficient merely to point out that both present the same tendencies and possess the same general features. But in order to prove that one system of art is derived from another, it is necessary to show that at a time which is either contemporary or anterior to the earliest specimens of the art which is supposed to be derived, the art supposed to be the origin possessed features common to the former."

Having established this general principle, M. Parmentier proceeds to discuss whether the primitive style of Cham art as exemplified at Myson has any common features with the art of Cambodge, Java or India as it existed in the seventh century A. D., the date of the Myson temples. He points out that Java may altogether be eliminated from the inquiry as its most ancient monument is posterior to this date. As regards Cambodge, the art of Angkor had not come into existence in the period in question, and the primitive Khmer Art was not only very different from but in a decidedly inferior state of development than the primitive Cham Art. Lastly, an examination of the Indian monuments earlier than the seventh century A. D. has led Parmentier to conclude that with the exception of the curved roof, no typical element of Indian architecture appears in Cham style, nor is any typical *motif* of the Cham art traceable in the old Indian style.

It is on this point that we must join issue with M. Parmentier. To us the characteristic feature of a Cham temple seems to be its storied roof of several stages, in gradually diminishing proportions, each of which is again a miniature of the whole. Now this is the characteristic feature of what is known as the Dravidian style and makes its appearance as early as the seventh century A. D. in the Mamallapuram Raths and the temples at Conjeeveram and Badami.[1] Any one who compares the Dharmarāja Rath and Arjuna Rath with the normal type of temples in Champā cannot but be struck with the essential resemblance between the 'Śikharas' of the two. It may not also be uninteresting to note that the Dharmarāja Rath is expressly designated as a temple of Śiva named after the king as 'Atyantakāma-Pallaveśvara', as was the case with the Myson temple which was known as that of Śambhu-Bhadreśvara after its founders. Again, some of the temples (e.g. Myson B-5, B-6, C 1-5) of Champā have an elongated curved roof with ogival ends and this has its counterpart in the Gaṇeśa Rath and Sahadeva Rath. The third type of Śikharas, viz. the curved ones, resembles Draupadi's Rath and is probably derived from those of North-Indian style, as Parmentier himself admits. The basement of the temples at Champā also resembles those at Conjeeveram and Badami. On the whole it seems impossible not to connect the style of Champā with the early Dravidian style both of which rise into prominence more or less about the same time. It is generally held that the rock-cut Raths at Mamallapuram and the other early temples of that type must have been preceded by similar structures of less imperishable materials and the existence of this style in India in and probably even before the 6th century A. D. may therefore be regarded as a certain fact. While we remember that Indians from the eastern part of India played a prominent part in the colonisation of the Far East, and also the great extent to which Indian civilisation had influenced that of Champā, we need not hesitate to trace the origin of Cham style to Indian temples at Badami, Conjeeveram and Mamallapuram—particularly as this part of India was the

1. cf. Fergusson, History of Indian and Eastern Architecture, Vol. I Bk. III, Chaps. III-VII

nearest by way of sea to the kingdom of Champā. It is quite true that the Chams did not blindly imitated the Indian prototypes and added new elements of their own, but the fact that their style was throughout based upon the essential and characteristic features of Indian style, seems to be beyond question.[1]

As regards Cham sculpture and iconography, their striking agreements with the Indian style in both essential and non-essential elements have been shown in the preceding pages, and nobody has doubted or can possibly doubt their Indian origin. As to the relative excellence of the two, opinions might, of course, differ. Both were dominated by religious ideas and the aesthetic sense of the artists in both countries had to be sacrificed in a considerable degree to his religious preconceptions. But even within this limitation Indian artists evolved what may be called high class of art even when judged from a purely aesthetic point of view. Whether the Chams were able to do this, at least to the same extent, may be doubted. M. Parmentier, however, thinks otherwise and prefers the works of Chams to those of the Indians as purer works of art.

---

1. I reserve, for separate treatment, a full discussion of the question involved. Here I merely indicate the conclusions which I shall try to prove by means of copious illustrations in a succeeding volume. It will be beyond the scope of the present work to go into technical details and produce illustrations for a comparative study which alone can lead to a decisive conclusion. For the present I rest content by merely stating my views, and I hope my readers and critics will bear this in mind in forming a judgment on this portion of my book.

After the last pages of the book were printed off, I have come across an article of H. Parmentier "Origine commune des Architectures Hindoues dans l 'inde et en Extreme Orient" published in "Etudes Asiatiques" in which Parmentier has considerably modified his views on the origin of Cham architecture. He now admits an Indian origin as I have contended on pp. 273-4, but instead of deriving the Cham temples from Mamallapuram Raths or similar structures, he traces the origin of all these to primitive Buddhist structures, specially the many-storied *saṅghārāmas* built of wood or perishable materials.

INDEX.

(Ca = Capital ; Co = Country ; dy = dynasty ; K = King ; Km = Kingdom ; pr = province ; t = town ; tr = tribe)

BOOK III.

THE INSCRIPTIONS OF CHAMPA.

PREFATORY REMARKS.

I. As regards the serial number of kings bearing the same name, some discrepancy will be noticed between the headings of Inscriptions and the historical account given in Part I. This is due to the fact that headings of inscriptions have been mostly kept identical with those in the original publications, while a different and independent arrangement has been followed in Part I.* Thus Indravarman and Jaya Indravarman have been usually regarded as two distinct names, whereas the two have been treated as the same in Part I for reasons given on p. 65. The following table shows the name as given in inscription-headings and historical account in parallel columns.

Nos. of Inscriptions.	Name in Inscription-headings.	Name in Part I.
29, 30.	Vikrāntavarman II	Vikrāntavarman III
47.	Jaya Indravarman I	Indravarman III
51.	Harivarman I	Harivarman II
52-58	Jaya Parameśvara-varman I	Jaya Parameśvara-varman III
60.	Rudravarman III	Rudravarman IV
61.	Harivarman II	Harivarman IV
65.	Jaya Indravarman II	Jaya Indravarman V
68.	Harivarma-deva III	Harivarman V
69, 71.	Jaya Indravarman III	Jaya Indravarman VI
72-78.	Jaya Harivarman I	Jaya Harivarman VI
79-83.	Jaya Indravarman IV	Jaya Indravarman VII

*The original idea was to publish only the inscriptions in a separate volume and they were printed before Part I.

Nos. of Inscriptions.	Name in Inscription-headings.	Name in Part I.
85-93.	Jaya Parameśvaravarman II	Jaya Parameśvaravarman IV
94, 95.	Jaya Indravarman V	Jaya Indravarman X
100, 104. 106-109.	Jaya Siṁhavarman II or Indravarman IV	Jaya Siṁhavarman III or Indravarman XI
110-116.	Jaya Siṁhavarman III	Jaya Siṁhavarman IV
122.	Indravarman	Indravarman XII

II. The attention of the reader is drawn to a few serious printing mistakes in the following pages.

Page.	Line.	Incorrect.	Correct.
122.	3.	Rudravarman III	Bhadravarman III
135.	2.	Add after the word "illustrious" in line 2 "King Śrī Jaya Śaktivarman, son of the illustrious."	
157.	17.	972.	986.
215.	13.	Indravarman IV	Indravarman XI
224.	3.	Of Jayasiṁhavarman IV	of Nauk Glaun Vijaya.

III. Please omit the Roman figures at the beginning of the headline of the Inscriptions Nos. 40, 77, 78 and 82.

BOOK III

The Inscriptions of Champa.

No. 1. Vo-Chanh Rock Inscription.

The inscription was edited by Bergaigne (Corpus. No. XX, p. 191), and further commented upon by M. Finot (B. E. F., Vol. XV, No. 2, p. 3).

The inscription is engraved on two faces of a block of Granite, found close to the village of Vo-Chanh in the province of Khánh-Hoà. It contains fifteen lines of writing in the first face, and seven lines of writing on the second face. As these last are line by line continuations of lines 8–14 of the first face, it appears that the first seven lines of the second face are lost. Very little, however, remains of the first seven lines of the first face. The inscription is composed in Sanskrit, and may be referred, on palaeographic grounds, to the third or second century A. D. There are two verses in *Vasantatilakā* metre, and the rest is in prose.

The inscription records the donation made by a king belonging to the family of Śrī Māra.

TEXT.

(६)......प्रजानां करुण......(७) प्रथम-विजय......
.......................(८)......णर्णामस्याम्[1] ।
आज्ञापितं सदसि राजवरेण.................
(९)................राजगण-वागमृतं पिवन्तु ॥
श्री-मार-राजकुल-व ˘ (१०) ˘—˘— न[2]
श्री-मार-लो ˘ न् ˘—[3] कुलनन्दनेन ।
आज्ञापितं स्वजन-स ˘ (११) ˘—˘ मध्ये
वाक्यं-प्रजा-हितकरं करिणोर्व्वरेण ॥

---

1. Bergaigne reads: "र्णमन्यम्". The above reading is that of Finot. It is no doubt the last portion of the word 'पूर्णिणामस्याम्'.
2. Finot Suggests 'वंशविभूषणेन'.
3. Finot Suggests 'लोकनृपतेः'.

लोकस्यास्य गतागति वि (१२)..............न सिंहासनाध्यासीनेन पुत्रे भ्रातरि नान्त्यके[1] स्वसमीकरणच्छन्देन (१३) (तृ)तेषु यत्किञ्चिद् रजतं सुवर्णमपि वा सस्थावरजङ्गमं कोष्ठागारक......
...............(१४) नं प्रियहिते सर्व्वं विसृष्टं[2] मया तदेवं मयानुज्ञातं भविष्यैरपि रा (१५) जभिरनुमन्तव्यं विदितमस्तु च मे भृत्यस्य वीरस्य... ....

TRANSLATION.

(6) Mercy for the people...........

(7) First conquest.....................

(8) Ordered by the excellent king in the assembly, on the full-moon day (?).

(9) Let them drink the nectar of the words of kings.

(10–11) Royal family of Śrī Māra...... .. .. He who is the delight of the family of Śrī Māra, and conversant with the ways of the world, being seated on the throne, said (the following) words, beneficial to the people, in the midst of his own kinsmen, (12) after having satisfied his sons, brothers and kinsmen (?) by enjoying wealth in common with them.[3]

(13) "Whatever silver, gold, movable and immovable property and stores (of grain ?) that I possess,

---

1. 'एकार' is doubtful.

2. Finot reads 'विषृष्ट'—apparently a slip for विसृष्ट which is clear on the estampage.

3. I do not understand the meaning of the word 'करिणोच्चरेण' and 'नान्त्यके'. The last, used along with sons and brothers, seems to denote 'kinsmen' or 'relatives'. Bergaigne takes it in the sense of 'no one else', but the use of the plural 'तृप्तेषु' in the absolute construction compels us to reject this view. That participle, being in the plural, requires at least one more subject other than 'भ्रातरि' and 'पुत्रे'.

(14) All that I consecrate to those who are dear and near to me. This is my commandment, and the future kings also should

(15) approve of it. Be it known to my heroic servant (or servant called Vira).

Nos. 2 and 3. Cho Dinh Rock inscriptions.

These inscriptions were edited by M. Bergaigne (Corpus No. XXI, p. 199), and commented upon by Finot (B. E. F., Vol. II, p. 186).

The inscriptions are engraved on a rock, situated in the village of Nhan-thap, in the province of Phu-yen, to the north of cape Varella. Cho Dinh is really the name of a market-place in the neighbourhood.

No. 2 contains 3 lines, and No. 3, one short line, in Sanskrit prose. The characters seem to be very ancient and may be referred to about 400 A. D.

No. 2 contains the name of king Bhadravarman and refers to a sacrifice offered to Śiva, called Bhadreśvarasvāmin, by Mahārāja Bhadravarman or one of his descendants.

No. 3 probably refers to human sacrifice, but it is not certain. Both the inscriptions seem to belong to the same age, and were probably written by the same individual.

TEXT.

No. 2.

(१) नमो देवाय भद्रेश्वरस्वामिपादप्रसादात् अग्नये त्वा जुष्टं करिष्यामि (२) धर्म्ममहाराज–श्रीभद्रवर्म्मणो यावच्चन्द्रादित्यौ तावत् पुत्रपौत्रं मोदयति (३) पृथिविप्रसादात्[1] कार्म्म[2]सिद्धिरस्तु॰।

---

1. Read पृथिवी–प्रसादात्.
2. Read 'कर्म्म'.

No. 3.

शिवो दासो बध्यते ।

TRANSLATION.

No. 2.

Reverence to God! By the favour of the feet of the Bhadreśvarasvāmin I shall make thee agreeable to Fire (*i. e.* sacrifice thee). So long as the Sun and the Moon endure, he (Agni) will save the sons and grandsons of Dharma-Mahārāja Śrī Bhadravarman. May the work (sacrifice) be successful through the grace of the earth.

No. 3.

Śiva,[1] the slave is bound (to the post).

No. 4. My-son Stelae Inscription of Bhadravarman.

The inscription was edited by M. Finot (B. E. F., Vol. II, p. 187).

The village of My-son, containing vestiges of many monuments of the past, is in the district of Quang Nam (for detailed accounts of the ruins of My-son, cf. B. E. F. Vol. IV, p. 805). The inscription, engraved on two faces of a stelae in front of the large temple of My-son to the east, contains 21 lines of writing. The language is Sanskrit, and the inscription is written throughout in prose. There are, however, mistakes in spelling and grammar.

The inscription records the donation of lands to the God Bhadreśvara. Although the author of the inscription speaks of himself in the first person, and refers to king Bhadra-

1. Bergaigne takes the word 'Śiva' as an adjective to 'dāsa', and translates it as 'auspicious' (propitiatoire).

varman in the third person, it is clear from lines 5 and 11, that the endowment was given by the king himself.

As the God Śiva is called Bhadreśvara, it would follow that the temple was also founded by Bhadravarman. For it was a well known usage in these countries to designate Śiva by a term composed of the first part of the king's name and the word Īśvara. It may be argued, of course, that the temple was founded by a predecessor of the king, also called Bhadravarman. But the endowment of lands, consisting practically of the entire valley in which the temple is situated, precludes this idea,—for if there had been a temple already in possession of any part of these territories, the fact would have been mentioned.

Judging from the number and beauty of temples which once surrounded the shrine, and the many endowments that have been made to it by successive kings, the temple of Bhadreśvara seems to have enjoyed a very high prestige in Champā.

TEXT.

(a).

(१) सि[1] द्धं नमो महेश्वर उमाञ्च प्र......(२) ब्रह्माणं विष्णुमेव च नमो पृथिवी वायुराकाशमप (:) (३) ज्योतिश्च पञ्चमं नमस्कृत्वाह मिच्छामि सर्वविशेषैरनुध्यातं दुस्कृ(त्क) (४) र्म्मव्यपोहन् (तु) सुकृतो नयुतन्तुदा[2] भद्रेश्वर स्वामिपदानुध्या(ने)न चास्माक(म्) महारा (जेन) (५) भद्रवर्म्मणा मानुष्यमध्वानं ज्ञा(त्वा) भद्रेश्वराय अक्षयी नीवी दत्ता यथा (पूर्वेण)[3] (६) सुलहपर्व्वतो दक्षिणेन महापर्व्वतः पश्चिमेन कुचकपर्व्वत उत्तरेण म(हानदी) (७) परिमाणाभ्यन्तरा सकुटुम्ब-

1. The इकार is doubtful.

2. The passage is corrupt. Apparently the writer intended to say "व्यपोहितुं सुकृतं नयश्च तनितुम्".

3. This is the corrected reading cf. B. E. F. Vol. XVIII, No. 10, p. 14.

जना भूमि[1] दत्ता जनपदमर्य्यादा (:) पड्भागे पि......(८) स्वामिना दशभागेनानुगृहीता देवस्य देय (आ) इन् (इ) तदेव यथाभिलिखितमकुर्व्व(तो) (९) देवस्य जन्मप्रभृति धर्म्मप्रसवो यः तत्फलं भद्रवर्म्मणः यदि कश्चिद् (आ)कस्य हर(नि) (१०) विनाशयति वा मुक्तदोषा[2] कुटुम्बिनः तस्योपरि अधर्म्म[3] स्यात् चातुर्व्वैद्यं राजा(नम्) (११) राजमात्रं वा सह कुटुम्बिभिः विज्ञापयामि ममानुकम्पार्थं यन्मया दत्तं मा विनाशय(त) ॥

(b).

(१) यदि विनाशयथ जन्मनि जन्मनि वो यत्सुकृतं तन्मम स्यात् (२) यच्च मम दुष्कृतं तद् युष्म्(आ)कं स्यात् अथ सम्यक् परिपालयथ तद् युष्माकमेव (३) धर्म्म[4] स्यादिति भूयो विज्ञायामि[5] य इह प्रभवति......................देवब्रलिकारकाः (ने-) (४) (पा)ङ् कर्म्म न कारयितव्यं स्याद्. ओर.........रत्रगतं वा राजकुलकार्य्यमनुष्ठेयं......(५) (अ)थ गुरो ऽस्माकं राजान् (ा)......यन् किञ्चित् ....फलाद्येषु पादेषु पदितव्यमिति (६)............[6] (७) कुशालायतनाः वहुलरत्न च.........[7] (८)..............[8] अयन् न स्वरतो धर्म्मभव.........(९)...............पालयति तस्यैव धर्म्म (:) यो नतु पालति[9] अभिनाशयतु अथ विनाशयति (१०)..................तस्य भद्रेश्वरस्वामि जानाति ॥

TRANSLATION.

(a).

(1) Perfection has been attained. Reverence to Maheśvara and to Umā.........(2) to Brahmā and to Viṣṇu. Reverence to the Earth, Wind, Sky, Water (3) and fifthly, the Fire.

1. Read 'भूमिर्'.
2. Read मुक्तदोषाः.
3. Read अधर्मः.
4. Read धर्मः.
5. Read विज्ञापयामि.
6. About 27 akṣaras.
7. About 16 akṣaras.
8. About 18 akṣaras.
9. Read पालयति.

Having saluted them I wish all eminent people to note the following: That with a view to (4) atone for all evil deeds, and to perform good and virtuous work,[1] and having realised the destiny of human life,[2] a perpetual endowment has been given to Bhadreśvara by our king Bhadravarman, who is devoted to the feet of Bhadreśvarasvāmi: To wit, (6–7) the land within (the boundaries *viz.*) Sulaha mountain in the east, the great mountain in the south, the Kucaka mountain in the west and the Great River in the north, together with its inhabitants, has been given. (8) The (royal share of the) revenue consisting of a sixth of the produce, but reduced, through the favour of the Lord (king ? or the owner of the temple to which land is given ?) to one-tenth, is to be given to the God. If what is written above is not done for the God by anybody, (9) the fruit of merits, acquired by him since his very birth, belongs to Bhadravarman. But if somebody plunders, or destroys it by force, then (10) the people are exempt from guilt which falls upon that man alone. To the king, versed in the four Vedas, and to his (11) officers and other people, I declare: Out of compassion for me don't destroy my gifts.

(b).

(1) If you destroy it, all your good deeds in your different births shall be mine, (2) and all the bad deeds done by me shall be yours. If, on the contrary, you properly maintain

1. This portion of the text is not quite intelligible, but the above rendering seems to bring out the sense intended to be conveyed.

2. Finot translates "ways of man". For the use of the word 'adhvan' in the above sense cf. Durmaraṃ purusheṇeha manye adhvanyanāgate. (Mahābhārata, Aśvamedhaparvan ch. 80, v. 24. Bombay Edition).

(the endowment), (3) the merit shall belong to you (alone). I again declare............[the broken fragments in Lines 4–8 do not yield any sense] (9) he who maintains. the merit belongs to him. He who does not maintain but destroys, will himself be destroyed......(10) Bhadreśvarasvāmi knows.

No. 5. Chiêm-Son Rock Inscription.

The inscription was edited by Finot (B. E. F., Vol. XVIII, No. 10, p. 13). It is engraved on a rock, overhanging the river Song-Thu-bon, a little to the east of My-son. It contains four lines, and describes the boundaries of the temple of Bhadreśvara. To the east. 'Sulaha mountain',—to the south, the Great (mountain),—to the west, Kucaka mountain,—and to the north, the Grand River *i. e.* Song-Thu-Bon. The writing belongs to the period of Bhadravarman (5th century A. D.).

Although similar boundaries are given in two other inscriptions (Nos. 4 and 7), the northern boundary is given here for the first time. It shows that the boundaries given are not those of My-son circle, but of the dominions belonging to the temple.

TEXT.

(१) पूर्व्वेण सु

(२) ह पर्व्वत

(३) दक्षिणेन महा............पश्चिमेन कुचक प-

(४) र्व्वत............उत्तरेण महानदी ।

Comparing the above with the relevant portions of Nos. 4 and 7, we may restore the text as follows:

पूर्व्वेण सुलहपर्व्वतो दक्षिणेन महापर्व्वतः ।
पश्चिमेन कुचोकपर्व्वत[1] उत्तरेण महानदी ॥

---

1. Finot formerly read it as 'कुचक°' but later on suggested the reading 'कुचोक°'. He takes it as an indigenous word meaning 'the august mountains'.

TRANSLATION.

To the east, the Sulaha mountain, to the south, the Great mountain, to the west, Kucoka mountain, to the north the Great River.

No. 6. Hon-Cuc Stone Inscription.

The inscription was noticed by Aymonier (J. A. 1896 part I, p. 149), and edited by Finot (B. E. F. Vol. II, p. 186).

It was engraved on a rock called Hon-Cuc near the village of Chim-Son in the province of Quang-Nam. It contains two lines in Sanskrit, and probably belongs to the time of king Bhadravarman.

TEXT.

(१) नमो भगवतो महादेवाय भद्रेश्वरस्वामिनः

(२) शिरसा प्रणिपत्य ।

TRANSLATION.

Reverence to the August Mahādeva Bhadreśvarasvāmi by bowing down the head in obeisance.

No. 7. My-son Stelae Inscription of Śambhuvarman.

The inscription was edited by M. Finot (B. E. F. Vol. III, p. 206) without any translation.

For localities cf. No. 4. It is engraved on a stelae close to the one containing No. 4, and is practically a continuation of the latter. It contains 24 lines of writing in Sanskrit. There are three verses in *mandākrāntā* metre. The rest is in prose.

The inscription refers to two kings Śrī Rudravarman and his successor (probably also son) Śambhuvarman. During the reign of the first, in the year four hundred and........... (the tenth and unit figures being lost), the temple of the God of Gods, *i. e.* the one erected by Bhadravarman I for Bhadreśvara (cf. No. 4), was destroyed by an incendiary. But king Śambhuvarman re-installed the God under the name Śambhu-Bhadreśvara (apparently so called after the original founder of the temple and its restorer). The inscription also confirms the grant of land made originally in No. 4.

TEXT.

(१) ....तिः ॥

गंगेशस्य ˘ र ˘ ˘ ˘— — ˘ — — ˘ — —

(२) — — — —˘ ˘ ˘ ˘ ˘— —˘—(स्य) गुणानाम् ।

बिभ्रद् गुर्वीं धुरमनवरात् (मा) ˘— —˘— —

(३) — — — —˘ ˘ ˘ ˘ ˘ (श्री रु) द्रवर्म्मा नरेन्द्रः ॥

तस्मिन् ब्रह्मक्षत्रियकुलतिलके श्रीरुद्र (४) (वर्म्मणि)...........
......युत्तरेषु चतुर्षु वर्षशतेषु शकानां व्यतीतेष्वग्निदग्धं देवदेवाल—
(५) (यम्)........................

स्थित्युत्पत्तिप्रलयवशिनश्शूलिनस्समराणां

संस्थि[1]—नां अदहदनहि—˘—˘ ˘— — ।

(६) — — — —˘ यममलिनो वद्यवेत्तृस्वभावः[2]

कृत्स्नं वेत्ति त्रिभुवनगुरु+कारणं स्थानुरेव ॥

(७) ....परिमाणे शककाले स्वपुण्यातिशयाद् दिवं अधिरूढस्य श्रीरुद्रवर्म्मणो (८)..............ति गुणा विभव ....प्रमहान्यशास्यमलि (९)..............रता स्वकृत्यमतिहान-सात्म्यं स. वे समस्तं इह यस्य तृ......(१०)..............लप्रसूतो नितान्तोर्ज्जितश्श्रीशम्भुवर्म्माभिषेकनामा ॥ धृतसुचरि (११)...... ....धाम्ना प्रकाशः वसतिरवनिसूर्य्यस्सम्पदा ख्यातवीर्य्यो (१२)..............श्री प्रशस्तधर्म्मदिण्डिकनामा ॥ प्रकृष्टधर्म्मसगुणो न्न (१३)..............मी शरत्प्रदोषेन्दुरिवाभ्युदेति...........(१४)

---

1. Read 'संस्थानानाम्'.

2. Read 'वेद्य'.

......................(१५) (ई) द्रयोगे भार्ग्गवदिवसे स्थिरहोराद्रेक्का णनवांशकत्रिशद्भागमौरिका............(१६).........(ल)ग्ने सुविशुद्धे[1] तृतीयादित्यकेतुचतुर्थासुरगुरुजीवबुधषष्ठराहु.........................
(१७).........मस सप्तचत्वारिंशत् कुड़वासु सप्तदश नालिकासु पुरस्कृत गोपस्व (१८).........ब्रह्म दुर्व्वलिरम्भसामि जातरूपाग्रसनिकसहितेन[2] ब्राह्मणेस्वतिशयाचार्य्ये (१९)...................न श्रीशम्भुवर्म्मणा प्रतिष्ठापितः ततश्शम्भुभद्रेश्वरः ॥

सृष्टं येन त्रितयमखिलं भूर्भुवस्स्वः (२०) स्वशक्त्या
येनोत्खातं भुवनदुरितं वह्निनेवान्धकारम् ।
यस्याचिन्त्यो जगति महिमा यस्य नादिर्न चान्तश्
(२१) चम्पादेशे जनयतु सुखं शम्भुभद्रेश्वरोऽयम् ॥

अपि च भद्रवर्म्मणा राज्ञा येयं अक्षयिणी भूमिः
(२२) सकुटुम्बिजना दत्ता तस्याः पूर्व्वेण सुल्लहपर्व्वतो दक्षिणेन महापर्व्वतः पश्चिमेन कुचकपर्व्वतः
(२३) ....भूमौ ये कुटुम्बिनो निवसन्ति तैर्द्दशमो भागो दातव्यो राजाधिराजे............
(२४) ....स्थितिमनुपालयाद्भिर्न विनाशयितृ—
(भिः).................

TRANSLATION.

(Fragmentary passages not conveying a complete sense are mostly left out.)

(1) ....of Gaṅgeśa.

(2) ....of qualities.........carrying weighty burdens

(3) King (Śrī Ru)dravarman.

During the reign of that Rudravarman, the ornament of the Brahma-Kṣatriya family, (4) while four hundred (and ....?) years of the Śakas had elapsed, the temple of the God of Gods was burnt by fire.

1. The एकार is not distinct. 2. Read जातरूपामात्तनिकस्सहितेन.

(5–6) The God with trident,[1] the controller of creation, maintenance and dissolution: who, though not unfriendly, yet burnt (*i. e.* destroyed) all forms including Gods; who is unblemished and by nature both a knower as well as an object of knowledge;[2] is one fixed cause of the universe, the preceptor of the three worlds, and knower of all things.

(7) Of Rudravarman who has ascended to heaven by the abundance of his virtues in the Śaka year.........

(10) Having Śrī Śambhuvarman as the coronation name.

(11) who, a Sun in earth, is famous for his prowess.

(12) Whose name is Śrī Praśastadharma [diṇḍika[3]].

(13) Possessing excellent qualities he shines like the moon of autumn evening.

(15–17) [Astronomical details.]

(18–19) Then Śambhu-Bhadreśvara was established by Śambhu-Varman, accompanied by Durvvalirambhasāmi, the priest, and Jātarūpa who is entitled to foremost seat of honour.[4]

(19–21) May this Śambhu-Bhadreśvara—by whom, by his own prowess, the three worlds, *bhūḥ*, *bhuvaḥ* and *svaḥ* have baen created, by whom the sin of the world has been removed even as darkness is expelled by fire, whose glory is unthinkable in this world, who has neither beginning nor end—(may He) cause happiness in the kingdom of Champā.

---

1. Here sixth case-ending is used for the first.

2. Cf. Gītā "वेत्तासि वेद्यञ्च परञ्चधाम त्वया ततो विश्वमनन्तरूपम्".

3. Finot takes 'दिण्डिक' as an ascetic, and is inclined to the view that Praśastadharma was his religious name as opposed to the coronation name. Most probably Praśastadharma was his ordinary name as opposed to coronation name.

4. This is the only interpretation of l. 18 that occurs to me. But the passage in very obscure.

(21) Again, the land, with its people, which was given as perpetual (endowment) by king Bhadravarman (22) is bounded by Sullaha mountain in the east, the Great mountain in the south, Kucaka mountain in the west,............... (23) tenth part is to be given by the people who live in the land..............

(24) This endowment is to be maintained, not destroyed.

No. 8. Hue Stelae Inscription.

It is mutilated and contains only the last seven lines of a Sanskrit Inscription. It contains an imprecation against those who would destroy the endowments given by............ Varman, king of Champā, to the God Kandarpa-Pureśvara.

As Bhavapura was the name of the capital of Bhavavarman of Cambodge, and Indrapura, that of Indravarman of Champā, so Kandarpapura might be the name of the capital in the time of Kandarpadharma. The inscription may therefore be referred to Kandarpadharma or one of his successors, and the capital of this king may be looked for in the neighbourhood of Hue.

B. E. F., Vol. XI, p. 259.

No. 9. Trà-kiêu Rock Inscription of Prakāśadharma.

The inscription was edited by M. Huber (B. E. F., Vol. XI, p. 263). It is engraved on one face of a cubic block of stone found at Trà-kiêu in the province of Qnang-Nam. It contains four lines of writing. The language is Sanskrit. The inscription is written throughout in verse, and contains 2 stanzas in Āryā metre.

The inscription refers to some gifts of king Śrī Prakāśadharma, king of Champā, in honour of king Kandarpadharma, the father of his great-grandmother (grandfather's mother).

TEXT.

(१) शक्तिः परस्य न रिपुं क्षपयति गमितापि दण्डभेदभयेन ।
(य)स्य त्वदण्डभेदा सकलमरिमभीर्भिनत्ति शक्तिभृत इव ॥
(२) स श्रीप्रकाशधर्म्मा नृपतिः कन्दर्प्पधर्म्मणो धरणिभुजः
प्रपितामहीपितुरिदं स्थापितवानर्चनाय हटकयुगलम् ॥

TRANSLATION.

(1) The power[1] (lance) of other (kings), even when aided by much dreaded political expedients like *daṇḍa* (punishment) and *bheda* (disunion)—(even when applied with such force as to make the staff of the lance liable to break)—is not able to crush the enemy. There is, however, a king, who, like Kumāra, breaks through all his enemies, without fear and unaided by the political expedients of *daṇḍa* (punishment), and *bheda* (disunion)—(without wielding the lance so powerfully as to break it).

(2) He, Śrī Prakāśadharmma, established this pair of haṭakas[2] in honour of king Kandarpadharma, the father of his great-grandmother (grandfather's mother).

---

1. The word śakti, and its adjectives, are throughout used in a double sense, as shown within the brackets.

2. The meaning of the word 'हटक' is unknown. The word is probably हाटक, which is the name of a God cf. 'हाटकेश्वर माहात्म्य' in the Skanda Purāṇa.

No. 10. Thach-Bich Rock Inscription of Prakāśadharma.

The inscription is engraved on a rock in a river-bed in Thach-Bích in the district of Quang-Nam.

TEXT.

(१) श्री चम्पेश्वरो विजयी महीपति...........श्री

(२) प्रकाशधर्म्मेति स्थापितवानमरेशमिह ॥

TRANSLATION.

Śrī Prakāśadharma, king of Champā, always victorious, master of the land,...................has installed here the God Śiva (Amareśa).

(As there is no room in the rock for a temple, possibly the image referred to is a Liṅga.)

B. E. F., Vol. XI, p. 261.

No. 11. Duong-Mong Pedestal Inscription of Prakāśadharma.

The inscription is engraved on one side of a stone pedestal at Duong-Mong in the district of Quang-Nam.

TEXT.

(१) इदं भगवतः पुरुषोत्तमस्य विष्णोरनादिनिधनस्याशेष-
भुवन—

(२) गुरोः पूजास्थानं श्रीप्रकाशधर्म्मणा कारितम् ॥

TRANSLATION.

This temple of God Viṣṇu Puruṣottama, who is without beginning or end, who is the preceptor of the whole world, was built by the order of Śrī Paakāśadharma.

B. E. F., Vol. XI, p. 262.

---

12. My-son Stelae Inscription of Prakāśa-dharma, dated 579 Saka.

The inscription was edited by M. Finot (B. E. F. Vol. IV, p. 918—No. III), and further commented upon by M. Coedes (B. E. F. Vol. XII,—No. 8, p. 15). (For localities etc. cf. No. 4). It is engraved on two faces of a stelae and contains 55 lines of writing. The language is Sanskrit. The first seven lines are illegible. Then follow 30 verses, mixed with two pieces of prose; the metre being vv. 1, 20, 27, 30 Śārdūlavikrīḍita; 2, 9, 13, 17-19, 22, 26, 28, 29, Upajāti; 3, 4, 6, 7, 15, 16, Śloka; 5, Vasantatilakā; 8, 24, Śikhariṇī; 10, 25, Mālinī; 11, 12, 14, 21, 23, Āryā.

The inscription records the donations made by king Prakāśadharma-Vikrānta Varman to the Gods Īśāneśvara, Śambhu-Bhadreśvara and Prabhāseśvara. It also gives the genealogy of the king.

TEXT.

(a).

(१) सिद्धिः............(२)..................न्यविशुद्ध.........
(३)..................(४)............धंशांतरचतुराननपुरपु......(५)
..................(६)................धराभ्रदीक्षितमूर्तिर्भगवतश् श्री-
शम्भुभद्रेश्वरस्य.........(७).........श्रीमत्याश्चम्पापुर्य्याम्

I आसीत्—˘ ˘—˘—˘ (८) ˘ ˘— — —˘ रः स्वैर्गुणैः
गंगाराज इति श्रुतो नृपगुणप्रख्यातवीर्य्यश्रुतिः ।
राज्यं दुस्त्य(जं) —˘—˘ ˘ ˘— (९) — — ˘—प्रग्रहे
गंगादर्शनजं सुखं महदिति प्रायाद्दतो जाह्नवीम् ॥

II दिलीपमन्धातृपुरस्स (रं —)
˘—˘— —˘ ˘—˘— —
(१०) सनातनीर्लंघयतिस्मनो हि
स्थितीरुदन्वानिव यः प्रभुत्वे ॥

III तस्य कीर्त्तियशो.........श्रीम (११) नोरथवर्म्म(णः)।
दौहित्रीतनयो योभूद्द्विजातप्रवरात्मजः ॥

IV श्रीरुद्रवर्म्मणस्तस्य नृपतेर्भूरिते(जसः)।
(१२)......तेजस्विनां योभूत् सूनुर्दीधितिमानिव ॥

V धर्म्मस्थितिं कृतयुगाखिलपादभाजं
यस्साम्प्रतेप्यनुसरत्यमलं ⏑ — —।
(१३) — —⏑ मुखतिरस्कृतमण्डलाभ-
स्सोम्यं[1] स्वकं न हि जहाति ⏑ — कृतोपि ॥

VI श्रीशम्भुवर्म्मणस्तस्य राज्ञः प्रथितते(जसः)।
(१४) (य) इमं शम्भुभद्रेशं पुनः स्थापितवान् भुवि ॥

VII यस्सूनुरौरसो राजा प्रादुरासीन्महायशाः।
श्रीमान् कन्दर्प्पधर्म्मेति (१५) साक्षाद्धर्म इवापरः ॥

VIII प्रजा यस्स्वैर्धर्म्मैर्व्यसनरहितः पाति सुतवन्
न तत्रास्त्याशा मे कलिरिति समुत्सेकविमु(खः)।
(१६) ⏑— — स्तेजोभिर्विधुतविरसः क्वाप्यपगतो
निदाघासह्याशोहिनकृत[2] इवद्ध्वान्तनिवहः ॥

IX यस्तस्य पुत्रत्वमुपसन् — —
(१७) — —⏑— — स्थितिनिग्रहेतुः।
सर्व्वप्रजानां समुदेति यत्र
मनोरथो विश्वसृजीव सर्ग्गः ॥

X स्वपरहितनिषेधप्राप्ति हेतुप्र — —
(१८) ⏑ ⏑ ⏑ ⏑ ⏑ गुणानां युक्तिमापादयन् यः।
प्रकृतिहितमधीप्सन् सन्तनोत्यात्मतेजो
मधुसमय विवस्वद्रश्मिधर्म्मानुपाती ॥

XI (१९) प्रभासधर्मनृपतेस्सोदर्या तस्य यानुजा समभूत्।
जगतां हितार्थजननी विश्वसृजः कर्म्मसिद्धिरिव ॥

XII ....जन्माच्छन्दस्यसत्यकौशिकस्वामी।
तस्याः पतित्वमागादनसूयाया इवात्रिमुनिः ॥

---

1. Read 'सौम्यं'. 2. Read 'निधायासह्यांशुं दिनकृत'.

XIII — — ˘ पत्यं किल योबभूव
प्रख्यातवीर्य्यश्रुतिरूपकान्तिः ।
क्षत्रं कुलं ब्राह्ममथ द्वयं हि
निरन्तरं यः प्रकटीचकार ॥

XIV (२२) (श्री भ)द्रेश्वरवर्म्मेत्यनङ्गरूपोथ विश्वरूप इति ।
च ते त्रयो बभूवुस्सोदर्यभ्रातरो य — ॥

XV (२३)………तश्श्री जगद्धर्म्मः प्रथितः प्राज्यविक्रमः ।
प्रायात् केनापि विधिना पुरं यद् भवसाह्व(यं) ॥

XVI (२४) (तत्र) स्थापितवाञ्छूलं कौण्डिन्यस्तद्द्विजर्षभः ।
अश्वत्थाम्नो द्विजश्रेष्ठाद्द्रोणपुत्रादवाप्य तं ॥

XVII (२५) — — कुलासीद् भुजगेन्द्रकन्या
सोमेति सा वंशकरी पृथिव्याम् ।
आश्रित्य भावेतिविशेषवस्तु
या मानुषावासमुवास — — ॥

XVIII (२६) कौण्डिन्यनाम्ना द्विजपुङ्गवेन
कार्यार्थपत्नीत्वमनायि यापि ।
भविष्यतोर्थस्य निमित्तभावे
विधेरचिन्त्यं खलु चेष्टितं हि ॥

XIX (२७) तदन्वयच्छेदिविशुद्धवंश-
परम्परोपात्तनृपत्वजन्मा ।
अद्यापि योलङ्कृतितां प्रजानाम्
आयात्यनिन्द्यप्रसवैर् ˘— —[1] ॥

(b).

XX (१) तस्य श्री भववर्म्मणः क्षितिपतेश्शक्ति-त्रय-श्लाघिनो
(२) वीर्योद्दामसपत्नसंघसमरस्पर्द्धाभिमानच्छिदः ।
भ्राता यः पृथिवीशुरस्समभवद् हतारिपक्षक्षय-
(३) स्तेजोवर्द्धितशासनो रविरिव प्राज्यप्रभावोदयः ॥

---

1. The word commences with an 'उ-कार'. Probably it is 'गुणानाम्'.

XXI स श्री महेन्द्रवर्म्मा त्रिदशाधिपतुल्यविक्रमः प्रथितः ।
(४)यमजनयत् प्रियतनयं नय इव सुधियां सुखप्रसवम् ॥

XXII श्रीशानवर्म्मा स नराधिपति-
स्समस्तदिक्प्रान्तविसर्पितेजा(ः) ।
(५) (प्रा)सूत यामद्वयवृद्धिहेतो-
र्व्यञ्जक्रियारम्भ इवोदयर्द्धिम् ॥

XXIII तस्यां श्री शर्व्वाण्यां सत्यां सोमान्वयप्रसूतायाम् ।
(६) वरविक्रमं प्रियसुतं यमजनयच्छ्रीजगद्धर्मः ॥

XXIV गुणानां साकल्यं भवति न किलैकत्रवशिनः
किमप्येव(म्) सृष्टेर्व्वर (७) कमलयोनेर्भ्भगवतो ।
गुणा यत्राशेषा दधति तु परार्द्ध्यामतिरतिम्
महार्हो रत्नो यो इव जलनिधौ दुस्तरजले ॥

XXV (८) अविरतनरदेवब्रह्मवश्यस्स्वतेजः-
शमितरिपुसनाथ(ः) श्रीसमुत्सेकहेतुः ।
दशरथनृपजोयं राम इत्याशया यं
(९) त्रयति[1] विधिपुरोगा श्रीरहो युक्तिरूपम् ॥

XXVI विवृद्धिमेति त्रितयं यमेत्य
पद्मा च कान्तिश्च सरस्वती च ।
प्रायेण (१०) सत्स्थानमभिप्रपन्न(म्)
सुवीजमानन्त्यफलाय कल्प्यम् ॥

सोयमुदितोदित—मानवेन्द्र—महतीयान्वयमहत्तर— (११) दुरवाप—पर्य्यन्त—क्षीरपयोनिधि—पूर्व्वभागोदित—निर्म्मल—मयूख-पर्य्याप्त—मण्डल—क्षपानाथः क्षपित—महाभिमान (१२)—दुष्कह—सपत्न — संघ — संस्तुत—निसर्ग—वीर्य्योवीर्य्यदृढतरैकसार्थ—पार्थिव—गुणोपात्त—पालित—सम्वर्द्धितार्हतीर्थापादितराज्यः (१३) लक्ष्मी—निरूपित—वैचक्षन्य श्रीमान् श्रीचम्पापुरपरमेश्वरो महाराजः श्रीविक्रान्तवर्म्मेत्युपात्तविजयाभिषेकनामा श्री प्रकाशधर्म्म(ो) (१४) नव—सप्तत्युत्तर—पञ्चवर्ष—शतातीत—शकाव-

1. Read 'श्रयति'.

नीन्द्र—कालपरिमाणम् नपस्यसितदशाहार्कवासरादित्यर्दवृषभो-
दयैकादश— (१५) घटिका—नवघहोरादि—पुरस्सरं मीनयुगाया—
तार्कबुधभार्गवं तुलाधरस्थभौमसौरं घटधरसंस्थवाचस्पतिनर-
युग्मोपगत—(१६) ताराधिपशोभनमित्याजवञ्जवी भावसामर्थ्य–बीज
—संहृति—चिकीर्षया सकलभुवनैकनाथं श्री प्रभासेश्वरं प्रतिष्ठा-
पितवान्[1]।

XXVII (१७) स्वाः शक्तीः प्रति योग्यतामुपगता क्षित्यादयोमूर्त्तयो
लोकस्थित्युदयादिकार्य्यपरता ताभिर्व्विना नास्ति हि।
(१८) इत्येवम् विगणय्य शक्तिवशिना येनाश्रियन्तेथ वा
का नामेह विभुः क्रिया न भजते या स्युः परार्थोदये॥

XXVIII (१९) यो ब्रह्मविष्णुत्रिदशाधिपादि
सुरासुरब्रह्मनृपर्षिमान्यः।
तथापि भूत्यै जगतामनृत्यच्=
छ्मशानभूमावतिचित्रमेतत्॥

XXIX (२०) यतो जगत् स्थाष्णुचरिष्णुरूपं
विवर्त्तते का[2]दिव रश्मिजालम्।
यत्रैव भूयः प्रनिलीयते तद्
अहो विचित्रो महतांनिसर्ग्गः॥

XXX (२१) यस्यातीतमनोगतेरपि सतो हेतोर्ज्जगज्जन्मनां
श्रेयोनन्त्य फलप्रदा स्मृतिरपि व्यक्तिः पुनः का कथा।
(२२) सौस्थित्य–प्रभवोपलब्धि–विषये चम्पानगर्य्यां स्थिरं
स्थेयादाभुवनस्थितेर्व्विभुरयं स श्री प्रभासेश्वरः॥

(२३) लोड्—कोष्ठागारं स—चौम्—विषयं हवौड् कर्श्रौय्—
चौ—पितौ—क्रौड्—नजोच्—वसौय्—कोष्ठा (२४) गार दि मिदित्
तत्रसहितं सर्व्वमिदं श्रीमाञ्छ्री—चम्पेश्वर—श्री—प्रकाशधर्म्मा
भगवतां ईशाने (२५) श्वर—श्रीशम्भुभद्रेश्वर—श्रीप्रभासेश्वराणां
सततपूजाविधये प्रादात्॥ ये ध्वंसयन्ति (२६) ते ब्रह्महत्याफलम—

1. The short strokes separating the elements of compound words are not in the original.

2. Read '°र्का'.

नन्तं कल्पेष्वजस्रमनुभवन्ति ये परिपालयन्ति तेऽश्वमेधफलं (२७) ब्रह्महत्याश्वमेधाभ्यां न परं पुण्यपापयोरित्यागमादिति प्रतिज्ञातम् तेन तद्देवताविशेष (२८) समत्तयो[1] ऽस्य सर्व्वस्य प्रदातेति ॥

TRANSLATION.

(a).

LL 1–7. Perfection has been attained............another family..............the town of Brahmā...............consecrated image of God Śrī Śambhu-Bhadreśvara.........in the prosperous city of Champā.

V. 1. There was a king called Gaṅgārāja, who was famed for the royal qualities of knowledge and heroism...... the sovereignty difficult to abandon.................... 'the joy arising from a view of Gaṅgā (Ganges) is very great', and so he went to the Jāhnavī (Ganges).

V. 2. Kings beginning with Dilīpa and Mandhātā...... he, in his majesty, never transgressed the eternal rules of conduct, even as the ocean never transgresses her boundaries fixed for eternity.[2]

V. 3. He, who was the son of an eminent Brāhmaṇa, and the 'son of the daughter's daughter' of glorious Manorathavarman.

V. 4. The son of this king Rudravarman, of great valour, was (foremost among) those who possessed splendour, like the Sun.

V. 5. He who, even at the present time, follows the pure rules of conduct which obtained in the Kṛta-Yuga,

---

1. Read '°समन्वयो'.

2. Finot translates "Celui qui était egal en puissance à l'Océan" (He was equal in power to the ocean) ignoring the double meaning of the word 'स्थिति' and a very well-known comparison with the ocean.

when Dharma prevailed in its entirety.[1]....................The beauty of his face surpasses that of the moon with a halo, but the moon, though cast into shade, still maintains his own.[2]

V. 6. Of that Śambhuvarman, renowned for his prowess, who re-established on this earth this Śambhubhadreśa.

V. 7. Was born a son of mighty fame, called Kandarpadharma, endowed with beauty, and like an incarnation of Dharma.

V. 8. "I have nothing to expect from a king who, free from passion, dutifully protects his subjects like his own sons,"—with this melancholy reflection, Kali, chased by the splendour of the king, sadly moved away, nobody knows where, even as the army of darkness flies before the Sun, leaving its unbearable rays behind.

V. 9. He who was his son,................The desires of all his subjects are centred on him, as those of all the creatures on the Creator.

V. 10. Wishing for the good of his subjects, he increased his own prowess, following in the wake of the Sun who extends his rays in spring time.[3]

V. 11. He, Prabhāsadharma, had a younger sister, who was the source of welfare and prosperity of the whole world, and the perfection, as it were, of the creation (Karmma) of God.

---

1. The poet here refers to the theory that Dharma which originally stood on four legs, in the Kṛta age, lost one in each of the succeeding ages viz. Tretā and Dvāpara. At present, in Kali, she stands on only one leg.

2. The last portion is only conjectural.

3. The first two fragmentary lines are not translated.

V. 12. For the birth of Chanda[1]....................Satya-kauśikasvāmī became her husband as the hermit Atri was of Anasūyā.

V. 13. He who was (his or her) son,[2] celebrated for his heroism, knowledge, and beauty, and who always shed lustre on both the Kṣatriya and Brāhmaṇa families,

V. 14. Was called Bhadreśvaravarman; he and Anaṅga-rūpa and Viśvarūpa were three brothers born of the same mother.

V. 15. (Then) the famous Śrī-Jagaddharma, of mighty prowess, went to the town called Bhava[3] on account of certain circumstances.

V. 16. It was there that Kauṇḍinya, the foremost among Brāhmaṇas, planted the spear which he had obtained from Droṇa's son Aśvatthāmā, the best of Brāhmaṇas.

V. 17. There was a daughter of the king of serpents, called Somā, who founded a family in this world. Having attained, through love, to a radically different element, she lived in the habitations of man.

V. 18. She was taken as wife by the excellent Brāhmaṇa Kauṇḍinya for the sake of (accomplishing) certain work. Verily, incomprehensible is the way of God in providing conditions leading to future events.

V. 19. (King Bhadravarman) who, being born in that pure unbroken line of kings, is, even to-day, the pride of his subjects by his unblamable (conduct).

(b).

V. 20. He, the king Bhavavarman, who boasted of his triple power, and broke the arrogant pride of his enemies

---

1. Finot takes चन्द्स्यसत्यकौशिकस्वामिन् as the name of the husband. This does not seem probable.

2. 'अपत्यं' but only the last two letters are distinct.

3. Bhavapura i. e. Cambodge.

about military strength caused by excess of heroism, had a brother, who was a hero in the world, who was a destroyer of the proud allies of enemies, whose power was increased by his strength, and whose supreme majesty, like that of the sun, brilliantly shone forth.

V. 21. He, the famous Śrī Mahendravarmā, equal in prowess to Indra, the king of gods, begat happily, with ease, a favourite son, even as the policy of wise men produces happy results.

V. 22. He, Śrī Īśānavarmā, king of men, whose splendour spread in all directions up to the very end, begat a daughter, for the sake of unique prosperity, as sacrificial ceremonies beget both material prosperity and supernatural power.

V. 23. Śrī Jagaddharma begat on that Śri Śarvvāṇī, chaste, and born in the family of Soma (or Somā), a favourite son of remarkable prowess.

V. 24. It is said that the sum-total of excellences is not to be found together in any creature. Is it applicable even to the creations of God Brahmā ?. To him (the king) (at least) all the excellences are very fondly attached; he is like a priceless jewel in the deep of the ocean.

25. Constantly devoted to the Brāhmaṇas, the gods among men, (he was) gracefully attended by enemies subdued by his own prowess; (he was) cause of Lakṣmī's pride; Śrī Lakṣmī, in fond hope that he was Rāma, son of king Daśaratha, dutifully followed[1] him, and this was well worthy of her indeed !

26. The Trio *viz.* Padmā (Lakṣmi *i. e.* Prosperity), Kānti (beauty) and Sarasvatī (knowledge), attain a luxuri-

---

1. I cannot understand the word 'नयति' as published in the text. I take it as 'श्रयति'.

ant growth in him. Very often good seeds, obtaining good soil, lead to eternal fruits.

He, the illustrious king of Champā, Mahārāja Śrī Prakāśadharma, who took the name of Śrī Vikrāntavarmā at the time of coronation,—who was the full moon,[1] with pure rays, rising in the east,[2] of the great and vast (lit. whose ends can be reached with difficulty) ocean of milk, which was the great, noble, and ever-prosperous[3] royal family,—whose natural prowess is familiar to his innumerable wicked enemies, whose great pride was humbled by him,—whose kingdom was bestowed on him by holy men, and was acquired, protected, and augmented, by means of a group of royal qualities, made all the firmer by heroism,—who was singled out by luck (Śrī) for his skill,—he, in the year 579 of the era of the Śaka king, (astronomical details follow)—established Śrī Prabhāseśvara, the one lord of all the world, with a view to destroy the seeds (of karma), which have the power of leading to births (lit. existence)[4] in quick succession.

27. His (*i. e.* Śiva's) forms like Earth etc. are suitable to his energy, and, without them, his activity for the maintenance and progress of the world cannot exist. It is from this consideration that (these forms) are held by the master of energy. What action is there that the Lord will not undertake for the welfare of others?

---

1. 'पर्यास मण्डल' applied to the king would mean the vast extent of his kingdom.

2. 'पूर्व्व भाग' applied to the king would mean in the forefront of the royal family.

3. 'उदितोदित' applied to ocean would mean 'surging'.

4. In other words, the king desired to escape from rebirths, a desire of all orthodox Hindus.

28. He, who, although revered by Brahmā, Viṣṇu, Indra and other gods, Asuras (Demons), Brāhmaṇas, kings and ascetics (or royal ascetics), yet danced in cemetery for the sake of the prosperity of the world—this is strange indeed!

29. From whom is evolved this static and dynamic world, like rays from the Sun, in whom again are they merged! How wonderful is this great creation.

30. Who, although having no desire of his own,[1] is yet the cause of the creation of the world; thoughts of whom, alone, are capable of yielding infinite bliss, not to speak, again, of his visible manifestation; may he, Śrī Prabhāseśvara, remain fixed here as long as the world lasts, as a means of securing the welfare of the city of Champā.

The store-house of Loṅ, with the district of Caum, and the store-houses of Havaun, Karnnauy, Cau, Pitau, Kraun, Najoc, and Vasauy at Midit,—all these have been given for the worship of the gods Īśāneśvara, Śrī Śambhu-Bhadreśvara and Śrī Prabhāseśvara, by Śrī Prakāśadharman, king of Champā. Those who will destroy, they will feel, without remission, the consequences of murdering a Brāhmaṇa, through the aeons. Those who will maintain, will enjoy the reward of an Aśvamedha sacrifice. And it has been said in the Śāstras 'that there is no greater meritorious act than the Aśvamedha, and no greater crime than the murder of a Brāhmaṇa.' Thus declares the donor of all these in the presence of that God.

No. 13. My-son Stelae Inscription of Prakāśadharma.

The inscription is engraved on another face of the same stelae which contains No. 7. It contains a date of which

1. Or 'although beyond mental perception.'

the hundredth figure alone is legible *viz.* 5xx, and refers to king Prakāśadharma, grand-son of...........(name lost).

B. E. F., Vol. III., p. 210.

No. 14. My-son pedestal Inscription of Prakāśadharma.

The inscription was edited by M. Finot (B. E. F., Vol. IV, p. 928 No. V.) (For localities cf. No. 4).

It is engraved on a pedestal, and contains 2 lines of writing in Sanskrit, consisting of 2 ślokas:

The object of the inscription is to record the erection of a temple to Kuvera, the friend of Maheśvara, by Prakāśadharma.

TEXT.

(१) महेश्वरसखस्येदं कुवेरस्य धनाकरं ।
प्रकाशधर्म्मनृपतिः पूजास्थानमकल्पयत् ॥

(२) एकाक्षपिङ्गलेत्येष देव्यादर्शनदूषितः ।
सम्वर्द्धयत्वीशधनं पायाच्चाहिततस्सदा ॥

TRANSLATION.

(1) This temple of Kuvera, the friend of Maheśvara, a mine of wealth, has been erected by king Prakāśadharma.

(2) May this (Kuvera), who is called 'ekākṣapiṅgala' for having (his eye) injured by the view of the Goddess (Umā), increase the wealth of this king, and always protect him from evils. (For the allusion to the story of Kuvera, cf. Rāmāyaṇa Uttara-kāṇḍa, ch. XIII, vv., 24, 30-31).

No. 15. Lai Cham Inscription of Prakāśadharma.

(For localities cf. No. 56.)

It contains two short lines.

TEXT.

(१) नमश्शिवाय ।

(२) श्री प्रकाशधर्मा जय(दानं) (?) ॥

TRANSLATION.

Homage to Śiva; the gift of victory (?) by Prakāśadharma.

B. E. F., Vol. XV., No. 2, p. 112.

No. 16. My-son Stelae Inscription of Vikrānta-Varman I, dated 609.

The inscription was edited by M. Finot (B. E. F. Vol. IV, p. 925, No. IV). (For localities etc. cf. No. 4). It is engraved on two faces of a stelae, and contains, besides the invocation, 23 lines of writing. The language is Sanskrit, and, with the exception of the invocation, the inscription is written throughout in verse. There are altogether 11 verses, six on the first, and five on the second face. The metres are, v. 1, Indravajrā; vv. 2–8, 11, Āryā; v. 9, Śārdūlavikrīḍita; v. 10, Sragdharā.

The first eight stanzas are written in the same character, and form one inscription, recording the donation of a *Kośa* to Īśāneśvara, and a *mukuṭa* to Bhadreśvara, by king Prakāśadharma in 609 (687 A. D.). The last three stanzas, which are written in a different style, record the same donations by king Vikrāntavarman.

TEXT.

(a).

ओं नमस् शिवाय.

(१) स्वस्ति

I यं सर्व्वदेवास्ससुरेशमुख्या
ध्यायन्ति तत्तत्त्वविदश्च सन्तः ।
(२) स्वस्थः सुशुद्धः परमो वरेण्य
ईशाननाथस्स जयत्यजस्रम् ॥

II (३) स्मृतिरपि यस्य सकृदपि प्रणिपतितान् तारयत्य-
पायेभ्यः ।
(४) सो श्रीभद्रेश्वरोस्तु प्रजाहितार्थं तथा प्रभासेशः ॥

III (५) आनन्दाम्बरषट्शतनियमितशकभूभुजाकृते समये ।
(६) शुचिशुक्लद्वैतादिनप्रपन्नसुपुनर्वसुव्यस्ते ॥

IV (७) सिंहहनिविष्टसुरगुरौ वृषभोपगतार्कभौमसोमसुते ।
(८) सौराध्यासिततौले मेषायातसुरेन्द्रगुरौ ॥

V (९) उपचयकृद्वविवारे युग्मायातोपकारिचन्द्रमसि ।
(१०) विश्वमुहूर्त्तोपन्नाम् त्रयोदशीम् नालिकामभितः ॥

VI (११) ईशानेश्वरकोशं संस्थाप्य यथाविधि स्वभक्तिवशात् ।
(१२) (श्रीमान् प्रकाशधर्म्मो) मुकुटं भद्रेश्वरायादात् ॥

(b).

VII (१) कोशमुकुटोभयं तत्कीर्त्तिस्तम्भद्वयोपमेयमिव ।
(२) यावच्चन्द्रादित्यौ तावदिदं सुस्थितं जगति ॥

VIII (३) इति यस्य कीर्त्तिरित्थंसंभूता लब्धभूमिका स्थाने ।
(४) स श्रीप्रकाशधर्म्मा चम्पात्तोणीश्वरो जयति ॥
(५) अथैव

IX सूर्य्येस्मिन्नुदयकृते हिमकरो यात्यस्तमिन्दूदये
तस्मिंश्चास्तमितो रवि(ः) (६) पुनरिति प्रायेण लोकस्थितिः ।

ईशानेश्वरकोशनिर्म्मलशशी भद्रेशमौल्यंशुमां
(७)स्ताव प—˘ ˘—˘ ताभिहितवान् विक्रान्तवर्म्मा नृपः ॥
X अच्छेद्याभेद्य आद्यः (८)कृतमिह सकलश्राशयश्राश्रितानाम
ईशानो यत् कृताङ्गस्स्वयमयमवदत् सद्भिराख्येयमेतत् ।
ईशानस्याष्टमूर्त्तिः कृतमभिलषितं रूप्यकोशेन्दुनाद्दो
(१०)राजा विक्रान्तवर्म्मा जयति बहुमतश्चाददयित्वैव नान्यं ॥
XI श्रीशानरूप्यभेदे (११) प्रकाशधर्म्मावनीन्द्र.........

....

TRANSLATION.

(a)

Reverence to Śiva !

Hail !

1. May Īśānanātha, who is meditated by all the gods, with Indra at their head, and by the good persons who know His essential nature,—who is calm, pure, supreme and sublime, triumph for ever !

2. Only the thought of Him saves from danger those who prostrate even once. May that Śrī Bhadreśvara, as well as Prabhāseśa, be for the good of the people.

3. When six hundred and nine[1] years had elapsed since the time of the Śaka kings.

(Astronomical details.)

6. After having installed, out of devotion, a *Kośa* of Īśāneśvara (*i. e.* a Linga of Śiva called Īśāneśvara) according to true rites, the illustrious Prakāśadharma gave a crown to Bhadreśvara.

1. Ānanda has been taken by Fleet to be equivalent to Nanda or 9. This is doubtful. There are four Ānandas according to Tantra (Caturānanda), and hence it may denote four.

(b).

7. May this pair of *Kośa* and crown, like two pillars of his fame, exist unimpaired in this world, as long as the Sun and the Moon last.

8. Victory to Śrī Prakāśadharma, king of Champā, whose fame, originating in the above manner, has very appropriately spread afar.

9. When the Sun rises, the Moon is gone; and when the Moon rises, the Sun sets—this is the rule of the Universe. But the spotless Moon which is the *Kośa* of Īśāneśvara, and the Sun which is the crown of Bhadreśvara, both (have been brought together ?) by the king Vikrāntavarmā.

10. That Īśāna who cannot be cut, or pierced, who is primordial, and who heals the wounds of all his followers, has his own limbs wounded, as he himself said. Let the pious men solve this problem. (The reply is) Īśāna cut himself into eight parts, and this mutilation is intentional. May the revered king Vikrāntavarmā triumph by his moon-like silver *Kośa*, without eclipsing any body else.

No. 17. My-son Stelae Inscription of Vikrāntavarman.

The inscription was edited by M. Finot (B. E. F., Vol. IV, p. 930, No. IX.) (For localities cf. No. 4). It is engraved on two faces of a stelae and contains, besides the invocation, 38 lines of writing. The second face, containing 20 lines, is illegible, the names Śambhuvarman and Vikrāntavarman alone being decipherable. The first face contains six verses and a piece in prose. It records an invocation to Śiva.

The metres being, vv. 1-2, Śārdūlavikrīḍita; v. 3, Mandākrāntā; vv. 4-5, Sragdharā; v. 6, Mālinī.

TEXT.

(4).

ओं नमस् शिवाय.

(१) स्वस्ति

I ऐश्वर्य्यातिशयप्रदो मखभुजां यस्तप्यमानस्तपः
कन्दर्प्पोत्तमविग्रहप्रदहनो हिमाद्रिजायाः पतिः ।
(२) लोकानां परमेश्वरत्वमसमं यातो नदद्वाहनो
याथातथ्यविशारदास्तु जगतामीशस्य नो सन्ति हि ॥

II इच्छातीतवर(३)प्रदानवशिनं भक्त्या समाराध्य यम्
त्रैलोक्यप्रभावप्रभावमहता[1] वृत्रस्य हन्त्वा विना ।
भुङ्क्तेऽद्याप्युपमन्युरिन्दु—(४) धवलं क्षीरार्णवं बान्धवैः
श्रीशानेश्वरनाथ एष भगवान् पायादपायात् स वः ॥

III यस्यात्मानस्सकल (५) मरुतां मानिनां माननीया
अष्टौ पुण्या वरहितकृतस्सर्व्वलोकान् वहन्ति ।
अन्योन्यस्य स्वगुणविदयागाढ—(६) संवध्यमाना
योग्यायुग्या इव पथि पथि स्यन्दनान् स्यन्दमानान् ॥

IV सावित्रीज्यासनाथप्रणवदृढधनुर्मुक्तबाणारिबाणं
(७) कृत्वा सोमोरुपुङ्खं स्फुरदनलमुखं सारथीडाविरिञ्चम् ।
अध्याऽऽब्रह्मधुर्य्यं सकलसुरमयस्यन्दनं विघ्नघानां
(८) शान्त्यर्थं येन दाहो युगपदपि पुरा त्रैपुराणां पुराणां

तेनान्य—देवता—विशेष—परम—दुरधिगमाणिमादि—गुणै-
श्वर्य्य(९)साध्यफल—निमित्त—तपश्चरण—परायणेन कटाक्षिचक-
दनलशिखश्रेणि—भूतिसात्कृत—मदन—निरुपमापघनेनापि (१०)
वल्लभ—तुहिनवदमलहितदुहितृकेन सकलभुवनैक—परमेश्वरेणा-
पि गगन—तल—गमन—कर्कश—कर्क—वरपत्रेण दुरव—(११)
गम—परमार्थ—भवेन वाङ्मानस—गोचरातीत—स्वरूपेणाप्य
वनि—वन—पवनसख—पवन—वनदपथ—दशशतकिरण—शतकि-
रण—(१२) दीक्षित—तनुभिरतनुप्रभावाभिः शर्व-भव-पशुपतीशान-

1. Read 'त्रैलोक्य-प्रभव-प्रभाव-महता', as required both by metre and sense.

भीम-रुद्र-महादेवोग्राभिधान-प्रधान-समुपबृंहिताभिराविर्भावित-
(१३) विश्वमूर्त्तिना नलिननाभ—नलिनविष्ट—हव्यवाहन—प्रमुख
—मुख्य—सहायेन स—सुर—मुनि—गन्धर्व्वादि—सकल—लोक-
विध्वंसन (१४) कर—त्रिपुर—महासुरोद्धरेणानुमितामित—प्रभावेण
भगवता श्रीशम्भुभद्रेश्वर—परमभट्टारकेण जितम् ॥

V (१५) इन्द्रादीनां सुराणां भुजबलमहतान्नित्य—जेताहमुच्चै-
जैंतम्—˘—र्व्यात्रिभुवनपद— —˘— —सहाय ।
(१६) सर्व्वीयो माधवो यज्जगती मम श — —˘— —˘— —
— — — —˘— —˘ ˘ ˘ ˘ ˘ ˘— —˘—प्राप यस्मात् ॥

VI (१७) दिशतु विभुरहेतुस्सर्व्वलोकैकहेतुः
˘ ˘ ˘ ˘ ˘ ˘ — — —˘—यादिमूर्त्ति
(१८) र्भुवि[1] शमिति सदेदम् श्री ˘— —˘— —

....

TRANSLATION.

(a).

Reverence to Śiva ! Hail !

(1) He, who, practising austerities, grants the highest supremacy to the gods (lit. those who enjoy sacrifice),—who burnt the fine figure of the God of love, and yet married the daughter of the icy Himālaya,—who, riding on a bellowing animal (bull), obtains the unique supremacy in all the worlds, —there is none in the world who knows that God in his true aspects.[2]

(2) By devotedly worshipping Him,—who has it in his gifts to grant boons beyond one's desire,—Upamanyu is en-

---

1. The vowel-sign उ is not distinct.

2. The first three lines imply the contradictory nature of the God. (viz.) [1] Giver of bounies to others, but himself practising austerities (for what ?). [2] Husband, yet destroying the Cupid [3] Lord of the Universe, yet riding on a mean animal. A further implication is that although of a fiery nature (evidenced by the burning of Madana), he was yet united to the daughter of the cold Himālaya.

joying even to day, with his friends and relations, the ocean of milk, white as the moon, to the exclusion of the destroyer of Vṛtra (*i. e.* Indra), whose great glory became manifest by having worked the miracle of creating the three worlds. May this Lord Śrī Īśāneśvara-Nātha protect you from all dangers.

(3) Whose eight holy forms, respected by all the proud Maruts, profoundly united with one another by appreciating the individual functions of each, and bestowers of excellent blessings, carry this world, as worthy pairs of horses carry rapidly moving chariots on different roads.

(4) He who, at one and the same time, destroyed the three cities belonging to Tripura-Asuras for the peace of the worlds, making Praṇava his strong bow, with the Sāvitrī as its bowstring; Viṣṇu, his arrow, with Soma as its excellent feather, and the blazing fire (Agni), its barb; all the gods, his chariot, with the four Vedas as its horses, and Iḍā and Viriñca as its charioteers.[2]

---

2. The story hinted at in this verse is thus described in **Mahābhārata [Anuśāsana Parva] vv. 7458 ff.**

There were in the sky three cities of the valorous Asuras, one of iron, another of silver, and a third of gold, which Maghavan [Indra] could not demolish, with all his weapons. Then all the great gods, distressed, went to the great Rudra as their refuge, and said to him, after they were assembled; 'Rudra, there shall be victims devoted to thee in all the sacrifices. Bestower of honour, destroy the Daityas with their cities and deliver the worlds.' He, being thus addressed, said, 'So be it'; and making Viṣṇu his arrow, Agni its barb, Yama, the son of Vivasvat, its feather, all the Vedas his bow, and the excellent Sāvitrī [the Gāyatrī] his bowstring, and having appointed Brahmā his charioteer, he in due time pierced through these cities with a three-jointed, three-barbed arrow, of the colours of the sun, and in fierceness like the fire which burns up the world. These Asuras with their cities were there burnt up by Rudra.

Victory to the Great Lord Śrī Śambhubhadreśvara,—who, although possessed of Aṇimā and other divine faculties which are very difficult to be obtained by other classes of gods, yet devotes himself to austerities without desiring any reward therefrom; who reduced to ashes the incomparable body of Madana by means of burning fire proceeding from his eyes, and yet became the husband of the daughter (of Himālaya), white as snow and benefactress; who is the unique lord of all the worlds, and yet selected a white vehicle (*i. e.* the bull) which has become rough by traversing the sky; who is the source of the supreme end of life, difficult to attain; whose true nature is beyond the domain of thought and speech, yet whose image, identical with the Universe, is manifested by his forms,—earth, water, fire, air, sky, sun, moon and sacrificer,—which are dignified by the titles of gods of very great power, named Śarva. Bhava, Paśupati, Īśāna, Bhīma, Rudra, Mahādeva and Ugra; and whose infinite power may be inferred from the fact that, aided by (the gods with) Brahmā, Viṣṇu, and Agni (Fire) at their head, he exterminated the great Asura (demon) Tripura, who had destroyed all the worlds with the gods, ascetics and the Gandharvas.

5. I am always victorious over Indra and other gods who are great on account of the strength of their arms.

6. May he, who is without cause, but who is the cause of all the worlds, grant blessings..............

(b).

Śambhuvarmā.......................Vikrāntavarmā.

No. 18. My son Stone Inscription of Vikrāntavarman

The inscription was edited by M. Finot (B. E. F., Vol. IV. p. 929, No. VII.) (For localities cf. No. 4). It was engraved on a block of stone, forming part of a circular pedestal. It contains one line, and records the installation of a golden image of a god by king Vikrāntavarmā.

TEXT.

नमस्सुवर्णाक्षाय.

चम्पावनिभुजार्च्चयम् काञ्चनी तत्ववेदिना ।
विक्रान्तवर्म्मणा भक्त्या स्थापिता पारमेश्वरी ॥

TRANSLATION.

Reverence to Suvarṇākṣa (Lit. God with golden eyes). This golden image of Parameśvara has been installed with devotion by Vikrāntavarman, king of Champā, who knows the truth.

No. 19. My-son Pedestal Inscription of Vikrāntavarman.

The inscription was edited by M. Finot (B. E. F., Vol. IV. p. 930, No. VIII.) (For localities cf. No. 4).

It is engraved on a circular pedestal and contains one line in Sanskrit verse.

TEXT.

स्थापितो राजसिंहेन श्रीमद्विक्रान्तवर्म्मणा ।
वामेश्वरस्य कोशोऽयं स्थेयानाभुवनस्थितेः ॥

TRANSLATION.

This Kośa of Vāmeśvara, (Śiva) installed by Śrī-Vikrāntavarmā, the best of kings (lit. the lion among kings), will endure as long as the world exists.

No. 20. My-son Stelae Inscription of Vikrāntavarman II, dated 63 x.

The inscription was edited by M. Finot (B. E. F., Vol. IV, p. 928, No. VI and vol. XV, No.2 p. 190) (For localities cf. No.4). It is engraved on three faces of a stelae, containing, besides the invocation, 40 lines of writing. The language is Sanskrit, and the inscription is written throughout in prose. It is mostly illegible,and contains a date, 63 x, the unit figure being effaced.

TEXT.

(a).

ओम् नमश्शिवाय......................(१२) चम्पा........
राज्यलक्ष्मी राज.................

(b).

(१)........चम्पा–पुर–परमेश्वर...........राजाधिराज......
(२).........श्री प्रकाशधर्म्मेण कृतप्रतिष्ठ..............(३).........
श्री प्रकाशधर्म्म............(६).........श्री प्रकाशधर्म्म.........(७)
.........श्री गङ्गेश्वरवंशजः..............(१०) श्री विक्रान्तवर्म्म—
महाराजाधि(११) राज.................विक्रा (१२)न्तवर्म्मनृपश्श्री
योगेश्वर—राजसूनु—शशिनो नप्त्रे..............(१३) मकुटकोश
.........आलङ्कृतम्.........(१४)शकपति—समये.........रामरसैष्
............फाल्गुनशुक्ल............

(c).

(१) नमश्श्रीशानेश्वर—श्रीभद्रेश्व(२)र—श्री प्रभासेश्वर
—श्रीवा (३)(म)भूतेश्वरेभ्यो (४) हेमरजत...................(६)
श्रीभद्रवर्म्म—श्रीरुद्रवर्म्म..............(१०) सह पुनः प्रादादिति
(११) तानि ये नाशयन्ति वा पाल(१२)यन्ति वा तेषाम् फलञ्च
श्रीशा(१३)नेशादय ईश्वरा जानन्ति ॥

TRANSLATION.

(a).

Reverence to Śiva....................(12) Champā...........
Goddess of sovereignty.........king.

(b).

(1) Lord of the city of Champā.........King of kings......
(2) installed by Śrī Prakāśadharma............ (3) Śrī Prakāśadharma.........(6) Śrī Prakāśadharma. (7) Belonging to the family of Gaṅgeśvara (Lord of Gaṅgā ?) (10-11) Śrī Vikrāntavarmā, the great king of kings, (11-12).........king Vikrāntavarmā..............to the grandson of king Yogeśvara's son, a moon............(13) Crown and Kośa.........decorated. (14) In the year 63.................of the Śaka king, bright fortnight of Phālguna.

(c).

(1) Reverence to Śrī Īśāneśvara, Śrī Bhadreśvara, (2) Śrī Prabhāseśvara (3) and Śrī Vāmabhūteśvara.........(4) gold and silver . .(9) Śrī Bhadravarmā and Rudravarmā (10) together again gave.........(11) He who destroys or maintains them—the consequence (of their action) is known to Śrī Īśāna and other gods.

No. 21. My-son Stelae Inscription of Vikrāntavarman II, dated 653 Śaka.

The inscription was first brought to notice by M. Finot (B. E. F., Vol. IV, pp. 932–33, No. x), who could read only a few words. Later, M. Huber has partially restored the text (B. E. F., Vol. XI, p. 265).

For localities cf. No. 4. The inscription is engraved on two faces of a stelae, containing respectively 11 and 12 lines of writing, besides the invocation.

It begins with 'Namaś Śivāya Svasti', and then follows an invocation to Śiva in two verses (metre Mālinī), LL. 1-4. (Verse 1 is given below).

The lines 5-11 contain each a śloka, and record that king Śambhuvarman built a brick *vedī* (quadrangular spot) covered with silver plates, with a statue of Lakṣmī thereon.

The four ślokas that follow give a poetical description of the splendour of the temple.

The first six lines of the second face each contain a śloka, and record that Śrī Prakāśadharma intended to build a *vedī* of stone, and that this was actually accomplished by one Naravāhana Varman, who further covered the stone *vedī* with silver and gold plates. It is difficult to decide whether Naravāhana Varman is identical with Vikrānta-Varman, the successor of Prakāśadharma, or a new king intermediate between the last two.

The lines 8-9 contain a prose passage glorifying Vikrāntavarman.

TEXT.

(a).

(V. I.) जयति जितमनोजो ब्रह्मविष्ण्वादिदेव–
प्रणतपदयुगाब्जो निष्कलोऽप्यष्टमूर्त्तिः ।
त्रिभुवनहितहेतुस्सर्व्वसङ्कल्पहारी
परपुरुष इह श्रीशानदेवो ऽयमाद्यः ॥
(LL. 6–7) श्रीशम्भुवर्म्मणा राज्ञा वेदी बद्धेष्टकमयी ।
बही रौप्यमयी लक्ष्मीं बिभ्रती वेदिका पुरा ॥
क्षीरोदधि............

(b).

(L. 2) स श्रीप्रकाशधर्म्म˘ कर्त्तुमिच्छन् शिलामयीम्.।
नरवाहनवर्म्म.........

(LL. 4–6) नरवाहनवर्म्मश्रीरकरोत्तां शिलामयीम् ।
रुग्मरौप्यवहिर्वेद्धां ब्रह्मा मेरुशिखामिव ॥
स्वर्णरौप्यमयी लक्ष्मीं बिभ्रती वेदिका पुनः ।
विद्युत्.........भाति शिखा हिमगिरेरिव ॥
तेनेदृशी महावेदी दुष्करा पूर्व्वजैर्नृपैः ।
कृता यद्......अहंकरो......किमद्भुतम् ॥

(LL. 8–9) श्रीशानेशादिदेवस्वपितृपदयुगाम्भोजरेणुप्रसादात्[1]
प्रोत्तुङ्गा यस्य कीर्त्तिः प्रथितपृथुयश......
स श्रीविक्रान्तवर्म्म......लक्ष्मीं कैलासशिखरोद्भवाम्
येनेदृशी......वेदी......स्थापिता पुनः

(L. 10) भुक्ते रामार्थवट्कैश्शकपतिसमये पञ्चमे मा(घ)......[2]
सादित्यर्क्षप्रपन्ने शशिदिवसयुते अङ्गिरश्शुक्लग्ने ।
मीनागारस्थसौरे वगतरविबुधे[3] नौलिभौमासुरेऽस्मिन्
श्रीमान् विक्रान्तवर्म्मा सुचिरवपुरिहास्थापयन् कीर्त्ति-
कायम् ॥

TRANSLATION.

(a).

LL. 1–4. Victorious is the Great Being, the primaeval God Śrī Īśānadeva, who conquered the Cupid, whose lotus-feet are saluted by Brahmā, Viṣṇu and other gods, who is without atoms, but has still eight forms, who is the cause of the welfare of the three worlds, and who fulfils all the desires.

---

1. Huber reads °म्बुजरेणु°. But apparently the fragment is the first line of a stanza in sragdharā metre, which requires the syllable म्बु to be long. The third and the fourth line are too corrupt to be restored.
2. This is Huber's reading. Possibly the missing word is मार्गशीर्षे which fits in with the metre here.
3. Could it possibly be विगतरविबुधे ?

LL. 6–7. King Śambhuvarman made a brick altar, covered with silver on the exterior, which supported Lakṣmī, —formerly the ocean of milk...........

(*b*).

L. 2. He, Śrī Prakāśadharma, desiring to make.........of stone.........Naravāhanavarman........

LL. 4–6. Śrī Naravāhana-varman covered (that altar) of stone with gold and silver on the outside, as Brahmā made the peak of Meru. Moreover this altar, of gold and silver, supporting Lakṣmī......shines like the peak of Himālaya. By him was made this great altar, (a task) difficult for the previous kings,......how wonderful.

LL. 8–9. Śrī Vikrāntavarman, whose great glory is well-known, and whose high fame is due to the grace of the lotus-feet of the primaeval God Śrī Īśāna and his (king's) father.........by whom Lakṣmī, born in the Kailāsa mountain, was again installed on such an altar.

LL. 10 ff. Vikrāntavarman, possessed of fortune and a beautiful body, established here the famous (image of Lakṣmī)[1] in the year denoted by 'Rāma-artha-ṣaṭ' *i. e.* 653.

(Astronomical details follow.)

No. 22. Po-Nagar Stelae Inscription of king Satyavarman dated 706 Śaka.

The inscription was edited by M. Bergaigne (Corpus No. XXVI, p. 242).

This inscription, along with five others (Nos. 29 a, 29 b, 29 c, 45, 47), is engraved on the four faces and the base of a stelae found at Po-Nagar. The language is Sanskrit.

---

1. कीर्त्ति means any work, calculated to render famous the name of its constructor (cf. Fleet, Gupta Inscriptions, p. 212).

It contains five verses in 18 lines, the metre being Śārdūlavikrīḍita.

It first gives a legendary account of the installation of a Mukhaliṅga, in the province of Kauṭhāra, by king Vicitrasagara. In the year 696 (=774 A. D.) the temple was destroyed, and the treasures of the temple, together with the Liṅga, were carried away. King Satyavarman pursued the plunderers and defeated them in a naval battle, but could not recover the treasures or the Liṅga. The king then built another temple, and installed a new Mukhaliṅga, called, after the king, Śrī-Satya-Mukhaliṅga, together with an image of 'Bhagavatī and Gaṇeśa' (?) in the year 706 (=784 A. D.).

TEXT.

ओम्

I येनोर्व्वीसकलाधिराज्यमसमं लब्ध्वा पुरा श्रीमता
श्रीशम्भोर्म्मुखलिङ्गमुज्वल[1]निभं सर्व्वोपभोगान्वितम् ।
कौठारे जगतस्तमोमयहरं संस्थाप्यते भूतले
विख्यातो नृपतिर्व्विचित्रसगरो नाम्ना स राजाधिकः ॥

II देवीशाननलिङ्गमन्यपुरजैः प्रेतातिकष्टाशनै-
र्भीमाभैरतिकृष्णरूक्षपुरुषैः कालोग्रपापात्मकैः ।
शाके कोशनवर्तुगे गतघृणैरुद्धृत्य पोतागतै-
र्दैत्यौघैरिव सायुधैस्सुरपुरन्दग्धन्तदेतैस्तदा ॥

III तन्नाशं सभटस्सवीरपुरुषश्श्रीसत्यवर्म्मा नृप-
श्श्रुत्वा तानुदधौ सुपोतसहितः पापात्मकान् दुर्ज्जनान् ।
हत्वा तद्वहनस्थितं शिवमुखं सस्वन्निमग्नञ्जले
तल्लिङ्गे निधनङ्गते मरपतिश्शोचन्भवेद्याकुलः ॥

IV देवेन्द्रानुमताधिराज्यपरमश्श्रीसत्यवर्म्मेति यः
कोशं साननमादितुल्यविभवं सश्रीभनारीवपुः ।

---

1. Read °ज्ज्वल° here.

श्रीदेवेश्वरसन्नतौ कृतमनाश्शाङ्कः प्रकर्तुं पुन-
र्व्विज्ञेयस्स नृपो विचित्रसगरो भूमौ तदन्यो न चेत् ॥

V वृद्धे कोशखभूवरेश्शकपतौ वैशाखधौतान्विते
जीवाग्र्ये रविभे तिथौ मुनिगते केत्वर्कचन्द्रात्मजाः ।
चा— —˘ ˘ —धरासुतगुरू द्वन्द्वोदुपो[1] गो भृगु-
र्म्मत्स्ये—˘ ˘—˘—˘ ˘ ˘— — —˘ येस्थापयत् ॥

TRANSLATION.

1. The fortunate king, who, obtaining unique sovereignty over the whole world, formerly established in this world, at Kauṭhāra, a Mukhaliṅga of Śambhu,—bright as gold and dispelling darkness from the world,—together with all articles of enjoyment, was famous by the name Vicitrasagara.

2. In the Śaka year, denoted by Kośa-nava-ṛtu (696), ferocious, pitiless, dark-coloured people of other cities, whose food was more horrible than that of the Vampires, and who was vicious and furious like Yama, came in ships, took away the Mukhaliṅga of the God, and set fire to the abode of the God, as the armed crowds of Daityas did in heaven.

3. Learning of this raid, king Śrī Satyavarmā (sailed) on good ships with his soldiers and other heroes (officers ?), and killed those wicked and vicious persons in the sea. But he was very much dejected to learn that the Śivamukha, together with its property, which was in their ship, was thrown into water, and that the Śivaliṅga was destroyed.

4. The king Śrī Satyavarmā, ruling over an excellent kingdom covetable to Indra, having resolved to devote himself to the worship of Śiva, was able to re-install with the pristine splendour, a Kośa (Liṅga) with a face (*i. e.* Śiva mukha), together with a beautiful female (Durgā ?) and an elephant (or Gaṇeśa, whose face was like that of an elephant ?).

---

1. Read °डुपो here.

He must be known as king Vicitrasagara, (if, as the tradition goes,) there be not a second king of that name on the earth.

5. Established in the year of the Śaka king denoted by Kośa-kha-bhūdhara (706)................(astronomical details follow).

No. 23. Yang Tikuh Stelae Inscription of Indravarman I dated 721 Śaka.

The inscription was edited by M. Bergaigne (Corpus, No. XXII, p. 207).

Yang Tikuh is the native appellation of a stelae, found near the village of Takoh, not far from the hill of Datrang in the plain of Phanrang. The inscription, engraved on two faces of the stelae, contains 37 lines of writing. The language is Sanskrit. The inscription is written partly in prose and partly in verse. There are altogether 14 verses, the metre being, vv. 1–2, Sragdharā; vv. 3–4 Śārdūlavikrīḍita; vv. 5–9 and vv. 11–14, Anusubh; and v. 10, Vaṁśastha.

The inscription records that in 709 Ś (=787 A. D.), the army of Java, coming to Champā by way of sea, destroyed the temple of Śiva known as Bhadrādhipatīśvara. King Indravarman reconstructed the temple in 721 Ś (=799 A. D.), installed an image of the god, to be henceforth worshipped under the name of Indrabhadreśvara, and made various donations.

TEXT.

(a.)

ओम्.

I (१) यस्सिद्धर्षिसङ्घैस्सुरवरनिचयैश्चारणैश्चोत्तमौजो
यं यस्माद्याति युक्तस्स ज(२)यति जगताञ्जायते जन्मजुष्टः ।

तात्यर्कोन्द्विन्द्रदैत्यैर्द्दिवि भुवि विभवैर्भावभोगस्य भोक्ता
(३) यत्तर्त्तुद्ररक्षः क्षणमपि शमभूत्तस्य भक्त्या स्मरेयम् ॥
तस्य भगवतोऽसुरासुररिपुपवि(४)त्रचरणयुगलसरोरुह-
मकरण्डस्य क्षीरार्णवतरङ्गगगणसिन्धुफेणशशिकरशुक्लतरभ(५)
स्मावदातधवलतरशरीरप्रदेशस्याशेषभुवनोपजीव्यमानविप्रती-
ततर[1]पङ्कजमृणालनालपा(६)दविम्बस्य सुरासुरपतिशिखरमङ्क-
लपदद्वयरेणुगङ्गाप्रवाहस्यापि सुरसिद्धविद्याधरगणमकुटकि-
(७)रीटवरकनककणनिकरसन्ध्यायमानचरणनखमणिदर्प्पणस्य
पादयुगलारविन्दस्य शरणमधिकृत्य स भगवान् श्रीमानिन्द्र-
वर्म्मा प्रतिदिवसमेवमखिलदिगन्तरालधर्म्मस्थितितरतम-
क्रमप्रती (६) तः क्षितितले पुण्यमकरोत् ॥

II श्रीमान् राजेन्द्रवर्म्मा वरजनमहितो यक्षरत्नप्रमुख्यः
ख्यातस्तेषां प्रभावैर्म्मनुरिव जगतो रक्षणे क्षेमयुक्तः ।
ब्रह्मक्षत्रप्रधानो जगति दिवि यथा यज्ञभागैर्म्महेन्द्रो
राज्ये वंशप्रतीतस्सरुचिरिव शशी निर्म्मलाकाशदेशे ॥

स जयति विक्रमतया (१२) भुजद्वयेनोद्वहन्निव धरणीं सकल-
चम्पाधिराज्यवसुमतीतलपतितशतमख इव धनञ्जय (१३) इवा-
प्रतिहतपराक्रमोऽपि हरिरिव विजिताशेषारिपुवृन्दवृन्दस्सुरासुरगुरु-
चरणाद्वया(१४)रविन्दजनितसुस्फीतदेशातिशयविक्रमस्तु भुवि
देवराजसदृशः पूर्व्वजन्मानवरतमखकुश(१५)लतपःफलतया धनद इव
धनत्यागातिशयेन राजलक्ष्म्यालिङ्गितमृदुतरशरीरप्रदेशः (१६)
प्रमुदितमनसा तस्य नगरीप्रतीततरवसुधातरतमानुक्रमरक्षणस्व-
शक्तिप्रभावोर्ज्जितनिरुपद्रववर्णाश्रमव्यवस्थितिस्सुरनगरीव राजधा-
न्यासीत् ॥

III स श्रीमान् नृपतिस्सदा विजयते भूमौ रिपोस्सर्व्वत-
श्चन्द्रेन्द्राग्नियमस्य विग्रहमधाद्यताधिपस्यौजसा ।

---

1. Read '°प्रतीपतर'.

ग्रहांशप्रभवः प्रभूतविभवो भाग्यप्रभावान्वितः
शक्त्या विष्णुरिव प्रमथ्य च रिपून्धर्म्मस्थितिं पालयेत् ॥

(b).

IV (१) श्रीभद्राधिपतीश्वरस्त्रिभुवने ख्यातस्स्वतेजोग्निभि-
र्गन्धर्व्वोरगराक्षसैश्च मुनिभिर्देवर्षिविद्याधरैः ।
(२) पातालप्रभवश्च वीर्य्यतपसा सात्वेन[1] वा योगिनो
युक्तस्तैर्म्मनसा प्रभावविभवैः संस्तूयते सर्व्वदा ॥

V (३) नगर्य्याः पश्चिमोद्भुतस्त्रिभिर्लोकैः[2] समर्च्चितः ।
दूरतस्तेजसो भक्त्या सोऽयं भाति महीतले ॥

VI भद्रं स्वस्थं शुभं यस्माज्जगतां पाति तेजसा ।
भद्रस्याधिपतिस्तस्मात्स भद्राधिपतीश्वरः ॥

अथ चिरकालेन कोशकोष्ठागारदासदासीरजतसुवर्णरत्नादि-परिभोगभुक्तस्स भुवनत्रयार्च्चितपादपङ्कजरेणुरेव स्वेन तेजसा सकल-जगद्धितकारणस्समभवत् ॥

ततश्च कलियुगदोषातिशयभावेन नावागतैर्ज्जववलसंघैर्न्निर्द्दह्यते-पि नवाम्बराद्रियमिते शककाले स एव शून्योऽभवत् ॥

VII बहुवर्षसहस्राणि स बभूव महीतले ।
स्वं स्थानं दहनं गन्तुं ह्यकरोत् स्वस्य मायया ॥

अथ तस्य तदपि राजेन्द्रवर्म्मणा पुनस्स्थापितमेव सकलकोश-कोष्ठागाररजतसुवर्णमकुटरत्नहारादिपरिभोगसान्तःपुरविलासिनी-दासदासीगोमहिषक्षेत्रादिद्रव्यं तस्मै तेन दत्तश्चिरसप्रसादेन ॥

VIII तस्यापि पार्थिवं लिङ्गं स्थापितं श्रीन्द्रवर्म्मणा ।
इन्द्रभद्रेश्वरो नाम्ना ततश्चाभूत् स एव वा ॥

IX तस्यैव स्थापितन्तेन द्रव्यं कोशश्चरस्थिरं ।
समुखश्चरकोशं हि शाके शशियमाद्रिगे ॥

X स एव राजा परिपालयन्महीं
यदा प्रजास्ताः मुदितास्स्वविक्रमैः ।

---

1. Read 'सत्त्वेन'.

2. Read °'भूतस्त्रि°'.

स्वधर्म्मयत्नात् प्रथितो महीतले
सदा रिपूनाञ्जयति स्म तेजसा ॥

XI स धर्म्मकुलसम्पन्नस्त्यागी शूरसमन्वितः ।
शक्त्या पराश्च निर्ज्जित्य महीं पायात्समन्ततः ॥

तस्मै भगवते सकललोकहितकारणाय श्रीन्द्रभद्रेश्वरायेद-
मिति स भगवान् श्रीमानिन्द्रवर्म्मा जअंकोष्ठागारं शिवयज्ञक्षेत्रद्वयं
शिखिशिखागिरिप्रदेशं भक्त्या शुद्धेन मनसैव दत्तवानिति ॥

XII इन्द्रभद्रेश्वरस्यैव सर्व्वद्रव्यं महीतले ।
ये रक्षन्ति रमन्त्येते स्वर्गे सुरगणैस्सदा ॥

XIII ये हरन्ति पतन्त्येते नरके वा कुलैस्सह ।
यावत् सूर्य्योऽस्ति चन्द्रश्च तावन्नरकदुःखिताः ॥

XIV लुब्धेन मनसा द्रव्यं यो हरेत् परमेश्वरात् ।
नरकात् न पुनर्ग्गच्छेन् न चिरन्तु स जीवति ॥

TRANSLATION.

Victorious in the world is He, who is the supreme energy; who is attended by the excellent Siddhas, the Ṛṣis, the excellent gods and the chanters of hymns; from whom are born all creatures liable to birth, and to whom they (ultimately) resort; and who enjoys pleasures in infinite varieties, along with Tārkṣya, the Sun, the Moon, Indra, and the Daityas in heaven, and by means of his mighty prowess, in the earth. Supreme Yakṣas as well as the mean Rakṣas are assured of happiness if they think of Him with devotion, even for a moment.

Taking protection in the pair of lotus-like feet of the God, —the honey of whose lotus-feet purifies the Asuras and their enemies; whose brilliantly white body is besmeared with ashes whiter than the waves of the milk-ocean, the foam of the celestial river, and the rays of the moon; the image of whose feet, the support of the three worlds, excites the jealousy of the stalk and roots of lotus; the holy dust of whose pair of feet, and the holy stream of the Ganges on whose head are the crest-jewels of the chiefs of Suras and Asuras;[1] and the nails of whose feet, wearing the crimson glow of twilight by the facets of the golden crown of the groups of gods, Siddhas, and Vidyādharas, appear like a bejewelled mirror:-His Majesty king Indravarman, whose fame for observing the law was spreading more and more[2] every day in all directions, made this pious work in the world.

2. The king Indravarman, who is honoured by good men; who is foremost among those who regard sacrifice as their principal treasure; who is celebrated in this world on account of the efficacy of these sacrifices, as Mahendra is in heaven by obtaining only a portion of them; who, like Manu, peacefully guards the world; who is the head of the Brahma-Ksatra clan;[3] and who is famous in his kingdom by the purity of his race, like the brilliant moon in a clear sky.

Glory to him, who like Vikrama (Viṣṇu) raised the world, as it were, by his two hands; who is like Indra, fallen to the earth for ruling over the whole of Champā; who like Dhanañjaya is of irrepressible valour, and yet, like Hari, prospered after having conquered many groups of enemies, and placed his foot in a large number of countries created by the lotus-like feet of the preceptor of the Suras and Asuras (*i. e.* Kāśyapa); who is like Indra in this world, by virtue of perfect austerities and constant sacrifices performed in previous births; who is like Dhanada by his liberality; and

---

1. The word 'अपि' seems to have no special meaning.

2. The use of the adjective 'तरतम' is unknown, though the noun derived from it viz. 'तारतम्य' is well-known.

3. Bergaigne translates : "who has, for ministers, only the Brāhmaṇas and the Kṣatriyas.

whose charming body is embraced with pleasure by the Goddess of sovereignty.[1]

The king who, on account of his capacity to govern better and better a country, celebrated for its towns, maintains intact the orders of castes and *āśramas*, had a capital like the city of the gods.

III. This fortunate king is always victorious over his enemies in the world in all directions. In the height of his strength, he combines in himself the prowess of Candra, Indra, Agni, Yama and Kubera;[2] originating partly from a Brāhmaṇa (or from a portion of Brahma), the master of immense wealth, possessed of fortune and prowess, crushing, like Viṣṇu, his enemies by means of his prowess, he established the proper law (in his kingdom).

(*b*).

IV. Śrī Bhadrādhipatīśvara, who originated from the nether world, who is celebrated in the three worlds by the fire of his own energy, and is possessed of heroism, asceticism, and the character of Yogin, is always eulogised at heart by the Gandharvvas, the Uragas, the Rākṣasas, the Munis, the divine sages, and the Vidyādharas, who have prowess as their treasure.

V. Coming out from the west of the town, worshipped in the three worlds, he shines in the world from afar, with splendour as his ornament.

---

1. The construction is not very happy.

2. Cf. Manu, Chap. VII, vv. 3-5. Bergaigne translates the verse in a quite different way: "He has carried a redoubtable war in the regions of Candra, Indra, etc." Senart proposes a correction: "He took by his strength the body of Candra, Indra, etc. i. e. he beca ne, in some way, the master of the northern, eastern, etc. regions"

VI. He is called Bhadrādhipatīśvara, because he is the master of welfare, and maintains, by his splendour, the welfare, the health and the good of the worlds.

Now, for a long time, having enjoyed treasures, grain-stores, male and female slaves, silver, gold, jewels etc., he, the dust of whose lotus-like feet is worshipped by the three worlds, became, by his own prowess, the cause of the prosperity of the entire world.

Then owing to the excess of faults in the Kali age it (*i. e.* the temple, also called Bhadrādhipatīśvara) was burnt by the army of Java coming by means of ships, and became empty, in the year of the Śakas denoted by 'nine-ambara-adri' (709).

VII. He was in the world for many thousands of years and then had his own abode burnt by his own *māyā* (illusion).

Then king Indravarmā re-installed it, and out of the goodness of his heart gave it treasures, grain-stores, silver, gold crown, jewel, necklace and other objects of enjoyment, together with women of the harem, male and female slaves, oxen, buffaloes, fields and other articles.

VIII. Indravarman also installed an earthen Liṅga of the God, which therefore came to be known as Indra-bhadreśvara.

IX. He also established, in the year of the Śakas 'Śaśī-yama-adri' (721), two treasures for the God, the one composed of moveable and immoveable property, and the other moveable and with a mouth (priests ?).

X. When this king protects the earth, his subjects are delighted at his prowess. Renowned in the world for his zeal in protecting Dharma (Law ?), he always triumphed over his enemies by his own prowess.

XI. Endowed with virtue, and born in a noble family,

charitable, surrounded by heroes, and defeating the enemies by his prowess, he protects the world on all sides.

To the God, Śrī Indrabhadreśvara, who is the cause of the happiness of the whole world, king Indravarmā, out of devotion and in pure heart, has given the country of Śikhi-śikhāgiri, comprising the two fields of Śivakṣetra and Yajña-kṣetra, and the grain-store called jaña (?).

XII. Those who protect all these goods of Indrabhadreśvara in the world, would enjoy the delights of heaven along with the gods.

XIII. Those who carry them away would fall into hell together with their family, and would suffer the sorrows of hell as long as the sun and the moon endure.

XIV. Those who, out of cupidity, rob Parameśvara of his goods, will not live long, and will never come out of the hell.

Nos. 24 a, 24 b. Glai Lamov Stelae Inscriptions of Indravarman I dated 723 Śaka.

These two inscriptions were edited by M. Bergaigne (Corpus No. XXIII, p. 218).

Glai Lamov is the name of a thicket amidst the rice fields in the valley south of Phanrang. The two inscriptions are engraved on two faces of a stelae. No. 24 (*a*) contains 22 lines, and No. 24 (*b*), 23. The language is Sanskrit. No. 24 (*a*) contains 14 verses and a fragment in prose, the metre being, v. 1, Anuṣṭubh, v. 2, Indravajrā, vv. 3-8, and vv. 10-14, śloka, and v. 9, Śārdūlavikrīḍita. No. 24 (*b*) has a long prose text at the beginning, then two verses (metre Vaṁśastha), then another prose text, and lastly one verse in Śloka metre.

The inscription No. 24 (*a*) gives a short genealogy, comprising three names, *viz.* Prathivīndravarman, his sister's son Satyavarman, and lastly, the brother of the latter, Indravarman. It refers to the installation of two images of Śiva, called, after the king, Indrabhogeśvara and Indrabhadreśvara, and records the installation of a third, called Indraparameśvara, in the year 723 Ś. (=801 A. D.).

No. 24 (*b*) records the donations made by Indravarman to the God Śaṅkara-Nārāyaṇa.

TEXT.

(*a*).

ओम्

I नमोऽस्तु सर्व्वदेवेभ्यः प्रजानां निरुपद्रवाः ।
राज्ञश्च विजयो नित्यं स्म भवन्तु महीतले ॥

II श्रीमान्नरेन्द्रः प्रथिवीन्द्रवर्म्मा
ख्यातस्स्ववंशैर्ज्जगति प्रभावैः ।
ह्यस्तीति लोके स भुनक्ति भूमिं
शक्त्या च निर्ज्जित्य रिपू[1] हि सर्व्वान् ॥

III चम्पाश्च सकलां भुक्त्वा स एव परमो नृपः ।
तस्य राज्ये सुभीक्षा[2] स्यान्नानाद्रव्याणि सन्ति च ॥

IV न्यहनत् तस्करान् सर्व्वान् तमो भानुरिव प्रभुः ।
शितरश्मिर्य्यथा व्योम्नि तथा वंशे स शोभते ॥

V अथ कालेन महता शम्भोर्भ्भक्तिपरायणात् ।
कीर्त्या च धर्म्मेण सता रुद्रलोकमगान्नृपः ॥

VI तस्यैव भागिनेयोऽसौ श्रीमान् वीर्य्यतमो नृपः ।
सत्यवर्म्मेति नामाख्यः ख्यातो लोके स्वकर्म्मभिः ॥

VII साद्रिद्रुमार्णवा भूमिर्द्दिशश्च विदिशस्तथा ।
तस्यं भावेन महता घूर्णिताश्च समन्ततः ॥

1. Read रिपून्
2. Read सुभिक्षं

VIII तस्य प्रमुखत स्थातुं न शक्तो वा परो युधि ।
विष्णोर्य्यथासुरश्चाभूद्दृष्ट्वा तन्तु पराङ्मुखः ॥

IX कान्त्योर्व्यां कुसुमायुधेन सदृशश्शक्रेण तुल्यो जये
शक्त्युग्रेण यशोर्थिनेऽतिबलवान् देवेन्द्रपुत्रोपमः ।
मान्यो मानवसंगमेषु च सतां तार्क्ष्योग्ररूपो विभु-
र्भावानाश्रयति प्रमथ्य च रिपून् श्रीसत्यवर्म्मा नृपः ॥

X चिरकालेन महता प्राप्ते स निधनं गतः ।
ज्ञानेन धर्म्मसंयुक्तो लोकमैश्वरमाप्नुयात् ॥

XI तस्यानुजश्च नृपतिश्श्रीमान् धर्म्मपरोऽभवत् ।
इन्द्रवर्म्मेति विख्यातस्तेजसा बलवान् भुवि ॥

XII स युद्धे न्यगमत् शत्रून्नृपोऽपि परवीरहा ।
समीक्ष्य वलसंयुक्तो मृगेन्द्र इव कुञ्जरान् ॥

XIII भूमौ विजयते राजा वीर्य्यवान् यशसान्वितः ।
सोऽहनत् परसैन्यानि वज्रहस्त इवासुरान् ॥

XIV व्यरोचत महाप्राज्ञो राजा शूरसमन्वितः ।
राज्ये हि धर्म्मसंयुक्तो धर्म्मराज इवाभवत् ।

स एव राजा श्रीमान् प्रथमतरन्तावदिन्द्रभोगेश्वरं वीरपुरे स्वयमेव स्थापयेत् तिथिकरणमुहूर्त्तनक्षत्रादिवसलग्नयोगेन तदनन्तर-मिन्द्रभद्रेश्वरमुपस्थापितवान् ॥

अथापि शरदि निर्म्मलकह[1]शशिराजवंशसंभूतेन धराधर-तनुजकान्तिकोमलशरीरप्रदेशेन तारागणोदयगिरिशिखरनिशाकरेणेव वरभवनगवाक्षप्रदेशविनिहितवदनकमलकुड्मलेन मृगदर्पणो-त्करसुगन्धचन्दनानुलेपनभवलिनोरस्थलवायुद्वयेन[2] प्रथुतरभाग्यसंप-दुपवृंहितपरमराज्यराजलक्ष्मीलक्षणोपचितकर्म्मस्वभावेन परबल-स्वबलधनुर्ज्यानिक्षेपनिर्घोषपरिकम्पितसमरभूमिभोगनिश्चलचित्तच-न्द्रप्रभावेन [ण] राज्ञेन्द्रवर्म्मणेह स भगवानिन्द्रपरमेश्वरस्सकल-

1. Read 'कल'.

2. Read '°नुलेपनधवलितोरुस्थलबाहुद्वयेन'.

जगद्धितकारणश्श्रीसत्यवर्म्मणो वरभवनस्थाने स्थापितश्चापि परम-शुद्धेन मनसा समस्तमुनिजनतपोधनविबुधविप्रगणेभ्यः परस्पर-मुदितप्रवृत्तचित्तेभ्योऽरिकृतप्रयत्नेन[1] धनदानैरपि शकपतिसमये लोकयमपर्व्वते क्याले[2] (?) यकसितपक्षनवम्याः निशायामुत्तराषाढर्क्षेण चन्द्रवारसहितेन कर्क्कटलग्नेन यावद्वसुमतीपर्व्वतमहार्णवाकाश-मित्यस्ति तावदित्येव स्थिरो भवतु ।

(b).

ओम्

जयति महासुरपुरत्रयावमर्द्दण[न] विविधविक्रमोऽपि सितभस्म-प्रभावयोगादिजपहुङ्कारनिर्म्मलतरशरीरप्रदेशश्च गगणान्तरस्फुरित-विद्युदनेकचञ्चच्चारुरुचिरविततशिखिशिखावलीज्वलितनेत्रत्रयज्यो-त्स्नो द्योतितसकलजगन्मण्डलस्थितिर्भाति बहुतरकनकरजततरु-लतावगुण्ठिततुहिनगिरिशिखरगह[न?]विवरान्तरस्थितोऽवनतसिद्ध-चारणहरिघणमुखशतमखमुखतियविबुधगणमस्तककिरीटमणिकिरण-विच्छुरितपादबिम्बो निपतितरक्तबन्धुजीवकुसुमरेणुरञ्जितचरणतल-कमलकोमलमृणालनालस्तु नभस्तलनिसृतगम्भीरगङ्गाजल-निपातधाराधौततरजटाधारोऽत्यहङ्कारकामाङ्गदहनस्ससुरासुरमुनि-सिद्धयक्षगन्धर्वकिन्नरवराप्सरोगणपवित्रचरणयुगलाम्भोरुहश्चातिव-लदर्प्पान्धासुरघ्नश्च स भगवान् महेश्वरोऽपि जगत[:]स्थित्युत्पत्ति-प्रलयकारणस्तु तथापि नारायणस्समस्त भुवनपरिरक्षणसमर्थभावः क्षीरार्णवतरङ्गसङ्घाततलशयनानन्तभोगभुजगपरिसेवितचतुर्भुजभुव-नस्तम्भश्चापि गोवर्धनगिरिधरणसुरासुरमुनिवन्दितचरणारविन्द-स्तु कृतमधुकंसासुरकेशिचानूररिष्टप्रलम्बनिधनोऽपि मधुकैटभरुधि-रसन्ध्यायमानचरणनखमणिदर्पणश्चापि यदेकमूर्त्तिस्थितस्तत इति शङ्करनारायणोऽपि भगवान् सुरचिताभरणकनकपिञ्जरीकृततनुवरैक-देशस्तु तस्य प्रसादोऽस्तु भगवते श्रीमत इन्द्रवर्म्मणे सर्व्वोपभोगान् स ददातु तस्मै सर्व्वैश्वर्य्याणीहामुत्र वा तस्य राज्ञो यथेप्सिताः भवन्तु

1. Read 'विकृत°' (रिकृत—does not offer any suitable meaning).

2. I think this is काले विकसितपक्षनवम्याः (i.e. ninth day of the bright fortnight.)

स्म ॥ तस्मै सकलकोशकोष्ठागारसान्तःपुरविलासिनीदासदासीगोमहिषक्षेत्रादिद्रव्यं हेमकटिसूत्रवलयनूपुरकिरीटमणिमुक्तिप्रवालहारादिभूषणं रजतकुम्भान्नभाजनव्यजनातपत्रकदवकलशचामरशरावादिपरिभोगं स श्रीमानिन्द्रवर्म्मेति परमेश्वरचरितनिरन्तरमनास् सुरपतिरिव दत्तवान् सकललोककारणप्रसादातिशयेभ्यो विगतकलुषचित्तभावेन ॥

I. य एव राजा परिरक्षति प्रभुः
परस्य दत्तन्तु नृपस्य शासनम् ।
हि तस्य राज्ञः परिरक्षतु स्वकम्
परोऽपि राजा वसुधातले धनम् ॥

II. य एव राजा तु विनाशयन् धनं
परस्य दत्तन्तु नृपस्य शासनम् ।
परोऽपि राजा तु विनाशयेत्पुनः
स तस्य राज्ञो वसुधातले स्वकम् ॥

प्रथमतरन्तावत् श्रीकोष्ठागारं पवित्रेश्वरस्य कोष्ठागारं ममौच्कोष्ठागारं भुवनाग्रपुरकोष्ठागारद्वयं क्लजदटीप्रदेशग्रामैकं चं(?)लैप्गिरिशिखरोत्तुंगदीर्घे सर्व्वाणि तेन दत्तानि तस्मै चित्तप्रसादेन ॥ ये केचित् साधुपुरुषाः स्वपुण्यपरिरक्षार्थं ते तानि सर्व्वाणि संरक्ष्य दीर्घायुषा[1] भवन्तु सर्व्वैः कुलसन्तानैस्स्वर्ग्गे नसन्तु यावदिन्द्रोऽपि दिवस्थो ह्यस्त्यनेकशतसहस्रकल्पेषु तावद्देवताविशेषैः रमन्तु स्म ॥ ये केचित् पापपुरुषाः नरकनिर्भयाः तानि द्रव्यानि[णि] वा हरन्ति नाशयन्ति ते ह्यल्पायुषा[1] भवन्तु नरके पतन्तु सर्वैः सप्तमकुलैः यावत् सूर्य्याचन्द्रमसौ ग्रहनक्षत्रतारागणास्सन्ति तावत् नरके वसन्तु स्म ॥ सर्वाणीमानि वचनानि पुरोहिताग्रासब्राह्मणपण्डिततापसगणानां यदा श्रीपरमपुरोहितेन हूयमाने वरर्णाले लिह्यमाने ज्वालमाने तदा सर्व्वं शापमवदन् ॥ ये तान्यनुचरन्ति ते दीर्घायुषा[1] भवन्तु ॥ उक्तं हि :—

III. पाकभेदः कृतघ्नश्च भूमिहर्त्ता च ते त्रयः ।
नरकात्[2] न निवर्त्तन्ते यावच्चन्द्रदिवाकरौ ॥

---

1. Read °षो 2. Read न्

TRANSLATION.

(a)

1. Reverence to all the gods ! May the people be free from calamities, and the king always victorious in this world.

2. The fortunate king Prathivīndravarmā[1], famous in the world for his family and prowess, enjoyed the lands by having conquered all his enemies by his own power, while he was in the world.

3. Having enjoyed the whole of Champā, he flourished as a great king. There were abundance of alms (*i. e.* means of subsistence) and various things in his kingdom.

4. The king destroyed all the thieves, as the sun dispels the darkness. He shone in his family as the moon does in the sky.

5. After a long time, on account of his devotion to Śaṁbhu, his glory, and his pursuit of good law, the king went to the world of Rudra (*i. e.* died and went to heaven).

6. The king called Satyavarmā, fortunate and very heroic, and renowned in the wo.ld by his own actions, was his nephew (sister's son).

7. The earth, with its mountains, trees, and oceans, as well as the directions, both cardinal and intermediary, turned round in all directions, by (the pressure of) his great power.

8. In the combat, the enemies could not stand (the ground) in his presence, but turned their face on seeing him, as the Asuras did on seeing Viṣṇu.

9. By his beauty he was like cupid in this world; by

---

1. It may be a mistake for 'पृथिवीन्द्रवर्मा' or the change of form may be deliberate. Elsewhere we have 'प्रथु' for 'पृथु'.

his victories he was comparable to Indra; by his prowess he was like Ugra (*i. e.* Śiva); among those who desire glory he was very strong, like the son of Indra;[1] in the assembly of men he was respected by honest persons; his appearance was terrible like that of Tārkṣya (Garuḍa); he, the king Satyavarmā, master of sentiments (or, master of all creatures), is victorious by having churned (*i. e.* exterminated) all his enemies.

10. The king died without reigning for a long time, and being devoted to his duty, he secured the world of Īśvara, by virtue of his great knowledge.

11. His younger brother Indravarmā became king; he was fortunate, dutiful, powerful and renowned in the world for his strength.

12. Although a king (nṛpa, lit. protector of men), he was a destroyer of enemies, heroes in combat, and accompanied by his army he attacked the enemies as soon as he saw them, as a lion attacks an elephant.

13. The powerful and renowned king triumphs in the world; he destroyed the army of the enemies as Indra destroyed that of the Asuras.

14. The king who was very wise, and surrounded by heroes,—flourished greatly. Faithful to law in his kingdom, he was like Dharmarāja (Yama or Yudhiṣṭhira).

The fortunate king kimself at first installed Indrabhogeśvara at Vīrapura after having selected the *tithi*, *Karana*, *muhūrtta*, *nakṣatra*, *divasa* and *lagna*. (15) Then he installed Indrabhadreśvara.

1. Bergaigne takes 'शक्तुप्रेण' as an ordinary adjective, and translates: among those who desire the glory . he was like Indra, terrible by his power of vanquishing. In 'यशोर्थिने' we have the fourth case ending instead of the seventh.

He, who is born in the family of the spotless moon of autumn,-whose body is delicate and beautiful like that of Cupid,[1]—who appears like the moon in the midst of the stars at the summit of the mountain Udayagiri, when he shows his face, fair as a lotus bud, from the window of his magnificent palace,—whose hands and breast have been made white by the application of an abundance of perfumed sandal and musk,—who is habituated to noble actions as indicated by signs of royalty fostered by his magnificent good fortune,—whose terrible majesty (is manifest when) his heart remains unmoved in the vast[2] battle-field thoroughly shaken by the noise arising from the striking of the bowstrings of his own and his enemies' armies,—he, king Indravarmā installed in the excellent house of Satyavarmā, the God Indra Parameśvara, the cause of the prosperity of the whole world,—in a pure mind, and after having given riches, by sincere efforts, to all the Munis, ascetics, and learned Brāhmaṇas of lofty thoughts and inclinations, in the year of the Śakas denoted by 'loka-yama-parvvata' (723) (astronomical details follow). May this endure as long as the earth, the mountains, the great oceans, and the sky.

(b).

Victorious is He,—who even having performed various feats of prowess in destroying the three cities of the great Asuras, has the body (of an ascetic)[3], white with ashes, and purified by means of miracles, *yoga*, *japa*, *huṅkāra*, etc.;—who is illumined by the three eyes which glow like many beautiful flickering sparks of fire, and shine like lightning

1. The son of 'धराधर' i. e. Viṣṇu.

2. Bhoga here stands for आभोग.

3. The underlying idea is that asceticism ill suits a ferocity described above, hence the virodha, i. e. contradiction.

traversing the sky;—who illumines the whole universe, and shines, being situated in a deep cavern on the summit of the Himālaya mountain which is covered with abundance of gold, silver, trees and creepers;—the disc of whose feet is anointed by the rays of the jewels of the crowns at the head of the Siddhas, Cāraṇas, Hari, Kārttika, Indra, and other gods prostrate before him;—the lower part of whose feet, soft as the stalk and root of the lotus, is dyed with the pollen of the red[1] *Bandhujīva* flowers scattered on the ground, while his matted hair is washed by the fall of the deep waters of the Gaṅgā descending from heaven; —who burnt the body of Kāma who was very proud; whose two feet, like two lotuses, cause purification to the multitude of gods, Asuras, Munis, Siddhas, Yakṣas, Gandharvvas, Kinnaras, and beautiful Apsaras; —who is destroyer of the Asuras blinded by the pride of their excessive strength;—who is the greatest God (Maheśvara), and the cause of the origin, maintenance and destruction of the world.

Again, Nārāyaṇa is also capable of protecting the whole world. His four arms—the pillars of the world—are served by the serpent king with infinite hood, whose fathomless bed is formed by the deep of the ocean of milk beneath its mighty waves, while homage is paid to his lotus-feet by the gods, Asuras and Munis, as he held aloft the mount Govardhana; he destroyed Madhu, Kaṅsa, the Asura, Keśi, Cāṇūra, Ariṣṭa and Pralamba, while the nail of his feet, dyed crimson (lit. made to appear like evening) by the blood of Madhukaiṭabha, appeared like a jewelled mirror.

These two gods are united in one image which is therefore called Gol Śaṅkaranārāyaṇa, one part of whose august

---

1. There may be a pun on the word 'रक्त'-meaning blood (of the victims sacrificed before Śiva.)

body appears to be made of gold on account of the excellent gold ornaments. May the grace of the God fall upon His Majesty king Indravarmā. May the God grant him all kinds of wealth and enjoyments and fulfil all desires of the king both in this world and in the next.

The fortunate king Indravarmā, who always thinks of the work of the great God, and is like the king of gods, has given Him all the treasures, grain-stores, together with women of the harem, male and female slaves, oxen, buffaloes, fields and other objects; golden waistband, bracelet, anklet, diadems, jewels, pearls, corals, necklaces and other ornaments; silver jug and dishes for rice, fans, umbrellas, pitchers for drinking water[1] (?), chowries, shallow earthen dishes, and other articles of enjoyment, for gaining an excess of favour from the cause of all the worlds (*i. e.* the God), and with a heart free from all sordid thoughts.

1. Whatsoever king, himself a master, guards the donations made by other kings, he will see his own wealth in this world respected by other kings.

II. Whatsoever king, on the other hand, destroys the donations made by other kings, he will see his own wealth in this world destroyed by other kings.

In the first place, the granary of Śrī, the granary of Pavitreśvara, the granary of *Mamauc*, the two granaries of Bhuvanāgrapura, a village in the district of Klajadaṭī extending as far as the high summit of the mountain *Chamlaip*—all these have been given to the God by the king with a pure heart. Let the virtuous persons desiring to gain religious merit protect the above (goods) and live long in this world, and afterwards live in the heaven with generations of their race, as long as Indra resides

1. 'Kadava' is not in the dictionary,–Kada means 'giving water'.

there; may they take delight there with other great gods for millions of aeons.

Those vicious persons who, fearless of hell, rob those goods or destroy them, let their lives be of short duration, and let them fall into hell, and reside there with seven generations, as long as the sun, the moon, the planets, the constellations and the stars endure.

All these words have been said by the multitude of priests, persons having right to seats in the first rank, the Brāhmaṇas, the learned men, and the ascetics; while the chief priest was offering to the fire barṇṇāla, ablaze as it was being licked, they uttered these imprecations.

Those who follow (the above regulations) would be of long life. It is said:

Those who destroy the ripe grains, those who are ungrateful and those who take others' lands,–these three never come back from hell as long as the sun and the moon endure.

No. 25. Po-Nagar Temple Inscription of Harivarman I dated 735 Śaka.

It records that in the year 735 (=813 A. D.), during the reign of king Vīra Jaya Śrī Harivarma Deva, victorious in battles, the Senāpati Pañroe living at Mani.........at Panrāṅ again made donations to God.........

J. A. 1888 (1), p. 76 No. 410
J. A. 1891 (1), p. 24.

No. 26. Po-Nagar Temple Inscription of Harivarman I dated 739 Śaka.

The inscription was edited by M. Bergaigne (Corpus No XXVIII, p. 263).

The inscription is engraved on the third face of the left door-pillar of the Po-Nagar temple to the left. It contains 31 lines of writing The language is Sanskrit. The inscription is written in prose with two verses at the end (metre-śārdūlavikrīḍita).

The inscription refers to 'Śrī Harivarmmadeva Rājādhirāja, lord of Champā, and to his young son Śrī Vikrāntavarman who was appointed the governor of Pāṇḍuraṅgapura and put in charge of a person who is called *senāpati*, but whose proper name consists of two syllables in Cham, the last of which is not intelligible, ('senāpati Pamr'), (cf. No. 25). The object of the inscription is to record the installation of a stone image of Bhagavatī, and the establishment of three temples, respectively for the Liṅga of Saṇḍaka, for Gaṇeśa, and for a God named Śrī-Maladā Kuṭhāra by Senāpati Pār (?), in the year 739 (=817 A. D.). The inscription incidentally refers to the victories of the king and the Senāpati.

Text

स्वस्ति श्रीहरिवर्म्मदेवराजाधिराजश्श्रीचम्पापुरपरमेश्वरो भूपतिरजितविक्रमो भुजगभुजोत्तम्भितजलधिकालिनिमग्नवसुन्धरामण्डलः मार्त्तण्डदो ?[दो]र्दण्डदग्धचीनतमिश्र[स्त्र]निचयो नारायणमूत्तिरि[1] वौजसा तस्यात्मजो ज्ञत्रोत्तमः पुल्याश्रीविक्रान्तवर्म्माख्यश्श्रीपाण्डुरङ्गपुराधिपत्यन्दत्त्वा तस्य रक्षणाय महाचमूपतिरेको राज्ञाभ्युदितस्सेनापतिपँरसमभिधानः मणिध्याम् पुर्य्यां द् (?) कजा महाग्रामे जन्मभूमिरतिगहनकम्बुजपुरकाननजनगजपदप्रमथनैकराजसिँहायमानस्तुहिनकरकिरणसदृशकीत्ति[2]प्रबोधितसज्जनहृदयकुमुदषण्डश्श्रीगौरीपतिचरणयुगहेमारविन्दप्रमुदितहँसायमान आकम्बुजार्धमाजितभुजौजसा गृह्य कौठारे श्रीभगवतीरूपं पुराणं जगत्प्रसिद्धं चिरेण शून्यमभूत् ।

---

1. Read 'मूर्त्तिरि°' 2. Read 'कीर्त्ति'

पुनः तत्प्रतिमां शिलामयीं सविचित्रालङ्कारां कृत्वा पराढकालिङ्गस्य प्रासादश्च श्रीविनायकस्य प्रासादश्च श्रीमलदाकुठारप्रासादमेतानि प्रासादानि वह[1] मराडपविचित्रद्वारेण विवरहराज्ञाद्रियुते शकराजे ज्येष्ठमासे इनग्रहणसमये जगत्पुरायार्थं इह कीर्त्यै परत्र मुक्त्यै संस्थापितवान्। तस्यै महाकगवत्यै[2] कनकरजतरत्नचित्रवस्त्रादीनि द्रव्यानि[णि]सन्ददौ कौठारजनपदे क्षेत्राणि सदासदासीमहिषाणि × × × × × [स] न्निवेद्येति,

I. यो धर्म्मेन [ण] युधिष्ठिरेण [सदृशो] वीर्य्येण कँसारिणा सौन्दर्य्येन मनोभुवा ⌣ ⌣ ⌣ — भूयोऽधिपत्येन ह। — — त्रेण भृगूत्त —⌣ ⌣ ⌣— — एन पुरुषोत्तमः श्रीसेनापतिपँर —⌣ ⌣ ⌣ — — — दमात्य [म्] शुभम् ॥

II. तुङ्गत्वं ज ⌣ —⌣ —⌣ ⌣ ⌣ — — —⌣ — —⌣ ⌣ —ौ कान्तिमता प—⌣ ⌣ ⌣— — —⌣— —⌣ ⌣

TRANSLATION.

Hail, the great king, king of kings, Harivarmmadeva, king of Champā, of irrepressible prowess. His arm was the serpent that held up the circle of earth, plunged in the ocean, which was Kali; his strong arm was the sun that expelled the darkness which was the Cinas; in splendour he was like the incarnation of Nārāyaṇa.

His son, the best of Kṣatriyas, was called *pulyā* Śrī Vikrāntavarmā. The king having given him sovereignty over Śrī Pāṇḍuraṅga, raised to the rank of Commander-in-chief, for guarding the prince, a person named Senāpati Pam̐r, born in the great village of *D (?)kjā*, depending on the town of Maṇidhi. Like a lion ravaging the elephants in an impenetrable forest he ravaged the towns of the Kamvujas, which contained men instead of elephants. His fame, white as the rays of the moon, delighted the hearts of the honest men which were like so many lotus flowers. He was

1 Read 'सह' 2. Read 'महाभगवत्यै'

the swan that took delight in the golden lotus which was the pair of feet of the lord of Gaurī (*i.e.* Mahādeva) ....as far as the middle of Kambuja, thanks to the invincible strength of his arm.[1]

An[2] old image of Bhagavatī in Kauṭhāra, famous all over the world, remained empty for a long time (*i.e.* the image was carried away and the temple remained empty and deserted).

Having made a new stone image of the Goddess adorned with a variety of ornaments, he again erected a temple of the Liṅga of Ṣaṇḍhaka, a temple of Śrī Vināyaka, and a temple of Śrī-Maladākuṭhāra, adorned with Maṇḍapas (Halls) and wonderful gates, in the year of the Śakarāja, denoted by 'Vivara-harākṣa-adri' (739), in the month of Jyaiṣṭha, at the time of the solar eclipse, in order to secure religious merit for the whole world, and for the sake of fame in this world, and salvation in the next.

He also offered to Mahābhagavatī, gold, silver, jewels, clothes of variegated colour, and other articles. He further dedicated fields in the Kauṭhāra country together with male and female slaves, buffaloes etc.

I. The king who resembles Yudhiṣṭhira for justice, the enemy of Kaṅsa for heroism, and the Cupid for beauty, to (Indra ?) for sovereignty,..............Bhṛgu..............the first among men (?) has (appointed) Śrī Senāpati Pam̐r an excellent minister.

---

1. The relation of the last phrase with the preceding one is difficult to understand. Does it mean that he adored Śiva, by visiting his temples as far as the middle of Kambuja ?

2. It is difficult to understand the significance of the word 'गृह्वथ्' which immediately precedes this sentence. It may be the end of a sentence introducing this old story.

No. 27. Glai Klong Anoh Stelae Inscription of Harivarman, dated 7 XX.

The Cham inscription on the stelae of Glai Klong Anoh, a small thicket in the fields of Panrang between the villages of Ram and Pralau, refers to king Śrī Harivarmadeva and his Senāpati (general) Panroe. It is dated, but only the hundredth figure '7' is legible. It apparently recorded some donations to God Viṣṇu.

J. A. 1888 (1), p. 77, No. 394.
J. A. 1891 (1), p. 23, No. 394.

No. 28. Bakul Stelae Inscription, dated Ś 751.

The Sanskrit portion of the inscription was edited by Bergaigne (Corpus No. XXV, p. 237) and the Cham portion by Aymonier (J. A., 1891, part I, pp. 25ff). It was commented upon by Finot (B. E. F., vol. III, p. 633, No. V.)

According to Finot, the unpolished stelae bearing this inscription was found about 3 miles to the west of the village of Chung-my in the valley south of Phanrang. (Aymonier and Bergaigne are wrong in stating Yangkur as the place of its origin).

The inscription, engraved on a single face of a rough stelae, contains 16 lines of writing, the first seven and the last two being in Sanskrit, and the rest in Cham. The Sanskrit portion, with the exception of Śrī at the beginning, is written in verse, the metre being vv. 1, 2, 4, Anuṣṭubh, and v. 3. Upajāti.

The inscription, which records the donations made to God Jina and Śaṅkara (that is to say, Buddha and Śiva) by a person named Samanta, was actually composed after the death of the donor by his son Buddhanirvāṇa. The donations consisted of two monasteries, two temples, and two pieces of land.

The Cham text gives the date 751 Ś (=829 A D.), records donations to God Mandara in the Parvata and God Praṇaveśvara, and refers to two fields and two monasteries, one of the latter being called Devarakṣa.

TEXT.

श्री

I. (1) विक्रान्तेश्वरलोकौ यौ तयोर्गुप्तौ स नायकः ।

(2) समन्तः प्रथितो नाम्ना तस्य पुण्यमिदं मतम् ॥

II. (3) विहारौ देवकुले द्वौ द्वे जिनशङ्करयोस्तयोः ।

(4) स्वजनार्थं प्रकुरुते ताङ्कतिं प्रगतश्शुभाम् ॥

III. (5) हुमातवोवसंगणितस्तु पात्मः

क्षेत्रन्तु खार्य्याः दशमस्ताङ्के[1] ।

(6) परत्र भूरीच्छति भोगमार्य्यं

प्रादाज्जिनायैव मनश्शुभेन ।

VI. (7) समन्तपुत्रस्स्थविरः बुद्धनिर्व्वाणसंज्ञकः ।

काव्यस्य करणञ्चक्रे ज्ञातये भूतले नृणाम् ॥

TRANSLATION.

(1) This is the meritorious act of the leader who is famous by the name of Samanta, and who is under the protection of the two, viz. Vikrānta and Īśvaraloka.[2]

---

1. Read "दशमस्तकाङ्के".

2. The first line of the first stanza is obscure, and the translation is merely conjectural. Bergaigne and Barth take the word 'loka' in the sense of 'world'. The former takes it to mean that Samanta was the guardian of the two worlds of Vikrānta (Buddha) and Śaṅkara (Śiva). The latter says that Samanta was the minister of a king called Vikrāntavarman in this world, and occupies the same post in heaven now that both of them were dead, Vikrāntavarman being called Vikrānteśvara after his death.

(2) Two temples and two monasteries for Jina[1] and Śaṅkara were made by him who has reached the state of bliss (i. e. gone to heaven) for the welfare of his kinsmen.

(3) Pātpluḥ added to (?) Humātavov (?), the field called Khāri in the neighbourhood of Daśamastaka. He desired moreover noble enjoyments in the other world.........these he has given to Jina alone, in the sincerity of his heart.

(4) The son of Samanta, Sthavira Buddhanirvāṇa, composed this poem for the instruction of men of this world.

Nos. 29 A, 29 B, 29 C.

Po Nagar Stelae Inscriptions of Vikrāntavarman II.

For localities, publications etc. cf No 22. No. 29 A contains two verses (one Anuṣṭubh, one Indra- vajrā), then a prose fragment, then four verses (one Upajāti, one Vasantatilakā and two Anuṣṭubh), then another prose fragment, and lastly oneverse in Vasantatilakā.—Total 22 lines.

No. 29 B contains one line in prose.

No. 29 C contains 5 lines in prose.

No. 29 A briefly recites the events recorded in No. 22, and records the erection of a new temple and the installation therein of an image of Śiva, called Mahādeva, by king Vikrāntavarmā. It also records donations made by king Satyavarman to his temple referred to in No. 22.

Nos. 29 B and 29 C. record donations made by king

1. Jina may denote either the Buddha or Mahāvīra. Here it probably denotes the former. Vikrānta (Siṁha) also refers to him (cf. Śākyasiṁha).

Vikrāntavarman to the Gods Śrī Mahādeva and Śrī Satyamukhaliṅga.

TEXT.

29 (A)

I. कृता विचित्रेण पुरा मुखलिङ्गस्य नामतः ।
श्रीसत्यमुखलिङ्गस्य स्थापना सत्यवर्म्मणा ॥

II. श्रीसत्यवर्म्माच्युतसत्यवर्म्मा
दैवस्वभावप्रविकीर्णकीर्त्तिः ।
भास्वत्मुखं श्रीमुखलिङ्गकोशम्
प्रास्थापयत् सद्गुणकर्मशुध्या ॥

पञ्चसहस्रनवशतैकादशे विगतकलिकलङ्कद्वापरवर्षे
श्रीविचित्रसगरसंस्थापितश्रीमुखलिङ्गदेवः ॥ तस्य
सकलकोष्ठागाररजतरत्नहेमकदवकलशभृङ्गाररुक्म-
दण्डसितातपत्रचामरहैमघटादिपरिभोगा वर्द्धमाना
भवन्तिस्म ॥ ततश्चिरकालकलियुगदोषाद्देशान्तरसमवागत-
पापनरभुग्गणसंहृतेषु प्रतिमापरिभोगभूषणेषु शून्यो
ऽभवत् ॥ पुनरद्यापि तत्पुण्यकीर्त्त्यविनाशाय श्रीसत्यवर्म्म-
नरपतिर्व्विचित्रसगरमूर्त्तिरिव माधवसप्तशुक्लपक्षे यथा
पुरा श्रीभगवतीश्वरमुखलिङ्गमतिष्ठिपत् ।

III. स्फुरद्वपुश्श्रीर्व्वरहेमलेपै
र्ज्ज्वलत्प्रभा श्रीवदनाम्बुजा सा ।
रत्नप्रभा रत्नकपोलबिम्बा
कौठारदेवी वरदा नतानाम् ॥

29 (B)

IV. चूडामणिज्वलितहेमशिरोरुहश्रीः
कौठारसागरसमीपनिवासिनी या ।
शुभ्रांशुरत्नरुचिराचितलम्बकर्णा
सा श्रीमती भगवती विबभौ त्रिलोके ॥

V. तस्य विक्रमवर्म्मेन्द्रोर्भ्भगिन्याः भूपतिस्सुतः ।

श्रीमान् विक्रान्तवर्म्माख्यः ख्यातो लोके स्वतेजसा ॥

VI. तेनैकलग्नसंयुक्ते तिथिनक्षत्रचारके ।

स्थापितश्श्रीमहादेवस्सकोशविभवान्वितः ॥

तस्मै श्रीभगवतीश्वराय वंधौणकोष्ठागारं कुङ्कोष्ठागारं

अरै कोष्ठागारं ……… स्त्रीगणैस्सहादित

श्रीसत्यवर्म्मा ॥

VII. रक्षन्ति ये सुरगणैस्स (हलोकगो) पैः

क्रीडन्त इष्टसुखिनो दिवि ये मनुष्या ।

ये वा हरन्ति पितृ (भिः पुरु) षाधमास्ते

देवीश्वरस्वनिचयं निपतन्त्यवीच्याम् ॥

29 (B)

द्रमदराद्रम्कुमारद्रम् दुरोटाक्-

पौर्न्हंग्मरडलन्नराकोष्ठागारम्

एव सर्व्वाण्येव श्रीविक्रान्तवर्म्मा

दद्यादिति चित्तप्रसादेन श्रीमहादेवेश्वराय ॥

29 (C)

[illegible]

संवरणं श्रीमहादेवस्य वेदिकायास्

संवरणं राजतमपि श्री विक्रान्तवर्म्मा दद्यादिति ॥

TRANSLATION.

29 (A)

1. Formerly a Mukhaliṅga was made by Vicitra. Satyavarman installed it under the name of Satya-mukhaliṅga.

2. Śrī Satyavarman, who has unflinching truth as his armour, and the fame of whose divine nature has spread in

all directions, has established a Śrīmukhaliṅgakośa of bright appearance, with purity caused by honest qualities and work.

In the year 5911 of the Dvāparayuga, free from the stains of Kaliyuga, Śrī Vicitrasagara established the God Śrī Mukhaliṅga. All articles of his enjoyment viz; grain-store, silver, jewels, gold, pitchers for drinking water, vase, white umbrella with golden rod, fly-whisk, golden vase, and other things were gradually increased. Then owing to the defects of the Kaliyuga existing for a long time, multitudes of vicious cannibals coming from other countries by means of ships, carried away the images, articles of enjoyment, and the ornaments, and the temple became empty. Again to-day, in order that the glory of this pious work may not be destroyed, king Satyavarman, like an incarnation of Vicitrasagara, re-installed, as before, the Mukhaliṅga of the lord of Bhagavatī on the seventh day of the bright fortnight of the month of Caitra.

III. The Goddess of Kauṭhāra, possessed of a body sparkling in beauty, on account of an excellent coating of gold, with her face glowing with splendour and beauty like a lotus, and cheeks aglow with rays of jewels, grants all the desires of those who bow down to her.

IV. She, the venerable Goddess, the beauty of whose golden hair is made brilliant by the jewels on her head; who lives close to the sea of Kauṭhāra, whose long ears are adorned with spotless jewels of splendid rays, shines in the three worlds.

V. The sister of this king, who is moon (i. e. foremost) among those who have prowess as their armours, had a son who was the fortunate king called Vikrāntavarman ,famous in the world by his own majesty.

VI. The king established the Mahādeva together with Kośa and riches (astronomical details follow).

Śrī Satyavarman gave to that Lord of Bhagavatī, the granary of *Vamdhauṇ*, the granary of *ktuṅ* and the granary of *Ñarai* with a large number of females.

VII. Those men who protect the goods of the Lord of the Goddess enjoy the wished for pleasures in heaven, being engaged in sports with the multitude of gods and the guardians of the world ; but those, who, worst among mankind, carry away those goods, fall into the Avīci (hell) together with their ancestors.

29 (B)

The draṃ Adairā, the draṃ Kumāra, the draṅ Duroṭāk, the granary of Vnarā in the district of Pauñrhag,—all these Śrī Vikrāntavarman has given, with a sincere heart, to Śrī Mahādeveśvara.

29 (C)

Śrī Vikrāntavarman has also given a diadem, and a dam over the drain, for the God Śrī Satyamukhaliṅga, as well as a silver cover for the pedestal of Mahādeva.

No. 30

Po-Nagar Stelae Inscription of Vikrānta-varman II, dated Ś 776.

The inscription was edited by M. Bergaigne (Corpus No. XXIV. p. 231) and noticed by Aymonier (J. A. 1891, Part I, p. 24.)

Po-Nagar is the name given to a stelae found near Panrang and must not be confounded with the celebrated temple of that name at Nha-Trang in Khanh-Hoa. The inscription engraved on a single face of the stelae is composed in Sanskrit, and contains 17 lines of writing. There are two verses at the beginning and two more at the end, the middle portion being written in prose. The Metres are:-v.1 Śārdūla-vikrīḍita, v. 2 Indravajrā, and vv. 3-4 Anuṣṭubh.

The inscription records that in the year 776 (=854 A. D.) the king Vikrāntavarman granted some lands to two temples of the God Śiva worshipped respectively under the names of Vikrāntarudreśvara and Vikrānta-devādhibhaveśvara.

TEXT.

I. श्री गङ्गा ˘ ˘—˘—˘ ˘ ˘ — — —˘——˘ य
चन्द्रांशस्य दधे पुरे स ˘ ˘ — — — ˘ — — ˘ सा
रा — नादि ˘ रा ˘ ना ˘ ˘ ˘ — — — ˘ — — ˘ ⏓
— दाराय ˘ — ˘ — पुनरिमा विक्रा(न्तरुद्रेश्वरः ॥)

II. (विक्रा)न्तवर्म्मा हि नराधिपश्श्री
र्य्यो मूर्त्तिमान् शक्र इवा ˘ — — ।
⏓ — ˘ — क्षेत्रमिदं विशालं
विक्रान्तरुद्राय स एव दद्यात् ॥
स एव राजा श्रीविक्रान्तवर्म्मदेवस्सकलपरिपूर्ण-
हरिणाङ्कदीप्तवैदूर्य्यमुक्तावलीलम्बहाटक............
सिन्धुतरगाम्भीर्य्यादिङ्मण्डलच्छदनसितातपत्र-
सन्धारितो ज्वलिततडिल्लताकनक..........
ण्ड पद्मरागरत्नबन्धकिरीटादेरबन्धहार-
कुण्डलभरितमूर्त्तिसमुपशोभितोऽनेकपरजन[1]-
ब्राह्मणपुरोहिताग्रासनक्षत्रान्यनरपति-

---

1. Read 'परिजन०'

वृन्दजुष्टचरणारविन्दः ××× सूक्ष्मप्रणवावसानैः सुवि-
शुद्धजन्म ××× श्रीविक्रान्तरुद्रेश्वराय सकलजगद्धित-
कारणाय त्रैलोक्यगुरवे [सं]तापातपहरणा[य द्यावा]
प्रथिव्योः परमकीर्त्तये श्रीमदीश्वरयज्ञार्थं शिवक्षेत्रीकृतं
दीर्घ ××× [क्षे]त्रवरमिदं कोशागमुनिभिश्शकराजे तदेव
दत्तवानिति तदनु श्रीविक्रान्तदेवाधिभवेश्वराय श्रीदे ××××
[व क्षेत्रं ?] अङ्कसान्निकृष्णमुभयत्र कीर्त्तये स एव
शुभमदात् ।

III. रुद्रक्षेत्रमिदं ख्यातं पालयन्तो यतीश्वरे ।
स्वर्गं यान्तु हरन्तस्ते पतन्तु नरकाधमे ॥

IV. वृत्तः किराटवृत्तं हि रुद्रक्षेत्रमिदं महत् ।
श्रीमता ×××× दत्तं विक्रान्तवर्म्मणा ॥

TRANSLATION.

1 Śrī Gaṅgā..................
of the portion of the moon..............
Again, he Vikr(āntarudreśvaraḥ).

2. King Śrī Vikrāntavarman, who is Indra personified, gave these vast fields to Vikrāntarudra. He, king Vikrāntavarmadeva, who was adorned with golden ornaments (?) containing pearls and lapislazuli which shone like full moon ; who was under the shade of a white umbrella which covered all the points of the direction (i.e. all horizon) because its profundity was greater than that of the sea ; whose whole body was decorated with diadem, waistband, necklace, and ear-rings, made of gold, ruby and other jewels, and shining like lightning ; whose feet, comparable to lotus, were worshipped by a host of retinue and multitude of Brāhmaṇas, priests, persons having right to seats in the first rank, Kṣatriyas and other kings........... ; by the inaudible end of the syllable Om...... who is of pure birth ; –(he, the king) gave, in the

year of the Śaka king 'Koṣa'-aga-muni' (776), for performing sacrifices to Īśvara (i.e. Śiva) and for the sake of great glory in heaven and earth, a long and excellent field, now made the fiield of Śiva, to Śrī Vikrāntarudreśvara,–who is the cause of the prosperity of the whole world, who is the preceptor of the three worlds, and who puts an end to the agonies of sorrow. Subsequently he gave to Śrī-Vikrānta-devādhibhaveśvara a field called Śrīdeva, lying close by, as a meritorious gift, for the sake of glory in the two worlds.

III. Those who protect this famous Rudrakṣetra (field of Rudra) for the lord of the ascetics (i.e. Śiva) would go to heaven; those who destroy would fall into damned hell.

IV. This great field of Rudra, full of Vṛlas and Kirāṭas has been given by the fortunate Vikrāntavarman.

No 31.

Dong Duong Stelae Inscription of Indravarman II, dated Ś 797.

The inscription was edited by M. Finot (B. E. F., Vol. IV, p. 84.)

The ruins of Dong-Duong are situated about 12 or 13 miles to the south-east of My-son in the province of Quang-Nam, the ancient Amarāvatī (for full details of the ruins and the position of the inscription, cf. Parmentier's account in B. E. F., Vol. III, p. 80)

The inscription is engraved on the four faces of a stelae containing respectively 24, 24, 23 and 31 lines. The language is Sanskrit, and with the exception of the benedictory formula at the beginning and two prose pieces at the end of the second and the fourth face, the inscription is written in verse. The metres are :

A. vv. 6, 7, 9, 10, 11, Sragdharā ; vv. 8, 12, 13, Śārdūlavikrīḍita; vv. 15, 17, 23, Indravajrā; vv. 18-21 Āryā; v. 14. Mālinī; v. 16, Upajāti; v. 22, Anuṣṭubh.

B. v. 2, Pṛthvī ; vv. 3, 4, Anuṣṭubh; vv. 5, 6, 8, 10, 13, Śārdūlavikrīḍita ; vv. 12, 15, Sragdharā; v. 7, Mālinī ; v. 11, Indravajrā; v. 14, Āryā ; v. 9; Vasantatilakā.

C. vv. 1–3, 5, 6. Anuṣṭubh ; v. 4, Śārdūlavikrīḍita ; vv. 7-9, Upajāti.

D. vv. 1-3, Anuṣṭubh.

The Inscription records the foundation of a Buddhist temple and a monastery dedicated to Lakṣmīndra Lokeśvara by king Jaya Indravarman in 797 Śaka (875 A. D.), and gives the following genealogy of the king.

Parameśvara.
⋮
Uroja.
⋮
Dharmmarāja.
⋮
King Śrī Rudravarmā.
⋮
King Bhadravarmā.
⋮
Indravarmā.

TEXT.

A

श्री लक्ष्मीन्द्र लोकेश्वराय (नमः)

I. (१) ....प्रियं परधनानि वाकाङ्क्षते
स्वयञ्च यदि जीवितं न खलु हिङ्सि...धरः

II. (२) न् (न्) उतमपि सुर(वर्)गणैर्य्यक्षगन्धर्व्वदैत्यैर्
....

III-V.(३) भद्रेश्वर..

(४) रवचनं बुद्धि..

(५) ....

......................(६) भृगुः प्रेषितश्च

VI. स श्री भद्रेश्वरोऽन्यो प्रतिहरत इत..........................

....

....

(७) नित्यञ्जानाति शम्भुः कथमपि मनसा तां विशेषान्
त्वया भोः

VII. ....स्थापितं लिङ्गमेत-
च्छ्रीमद्भद्रेश्वरस्ये..................................
....

VIII. (८) स्वर्गस्थानविविक्तबुद्धिनिचयास्स्वर्गस्थिता
ये सुरा
मोक्षे पादयुगे च यान्ति शरणं सात्मैर्यथा भक्तिभिः ।
गवन्ते भुवि संस्थिताः सुरगणाः क्ष्मेन्द्रा ⏑ — — ⏑ —
(९) श्रीभद्रेश्वरपादयोरवनताश्श्रीमन्त एवन्तथा ॥

IX. सर्व्वे देवेन्द्र — — स्वविषयनिरतास्ते दुरापाधिलोकं
...............प्रवरमनुपमं ते विलब्ध्वा............ ।
(१०) सन्तानं प्राप्नुवन्ति स्वयमिव सहसा स्वं पुनर्यान्ति लोकं
शम्भुर्जानाति चैवं प्रहसितं महोरोजमेवं ब्रवीति ॥

X. सन्तानं सर्व्वदेवाः सुरुचिरमनसा लब्धवन्त ⏑ — स्मात्
सञ्चिन्त्यैवञ्च शम्भुस्स्मितमुखनयनः प्रेषितोरोज एव ।
स त्वं श्रीमानुरोजस्फुटतरसुयशाः श्रीनिधिः क्ष्माञ्च याहि
प्राप्तं राज्यञ्च – – ⏑ (१२) गुरुचरणरजश्शम्भुभद्रेश्वरस्य ॥

XI. राज्यं स प्राप्तवांश्चाप्रतिहरत इदं लिङ्गमीशस्य कार्य्यं
लोके संस्थापितन्ते सकलनृपतिभिर्धार्य्यमानं[1] शिरोभिः

1. Read °र्यं

एवो(१३)रोजः प्रतिज्ञे स्वयमिह कथयन् स्वात्मनःकीर्त्तिमेताम्
दिक्श्रेष्ठं स्याच्च लिङ्गजगदुपकरणाद् भूर्भुवस्स्वस्समुदीतम् ॥

XII. मोक्षे लिङ्गमुदीरितन्तदधीशस्येशात् पुरा (१४) यद् भृगुः
तस्माच्चैवमुरोज एव तदिदं लेभे जगन्नीयते ।
चम्पायां सततञ्जगद्धितकरं लिङ्गं प्रतिष्ठापितन्
तेनोर प्रभुना त्वया हितकृतमस्याप्येव साङ्ग्रिभ्भवेत् ॥

XIII. (१५) स्वर्गस्थाः परमेश्वरात्तु च वरं देवा न मोक्षे च्युते
तेनोपाददिरे सुराहितकृताश्श्लाघ्यैर्व्विहीनास्सदा ।
लोकस्थाश्च सुरा नृपा भगवतो भद्रेश्वरात्तु क्षितौ
(१६) तस्मान्न प्रभवन्ति ते सुरनृपाश्श्रीवर्द्धमानास्तदा ॥

XIV. स्तुतिनिलयनिधीनाङ्कीर्त्तिराशेरतीतं
स्तवनमभिमतार्थं मङ्गलं स्यात् मुनीनाम् ।
जनयति नृपतीनां संपदं न (१७) स्य तस्मै
जगत इह नमो भूच्छम्भुभद्रेश्वराय ॥

XV. यस्स्वप्रभावातिशयात् सुरेशा-
वैभुत्वमाप्नोति यशोभिरेव ।
तस्मै स्तुतिर्म्मे भवतु स्वभक्त्या
श्री शम्भुभद्रे(१८)श्वरविश्रुताय ॥

XVI. विराजितो देवगणैरनेकै—
श्श्री शम्भुभद्रेश्वर एव पूज्यः ।
चम्पापुरीं दर्शितसर्व्वधर्म्मा-
मपालयत् पावनसारभूतः ॥

XVII. ये तेपि चोपाद(१९)दिरेथ राज्यं
चम्पापुरे सन्ततिराज्यसारे ।
श्रीमन्युरोजस्य सुशासनाच्च
भद्रेश्वरे ते प्रथिताः पृथिव्याम् ॥

XVIII. परमेश्वरसन्तानाज्जात उरोजो धरापति(२०)र्य्यश्च ।
तस्माज्जातश्श्रीमाञ्छ्रीमतिमान् धर्म्मराजेति ॥

XIX. तस्माज्जज्ञे राजा श्रीधिश्र्श्रीरुद्रवर्म्मनामा यः।
तस्य सुतः ख्यातयशाः श्रीसहितो भद्रवर्म्मविभुः॥

XX. (२१) श्री इन्द्रवर्म्मविदितस्सूनुश्श्रीभद्रवर्म्मणस्तस्य।
माहेश्वरप्रभावाच्चम्पानगरे नृपो भवति॥

XXI. तेभ्यस्सन्तानेभ्यो राज्यं जातं नृपस्य संपूर्णं।
न पितामहे(२२)न दत्तं पित्रा च तथा न दत्तन्ते॥

XXII तपःफलविशेषाच्च पुण्यबुद्धिपराक्रमात्।
............मो नृपः प्राप्तो न पितुर्न पितामहात्॥

XXIII. संप्राप्तवान् राज्यमि(२३)दन्नरेन्द्रो
भद्रेश्वराद् यश्च तदिन्द्रवर्म्मा।
एवं ह्युरोजस्य विशे ⏑ — —
— — ⏑ — — ⏑ ⏑ — ⏑ — — ॥
......स्वामी जानती भूमि (२४) प्रसाद...(२५)...णम्॥

B.

I. (१)......(२)......बुद्ध्या......नु स्थापितवान्तं ह्यग्निनृपतिः।

II. सते मलयवासिने भगवते जगत्मुक्तये
नृणाञ्च ⏑ ⏑ — ⏑ — ⏑ ⏑ ⏑ — ⏑ ⏑ — ⏑ —
⏑ — ⏑ — (३) तकोशरूपमधिकं सुवर्णाननं
प्रतिष्ठितमरं नृपेन कृतिना च तस्मै पुनः॥

III. इत्येवं राजसन्तानात् समासञ्च मया कृतम्।
शम्भुलिङ्गं य.........(४) यत्नेन चेतसा॥

IV. इमञ्च परमं लोके बुद्धसन्तानजं वरम्।
अहं लोकेश्वरं कर्तुं जगतां स्यां विमुक्तये॥

V. के देवाः करुणात्मकाः पृथुधिया त्रा(५)णेषु सत्वेषु च
लोकेशस्सततं कृपातिमतिमाड्क्षान्त्या त्वजेयोऽभवत्।
एवं यो नृपतिर्व्विचिन्त्य हृदयैर्धर्मस्य जिज्ञासया
लोकेशं परमार्थतत्वविश(६)द्रो हस्तेन सोऽत्राकरोत्॥

VI. पूर्व्वं भूमिरियं प्रकृष्टसतता शोभेन पूर्णा चिर-
न्तस्यां ये मनुजा महर्द्धिधनिनो जाताः कुलेश्चोत्तमाः ।
लब्ध्वा तेन नृपं क (७) चिच्च धनिनस्तस्याञ्च राजाभव-
स्त्वेकस्त्वं पृथिवीन्द्रवर्म्मविदितो देवेन्द्रकल्पः क्षितौ ॥

VII. क्वचिदपि वलभिज्जो ब्रह्मजो विष्णुजश्च
क्वचिदपि भुजगेन्द्रश्शङ्करश्च (८) क्वचिद् वा ।
क्वचिदपिरविचन्द्रो पाम्पतिर्वह्निरूपः
क्वचिदभयदविम्बस्सत्वमोहाद् वभूव ॥

VIII. दुःखेनाभिहता नराश्च नरके केचित् तथा नारका
रात्रौ (९) वा च दिवा तदा च सततं काङ्क्षन्ति ते दर्शनम् ।
तर्षाभिश्च नरा दिवाकरहता ग्रीष्मे जलं शीतलं
ये ते द्रष्टुमनेकदुःखविहता वेच्छन्ति भूमौ यथा ॥

IX. अन्य (१०) न्तजन्मपरिशुद्धविशिष्टचित्तो
राजा महाजनवरैरनुगम्यमानः ।
चम्पापुरीमभिमतामखिलाञ्च पातु-
न्त्वाम् रक्षतु त्विह तमेव चिरं सदा श्रीः ॥

X. (११) यावद् धर्म्मनयेन रक्षति दिवं देवेन्द्र इष्टयाज्ञया
यावच्चाम्वुनिधिर्जलानि सरितां गाम्भीर्य्यतो धारयन् ।
यावद् वायुधरो शशाङ्करविकौ तारान (१२) णाङ्खोपि वा
तावद् वुद्धधुरं पदञ्च नयतु श्रीधीरराजा सदा ॥

XI. लक्ष्मीन्द्रभूमीश्वरविश्रुतो यो
ग्रामोपि नाम्ना त्रिदशोत्तमौजाः ।
सन्दर्शि(१३)तो भूपतिना च पूर्व्वं
पश्चात् कवीन्द्रैः स्तुतिभिः प्रतीतः ॥

XII. मर्यादाभेदिनापि श्रुतिवचनपदो तेन दुःखार्त्तचित्ता
नात्याज्यस्पष्ट(१४)नेत्राश्शरणमुपगताश्शत्रवोपि प्रियास्स्युः ।
लोकेशस्स्थापितोपीश्वरगुणनिपुनो[1] विस्मयो नाप्यकार्य्य-

1. Read निपुणो ।

त्रासेवीहाज्ञयानाविनमि (१५) तमनिना दुष्टवाक्यञ्च धर्म्मे ॥[1]

XIII. लोके सोप्यसमो नरेन्द्रयशसा त्वं ज्ञानबुद्धिद्युति-

प्रख्यातिश्रुतिनीतिकीर्त्तिगतिभिश्श्रीसम्पदाल (१६) ङ्कृतः।

सौम्याङ्गारबृहस्पतीन्दुदिनकृत्काव्यार्कजैः पालित—

श्श्रीमाञ्छ्रीजय-इन्द्रवर्म्मविदितो देदीप्यते प्रज्ञया ॥

XIV इयमस्य लक्ष (१७) णश्रीरङ्गं सर्व्वञ्च सङ्गमारूढा।

वर्द्धयति भावि भूमौ राज्यन्वमवार्य्यवीर्य्यत्वम् ॥

XV. दीप्ते श्री शाकराजे मुनिनवगिरिभिस्तोयधृन्नसू (१८) र्य्यपुत्रे

श्रृङ्गीनद्वन्द्वजीवोदयभृगुजयुते काव्यवारे जभूजे।

कौलीरेन्दौ च पुष्ये शुचिसितदिवसे पञ्चमे श्रीविबुद्धे

स श्रीमानिन्द्रवर्म्मा स्व (१९) भयदमधिकं स्वाज्ञयातिष्ठिपद् यः ॥

अथ स एव नरपतिश्श्री जय-इन्द्रवर्म्मा महाराजाधिराजोऽ-
नेकपूर्व्वजन्मा-तरतपः फल (२०) विशेषात् समधिगत—
चम्पाधिराजो दैवप्रसादयोगात् सकलदिङ्मण्डलाकाशव्याप्य-
नेकबुद्धिप्रकर्षसम्पदतुलकीर्त्तिः कीर्त्तिसम्पदश्श्रीसमुदया (२१)-
भिवर्द्धितचित्तप्रसादनयनवदनश्श्रीमहेश्वरलोकसन्तानजादि
(पू) रभव (ते)..................इश्वर श्री लक्ष्मीन्द्रभूमीश्वर-
ग्रामस्वामिभूतस्सकलभुव (२२) नगुरुवरेण्यो भवदिति ॥ पुन-

---

1. V. XII. As it stands, the text offers no suitable meaning but I propose the following emendation :—

मर्यादाभेदिनोपि स्तुतिवचनपरास्तेन दुःखार्त्तचित्ता

न त्याज्या स्युः सुनेत्रा शरणमुपगताश्शत्रवोपि प्रियास्स्युः।

लोकेशस्स्थापितोपीश्वरगुणनिपुणो विस्मयो नापि कार्य्यो

त्रासेवीहज्ञया नो विनमितमतिना दुष्टवाक्यञ्च धर्मे ॥

Even enemies who had transgressed the boundaries are not forsaken by that good leader but become dear unto him when, repentant for their action they seek his protection with flattering words. Although he consecrated the image of Lokeśa, eminent in all the attributes of God, he felt no pride in his work. Docile as he was, he did not practise the faulty doctrine, if any, recorded in scriptures.

रपि तथैव षष्...न...श्री अवलोकि(२३)तेश्वर......(अ)ि
इन्द्(र)वर्म्म(द्)प(व)...निधिरधि(२४)......(२५)व्यद्वयम्
सुवर्ण.........

C.

I. (१)......(ध)र्म्मार्थं विहारस्स्थापितो(२)...... ।
(रा)ज्ञो न त्वाकरादानाद् भिक्षुसङ्घ(३) (प्रयो)जनम् ॥
II. परिभोगानि सर्व्वाणि वि(४)हारे स्थापितानि मे ।
भिक्षुसङ्घोप(५)भोगार्थं सत्वानाञ्च प्रयोजनम् ॥
III. (६)न राज्ञःपरिभोगार्थो नाकरादानसन्त (७)तिः ।
भिक्षुसङ्घोपभोगार्थो विहा(८)रस्स्थापितस्सदा ॥
IV. भिक्षूनाञ्च धना(९)नि तानि सकलान्येवञ्च रक्षन्ति ये
(१०)विद्वद्ब्राह्मणतापसक्षितिपतिज्ञात्या(११)दयो भुक्तये ।
बौद्धं मोक्षपरं स(१२)मीयुरसमं सर्व्वे च बान्धवैर्य्ये
(१३)गृह्णन्ति च नाशयन्ति नरकं रौद्रं पतन्तु(१४)स्वयम् ॥
V. श्रुत्वा जानन्ति पश्यन्ति तद्द्रव्य(१५)ञ्च हरन्ति ये ।
निवेदयन्ति राज्ञे न स(१६)र्व्वे ते नरकं ययुः ॥
VI. निवेदयन्ति(१७)राज्ञे च सर्व्वे ते च पुनः पुनः ।
बा(१८)न्धवैस्सह पित्रा वा नरकं वै प(१९)तन्तु न ॥

VII. हरन्ति सर्व्वाणि धनानि(२०)तानि
ये क्षत्रिया वाथ नृपा(२१)द्विजा वा ।
सर्व्वे च ते नरकमे(२२)व दुःखं
मात्रा च पित्रा च पत(२३)न्तु नित्यम् ॥

VIII. रक्षन्ति ते तानि ध(२४)नानि सर्व्वे
सङ्घोपभोगा(२)य ममापि वाचा ।
क्षेत्रं सुव(२६)र्णं रजतञ्च कङ्सं
दासादिभि(२७)र्बुद्धपदं समीयुः ॥

IX. त्यक्त्वा(२८)वचो मे च हरन्ति केचित्
(नृ) प्(ा) (२९)दयो विप्रधनेश्वराश्च ।
अष्ट् (ौ) (३०)समीयुर्न्नरकान् समस्तान्
पित्रा(३१)च मात्रा च सबन्धुवर्ग्गैः ॥

D.

I. (१)...लाय क्षेत्रं असौ क्षेत्रं गमु(२) याङक्षेत्रम् तथैव ।
क्षौङ् अपङ्(३)सलवङ् क्षेत्रं सदमान्दिङ् धन्यद्वयं ॥
II. (४)दमनुष् क्लुर्वन्दाङ् क्षेत्रं दन्दाल् क्षू (`) (५) त्रं वतेङ् तथा
डौकम्विल् च(६)पताक् क्षेत्रं रडौल क्षेत्रमतौ(७)गिंवः ॥
III. ल्वुक् तन्द्रील वुक् कवोव् क्षेत्रं(८)वमनौङ् च अवं तथा ।
क्षेत्रा(९)ण्येतानि सर्व्वाणि लोकेशाय नृपोऽददत् ॥

अपि च यशश्री इ(११)न्द्रवर्म्मा क्षेत्राणि सधान्यानि दासीदा(१२)सान् सरजतसुवर्णकंसलोह(१३)ताम्रादीनि द्रव्याणि श्री-लक्ष्मीन्द्रलो(१४)केश्वराय भिक्षुसङ्घपरिभोगा(१५)य धर्म्म-सन्ततिपरिपूरणार्थाय द(१६)त्तवानिति ॥ ये राजानः क्षत्रिय ......(१७)ब्राह्मणा वामात्या वा......(१८)वा वनिजो वा हरन्ति नाशयन्ति ढयन्ति वा ते सर्व्वे महारौरवं ग(२०)च्छन्तु ॥ पुनरपि ते रक्षन्ति परि...(२१)पालयन्ति आविष्कुर्व्वन्ति सर्व्वे स्व(२२)र्गपुरं मोक्षपुरञ्च यथेष्टं(२३)गच्छन्तु भवन्तस्सर्व्वे ॥

TRANSLATION.

A.

Reverence to Lakṣmīndra-Lokeśvara.

1...Longs for other's wealth.........

2...By the gods, Yakṣas, Gandharvvas and Daityas...

3–5. Bhadreśvara......Bhṛgu was sent.

6. He, another Bhadreśvara......Śambhu always knows, in his mind......

7. This liṅga of Bhadreśvara was installed.

8. As the gods who dwell in heaven, and whose profound intelligence has been purified by residence in heaven, take shelter to his feet, out of devotion, for obtaining salvation, even so the kings, the gods dwelling upon the earth, bow down to the feet of Bhadreśvara, and thereby become prosperous.

9. All the excellent gods, devoted to their own work, having obtained thy world which is difficult to gain, excellent and incomparable,......obtain progeny and then suddenly go back to their own world. Śambhu knows this and says thus in laughter, to the grand Uroja.

10. "All the gods, possessed of a gracious heart, have obtained children." Having made this reflection, Śambhu, with smiling face and eyes, sent Uroja (with the following words:) 'Thou art fortunate Uroja, and a receptacle of prosperity; thy fame, too, is more widely spread; go thou to the earth, and take the kingdom along with the dust of the feet of your lord, Śambhubhadreśvara.'

11. He obtained the kingdom, and this *liṅga*, the work of Īśa the irrepressible and fit to be placed on the heads by all the kings, was installed in the world. And Uroja himself thus announced its glory, saying: "Let this *liṅga* be the best that shines in the three worlds (*bhu*, *bhuva* and *sva*) for doing good to the world.

12. The *liṅga* of Adhīśa, the well-known means of deliverance (of the world), which Bhṛgu got from Īśa, was again obtained from Bhṛgu by Uroja. (By this) the world is directed. May this *liṅga*, established at Champā by your Lordship O Ura, and always doing good to the world, be also beneficial to me by (the merits of) honest persons.[1]

13. The gods in heaven did not obtain any boon from Parameśvara, (as) the deliverance, *i. e.* the *liṅga*, the symbol of deliverance, had fallen to the earth below. Hence the gods, injured by the Asuras, were bereft of their pride. But

1. The idea probably is 'that honest persons would give to the author of the poem a share of the merit which they would obtain by worshipping the Liṅga.

the gods below, *viz.*, the kings, are prosperous in the world on account of the god Bhadreśvara. Hence while the gods were not powerful, the prosperity of the kings is on the increase.

14. May this pious hymn, surpassing a mass of glory, be agreeable to the Munis (ascetics) who are the abode of hymns of praises (*i. e.* who are skilful in composing hymns of praises). May this increase the prosperity of the kings. Let the world bow to Śambhubhadreśvara.

15. He who has obtained the position of the head of the gods by means of his extra-ordinary power and fame, who is called Śambhubhadreśvara, to him I address this hymn out of devotion.

16. Śambhubhadreśvara, shining in the company of a number of gods, is alone fit to be worshipped. He, the very quintessence of purification, protected the city of Champā where all the religions were prevalent.

17. All the kings who have reigned in prosperous Champā, have become famous in the world, as Bhadreśvara there forms the essence of perpetuity and sovereignty, and also on account of the good rule of Uroja.

18. From the son (or family) of Parameśvara was born Uroja, the king of the world. From him was born the fortunate and intelligent Dharmarāja.

19. From him was born the intelligent king Śrī Rudravarmmā. The son of the latter was the far-famed king Śrī Bhadravarmmā.

20. The son of Śrī Bhadravarmmā, known as Śrī Indravarman has become the king of Champā through the grace of Maheśvara.

21. Thus the sovereignty of the king was transmitted in its entirety from those kings (lit. sons). It was not given by the grandfather or the father.

22. By the special merit of his austerities, and by virtue of his pure intelligence, he gained (the kingdom), not from his grandfather or father.

23. It is from Bhadreśvara that Indravarmman got the sovereignty......for thus......Uroja......lord (through) the grace of mother earth.

B.

1. By the intelligence......king Hari installed it.

2. To the august god, who dwells in Malaya, and causes the deliverance of the world......of the men...(a liṅga) in the form of a Kośa with golden face, was promptly established again by the sage king.

3. Thus this *liṅga* of Śambhu has come down through a line of kings and carefully made by me........

4. And in making (*i. e.* establishing) this supreme and eminent Lokeśvara, born from a succession of Buddhas, I shall contribute to the deliverance of (the beings of) the world.

5. "Who are the gods, the essence of whose soul is pity, and whose intelligence is wide awake in saving creatures? Lokeśa was always full of kindness and his patience was incomparable." Desiring to learn what Dharma is, the king thought thus in his heart, and being skilful in finding out the essence of supreme truth, he made this Lokeśa by his own hand.

6. Formerly this land was wide and excellent, and for a long time adorned with beauty.[1] The men there who were very rich, excellent, and born in good family had no king[2],

---

1. 'Śobha' for śobhā is an unusual form, but cf. 'Ceṣṭa' for 'Ceṣṭā'.

2. Here the finite and infinite verbs have different nominatives against the rule of grammar.

and (therefore) some rich man made himself king in some locality; but thou, known as Pṛthivīndravarmman, were the unique king of the world, almost equal to Indra.

7. In some places Indra, Brahmā, and Viṣṇu,[1] in some places Vāsuki, in some places Śaṅkara, in some places, ascetics (ṛṣis), Sun, Moon, Varuṇa, Agni (fire), and in some places image of Abhayada (Buddha) appeared for the deliverance of creatures.

8. Men, over-powered by sorrows, and the dwellers in hell, long to see thee, day and night; as thirsty men over-powered by sun's heat long for cool water in summer, so they, suffering from many sorrows, wish to have a view of thine.

9. May the king, whose superior mind has been purified by successive births, followed by excellent men, protect you in order to rule the whole of beloved Champā. May the Goddess of Sovereignty in her turn always protect him.

10. As long as Indra protects the heaven according to the rule of Dharma, and by virtue of sacrifice; as long as the ocean, in its profundity, holds the water of the rivers; as long as the atmosphere, decorated with stars, maintains the Sun and the Moon; so long may the pious and auspicious king bear the yoke and dignity of Buddha.

11. Equal in splendour to the gods, and named Lakṣmīndra-Bhūmīśvara-Grāma, he was first introduced by the king, and then celebrated by the hymns of the best of poets.

12. (See Text, above, on p. 80 and footnote).

13. Adorned with the riches of Fortune, without equal in respect of royal glory, knowledge, wisdom, splendour, fame, sacred learning, polity, renown, and conduct; protected by

---

1. The letter 'ja' at the end of Brahmā, Viṣṇu and Valabhit would mean their sons, but that does not seem to be the sense.

Mercury, Mars, Jupiter, the Moon, the Sun, Venus and Saturn ; the illustrious Jaya Indravarmman shines forth in wisdom.

14. The marks of fortune which are spread all over his body increase his future sovereignty and invincible prowess in the world.

15. In the year of the Śaka king, denoted by *muni*, *nava* and *giri* (797), (astronomical details) he, Indravarmā, by means of his own command, erected (the image of) Svabhayada *i. e.* Buddha.

16. Now the king Śrī Jaya Indravarmmā, Mahārājādhirāja,—who became king of Champā by virtue of peculiar merits accruing from austerities of many previous births ; whose fame for high intelligence obtained by divine favour spread in all directions and in the sky ; whose fame is unparalleled ; whose only possession is fame ; whose fortune has increased the satisfaction of whose heart and beautified the eyes and face ;—became Śri Lakṣmíndra-Grāmasvāmi and the best of all the teachers in the world. Again.........Śrī Avalokiteśvara......Śrī Indravarmmadeva......two......gold.

C.

1. For the sake of Dharma, and not for revenue, a monastery has been founded for the community of monks (?).

2. I have placed all necessaries in the monastery for the enjoyment of the community of monks as well as other creatures.

3. This monastery has been founded for the perpetual enjoyment of the community of monks, and not for the enjoyment of the king, nor as a permanent source of revenue.

4. Those who will protect all these riches of the monks—the learned Brāhmaṇas, ascetics, relations of the king—will,

with their friends and kindreds, attain the Buddhist Nirvāṇa to which there is no parallel. Those who take or destroy (the riches) go to the hell called 'Rudra'.

5. Those who see or hear about persons taking away those goods, and yet do not report to the king, go to the hell.

6. Those who, again and again, report to the king, do not fall into the hell with their father and other relations.

7. Those who take away those goods—Kṣatriyas, kings or Brāhmaṇas—fall every day into the doleful hell along with their father and mother.

8. Those who, out of regard for my words, or for the enjoyment of the community of monks, protect the goods—fields, gold, silver and bell-metal—reach the abode of Buddha with servants etc.

9. Those who take away (the goods), disregarding my words,—kings, Brāhmaṇas, and wealthy men—go to all the eight hells with their father, mother and other relations.

D.

(1--3) (Enumeration of fields) All these fields the king has given to Lokeśa.

Now the king Śrī Indravarmmā has given these fields together with their corns, male and female slaves and other goods, such as gold, silver, bell-metal, iron, copper etc. to Lokeśvara, for the enjoyment of the community of monks and for the sake of the propagation of Dharma. Those kings, Kṣatriyas......Brāhmaṇas, ministers.....merchants who take away or destroy (these), they should go to (the hell called) Mahāraurava. Again, those who protect, maintain, and discover (what others have taken away), would go to heaven or attain Nirvāṇa as they like.

No. 32.

Bo-Mang Stelae Inscription of Indravarman II dated 811 Śaka.

The Inscription was edited by M. Huber (B. E. F. Vol. XI, p. 269).

This inscription, together with No. 34, was engraved on the four faces of a stelae found at Bo-Mang, a village about 10 miles to the south-west of Touranne in the district of Quang-Nam.

The inscription contains 42 lines of writing, the first 14 lines in Sanskrit and the rest in Cham. The Sanskrit portion contains, besides the invocation, seven verses and one prose text. The metres used are VV. 1, 2, 5, Āryā; V. 3, Śārdūla-Vikrīḍita, VV. 4, 6, 7, Anuṣṭubh.

The inscription records the erection of Śaiva images by the minister of king Śrī Jaya Indravarman and the religious donations of the latter consisting of lands and slaves. It is dated in the year 811 (=889 A. D.).

TEXT.

(क).

I. (१) ओं नमश्शिवाय ।
ब्रह्मादिमुनिसुरनुतस्सर्व्वभद्रेश्वरः प्रभुर्भगवान् ।
जयति जगद्गुरुराद्यस्त्रिपुरजयी योगिभिः साध्यः ॥

II. मन्त्रीनृपतेः ख्यातो विविधगुणैराशयेशभक्त्याश्च ।
त्मायां विभाति धर्म्मैराज्ञा मणिचैत्यनामायम् ॥

III. शकाब्दे शशिरूपमङ्गलयुते मैत्रे घतेनग्रहे
कुम्भस्थे भृगुजे ⏑—⏑ भुजगेसौरवारे शुभा ।
स्थाप्या तेन कुमारिकासुरगुरौ नागेन्द्रसौरे महा-
देवी फाल्गुणनीलपञ्चदिवसे गोलग्न ईशप्रिया ॥

IV. श्रीमहालिङ्गदेवोऽयं स्थापितस्तेन तत्पितुः ।
स्थापिताच महादेवी श्रीमती मातरि प्रिया ॥

V. तस्येश्वरदेवाख्योऽनुजः स्वकीर्त्यैः पितुर्धरायाश्च ।
येन स्थाप्यः सुमुदाश्रीश्वरदेवादिदेवोऽयम् ॥

VI. श्रीमहालिङ्गदेवाय प्रादात् क्षेत्रं सदासकम् ।
श्रीजयइन्द्रवर्मेदं शास्त्रज्ञो लोकधर्मवित् ॥

VII. चम्पेश्वरा वरनृपा आचन्द्रार्कात् पदाशयाः ।
शृणुयुः वचनमिदं परमार्थं सु[धर्मिकम्] ॥
श्रीजय इन्द्रवर्म राजस्य ॥
श्रीमहालिङ्गदेवं केचिद् अतिक्रत्य नरके पतन्तु
केचिद् बलात्कारेनास्य द्रव्यदास- ।

(b).

I. क्षेत्रगोमहिषान् हरिष्यन्ति
दहनशिखा कराळे महानिरये
पतन्तु ये धर्मज्ञा न्यायेन पालयन्ति
शक्तिमन्तमिमं ते दिवि वसन्तु ॥

TRANSLATION.

(a).

Reverence to Śiva !

1. Victory to Lord Śrī Bhadreśvara, who is extolled by the sages and gods like Brahmā and others, who is the supreme deity, who is the primeval Being, who conquered Tripura (demon), and who is the object of meditation of the ascetics,

2. The royal minister was named Ājñā Manicaitya; he was famous in all directions for his manifold qualities, he reposed confidence in his faith in God (Mahādeva), and he shone in the world by his virtues.

3. In the Śaka year denoted by 'Śaṣi-rūpa-maṅgala' (811)—(astronomical details follow)—he has installed this

beautiful statue of the great goddess, the wife of Īśa (i. e. Bhagavatī).

4. He has installed this Śrī Mahāliṅgadeva (in honour ?) of his father, and also a beautiful (image of) Mahādevī, dear to his mother.

5. His younger brother, called Īśvaradeva, for the sake of his own glory and that of his father in this world, installed, with joy, this (image of) Śrī Īśavaradevādideva.

6. Śrī Jaya Indravarman, who is versed in scriptures and the usages of the world, dedicated a field, together with slaves to Śrī-Mahāliṅgadeva

7. Let the lords of Champā, noble kings, who are desirous of retaining their position as long as the Sun and the Moon endure, listen to these words of king Śrī Jaya Indravarman which conform to the Dharma and express supreme truth.

Those who do any injury to Śrī Mahāliṅgadeva would fall into hell; those who forcibly take away any of its articles, slaves, fields, oxen and buffaloes would fall into a great hell terrible on account of burning fire. Those conversant with Dharma, who justly protect (the temple of) the mighty god, would reside in heaven.

b-d. (Cham).

The king Jaya Indravarman has given a religious endowment to the god Mahāliṅga for defraying the expenses of his worship. If any man destroy the goods of the god Mahāliṅga or have it destroyed by somebody else, the mother of this man would be haunted by multitude of dogs, and after his death he would live in the dark hell and remain there till the end of the *yuga* and the destruction of the world. Let the persons who observe fast, practise austerities and know the Dharma, and the sacrificers who practise austerities and know the Dharma, protect and embellish this temple of God Mahālinga; they will go to heaven. (Then follows an enumeration of 15 fields). All these fields king Jaya Indravarman has given to the god Mahālinga.

No. 33.

Phu Thuan Stelae Inscription of Indravarman II (?).

The inscription was edited by E. Huber (B. E. F., Vol. XI, p. 10).

Phu Thuan is a village in the Subdivision of Que-Son to the west of My-son. The inscription is written in Cham and records a donation made by king Indravarman to the god Bhāgya-kānteśvara. On palaeographical evidence, the inscription may be referred to the 9th or 10th century A. D. So it belongs to the reign of either Indravarman II or Indravarman III.

TRANSLATION.

Hail! Here is what I command, I, Śrī Indravarmadeva, king of kings, of the country of Champā. I exempt the (temple of) god Śrī Bhāgya-kānteśvara from all taxes. I employ four priests who would serve as sacrificers at his service, and give (the taxes) to them for defraying their own expenses and those of the worship. In regard to my donations to these priests, I implore the future kings and the future inhabitants of this country to respect my endowments. Because in acting thus they will be happy in this kingdom or elsewhere, and after death gain the heaven of Śiva. But if the men destroy my pious foundation made in favour of the curates of the temple, or have it destroyed by others, then they would go to the Avīci hell.

No. 34.

Bo-Mang Stelae Inscription of Jaya Siṁhavarman I.

The inscription was first noticed by Aymonier (J. A. 1896, part I, p. 150) and then edited by M. Huber (B. E. F., Vol. XI, p. 275) (for details cf. No. 32). It records the pious donations of the king Śrī Jaya Siṁhavarman. It contains two Sanskrit verses, the metre being; v. 1, Indravajrā, v. 2 Anuṣṭubh.

TEXT.

I. चम्पेश्वरश्श्रीजयसिंहवर्म्मा राजाधिराजः प्रथितोऽग्रवीर्यः ।
देशान्तरी श्रीश्रुतशक्तितेजः पुण्यं करोतीह दिवादिवाय[1] ॥
II. श्रीमहालिङ्गदेवाय लोकास्पदकृते भुवि ।
प्रदत्तस्स महाकीर्त्तिर्म्मुक्तिञ्च ससितध्वजाम् ॥

TRANSLATION.

1. Śrī Jaya Siṁhavarman, king of Champā, king of kings, famous and of unequalled prowess, (the fame of) whose fortune, knowledge, and power has reached other lands, made this pious work for the god of gods.

2. He, of great fame has given the Mukti[2] (?) and a white banner to Śrī Mahāliṅgadeva who is refuge of all in this world.

---

1. Read 'देवदेवाय'.

2. This probably stands for 'Bhukti' denoting territory.

No. 35.

Ban-lanh stelae Inscription of Jaya Siṁha-varman I Dated 820 Śaka.

The inscription was edited by M. Finot (B. E. F., Vol. IV, p. 99). Ban-lanh is the name of a village about 12 miles to the north of Dong Duong (cf. No. 31). The inscription is engraved on the three faces of a stelae which has been removed from its original position. The first face contains, besides the invocation, 15 lines of writing, of which LL. 1–10 are in Sanskrit and LL. 10–15 in Cham. The second face contains 18 lines: LL. 1–5 in Cham, LL. 5–10 in Sanskrit, and LL. 10–18 in Cham. The third face contains 11 lines in Cham. The Sanskrit portion contains 9 verses and one prose piece, the metre being vv. 1, 8, Anusṭubh; vv. 3 and 5, Śārdūlavikrīḍita; v. 2, Mandākrāntā; v. 4, Puṣpitāgrā; vv. 6, 7, 9, Indravajrā.

The inscription purports to be a deed of protection and immunity granted by king Jaya Siṁhavarman in favour of two temples *viz.*, a temple of Rudramadhyeśvara founded by a royal official called Śrīkalpa, and a temple of Śivaliṅgeśa founded by *muni* Śivāchārya in 820 Śaka (=898 A. D.). This last date is probably also that of the inscription itself. King Jaya Siṁhavarman appears to be a successor of Śrī Jaya Indravarman.

TEXT.

(a).

ओँनमश्शिवाय.

I. स्वस्ति

त्रैलोक्ये जयति श्रेष्ठस्सश्री जय गुहेश्वरः ।

देवासुरमुनिसङ्घैर्नताङ्घ्रिद्वितयाम्बुजः ॥

II. भुक्त्वा राज्यं भुवि च महता येन चिह्नेन विष्णोः
संहार्य्योतिः कलिविषतरुं राजलक्ष्मीविरुद्धं ।
नानादानो विविधविभवः कीर्त्तिकल्पद्रुमोघः
तद्धेमाढ्यस्सुरजतमयो भूतले स्थापितश्च ॥

III. तस्य श्री जयसिंहवर्मनृपतेर्यो दण्डवासो भटो
धर्म्मिष्ठः पतिभक्तितत्परमनाः कीर्त्यास्पदः सम्पदः ।
ख्यातोऽगाधविशालबुद्धिजलधिर्लब्ध्वाशयाशापदो
यः प्रीतिर्जगतां महामणिरिव स्थानं स्थिरं रक्षति ॥

IV. कृतमतिरधिको नरेन्द्रभाग्ये
समहिमा सगुणक्रियाविदग्धः ।
मुखविजितरवेर्वि रर्त्ति लक्ष्मीम्
निशि सकलान् नभविद् दिवा मुखेन ॥

V. लेभे श्रीजय इन्द्रवर्मनृपतेर्नामानि यस्त्रीणि सन्
राज्येन्द्वेश्वरकल्पनामभृदतस्संस्तूयमानोधिया ।
विद्वद्भिश्शिवकल्पसंज्ञकधरो रत्नप्रभादीपित
श्श्रीकल्पाह्वयभृत् पयोनिधिरिव श्रीमत्कलालङ्कृतः ॥

VI. श्रीरुद्रमध्येश्वरमद्भुताङ्गम्
स धर्मकाङ्क्षी शिवतत्वसेवी ।
तद्भक्तये श्रीजय सिंहवर्म-
प्रसादतः स्थापितवान् धरित्र्याम् ॥

(b).

श्रीवृद्धेश्वरे पूर्व्वं प्रपितामहेन स्थापिते परचक्रभिन्ने यं श्री-
शिवलिङ्गेशं यो मुनिश्शिवाचार्य्यनामधेयः पुनः स्थापितवान्
इति ।

VII. शैवक्रियावित् सुकृतप्रसक्तो
देवार्चनज्ञानसमर्थबुद्धिः ।
पित्रोर्गुणान् भारतरान् स चित्ते
सञ्चिन्त्य पुण्यं स करोतु कीर्त्यै ॥

VIII. शाके खद्वयष्टभिर्युक्ते पञ्चाहे शुच्यपाण्डरे
स्थापितश्शिवलिङ्गेशः शिवाचार्य्येण धीमता ॥

IX. श्रीरुद्रमध्येश्वर इद्धसिद्धिः
सिद्धेश्वरश्श्री शिवलिङ्गदेवः ।
ताभ्यां नृपश्श्री जयसिंहवर्मा
प्रादात् स मुक्तिं कृपया समस्ताम् ॥

TRANSLATION.

Reverence to Śiva.

(1) Hail !

I. The supreme Śrī Jaya Guheśvara, before whose two lotus-like feet multitudes of gods, Asuras (demons) and Munis (sages) prostrate themselves, triumphs in the three worlds.

II. (An image) of that (god), made of gold and excellent silver, together with various gifts and a variety of wealth, was established in the world, like a *kalpa-tree* of glory, by the great (king) who reigned with the great standard of Viṣṇu and killed the poisonous tree which is Kali, antagonistic to the prosperity of kings.

III. The captain of guards of that king Śrī-Jaya Siṁhavarman, was virtuous, wholly devoted to his master, asylumn of glory arising from his prosperity, and famous as a vast and profound ocean of intelligence. Having secured the desires of his heart and being beloved by the whole world like a precious stone, he guards his place without any disturbance.

IV. Resolute, having a fortune superior to that of the king, full of nobility, well-practised in meritorious deeds, his celestial face is superior to that of the Sun as it carries the entire Lakṣmī (splendour) both day and night.

V. He received from king Jaya Indravarman, three names: He bore in the kingdom the name Īśvarakalpa, praised by the learned men for intelligence; he was also called Śivakalpa, illumined by the splendour of gems; he was also called Śrīkalpa, like an ocean, full of magnificent talents (or decorated by Lakṣmī and Moon in the case of ocean).

VI. Desirous of spiritual merit, and devoted to the philosophy of Śiva, he installed in the world, by the favour of king Śrī Jaya Siṁhavarman, the god Śrī Rudramadhyeśvara, of a strange body, out of devotion for Him.

(Cham) The king protects the divine Guru (Śiva) in the temple (?). At the end of four years.........for the use of divine Guru.........the goods of men belonging to the temple .... There was an order of king Śrī Jaya Siṁhavarmadeva to four ascetics. The men belonging to this temple who would protect all the goods of the gods Śrī Rudramadhyeśvara and Śivaliṅgeśvara, slaves, oxen, buffaloes, fields, gold, silver...........these men would eternally live in heaven with their parents.

(b).

(Cham) The men who...........would take away those goods for themselves would fall into the hell called Mahāraurava........... All those who...........the mother of these people. Order of king Śrī Jaya Siṁhavarmadeva,—he gives to these two.........servants, wealth, food.........

(Sanskrit) Śrī Vṛddheśvara, formerly installed by great-grandfather, having been overthrown by the strangers, the *muni* (ascetic) named Śivācārya has re-installed (it under the name of) Śrī Śivaliṅgeśa.

VII. Well versed in Śaiva rites, fond of good works, with an intelligence capable of understanding the nature of divine worship, and meditating in his mind on the immense virtues of his parents, he made this pious work for the sake of glory.

VIII. In the year of the Śakas denoted by 'kha-dvi-aṣṭa' (820), the fifth day of the dark fortnight of the month of śuci, the Śivaliṅga was installed by the intelligent Śivācārya.

IX. King Śrī Jaya Siṁhavarman has kindly made all exemptions in favour of the two gods, Śrī Rudramadhyeśvara, who has wonderful divine faculties, and Śivaliṅgadeva, the lord of the Siddhas (a class of semi-divine-beings).

(Cham). Enumeration of fields granted by Śrī Jaya Siṁhavarmadeva.

(c).

The men who would protect this good work............who would conduct their sons and daughters to the temple for living therein as its property (?) (Enumeration of fields).

No 36.

Dong Duong Stelae Inscription of Jayasiṁhavarman I.

The inscription was edited by M. Finot (B. E. F., Vol. IV, p. 105). For localities cf. No. 31. The inscription is engraved on four faces of a stelae found outside the boundary of the temple. The first face has, besides the invocation, 17 lines in Sanskrit verse. The second face is very much damaged and has, besides the invocation, 15 lines in Sanskrit. There are six verses with a prose-piece between verses IV and V. The third face has 14 lines in Cham besides the invocation. The fourth face has six lines in Cham. The metres used are: Face A:—vv. 1, 6, Indravajrā; vv. 2, 3, Pṛthvī; v. 4, Āryā; v. 5, Sragdharā; v. 7, Anuṣṭubh; v. 8, Śārdūlavikrīḍita: vv. 9–10, Nardaṭaka. Face B:—v. 5, Āryā; v. 6, Vasantatilakā.

The inscription commences with an invocation in honour of Parameśvara Guheśvara, and then follows an eulogy of king Jaya Siṁhavarman. It records some pious foundations by princess Haradevī Rājakula, younger sister of the mother of the king. Haradevī Rājakula was the widow of a king who had the posthumous name Parama-Buddhaloka. The *Abhiṣekanāma* of this king is not recorded, but as the god installed in his memory by his widow is called Indraparameśvara, it may be safely inferred that the proper name of the king was Indravarman. This Indravarman is probably no other than the king of the same name referred to in Nos. 31 and 35. We know from No. 31 that he was greatly attached to Buddhism, and this accords full well with the posthumous name Parama Buddhaloka. We gather from No. 35 that Jaya Siṁhavarman succeeded Indravarman, and it would thus follow that after the death of the latter the throne passed on to the son of the elder sister of his queen Haradevī.

TEXT.

(*a*).

नमश्शिवाय.

I. — — अनङ्गत्वमुपागतोसौ
यस्माद्धराङ्गं पुनरेव कामः ।
यस्यादितामुत्तरभूद — —
यस्याङ्घ्रिपद्मं प्रणमन्ति देवाः ॥

II. स एव परमेश्वर — ˘ ˘ गुहेश्वराख्यः क्षितौ
˘ — यतकुमारशान्तिजयमङ्गलोत्पादकः ।
स्वपुत्रवरकीर्त्ति — ˘ ˘ ˘ — ˘ पदाम्बुजः
स्थिराय निजराज्यसंपदुदयाय जेजीयते ॥

III. पुरीन्द्रपुरसम्पदाभरित —˘— —˘ ना
सिताम्बुरुहरञ्जिताम्बुरुहिणीवरालङ्कृता ।

कृता च भृगुणा पुराणसमये ⏑— —⏑—
⏑— रिरजितार्द्धिमत्र च विभर्त्ति चम्पाह्वया ॥

IV. सा रक्षितातिशयिनी श्रीमज्जयसिंहवर्म......ण ।
शक्त्याभिर्नवसमृद्धिः सम्पदभिन्ना प्रभातीह ॥

V. आधारो यो गुणानां जनितसुखधियां गौरवाणां नरेन्द्रो
दिव्याचाराश्रयाणां पुनरपि गुणिनां धर्मनम्राशयानाम् ।
मन्वयादीनां बहूनां कनकगिरिरिवाकम्पितोऽद्भूत संप-
च्छोभानां कल्पवृक्षस्य मणिरुचिरुचालङ्कृतस्यापि लोके ॥

VI. शुभ्रीकृताशो भुवि योऽस्ति कीर्त्या
स्वच्छीकृताशेषजनः प्रभावैः ।
अन्धीकृतारिः स्वरुचा स्वरुग्भिः
स्निग्धीकृताशेषकलत्रवर्गः ॥

VII. तस्यामन्दगताबुद्धिर्धर्मेष्वतितरां शुभा ।
पापेषु सद्भिरुद्धेषु मृदु भवति सास्तुला ॥

VIII. तस्य श्री जयसिंहवर्मनृपतेर्मातृष्वसा सन्ततं
या पुण्ये निपुणा विशेषगुणभाग् भाग्योदयालङ्कृता ।
कीर्त्याशाभिरता मनोविहितसच्चिन्तास्पदा भ्राजते
गन्धे पुष्पनिबन्धवस्त्ररचनास्वेवं विदग्धोचिता ॥

IX. प्रियपतिपादभक्त्यभिरता परमार्थहिता
विधिगुणसंपदा कृतविभोगविभूतिरियं ।
द्विजयतिसज्जनाविरतदानकरी भुवि या
शिवपदपूजनाशयतनुः सततं भवति ॥

X. गुरुजनसाधुकारपरिपूतसुकीर्त्तिरियं
तदमलतुष्टिहेतुकृतभाग्ययुता महती ।
उपरुचितत्प्रसादहितपावनलब्धवरा-
भवदचलाशयोपहितसंपदानन्दितधीः ॥

(b).

नमः परमेश्वराय.

I. पुल्यङ्ग राजकुलाख्या सा धर्मपदवी वरानना
— — — — — — — — — — —

II. सत्यं वदति नासत्यं नाशौचं शौचमेवसा
श्रद्धेयं नाम — — — — — — — — — — —

III. — — — — — — — — — — — — —
— — — — — — — — — — — — —

IV. — — — — — — — — — — — — —
— — — — — — — — — — — — —शुभे
ग — — — — — — — — — ज्यैष्ठे शुचौ मासके
देवा इन्द्रपुरे तया सुमनसा कीर्त्यै प्रतिष्ठापितः ॥

त.................श्री जयसिंहवर्मदेवेन चम्पापुरपरमेश्वरेण सज्जनगुणविदा विदग्धमतिना मति — — — — — — — — श्रीमती हरोमादेवीविदिता हरदेवीसंज्ञापरनामधेयाया आज्ञा पोव् कुल्यङ् श्री राजकुलाख्यायाः स्वाम्बानुजायाः पुण्यवृद्धये प्रतिष्ठापितेयं इन्द्रपुरनाम्नि पुरेऽस्मिन्निति।..............श्री परमबुद्धलोकस्य नृपतेः स्वभर्तुः पुण्याय साधुमनसाज्ञा पोव् कुल्यङ् श्री राजकुलाख्यया...............गुणज्ञया प्रतिष्ठापितः श्रीन्द्रपरमेश्वरो नाम्नेति ॥ तस्मिन्नेव शकराजे श्री रुद्रपरमेश्वरः स देवः प्रतिष्ठापितस्तयाज्ञा पो कुल्यङ् श्रीराजकुलाख्यया स्वपितुः पुण्यवृद्ध्यै ॥ तदपि मातुर्निजायाः पुण्यसंवर्धनायाज्ञा पोव् कुल्यङ् श्री राजकुलनामधेया श्री रुद्रोमामिमामतिष्ठिपत् सद्भक्त्येति ॥

V. जयति हरोमादेवीसंज्ञा देवी महीमहाकीर्त्तिः ।
ल्यङ् श्री राजकुलाख्यायाः प्रतिबिम्बा च हरदेव्याः ॥

VI. श्रीमान् भुवीन्द्रपरमेश्वरनामधेयः
श्रीमान् स रुद्रपरमेश्वरनामधेयः ।
सा श्रीमती जयति लोकधरा च रुद्रो-
माख्या त्रयः सुरनरैः किल वन्दितास्ते ॥

TRANSLATION.

(a).

Reverence to Śiva.

1. Who reduced Kāma (Cupid) to ashes (lit. condition or state of being without a body); and from whom Kāma

again got back his beautiful body; before whose feet, like lotus, the gods bow down.

2. He is Paramesvara, called in this world Guhesvara, who brings about peace, victory and happiness to Kumāra; whose feet, like lotus............glory of his excellent son; he gains repeated victories for the steady growth of the prosperity of his own kingdom.

3. This city called Champā, decorated with the wealth of Indrapura (city of Indra—may denote also a town of that name in Champā), beautified by white lotus, and ornamented with excellent lotus flowers, was made in ancient days by Bhrgu, and contains splendour which yet remains unsurpassed.

4. This excellent city, protected by fortunate Jaya Simhavarman............gaining new splendour by his prowess, shines here, inseparably united with fortune.

5. The king, who is the receptacle of dignity and qualities that cause delight to the intellect;[1] who is the refuge of virtuous men following divine course of conduct, and whose heart has been made generous by religious impulse: who possesses many jewels and precious stones, and is therefore like the unshaken Mountain of Gold which possesses wonderful riches; and who is beautiful like a *kalpa* tree decorated with fine gems.

6. Who, by his own (white) fame, has made all the directions in this world white; who has illumined all the men by his prowess; who has blinded the enemies by his anger, and made his wives affectionate by his lustre.

---

1. The poet probably has in mind the conventional group of qualities called धि गुणाः and defined in Kāmandaka as follows:

शुश्रूषा श्रवण चैव ग्रहण धारण तथा ।
ऊहापोहोऽर्थ विज्ञान तत्त्वज्ञानं च धिगुणाः ॥

7. His laudable spirit, not inclined to evils, is very beneficial in religious matters, and is chary of vices, condemned by honest men.

8. King Jayasiṁhavarman has a maternal aunt (mother's sister); she is always skilful in virtuous work, endowed with exceptional qualities, and decorated by the increase of fortune; she takes delight in her fame and hopes; she is an asylumn of pious thoughts formed in her mind, and she is very skilful in making perfumes and arranging flowers and clothes.

9. She takes delight in her devotion to the feet of her dear husband; she is well disposed towards the supreme truth; she makes the best use of her wealth according to religious precepts and her inborn qualities; she constantly makes gifts to Brāhmaṇas, ascetics (yati) and virtuous people in the world, and she lives with the sole object of worshipping the feet of Śiva.

10. Her fame was purified by the praises of elderly relatives; she was united with fortune merely to cause unmixed delight to them; she was noble; she obtained dear and pure boons from the favour (of those elderly persons); her riches were produced by unshakable determination and her intelligence was without blemish.

(b).

Reverence to Parameśvara.

1. She, Pu lyaṅ Rājakula, was adept in virtue and had a beautiful face...............

2. She says what is true, not what is untrue; what is pure and not what is impure. The absence of jealousy......

4. In the pure month of Jyaiṣṭha, gods have been installed at Indrapur by that benevolent lady for the sake of glory.

..................By Śrī Jayasiṁhavarmadeva, lord of the city of Champā, who appreciates (lit. knows) the qualities of honest persons, and who possesses a penetrating intelligence ....has been installed, in this city named Indrapura, the august goddess known as Haromā[1] for increasing the religious merit of his mother's younger sister princess Ājñā Pov Ku lyaṅ Śrī Rājakula, also known as Haradevī. Śrī Indraparameśvara was installed by princess Ājñā Pov ku lyaṅ Śrī Rājakula, who is of virtuous mind and is a connoisseur of qualities.................for the sake of religious merit of her own husband king Śrī Paramabuddhaloka. In the same Śaka year the princess Ājñā Po ku lyaṅ Śrī Rājakula has installed the god Rudraparameśvara for increasing the religious merit of her father. And for increasing the religious merit of her own mother, princess Ājñā Pov ku lyaṅ Rājakula installed, with pious devotion, this goddess Śrī Rudromā.

5. Victorious is the goddess called Haromādevī, the great glory in the world, and a reflected image, as it were, of Haradevī Rājakula.

6. The august god Indraparameśvara, the august god Rudraparameśvara, and the august goddess Rudromā, supporter of the world, these three deities, adored by gods and men, are triumphant in this world.

(c).

Reverence to all...........

His majesty king Śrī Jaya Siṁhavarmadeva grants exemption from taxes to the god Śrī Indraparameśvara, to the goddess Śrī Haromādevī, to the god Śrī Rudraparameśvara and to the goddess Śrī Rudromā. If any wretch

1. Haromā (=Hara+Umā) may denote the 'अर्धनारीश्वर' in which Śiva and Umā are combined. More probably the question here is only of goddess Umā, called after Haradevī, Haromā.

carries away the servants or any articles of these deities he would fall into the hell called Mahāraurava. Moreover, if any noble soul protects these deities or their goods, he would obtain complete salvation and go to heaven. All these divinities have the use...........I, princess lyaṅ Rājakula, I leave this pious work as a legacy in this world. If any distinguished man maintains this pious foundation, his virtues will be recognised by the gods. I, woman as I am, I adore the god Parameśvara.

(d).

Order of........... If this man abstains from doing evil to me, to my family, and to all the creatures, and if this man follows the order of his Majesty Śrī Jaya Siṁhavarmadeva addressed to me, lyaṅ Rājakula...........this man...........he will enable all the men, without distinction, promptly to gain deliverance and enjoy heaven.

No. 37.

An-Thai Stelae Inscription dated 824 Ś.

The inscription was edited by M. Huber (B. E. F., Vol. XI, p. 277). It was engraved on two faces of a stelae found at An-Thai in the district of Quang-Nam. It contains 22 lines of writing, the last three lines being in Cham, and the rest in Sanskrit. The Sanskrit portion contains two prose passages and twelve verses, besides the invocation. The first two verses are almost entirely lost. The metres used are: v. 3, Sragdharā; vv. 4 and 7, Āryā; vv. 5, 8–11, Anuṣṭubh; v. 6, Indravajrā; v. 12, Upajāti.

The inscription records the erection of a statue of Lokanātha in 824 Śaka (=902 A. D.) by Sthavira Nāga-Puṣpa the abbot of the monastery of Pramudita-Lokeśvara. It further relates that the monastery was founded by Bhadravarman II, and confirmed in its possessions by Indravarman II. This is the earliest Buddhist Inscription found at Champā.

TEXT.

(a).

(नमो लो)कनाथा(य).

स्वस्ति ।

येन — — मूर्त्तिर्व्यक्तैक......तस्मैनमः कारुणिकाय नित्यं ।

— — — — — विगतसुखा लोहदण्डाभिघाताः ।

स्मृत्वा लोकेश्वर — — — — — — केवलमोक्षमापुः ॥

III. मारैरुग्रैः परीताश्चिरमपि मनुजाः पूर्व्वकर्मानुरक्ता

निस्त्राणा — ˘ — परमकलुषिताः क्षुत्पिपासाभिभूताः ।

पूर्वश्चादानदोषात् सुगतविमुखतः प्राप्त — ˘ —

— — — वज्रपाणिप्रशमितनिरयं बुद्धमार्गं समापुः ॥

IV. श्रीभद्रवर्मनृपतेः तस्य मतोऽत्यन्तवल्लभत्वमतिः ।

सुजनाङ्घ्रियुगलसेवी नागपुष्पस्थाविर[1]नामा ॥

V. लोकेश्वरञ्जगद्व्याप्तं श्रद्धाभावैरतिष्ठिपत् ।

पृथिवीकीर्त्तये सोऽस्मै धर्मदेशनया हितः ॥

VI. लोक ˘ — ˘ यशोंशुशुद्धः

चम्पाधिपस्सर्वसुखप्रदाता ।

श्री-इन्द्रवर्मा स सुरेन्द्रवर्मा

तद्वत्कृतमेव चकार तस्मिन् ॥

VII. करुणामृतरसरसिकः केवलमेव प्रजाहितास्पदकृत् ।

यो मुक्तिं स च निखिलां प्रमुदितलोकेश्वरायादात् ॥

VIII. वज्रधातुरसौपूर्वं श्रीशाक्यमुनि शासनात् ।

शून्योपि वज्रधृद्धेतुः बुद्धानामालयोऽभवत् ॥

IX. पद्मधातुरतो लोकेश्वरहेतुर्जिनालयः ।

अमिताभवचो युक्त्या महाशून्यो बभूव ह ॥

---

1. Read °स्थविर.

(b).

X. चक्रधातुरसौ शून्यातीतो वैरोचनाह्वया ।
वज्रसत्वस्य हेतुः स्यात् तृतीयोऽभूज्जिनालयः ॥

XI. नागपुष्पाह्वयो भाति स्थाविर[1]स्तुल्य शीलधीः ।
पूर्वेण नगपुष्पाख्येनात्मवंशेन भिक्षुणा ॥
अस्मै श्रीप्रमुदितलोकेश्वरविह[2]राय तत्पुण्याय यत् सर्वमिदं
क्षेत्रं श्रीभद्रवर्मदेवस्तदनुज्ञया दत्तवान् पुनरपि स श्री
इन्द्रवर्मदेवः सकलराजाधिराजः तदनुग्रहसंभावात् तदेव
नियुक्तं ॥

XII. गते शकाब्दे युगकर्णकायैः
ज्येष्ठस्य शुक्ले नवमे दिनेयं ।
तेन प्रतिष्ठापितयात्मकीर्त्यै
श्रीलोकनाथस्तु स जीववारे ॥

TRANSLATION.

(a).

Reverence to Lokanātha.

I. Hail ! constant reverence to that merciful one by whom............one form............has been manifested. Those whose happiness was over, and who were being struck by iron rods..............got the highest salvation by thinking of Lokeśvara.

III. Sinful men, attached to their works in former lives, and without any hope of deliverance, were eternally surrounded by the terrible hosts of Māra, and overpowered by hunger and thirst, on account of their want of liberality and aversion to Sugata (*i. e.* Buddha) in former times.

---

1. Read °स्थविर.

2. Read विहाराय.

But being rescued by Vajrapāṇi from the hell, they secured the way (to salvation) pointed out by the Buddha.

IV. The monk (*sthavira*) named Nāgapuṣpa, who adored the feet of virtuous men, was highly esteemed by king Bhadravarman, and cherished very loyal and friendly feelings towards him.

V. He, (the king), established, for Nāgapuṣpa, with sentiments full of devotion, the (monastery) of Lokeśvara, who is omnipresent in the world. May He (Lokeśvara), consecrated for the sake of religious instruction, lead to his (the king's ?) glory in the world.[1]

VI. Śrī Indravarman, king of Champā, who was purified by the rays of glory..............world, who bestows all kinds of happiness, and who is (protected) by Indra (as an) armour, did the same kind of things to him (Nāgapuṣpa).

VII. Having drunk the nectar of mercy, and being devoted to the good of his subjects in a unique manner, he gave all exemptions (*i. e.* from imposts) to Pramuditalokeśvara.

VIII. This Vajradhātu, who, although non-existent, is the cause of the Vajra-wielder, became by the command of Śrī Śākyamuni, the abode of the Buddhas.

IX. Then Padmadhātu, the great non-existent, (but) the cause of Lokeśvara, became, by the logic of Amitābha's words (commands), the abode of the Jinas (*i. e.* the Buddhas).

1. Huber translates: 'Desiring to extend his glory all over the world, and delighted to hear religious instruction, he constructed for Nāgapuṣpa (a monastery placed under the name of) Avalokiteśvara, for the king was full of faith and love for him who is omnipresent in the world.'

(b).

X. This Cakradhātu, who, although beyond the state of non-existence, would be the cause of Vajrasattva, became, by the command of Vairocana, the third abode of the Jinas (*i. e.* Buddhas).

XI. The monk (*sthavira*) Nāgapuṣpa, equal in intelligence and piety to a former monk of his own family, called Nagapuṣpa, flourishes in this world.

Whatever fields etc. king Śrī Bhadravarman granted to the monastery of Pramuditalokeśvara, by his command and for the sake of his religious merit, all that has been confirmed by Śrī Indravarman, king of all kings, for the sake of his favour.

XII. When the year of the Śakas, denoted by 'yuga-karṇṇa-kāya' (824) had elapsed, (astronomical details) he established this Lokanātha for the sake of his glory.

(The concluding portion in Cham contains an enumeration of the fields granted).

No. 38.

The Châu-sa stelae Inscription of Jayasiṁhavarman I dated 825 Śaka.

The inscription was edited by M. Huber (B. E. F., Vol. XI, p. 282). It was engraved on the four faces of a stelae found at Châu-sa in the district of Quang-Ngai. The first face contains 21 lines besides the invocation, of which nearly 15 lines are almost wholly illegible. In line 3 the name of king Śrī-Jaya-Indravarman, and in L. 5, that of two dignitaries *viz.*, Po kluñ Pimilis and Danāy Pinān can be read. In line 7 we have "......yena sthāpita Īśaś Śrī-Indra-devâhvaya śaraikamūrttibhir-yukte śakābde śraddhayā........"

It may be supposed, therefore, that this part of the inscription records the consecration of a *liṅga*, called Indradeva, in honour of the king Indravarman, by a dignitary, in the year 815 (=893 A.D.). Line 13 refers to king Śrī Jayasiṁhavarman. The text from L. 16 onwards is given below. It relates the erection of another *liṅga*, called Śrī Śaṅkareśa, by the same person in 825 (=903 A. D.), and the donations of the king to this god.

The second face of the inscription is totally lost. The last two sides contain a description in Cham, of the lands granted to the temple.

TEXT.

पञ्चद्विकायोपगते शकाब्दे
......धानेन भुवि स्वकीर्त्यै ।
येन प्रतिष्ठापित ईश्वरोऽयं
श्रीशङ्करेशाह्व स एव भूयः[1] ॥
श्रीजयसिंहवर्मा श्री शङ्करेशे नराधिपः ।
......त्रिश्च शङ्खश्चादाद् रौप्यं कलशान् तथा[2] ॥
यस्यानुजा श्री जय —˘ (वर्मा) —
वनीशभार्य्या परिशुद्धभावा
साध्वी द्वनायगोपुरेश्वर्.........
— ष्येव भातीह सुरेन्द्रदेवी[3] ॥

TRANSLATION.

In the year of the Śakas denoted by 'pañca-dvi-kāya' (825) the god called Śaṅkareśa was again established by him in this world for his own glory.

---

1. Metre 'Indravajrā'.
2. Metre 'Anuṣṭubh'.
3. Metre 'Indravajrā'.

King Śrī Jayasiṁhavarman dedicated to Śrī Śaṅkara three conch-shells and one silver jug.

His younger sister Surendradevī, wife of the king Śrī Jaya (Siṁha) (varman), who is chaste, and whose sentiments are quite pure, flourishes here below (?).[1]

No. 39.

Hoá-Quê stelae Inscription of Bhadravarman III, dated 831 Śaka.

The inscription was edited by M. Huber (B. E. F., Vol. XI, p. 285), Hoá-Quê is situated close to Tourane. The inscription is engraved on the four faces of a stelae containing respectively 17, 19, 17 and 19 lines, besides the invocation at the beginning. The inscription on the first three faces is written in Sanskrit verse with three prose texts. That on the fourth face is written in Cham, but it contains a short prose passage and a verse in Sanskrit. There are altogether 27 Sanskrit verses. The metres used are: vv. 1, 17, 20, Sragdharā; vv. 2, 3, 9–12, 14, 18, 19, 21, 25–27, Anuṣṭubh; vv. 4–7, 24, Vasantatilakā; v. 8. Śārdūlavikrīḍita; vv. 13, 15, Pṛthvī; vv. 16, 23, Āryā; v. 22, Upajāti.

The object of the inscription is to record the various pious foundations made by three brothers, councillors of king Bhadravarman, and sons of Sārthavāha, brother of the first queen of Indravarman II, in the years 820, 830 and 831 Śaka. It further records a foundation by Jayendrapati in the year 829. The first of these dates falls in the reign of Jayasiṁhavarman, and the three others in that of his successor Bhadravarman.

1. What 'Danñy Gopureśvar' means it is difficult to understand, and it is therefore left untranslated.

TEXT.

(a).

ओं नमःशिवाय.

स्वस्ति ।

I. नानारूपाणि यस्याखिलजगदुदितैश्वर्य्यसम्भावितानि
क्षित्तोणीदुरात्मप्रभृतिभयतमांसीद्धतेजांसि नित्यं ।
पूर्वप्रख्यातयोगानवसितमहिमालिङ्गिताङ्गैः प्रकामं
नम्यस्तुत्यानि सन्तु त्रिभुवनवसतां भो हि लिङ्गानि भूत्यै ॥

II. अनादिमध्यनिधनं लिङ्गं यस्य पुरातनम् ।
सर्वलोकप्रशान्त्यासीच्चराचरनमस्कृतम् ॥

III. यल्लिङ्गेन जितं शश्वद् भावानां हितधारिणा ।
साधकानाञ्च मोक्षत्वं ददता हेतुना विना ॥

IV. आकाशमण्डलमतीत्य महीमनेक–
भूताधिकारपरिवारितमण्डलाभः ।
यल्लिङ्गमिन्दुदिनकृद्ग्रहसेविताभ–
दत्तक्रमागतसुखोदयमप्रपायात् ॥

V. लिङ्गानि यस्य सकृदप्युत ये नमन्ति
कामान्यथा हृदयवीप्सुपदाल्लभन्ते ।
ते सर्वसाधकविशेषगुणस्तुताश्च
देवालयेऽपि सुरवत् सुरमाननीयाः ॥

VI. लिङ्गावसानमतिगाढतमन्त्वधस्ताद्
वाराहरूपवहता हरिणापि जेत्रं ।
वीर्येण साधयितुमुत्तम योगवेत्रा
शक्यम यस्य यदनिष्ठवरप्रसादात् ॥

VII. लिङ्गावसानमनभिक्षतयोपरिष्टाद्
मानोज्झितेन सरसीरुहयोनिनाद्ः ।
स्वध्यानवीर्यरुचिरेण तथापि वेत्तुं
शक्यं न यस्य यदनिष्टवरप्रसादात् ॥

VIII. यो विज्ञाय मुरारिपद्मवरजावज्ञानदोषोद्गति-
प्रालेयग्लपिताननाम्बुजनिभौ प्रोवाच वाणीमिमां ।
"हे गोविन्दसरोजजौ किमपरं साद्ध्वा युवाभ्यां मनाग्
यन्मूलाग्रबुभुत्सया मम नतिः कृत्या मुदा नान्यथा" ॥

IX. इति यस्य वचः श्लाघ्यं श्रुतवन्तौ च सादारौ[1] ।
मुरारिपद्मयोनी तौ नेमतुर्य्यमनुत्तरम् ॥

X. आहतुर्गाश्च यत्सूर्य्यप्रबोधितमुखाम्बुजौ ।
तौ महान् देवदेवस्त्वं कुर्य्या यद् वरमावयोः ॥

XI. इति यो दर्शयन्मध्यलिङ्गाद् निर्गतमाननं ।
नेत्रत्रयाग्निचन्द्रार्कप्रभाभासितमास्थितः ॥

XII. ततश्च दक्षिणे ब्रह्मा संस्थितो वामतो हरिः ।
इत्येकत्वं इमौ येन लभेते यदनुज्ञया ॥

XIII. स एव भगवान् सुरासुरगुरुस्तदच्छब्रह्मा[2]
महेश्वर इतस्ततः प्रणतपादपद्मद्वयः ।
द्वयेन रहितो महीधरसुताह्वयो योऽजितो
जितोत्तरगुणास्पदोऽभवद्गोऽनुदोस्ता[3] चिरम् ॥

XIV. स श्रीशानेश्वरो यत्र जातिपुष्टभुवि श्रिया
सुखासीनो नमस्कारधनान् नः पातु साध्वसात् ॥

(b).

XV. ⏑—⏑⏑⏑—⏑—⏑—⏑⏑ कलङ्कमलोज्झिता
महाजनगणप्र —⏑⏑⏑—स्त चम्पाह्वया ।
विभूतिपरिभोगसंपदुचिता सुतेजस्विना
पुराणभृगुशासनेन किल रक्षिता —⏑— ॥

XVI. श्रीभद्रवर्मनृपतिर्भृगुवरवंशाम्बरामलशशाङ्को ।
लोकाशयकुमुदानि स्वाकरकिरणैः प्रबोधयति ॥

---

1. Read सादरौ.

2. Read '°स्ततच्छब्रह्मा'.

3. Read '°दस्त'.

XVII. तुङ्गत्वङ्गत्तुरङ्गत्वरितखरखुरोद्धूतधूलिप्रधूम्रे
नानानाराचधाराहतखरुधिरकणाशोकपुष्पाङ्किताग्रे ।
गर्जद्राजद्गजेन्द्रध्वनिहतपटहोन्नादिताशान्तराले
चम्पाराजाधिराजः स जयति महसाजौ यथा पाण्डुसूनुः ॥

XVIII. न्यायेन महता तेन जनिता धर्मपद्धतिः ।
तया श्रेयस्तु जनितं राज्ञोऽर्वावृषदेश्वरम् ॥

XIX. श्रीसंपदं विचित्रार्थाधिरधीशप्रसादतः ।
अमात्योऽवाप यश्चाज्ञा महासामन्तसंज्ञकः ॥

XX. मालाशीर्षोत्तमश्चीर्वरतिलकरुचिः कर्णभूषा समस्ता
श्रेष्ठः कर्णावतंसोऽपि युगळवसनं रुग्म[1]काञ्चीगुणश्रीः ।
सत् खड्गो रुग्म[1]कोशोपि च रजतनिभं भाजनं वा चिराण्डं
मायूरच्छत्रभृङ्गारकळशनिचयो दौलिका रौप्यदण्डा ॥

XXI. इत्येतानि च यस्यैव राजाज्ञासुप्रयत्नतः ।
दुर्लभानीह लोकेऽन्यैरपि प्रादान्महीपतिः ॥
यस्तु दौलिका मधिवसन् राजपरत उच्छ्रितमायूरच्छत्र-
प्रियायाशेप[2] वाद्यैस्सह वलैरस्याश्चावतराति पुमरिदं श्रेयः॥

XXII. नागेन्द्रमारुह्य वलैरसङ्ख्यैः
परापरैरावृतपादचारं ।
लक्ष्म्या विभात्युच्छ्रितसन्मयूर-
प्रच्छादितस्वात्मरविप्रतापः ॥

XXIII. भ्राता यस्यास्त्याज्ञा नरेन्द्रनृपविश्रसंज्ञकोऽमात्यः ।
कल्पक्रियाविधिज्ञः परमेश्वरधर्म्मसर्व्वतन्त्रज्ञः ॥

XXIV. यस्यानुजस्सकलशास्त्रसमर्थबुद्धि-
र्बुद्धिश्रिया भुवि समोऽङ्गिरसाऽभिगीतः ।
आज्ञा जयेन्द्रपतिसंज्ञक उत्तमात्मा-
मात्यः पवित्रकुशलेन पवित्रिताङ्गः ॥

---

1. Read 'रुक्म°'.

2. Read 'प्रियामशेष'.

XXV. सर्व्वदेशान्तरायातभूभुक्सन्देशमागतम् ।
निरीक्ष्यैकक्षणं वेत्ति निश्शेषार्थं अतीहया ॥

श्रीजयसिंहवर्मदेवस्य पुण्यः श्री जयगुहेश्वरो देवो विष्णुश्च विष्णुपुरे श्रीभद्रवर्मदेवस्य पुण्यः श्री प्रकाशभद्रेश्वरः श्री रुद्रकोटीश्वरश्च श्रीभद्रमलयेश्वरश्च श्रीभद्रचम्पेश्वरश्च श्रीभद्रमण्डलेश्वरश्च श्रीधर्मेश्वरश्च श्रीभद्रपुरेश्वरश्च तेषु प्रशस्तानि शिलालेखाक्षरालङ्कृतान्यकरोदाज्ञाजयेन्द्रपतिनामाऽमात्योऽनेकपरिभोगदौलिकामायूरकनकनिबद्धखड्गकोशकलशभृङ्गाररजतभजनकटिसूत्रकुण्डलकुण्डलगण्चिराण्डयुगलवसनादीनि प्राप्तवान् राजप्रसादादिति ॥

(c).

XXVI. — — — अनुजा यस्य साधुवृत्त्याश्रिताशया ।
उग्रदेवी सती नाम्ना ख्यायते पुण्यकांक्षिणी ॥

तैस्तत्सहोदरैरेकमतिभिर्म्मात्रानुज्ञया श्री महारुद्रदेवः प्रतिष्ठापितो मद्ध्यतः गगखद्विमङ्गलशके पितुराज्ञा सार्थवाहनाम्नः श्रीइन्द्रवर्म्मनृपतिमहादेव्या श्रीरुद्रवर्म्मभूपभ्रात्रीययास्य सहोदरस्य प्रतिरुपतः पितरि तद्भक्त्यै स्वजननीभूमौ ॥

अथ तेनोत्तरत इयं भगवती प्रतिष्ठापिता खवह्नितनुशके मातुरतीनकल्पसन्तानकुलोद्भवायाः पु पोव कु रुद्रपुरसंज्ञिकाया देवीगणपतिकुमारानिमान्देवान् प्रतिष्ठापयन्त्याश्चन्द्राग्नितनुशके प्रतिरूपतो मातरि तद्भक्त्ये स्वभूमौ ॥

अपि चामात्य आज्ञा जयेन्द्रपतिनामेति दक्षिनत इमं श्रीमहाशिवलिङ्गेश्वरदेवमस्थापयन्नवह्निमङ्गलशके परमेश्वरपूजार्थमिह जननीभूमौ स्वकीर्त्तये वेति ॥

(d).

राजाज्ञा न लङ्घनीया भवद्भिः
(ऐ)न्दवी या कला यावद् यावत् सूर्य्यकरावली-
दीपमानास्ति रोदस्योरस्मिंस्तावद् सुमुक्तिका ॥

TRANSLATION.

(a).

Reverence to Śiva!

Hail! May the *liṅgas* (of Śiva)—which assume various forms, creating prosperity of the whole world; whose glowing splendour everyday dispels the darkness which is the fear caused by vicious persons in the world; which are worthy of reverence and praise by the *yogis* (ascetics) who are distinguished by the merits of asceticism, renowned in olden times, but not yet exhausted—be for the prosperity of the inhabitants of the three worlds.

2. Whose primaeval *liṅga*, having no beginning, middle, or end, and revered by all things movable and immovable, was for the peace of all the worlds.

3. Whose *liṅga*, leading to the welfare of creatures, and granting, without reason, salvation to the devotees, is ever victorious.

4. Whose *liṅga*,—which has surpassed the earth and has sky as its horizon; which has got a shining orb surrounded by a large number of dependent spirits (bhūta); and whose splendour, to which homage is paid by the Moon, the Sun and the Planets, grants series of benefits to the world,—may it protect this world!

5. Those who even once bow down to these *liṅgas*, realise their desires.[1] They are praised by a multitude of special devotees, and even in heaven they are revered, like gods, by the gods themselves.

6. The lower end of that victorious *liṅga*, on account of its great depth below, could not be forcibly reached even by

---

1. The phrase 'हृद्यवोप्सुगद्राङ्ग°' is unintelligible and evidently requires emendation.

Hari, when he had assumed the form of a Boar; for although he was practised in excellent yoga, he had not the desired boon from Śiva.

7. The proud Brahmā, although shining in meditation and heroism, could not, owing to ignorance, know the (upper) end of the *liṅga* from above, because he had not the desired boon from Śiva.

8. Who addressed the following words to Viṣṇu and Brahmā, when he came to know that their faces were pale like frost-bitten lotuses on account of humiliation arising from ignorance: "Ho Govinda and Brahmā! what else, even so little, can you do? He who wants to know my bottom and top can only do so by gladly making obeisance to me, and in no other way.

9. Hearing whose august words, Viṣṇu and Brahmā bowed down, with respect, to the excellent god.

10. They, with faces like lotuses awakened by the Sun, said these words; "Thou great god of gods; please grant a boon to us."

11. Who, thereupon, showed them his face, issued from the middle part of the *liṅga*, and resplendent with three eyes which were the fire, the Moon and the Sun.

12. By whose command, then, Brahmā and Hari were united with him, Brahmā standing on the right, and Hari on the left.

13. He, the god Maheśvara,—the preceptor of gods and demons, and dispeller of illusions spread afar; whose pair of lotus-feet is saluted here and there (*i. e.* everywhere); who, though divested of duality, was made double by Gaurī; who, unconquered, was victorious over those who are the refuge of good qualities;—remained fixed and immovable.

14. May Śrī-Īśāneśvara, seated with ease, protect us, who have salutation as the only treasure, from terror, by his charm, in this land which has been enriched by our race.

(b).

15. ....city named Champā full of riches, wealth, and enjoyments, protected by the commandments of the old Bhṛgu.........of great energy.

16. King Śrī Bhadravarman, a spotless moon in the sky which is the excellent family of Bhṛgu, awakens the lotus, which is the heart of men, by means of his excellent rays (splendour).

17. He, the king of Champā, like the son of Pāṇḍu, shines by his splendour in the battlefield;—which is grey with the dust raised by the swift-moving sharp hoofs of horses galloping high; whose surface has been dyed red with drops of blood, like Aśoka flowers, shed by means of various weapons; and in the four regions of which the sounds of war-drums were drowned by the roars of gigantic beautiful elephants.

18. By a strict course of justice the king established a new era of righteousness (dharmapaddhatiḥ). The bliss engendered thereby made the king flourish.

19. The minister called Ājñā Mahāsāmanta, owner of various riches, obtained wealth and riches by the favour of his king.

20. The honour of putting a garland on his head, the distinction of being marked by an excellent *tilaka* (mark on the forehead), a complete ornament for the ears, best ear-ring, a pair of robes, decoration by golden girdle string, an excellent dagger with a golden sheath, a vessel and a cirāṇḍa[1] white

---

1. Cira = Viṣṇu and Aṇḍa = Śiva.—Does Cirāṇḍa denote an image of the two gods combined in one?

as silver; an umbrella made of the feathers of a peacock and a multitude of pitchers and vases, and a palanquin with silver staff.

21. These, difficult to be attained by others in this world, were granted him by the king on account of his faithful performance of royal commands.

He who having been seated next to the king in the palanquin, made beautiful by the parasol of peacock-feathers raised over it, and accompanied by soldiers and musical instruments, again gets down from it.

22. Having mounted an elephant, surrounded by innumerable forces both in front and rear, he shone in his majesty, while his own splendour like, that of the Sun, was screened by the umbrella of peacock-feathers raised over him.

23. He had a brother, the minister called Ājñā Narendra nṛpavitra, who was versed in all sacrificial ceremonies, and in all treatises dealing with the Śaiva religion.

24. His younger brother, whose intelligence was capable of penetrating into all the śāstras, and who was renowned in the world like Aṅgirasa for his intelligence and fortune, was called Ājñā Jayendrapati, a minister of good soul, whose body was purified by holy virtues.

25. Who, by hard exertion, was able to understand thoroughly the meaning of messages sent by kings from different countries, after looking over them only for an instant.

The pious works of Śrī Jayasiṁha-varmadeva, *viz.* (the temples of) Śrī Jayaguheśvara and of Viṣṇu at Viṣṇupur. The pious works of Śrī Bhadravarmadeva *viz.* (the temples of) Śrī Prakāśabhadreśvara, Śrī Rudrakoṭiśvara, Śrī Bhadra-malayeśvara, Śrī Bhadracampeśvara, Śrī Bhadramaṇḍaleśvara, Śrī Dharmeśvara, Śrī Bhadrapureśvara:

In all these the minister Ājñā Jayendrapati composed poetical inscriptions engraved on stones, and obtained by the favour of the king various distinctions, such as the palanquin, parasol decorated with peacock feathers, golden sheath of a sword, vases, pitchers, silver vessels, girdle, ear-rings, *Cirāṇḍa*, pair of robes etc.

(*c*).

......................His chaste younger sister, who had a pious heart, and was always anxious to do good deeds, was known as Ugradevī.

Her three brothers, being of one mind and with the permission of their mother, have erected in the middle of their native place, in the śaka year denoted by '*gagana-dvi-maṅgala*' (820), an image of Śrī Mahārudradeva, out of devotion to, and in imitation of the features of their father, named Ājñā Sārthavāha, brother of the chief queen of king Śrī Indravarman, the niece (?) of king Śrī Rudravarman, ...

To the north of this they erected, in their native place, in the śaka year denoted by '*kha-vahni-tanu*' (830), an image of Bhagavatī, out of devotion to and in imitation of the features of their mother named Pu Pov ku Rudrapura, ...who had issued from a family, pure from time immemorial, and who had herself established in the śaka year denoted by '*Candra-Agni-tanu*'—(831), the images of Devī, Gaṇeśa and Kumāra...............

Again, to the south of this the minister named Ājñā Jayendrapati has established in his native place the god Śrī Mahāśivaliṅgeśvara in the śaka year denoted by '*nava-*

dvi-maṅgala' (829), for the worship of Śiva and for the sake of his own glory.

(*d*).

...............15th day of the bright fortnight of the fifth month.........garden as far as the town,............as far as the temple..............a religious foundation............... He who would carry away the goods of the temple would go to hell. He who would protect them would live in heaven as long as he desires.

The royal order must not be transgressed. May this pious work endure as long as the phase of the Moon and the rays of the Sun illumine the universe (lit. heaven and earth).

(The seven concluding lines in Cham contain details about arrangements of the temple; they contain several unknown words and have not been translated by the editor).

No. 40.

57 Lac-Thành fragmentary stelae Inscription of Bhadravarman III, dated 832 Śaka.

It is engraved on four faces of the great stelae at Lac-Thành in the district of Quang-Nam. It begins with an invocation to Śiva followed by the eulogy of king Bhadravarman. It is dated "Pakṣa-Paśupati-nayana-maṅgala-samupagate-śakapati-samaye" *i. e.* 832 (=910 A. D.). It concludes with imprecation and enumeration of fields.

B. E. F., Vol. XI, p. 285.

No. 41.

The Phu-Luong Stelae Inscription of Rudravarman III, dated 83x Śaka.

The inscription was edited by M. Huber (B. E. F., Vol. XI, p. 283) It is engraved on two faces of a stelae at Phu-Luong in the district of Hue. Although very fragmentary, it contains much that is of historical interest. The first face contains 18 lines, but the last 10 are nearly illegible. The second face contains traces of 16 lines, the first five in Sanskrit, and the rest in Cham;—the latter only containing the descriptions of lands belonging to the temple. There are six verses in the first face, the metre being v. 1, Upendravajrā; v. 2, Vasantatilakā; vv. 3–4, Anuṣṭubh; v. 5, Śārdūla-Vikrīḍita; v. 6, Indravajrā.

The inscription records the foundation in 83x (unit figure being lost, *i. e.* some time between 908 and 917 A. D.) of a temple of Śiva, called Dharmaliṅgeśvara, by one Pādarakṣa, an officer of king Bhadravarman. The king is apparently Bhadravarman III.

TEXT.

(a).

I. जयत्यसौ यः सुरराजचूडा-
मणीद्धरश्म्याच्छुरिताङ्घ्रियुग्मः ।
उमामुखाम्भोज ˘ — ˘ गेन
˘ — सितादिर्निरपेक्षनेत्रः ॥

II. संमोहनेन किल विद्ध्यति यं शरेण
कामो जगत्त्रयमनोहरविभ्र — ˘ ।
— — पुनः स लभते यदनङ्ग[1] भूयस् [:]
धृत्वा सकृदपि[2] यमभवत् पुरुषार्त्तमुक्तः ॥

---

1. The line is grammatically defective.

2. The line is metrically defective. I suggest: धृत्वा सकृद् यमभवत् etc., which mends the line.

III. स एव भगवान् ईशो दत्तलोकसुखोदयः ।
एव श्रीशानभद्रेशो राजश्रियां[1] अकारयत् ॥

IV. नमितव्यो महीभुग्भिः प्रजापालनकांक्षिभिः ।
राजश्रियां कराम्भोजालिङ्गितैर्भुवि भूतये ॥

V. स्वस्ति प्राप्तजनानुरागमुदयुर्व्वी[2]स्त्रीवतंसीभुवे
चम्पायै धनधान्यवर्धनभृते भूपेन्द्रकीर्त्तीन्दुना ।
शश्वद्भूषितभूमिमण्डलरुचा संपादित[3]र्य्यश्रियै
सूतायै चरणद्वयाद् भगवतस्तस्योद्गतेनांशुना[4] ॥

VI. श्रीकीर्त्तिलम्पद्बलवीर्यशूर-
त्यागक्षमाधर्मगुणानुरागैः ।
श्रीभद्रवर्मा पृथिवीश्वरो यं
नित्यानुयातो ˘ ˘ — इवेन्द्रः ॥

LL. 9-11 युधिष्ठिरो ऽसौ......दुर्योधनाद्यैः......युयुत्सु-
र्व्वरसेवकः नाम्ना यः पादरत्न............ ॥

(b).

पशुपतिनयनमङ्गलसमुपगते शाकपतिसमये मिथुनदिवाकर-
केतुरजनिकरधरणितनये जलधर.........घृष्मर्त्तु[5].........कृष्णाष्टम्याह
पादरत्ननाम्ना नरपतिदृढभक्तिहृदयेन श्रीधर्मलिङ्गेश्वरः प्रतिष्ठापितः
लिङ्गभूमिग्रामे ऽस्मिनिति ॥

TRANSLATION.

(a).

1. Victory to (Mahādeva), whose feet are illumined by the blazing rays of the crest-jewels of the king of gods, whose eyes are............face of Umā like a lotus, and whose eyes are indifferent to all attachment.

---

1. Read °श्रयं. The two एव's appear redundant.
2. Read °मुदयोर्व्वी°.
3. Read °तार्यं°.
4. Read °नांशुना°.
5. Probably ग्रीष्मर्त्तु.

2. Who was struck with the arrow called Saṁmohana[1] by Cupid, who had (a body) charming in the three worlds. Although Cupid again became bodiless, still he was relieved of the miseries of soul by even once getting hold of him (Śiva).

3. He, the powerful god Śrīśānabhadreśa, who bestows happiness and prosperity on the world, brought about the prosperity of the king.

4. He is to be adored by the kings who are embraced by the lotus-like hands of the goddess of sovereignty and who are desirous of protecting their subjects, for the sake of the prosperity of sovereignty in this world.

5. Hail to Champā, the crowning ornament of the land of the rising Sun, and created by the rays issuing from the pair of feet of that god! By the glory of the king, like the moon, which eternally decorated the beauty of the circle of the earth, she has come to possess immense wealth and prosperity and a noble dignity (in a way) that has won for her the esteem of the people at large.

6. King Bhadravarmā, lord of the world, who is constantly attended by..............like Indra, on account of fortune, fame, riches, power, strength, heroism, liberality, forbearance, and attachment to religion and good qualities.

He is Yudhiṣṭhira, Yujutsu......................by (or with) Duryodhana and others, the good servant who was called Pādarakṣa...........

(b).

In the year of the śaka king denoted by "..........eyes of Śiva, Maṅgala." (83x) (astronomical details follow) Dharma-

1. Lit. 'Fascination—name of one of the five arrows of the cupid.'

liṅgeśvara was established in this village of Liṅgabhūmi by Pādarakṣa who had a great devotion for the king in his heart.

No. 42.

Bang-An Stelae Inscription of Bhadravarman (III).

The inscription was edited by M. Huber (B. E. F., Vol. XI, p. 5). It was engraved on two faces of a stelae found at Bang-An in the district of Quang-Nam. It contains 32 lines of writing. The language is Sanskrit. The inscription contains 11 verses and fragments of verse and prose texts. The metres used are:—vv. 1, 2, 5, 6, Indravajrā; v. 3, Śārdūlavikrīḍita; vv. 4, 10, 11, Anuṣṭubh; vv. 7, 8, Upajāti; v. 9, Vasantatilakā.

The object of the inscription is to record the installation of a *liṅga* by king Bhadravarman (III) (?). It was dated, but the symbols denoting unit and tenth figures are lost. The hundredth figure is Maṅgala = 8.

TEXT.

ओं नमश्शिवाय.

स्वस्ति ।

I. यो भस्मराश्यां बहुसञ्चयायां
दिव्यः सुखासीन उरुप्रभावः ।
देदीप्यते सूर्य इवांशुमाला-
प्रद्योतितः खे विगताम्बुदेये ॥

II. ब्रह्मेन्द्रविष्णवादय[1] एव देवा
दृष्ट्वा तदा विस्मयमागताःस्युः ।

---

1. Read विष्णवादयः ।

तत्प्रज्वलन्तं यमखण्डिताभम्
निर्धूमकं वह्निमिवाज्ययुक्तम् ॥

III. देवेन्द्रः किल पूर्वतोऽस्थित तदा[1] याम्यां सरोजोद्भव-
श्चन्द्रार्काविह पृष्ठतश्च भगवान् नारायणो वामतः ।
मध्यस्थो ज्वलिताभरश्मिसहितश्चोंकारपूर्वैस्स्वधा-
स्वाहान्तैर्निजमन्त्रकैस्स्तुतनतो योऽसौ तदाद्यैः सुरैः ॥

IV. अथ तद्भस्मराश्या यः समुत्थायातिनिर्मलः ।
तिष्ठत्येव नभोमध्ये सूर्यकोटिसमप्रभः ॥

V. दीक्षानिमित्तं किल सर्वभावान्
आस्वा[2]वशेषं वरभस्म तत्र ।
यः पद्मयोनौ गुणमङ्गलार्थं
ददौ च पीयूषभुजां सभायाम् ॥

VI. संपद्य शेषां पृथिवीं नियोगाद्
यो भस्मदेशां अनुशास्ति विष्णुम् ।
योंतर्हितोऽभूत् तत एव देवा
ब्रह्मादयः स्वालयमाशु जग्मुः ॥

VII. (स) एव देवः परमात्मकः श्रीशानेश्वरो लोकगुरुर्नृपाणाम् ।
पूज्यः प्रणम्यः स[ह]भृत्यवर्गैश्चस्पर्धिहेतोर्जयतीह नित्यं ॥

VIII. श्रीभद्रवर्मा भृगुवंशनाकचन्द्र.........नगरीन् नरेन्द्रः ।
गुणेन वृद्धया च शतानवृत्तिं अलङ्करोत्युत्तमधीरिवेयम् ॥
नि जितवतः । केयूरांशुप्रभासितभुजबलेन याता जयदिन्दु-
मितां नु............घोरघोषसङ्कुलितान्ताः ॥

IX. देशान्तरागतमहीपतिदूतसङ्घ
ज — ˘ — ˘ युगळस्य नृपस्य कीर्त्तिः ।
संपूर्णचन्द्रधवला भुवनप्रकीर्णा
प्र —˘— ˘ ˘— ˘ ˘—˘— — ॥
विहिततपसः...सज्जनगीतो...भुवि......क्षे शुचिमतिचतुरः
अग्निस्सुराश्च...................मतिचतुरः ।

---

1. The line is grammatically defective.
2. Read आज्य॰.

X. संपातु विदुषो कर्म संपातु विदुषो वचः......................
कैलासशिश..................... ॥ स एव तपस्वी तपस्यामनु
...................रितदुरितदुरितकर्म्मा ....असुर
पिशाचवर्ज्जितो जितेन्द्रियोऽपि पुण्य............हितोपदेशं
............धन्यो मानितसकलजनो जनितकुशलो लोकयात्रा
..............धीरं..............वेलायां ध्याने समधिगत
............धवलीकृतं स्वशरीरं...........यतीदृशं इदं भस्म
हि क्षीरार्णवतरङ्गफेनधवलं कुन्देन्दुद्युति............पशुपतेः
वन्दितचरणयुगळस्येदं...................एव परमेश्वरस्थापना
कर्त्तव्या मया सर्वमुक्तये इति ॥ ....मङ्गलनियमित
शकपति समये प्रथमभवभानुभानुसुतके बुधपति...........
मिथुनलग्नसुरगुरु.............. मकरराहुजलधरदीतिजगुरु-
(ष)ष्ठाह...........रविवार पुनर्वसु........परमः परमेश्वर
............वान्तरेश्वर ....नाथमहामुनिमत ....
प्रतिष्ठापित इति ॥

XI. श्रीभद्रवर्मणा दत्ता तस्मै मुक्तिरियं —
(यावत् सू)र्यश्च चन्द्रश्च तावदस्ति महीतले ॥
सियमप........निय् अपुव्...........न्दो-इना ॥

TRANSLATION.

Reverence to Śiva.

Hail!

1. He, the divine (being), and of great power, seated with ease upon a mass of ashes, shines very much, like the Sun, aglow with rays, in a cloudless sky.

2. Seeing him shine with an unbroken splendour, like a smokeless fire, nourished by clarified butter, Brahmā, Indra, Viṣṇu and other gods are filled with astonishment.

3. With Indra in front, Brahmā to the right, the Moon and the Sun at the back, and the god Nārāyaṇa to the left,

he was sitting in the middle, glowing with splendid rays while those and other gods were bowing down before him and prasing him in his proper hymns which begin with 'Oṁ' and end with '*Svadhā-svāhā*.'

4. Then rising from the heap of ashes, he, the very pure, remained in the middle of the firmament, (shining) with a splendour equal to that of millions of suns.

5. For the sake of consecration, and for virtue and welfare, he gave everything, even the excellent ashes, the remains of sacrifice, to Brahmā, in the assembly of the gods.

6. Having transformed the ashes into the complete universe, he committed it to the care of Viṣṇu. Then he disappeared and all the gods, commencing with Brahmā, went to their respective homes.

This god Śrī Īśāneśvara, the preceptor of the world, who possesses the characteristics of the absolute, and who is worthy of worship and salutation by the kings, lives here triumphantly together with his multitude of servants for the sake of the prosperity of Champā. Śrī Bhadravarman, the moon in the heaven of the Bhṛgu family.......................... adorns hundreds (?) of towns................................ The multitude of royal ambassadors coming from different countries..............the white fame of the king has spread all over the world..............praised by virtuous men..............may he protect (?) the words and deeds of learned men !........... He is ascetic....................removed his sins,.................. devoted of *asuras* and *piśāchas*, having control over his passions..............respected by all.................these ashes white as the foam of the waves of the ocean of milk and shining like *kunda* (flarer)[1] and Moon..............of Paśupati

1. The text has 'kuṇḍa' = probably a mistake for 'kunda.'

..............whose feet are adorned.............. It is my duty to install the Parameśvara for the salvation of all.............. installed in the year of the śaka king denoted by x x *maṅgala* (8xx) (astronomical details follow...........)......... Exemption given to him by Śrī Bhadravarman—It will endure in the world as long as the Sun and the Moon.[1]

No. 43.

Nhan-Biéu Stelae Incription of Indravarman III, dated 833.

The inscription was edited by M. Huber (B. E. F., Vol. XI, p. 299). Nhan-Biéu is in the district of Quang-Tri. The inscription is engraved on the four faces of a stelae containing respectively 13, 14, 11 and 12 lines in addition to the invocation at the beginning. The inscription on the first three faces is written in Sanskrit, and the rest in Cham. There are altogether 21 verses in the Sanskrit portion with a number of small prose passages. The metres used are: vv. 1, 15, 20, Upajāti; vv. 2, 9, 12, Śārdūlavikrīḍita; v. 3, Śikhariṇī; vv. 4, 6, Gīti; v. 5, Upagīti; vv. 7, 8, 11, 19, Anuṣṭubh; v. 13, Indravajrā; vv. 14, 17, Āryā; v. 16, Pṛthvī; vv. 18, 21, Vaṁśasatha; v. 10, Sragdharā.

The inscription records that a dignitary of Champā named Po klun Pilih Rājadvāra and his eldest son Sukṛtī Po klun Dharmapātha, consecrated in the year 830 (=908 A. D.) a temple of Śiva called Devaliṅgeśvara, and in the year 833 (=911 A. D.) a Buddhist monastery of Avalokiteśvara. in honour of their grandmother, the princess Lyaṅ Vṛddhakula, who was also the grandmother of Tribhuvanadevī (cf.

1. In this fragmentary portion only important passages have been translated and many isolated words and phrases have been left out.

No. 44) queen of Jaya Siṁhavarman I. The father, Rājadvāra boasted of having served under four kings of Champā *viz.*, Jaya Siṁhavarman, his son king Jaya Śaktivarman, king Bhadravarman (III) and his son Indravarman III. He got the titles of Povkluñ Sudaṇḍavāsa and Akālādhipati.

TEXT.

(a).

ओं नमश्शिवाय.

स्वस्ति ।

I. यं भूर्भुवः स्वस् ˘ ˘ — ˘ — —
स्म वर्णयिष्यन्ति च वर्णयन्ति
त्रयस्त्रिंशकास्सन्ति ˘ — ˘ — —
— — ˘ — — ˘ नमोस्तु तस्मै ॥

II. येन श्रीपतितुल्यविक्रमवता निश्शङ्कया रक्षता
चम्पाभूमिं अखण्डितस्वतरसां लक्ष्मीमिवाचञ्चलां ।
दत्ता दत्तमनोरथा बहुविधा सम्पत्प्रजाभ्यस्सदा
श्रीमच्छ्रीजयसिंहवर्म्मनृपतिस्स ख्यायते भूतले ॥

III. सती नाम्ना या श्रीत्रिभुवनमहादेव्यनुपमा
नृपस्त्रीणां तस्यावनिपभवनेष्वग्रमहिषी ।
प्रधाना सर्वासां सुचरितरतापत्यसहिता
विभाति प्रायेण स्वपतिभवने श्रीरिव रुचा ॥

IV. सा ल्यङ् वृद्धकुलायाः पौत्री समभुक्तिशुद्धवंशायाः ।
सम्पूर्णेन्दुसमायाः दीपितवंशद्वयाम्बरायाश्च ॥

अपि च ।

V. नरेन्द्राधिपतेरवनिपचरणारविन्दभक्तिभृतः ।
प्रकृतेरिष्टप्रकृतेर्ल्यङ् वृद्धकुलाग्रजस्य सतः ॥

VI. श्रेष्ठायास्तनयायाः प्रकृतिसुपरिशुद्धनैजवंशायाः ।
तनयः प्रख्यातनयः क्षितिपचरणसेवानिपुणमतिरभूत् ॥

VII. यो धीमान् स्वनयोपेतो धर्म्यः कुशलनीतिमान् ।
भूपशासननम्रात्माभवदत्यन्तभक्तितः ॥

यश्श्रीजयसिंहवर्म्मनृपतेरतिवल्लभो नायकोऽयं
अभिमतसम्पदस्ति तदा यः
पोव् क्लुअ् पिलिः राजद्वारनामाभूत्। किन्तु

VIII. यवद्वीपपुरं भूपानुज्ञातो दूतकर्म्मणि।
गत्वा यः प्रतिपत्तिस्थः सिद्धयत्रां[1] समागमत्॥
अतो विभवसंपद्मधिगतवानिति॥

IX. पश्चाच्छ्रीजयशक्तिवर्म्मनृपतेरिच्छाशया रक्षत-
श्श्रीमच्छ्रीजयसिंहवर्म्मवसुधापालात्मजस्य क्षितिम्॥
राज्ये श्रीमति सर्वसंपदुदयैरापूरिते सर्व्वतो-

(b).

— — —⏑ ⏑—⏑—⏑ ⏑ ⏑—यद्वत् प्रभुतोऽभवत्॥

अपि च—

X. श्रीमच्छ्रीः भद्रवर्मावनिभुज इह दिक्प्र ⏑— —⏑— —
— — —⏑— —⏑ ⏑ ⏑ ⏑ ⏑ ⏑— —⏑—आचरीणाम्
— — — —⏑— —⏑ ⏑ ⏑ ⏑ ⏑ ⏑— —⏑— —⏑ वीर्य्यं
दिव्वाकर्ण्य द्विषस्ते पुलकितवपुषोऽतिज्वरं यान्ति सर्वे॥
तत्र तस्य पौव् क्लुअ् सुदण्डवासनामधेयस्समभूत्।
तत्रापि

XI. यवद्वीपपुरं भूयः क्षितिपानुज्ञया ⏑ —
द्विवारमपि यो गत्वा सिद्धयात्रामुपागमत्॥
अतो यस्मिंश्च श्रीभद्रवर्मावनिभुजो.........क्ष्मायां
स्सुदाङकुमुवेलक्षेत्राणि योऽधिगतवानिति॥ अपि च

XII. यस्यैराजवतः पुनःस्थिर ⏑ — श्रीभद्रवर्माह्वय-
क्षोणीपालसुतस्य दुर्जयजयश्रीविस्तरस्थायिनाम्।
कीर्त्तिर्विभ्रमती च दिक्षु वि ⏑ — निर्गन्तु अस्मात्परं
पूयत्प्रधनाय सर्वांदिगियं हासङ्करेत्यब्रवीत्॥

---

1. Read °यात्रां.

XIII. श्रीइन्द्रवर्माणमधीश्वरं तं
देशान्तरे व्याप्तयशःप्रकाण्डम् ।
प्रीत्या समाकर्ण्य नृपाश्चतुष्टास्
तं संस्तुवन्तिस्म निरन्तरं ते ॥

XIV. तद्राज्ये यस्तु प्रायशो भूपतेराज्ञासुप्रयत्न-
कृतायासत्वादकालाधिपतिनामधेयमवाप ॥

XV. — — ⏑ कर्म्मोपचितात्मभावः
क्षितीशनीतिप्रतिबद्धबुद्धिः ।
इष्टेष्वनिष्टेषु नराधिपस्य
किञ्चित्प्र — — खलु यः समर्थः ॥
अस्ति यदग्रजस्सुकृती पोवक्लुअधर्मपाथाख्यः
श्रीइन्द्रवर्मावनिपालानुग्रहोऽभूत् ॥

XVI. विदग्धमतिसंपदामिहपरं गुणाम्भोनिधेः
निधिः प्रकृतिभः पुरस्सरिकशुद्धचित्तोदयः ।
तथा सुविपुला...
....

(c).

योऽयमग्रज...............एवमकथयत् ।

XVII. कुमुवेलभूमिक्षेत्राणि राजप्रसादादधिगतान्यभूवन्
खिकिर्ग्रामोवात्मजननीनिवासभूमि............ ॥
.........हृदयोः देवः प्रतिष्ठापयितव्य इति । कुतः

XVIII. विभूतिरेषा विपुलाप्यसार्थिका
समुच्छ्रितापि क्षणभङ्गताङ्किता ।
अनीव निस्सारतमा महीतले
महर्षिणोक्ता सकले सदागमे ॥

XIX. एतत् सञ्चिन्त्य मतिमानत्र कीर्तिपरायणः ।
तयोरेव प्रतिष्ठां यः कर्तुमुत्सहते तदा ॥
स एव परमकुशलपुण्यसंभारभारावर्जितहृदयोऽम्बर
दहनमङ्गलोऽपगते शकराजे मिथुनादित्यकेत्विन्दुतनये

मृगेन्द्रलग्ने मृगराजाखण्डतुषरांशौ कन्याभूतनये मकर
राहौ मेषसुरगुरुरविजे मघर्दे सोमवारे जेष्ठसितपञ्चाहे देव-
लिङ्गेश्वरमतिष्ठिपत् स्वाग्रजेन सह कीर्त्तय इति ॥

XX. ततः प्रतिष्ठापित एव तेन श्रीवृद्धलोकेश्वरनामधेयः
त्रिव्यष्टयुक्ते च शके विहारोग्रामे चिकिर्नाम्नि तु साग्रजेन ॥

XXI. यथा धराश्रित्य वसुन्धराधरम्
चलाचलापि स्थिरतामुपैति सा ।
तथा प्रदेशोऽयमसौ महेश्वरम्
कूपात्मकं वापि च तत्प्रभावतः ॥

TRANSLATION.

(a).

Reverence to Śiva.

Hail !

I. Whom all the three words, *Bhū*, *Bhuvas*, and *Sva* (praised), praise, and will praise.. ......salutation to Him !

Again :

II. There was the illustrious king, famous in this world as Śrī Jayasiṁha Varman, who was equal in prowess to Viṣṇu, who protected, without fear, the kingdom of Champā, which was in the fulness of its power, and resembled Lakṣmī without (the proverbial) inconstancy; and who always gave various riches to his subjects to the fulfilment of their utmost desires.

III. In the house of that king, the chaste and incomparable Tribhuvana Mahādevī was the chief among all the queens. She was the foremost among all (the queens) and virtuous, and shone with her children[1] in her husband's house almost like Śri.

1. Huber translates "bereft of husband."

IV. She was the grand-daughter of Lyaṅ Vṛddhakulā, who was born in a pure family, and illumined both the families (*i. e.*, family of her father and husband) as the full moon illumines the sky.

Again:

V. Of the eldest son of Lyaṅ Vṛddhakulā Narendrādhipati[1] who was devoted to the lotus-feet of the king, who was a good person and whose character was agreeable.[2]

VI. He (Narendrādhipati) had an excellent daughter who had purified her own family by her character. This daughter had a son who was skilful and devoted in the service of the king and whose prudence was well-known.

VII. He was intelligent, prudent, religious and politic; out of great devotion for the king he was very obedient to his commands.

VIII. He was a favourite captain of the king Śrī Jayasiṁhavarman and had riches equal to his desires. He was named Pov Kluñ Pilih Rājadvāraḥ.

At the command of the king he went to the capital of Yavadvīpa on a diplomatic mission, and obtained credit by the success of his undertaking.[3]

From that time he obtained wealth and riches.

---

1. This may be the proper name or an epithet i. e. king of men.

2. Huber translates "who was the best product of nature." 'Prakṛteḥ' seems to be redundant.

3. Huber translates 'Siddhayatrām Samāgamat' as 'acquired the science of magic.' This seems to be farfetched. Huber reads 'nūta' in the first line of the verse which seems to be a mistake for 'dūta'. 'Nūta' means 'praiseworthy'—so it also leads nearly to the same conclusion.

IX. Then, in the prosperous kingdom,—filled everywhere with riches of all kinds,—of the illustrious king Śri Jaya Siṁhavarman, who protected the world with his stern commands.

(b).

He (Po Kluñ Piliḥ Rājadvāraḥ) continued to occupy a high position.

Again:

X. Fortunate king Śrī Bhadravarman.................his enemies hearing of him become afflicted with fear and the hairs of their bodies stand on end.

Under this reign he obtained the title of Pov Kluñ Sudaṇḍa(vā)sa.

XI. Again, at the commands of the king he went to Yavadvīpa a second time and was successful in his undertaking.

He obtained from king Śrī Bhadravarman the fields in the villages of Sudāñ and Kumuvel.

Again:

XII. ....the son of king Bhadravarman,............ whose fame and sovereignty had spread in all directions by hard-won victories.[1]..............

XIII. Delighted kings heard with pleasure of king-emperor Śrī Indravarmā, whose mighty fame had spread to other countries, and constantly praised him.

XIV. During his rule he (Piliḥ Rājadvāraḥ) had obtained the title of Akālādhipati as a reward for the zeal with which he served the king.

1. The passage is very obscure and I cannot offer any complete translation.

XV. Devoting himself exclusively to the study of politics he was enabied to advise the king as to what was good and what was bad.

His eldest son (or brother ?) called Sukṛti Pov Kluñ Dharmapātha was a favourite of king Indravarman.

XVI. (Eulogy of Dharmapātha........................... mutilated).

(c).

Who spoke thus to his eldest son (brother ?).

XVII. I have obtained the fields of Kumuvel by the favour of the king. The village of Cikir is the place of residence both of mine as well as of my mother. It is therefore necessary to establish god...........; for:

XVIII. This wealth, although very great, is unsubstantial; although accumulated with care it is liable to be destroyed in a moment. It is most useless in this world. Thus has the wealth been described by the great sage in all scriptures.

XIX. Having thought thus, he, the intelligent man and desirous of fame, resolved to install gods in the two places.

Then he, with his heart bent down under the burden of many excellent meritorious works, together with his eldest son (Brother ?) installed a Devalingeśvara, for the sake of glory, in the year of Śaka king denoted by '*ambara-dahana-maṅgala* (830) (astronomical details).

Then, in the Śaka year 833, he established, together with his eldest son (brother ?) a monastery called Śrī Vṛddhalokeśvara in the village of Cikir.

XX. As both the movable and immovable things in the world become fixed by the support of the mountains, so this region would find a stable support in the two sanctuaries of Śiva and Avalokiteśvara.

(d).

The Cham portion enumerates the lands granted to the temple of Devaliṅgeśvara.

No. 44.

Ha-Trung Stelae Inscription of Indravarman III, dated 838.

The inscription was edited by M. Huber (B. E. F., Vol. XI, p. 298). It was engraved on the four faces of a stelae found at Hà-Trung in the district of Quang-Tri. There were altogether 57 lines of writing in Sanskrit, and 71 lines in Cham. Only the last five lines of the Sanskrit portion can be read. It records the erection of a temple of Śiva, called Indrakānteśvara, by Tribhuvanadevī, in the year 838 (=916 A. D.) during the reign of Indravarman, son of Bhadravarman. The Cham portion describes the lands which belonged "to the temple of Śrī Indrakānteśvara in the town of Navap."

TEXT.

I. कायाग्निमङ्गळयुते शकपतिसमये मधोरसितपक्षे ।
षष्ठाहे बुधवारे प्रवरवसन्तर्तुकालेऽस्मिन् ॥

II. प्रथमभव..............घटगते रविपुत्रे ।
......तुल......सौरसुरगुरुचन्द्रागाते धनुषि......लग्ने ॥

III. भौम मकरे (मे)ष भृगुजे श्रीमतीन्द्रकान्तेशम् ।
सातिष्ठिपत् स्वभक्त्या साध्वी श्रीइन्द्रवर्मनृपे ॥

IV. श्रीत्रिभुवनदेव्याः श्रीः पुण्यानां स्थानमूढकीर्त्ति स्यात् ।
प्रतिमालिङ्गो देवो नित्यं श्रीइन्द्रकान्तेशः ॥

TRANSLATION.

In the year of the śaka king denoted by "*kāya-agni-maṅgala*" (838), (astronomical details)..................during the reign of the illustrious king Indravarman, the chaste (Tribhuvanadevī) installed the image of Indrakānteśa out of devotion.

The holy shrine and the image of god Śrī Indrakānteśa will be for ever to the great glory of Śrī Tribhuvanadevī.

No. 45.

Po-Nagar Stelae Inscription of Indravarman III, dated 840 Śaka.

For localities, publications etc. cf. No. 22. The reading was corrected by M. Huber (B. E. F., Vol. XI, p. 268). It contains 4 verses in 13 lines, the metre being: vv. 1-2, Anuṣṭubh, v. 3, Upajāti, and v. 4, Vasantatilakā.

TEXT.

I. श्रीभद्रवर्मनृपतिर्ज्जगद्विभवदायकः ।
भुनक्ति सकलां भूमिं पयोनिधिपयोम्बराम् ॥
II. तस्य सूनुर्म्महीपालश्चम्पारक्षणतत्परः ।
श्री इन्द्रवर्म्मनामास्थात् पूर्णचन्द्र इवाम्बरे ॥
III. मीमांसषट्तर्कजिनेन्द्रसूर्म्मि-
स्सकाशिकाव्याकरणोदकौघः ।
आख्यानशैवोत्तरकल्पमीनः
पटिष्ठ एतेष्विति सत्कवीनाम् ॥
IV. व्योमाम्बुराशितनुगे शकराजकाले
देवीमिमां भगवतीं कलधौतदेहाम् ।
एकादशेहनि शुचेरसितेर्कवारे
(सो)तिष्ठिपद्भुवनमण्डलकीर्त्तिकाङ्क्षी ॥

TRANSLATION.

I. The king Śrī Bhadravarmā, who is the giver of riches to the world, enjoys all the lands up to the ocean (lit. which have got as its dress the water of the ocean).

II. His son, king Śrī Indravarman, skilful in protecting Champā, was like full moon in the sky.

III. He who (skilfully played in the) good waves which were the six systems of Philosophy beginning with Mīmāṁsā and those of Jinendra (*i. e.* Buddha), and in the mass of water which was (Pāṇini's) Grammar with Kāśikā, who was a fish (in the water) which was the Ākhyāna and the Uttarakalpa of the Śaivas; because among the learned, he was the most skilful in all these subjects.

IV. In the year of the Śakas denoted by '*vyoma-amburāśi-tanu*' (840), on Sunday, the eleventh day of the dark fortnight of the month of Śuci (Jyaiṣṭha or Āṣāḍha), he has installed this golden image of the goddess Bhagavatī in order to gain fame in the whole world.

No. 46.

Lai-trung Stelae Inscription of Indravarman III (or Jaya-Indravarman I ?) dated 843 (?).

The inscription was edited by M. Huber (B. E. F., Vol. XI, p. 15). It was engraved on two faces of a stelae found at Lai-Trung in the district of Hue. The whole of the first face and about 8 lines of the second face are in Sanskrit and the rest is in Cham. The Sanskrit portion contains 5 verses and 1 prose passage. The metres used are: vv. 1, 3, 5, Śārdūlavikrīḍita; v. 4, Sragdharā; v. 2, Indravajrā.

The inscription refers to king Śrī Jaya Indravarman and records the erection of a temple of Śiva by one Danāy Pinān, a noble of Champā. It is dated as follows:

"Niy Śakarājakāla vuḥ yāp triḥ catvāra-aṣṭa." M. Huber and M. Finot take it to mean 840, taking 'triḥ' as a Cham word.

But 'triḥ' should, in my opinion, be taken as Sanskrit 'triḥ'=3. For, in the first place, the word 'yāp=counting' immediately precedes it; and secondly, the date would otherwise be merely 84, as there is no justification for taking 'catvāra' as equivalent to 40.

TEXT.

(a).

स्वस्ति । ओं नमश्शिवाय सिद्धिरस्तु.

I. यो व्यापी त्रिभवोत्तमो गुरुयशास्सर्वैः सुरैः पूजितो
भक्त्या योगविशुद्धया पृथुतमौजोभिश्च सिद्धर्षिभिः ।
देवामित्रगणैरगेन्द्रविवरे देवाङ्गनाभिस्तथा
पापापत्तिविनाशकृत्प्रणयिनां नृणां विभूतिन्ददौ ॥

II. श्रीशानदेवस्य हरस्य तस्यैवाङ्घ्रिद्वयाम्भोरुहरेणुभिर्य्या ।
चम्पापुरीसम्पदनूनशोभासंभोगभाराढ्यतरा समृद्धा ॥

III. तस्यां श्रीजयइन्द्रवर्मनृपतिः संपादितश्रीः सतां
सेनाभिस्सकलाभिरिन्दुरिव वा ताराभिरासेवितः ।
दीप्ताज्ञापरिरक्षिताखिलजगद् यः पुण्यकर्मोदयः
कान्त्या लोकमनोविशोधनकरश्शक्त्या प्रजा रक्षतु ॥

IV. तस्यामत्य[1]स्समस्तेश गुण पटुतरोऽशेषधर्मास्पदार्थी
नानापुण्यावसानाञ्जनितमुनिमनोमोदनो योऽमलात्मा ।
शान्त्या राकेन्दुवत् सज्जन[2]विरुतो लब्धकीर्त्यागमश्रीः
शास्त्री शास्त्रज्ञसङ्घैः स्तुतिपदुमतिभिर्दिङ्मुखे गीयते स्म ॥

---

1. Read °मात्य.

2. Metrically defective. We expect सज्जनगणविरुतो.

V. पो याङ्पोव् कुदनायपिनाङ् पृथुजनः शैवक्रियाज्ञानविद्
योगध्यानसमाधिकृच्छिवपदेच्छा यो निजात्मश्रियः।
स्मृत्वाम्भःप्लवमानफेनसदृशं कायं त्वनित्यं महत्
तत्पुण्यं भवसागरात् स्म कुरुते पित्रोर्मुचे स्वात्मनः॥
श्री अमरेन्द्रपुरेश्वरस्य धनानि क्षेत्रगोदासदासीमहिषादीनि धान्यतण्डुलवसनरजतकनककंसलोहताम्रादीनि च ये के पापपुरुषा हरन्ति बलतया तृष्णतया वा

(b).

कल्कनतया वातिभीममहानरके घोरतरहुताशनशिखाकराळे पतन्तु ते पितृबन्धुपक्षैर्मातृबन्धुपक्षैः। पुना रक्षन्ति न हरन्ति वा ये के साधुपुरुषा धर्मक[1]ङ्क्षिणः प्र[2]प्नुवन्तु ते नित्यं स्वर्गफलमिति॥

TRANSLATION.

(a).

Hail ! Reverence to Śiva ! Let there be success !

I. The god who penetrates everywhere; who is the best in the three worlds; who possesses a great glory; who is worshipped with devotion purified by yoga, in the caverns of Himālaya, by all gods, the Asuras (demons), the celestial nymphs, and the most powerful Siddhas and Ṛishis; and who destroys the sins; gaves strength and power to the men who are devoted to him.

II. By the pollens of the pair of lotus-feet of Śrī Īśānadeva Hara, the prosperity of the city of Champā increased with abundance of wealth, beauty and enjoyment.

III. May the king Śrī Jaya Indravarman,—who procures good fortune to the virtuous, who is served by his entire army as the moon is served by the stars, who protects

1. Read °कां°. 2. Read प्रा°.

the entire world by his brilliant strength, who is the source of all meritorious works, and who delights the mind of the people by his beauty,—protect his subjects in that city by his strength.

IV. He had a minister who was very skilful in all the qualities of Īśa (Śiva or of a master); who was desirous of being the receptacle of infinite religious merit; who ha . caused pleasure in the hearts of *munis* (hermits) by the successful performance of a number of meritorious works; whose soul was without stain; who was tranquil as the full moon; who (*i. e.* whose name) was sung by the virtuous; who had acquired fame, knowledge of scriptures and riches; who was versed in the sacred scriptures, and who (*i. e.* whose praise) was sung in all the regions by the assembly of men, learned in scriptures, and skilful in (composing) hymns of praise.

V. Po yāṅ pov ku Daṅāy Pināṅ, a dignitary, versed in the knowledge of Śaiva rites, and performing *yoga*, *dhyāna*, and *samādhi* for gaining the heaven of Śiva for the sake of his own salvation, thinking that this body is as impermanent as the foam floating on waters, made this great meritorious work for emancipating himself and his parents from this ocean of existence.

If the riches of Śrī Amarendrapureśvara *viz.*, fields, oxen, male and female slaves, buffaloes, rice, both husked and unhusked, clothes, silver, gold, bell-metal, iron, copper etc., are forcibly carried away by wicked men, out of greed or sheer wickedness, then they would fall into the deep abyss of hell, made horrible by the burning flames, together with their paternal and maternal relations. But those virtuous persons, who desiring religious merit, maintain and do not carry away (those goods), would secure the enjoyment of heaven for ever.

May the black dog, the white dog, the red dog and the dog of motley colour haunt the mother of him who incurs this curse.

Written in the year 843 of the śakas.

No. 47.

Po-Nagar Stelae Inscription of Jaya Indravarman I dated 887 Śaka.

(For localities, publications etc cf. No. 22). It contains two Anuṣṭubh verses in 7 lines. It records that in 887 śaka (=965 A. D.) king Śrī Jaya Indravarman installed a stone image of Bhagavatī to replace the golden one installed by king Śrī Indravarman (cf. No. 45), as the latter was carried away by the Cambodgians. This shows that between 918 and 965 A. D., the dates of Nos. 45 and 47, Champā was conquered by a king of Cambodge. This inference agrees well with the Baksei Cankran and Prasat Bat Chum inscriptions of Rājendravarman II (944–968 A. D.) according to which this Cambodgian king conquered the kingdom of Champā.

TEXT.

अपि स्त्र

I. हैमीम् यत्प्रतिमां पूर्व्वं येन दुष्प्रापतेजसा ।
न्यस्तां लोभादिसंक्रान्ता मृता उद्धृत्य काम्बुजाः ॥

II. श्रीजयइन्द्रवर्म्माख्यः सोऽब्धष्टाङ्गशकाधिपे ।
पुनः शैलमयीम् कीर्त्यैं कौठारे तामनिष्ठिपत् ॥

TRANSLATION.

Again,

I. The golden image which was formerly installed by (the king), of a majesty difficult to attain, the Kāmbujas, dominated by cupidity and other vices, had carried away and died.

II. In the year of the Śaka king denoted by '*adri-asta-anga*' (887) Śrī-Jaya-Indravarman again installed the stone image of the goddess, in Kauṭhāra, for the sake of glory.

No. 48.

Po-Nagar Temple Inscription.

Illegible. Doubtfully attributed to Jaya Indravarman I.

J. A. 1888 (I) pp. 78–79, No 403;
J. A. 1891 (I) pp. 27–28.

No. 49.

Po-Nagar Temple Inscription.

The reading is very doubtful.

It probably contains an invocation to the god of Yāpu-Nagara. The name of the king may be doubtfully restored as Śrī-Jaya-Indravarman.

Corpus, No. XXVII, p. 260.

No. 50.

Po-Nagar Image Inscription.

This Cham inscription is engraved on a small image of a goddess, placed close to the large statue of Bhagavatī.

It refers to king Śrī-Jaya-Indravarman, god Śiva and goddess Bhūmiśvarī.

J. A. 1888 (I) p. 79, No. 400;
J. A. 1891 (I) p. 28.

No. 51.

Myson Stone Inscription of Harivarman I dated 913 Śaka.

This short Cham inscription of 4 lines is engraved on a block of sandstone lying in the vestibule of a temple in the western group. It records the re-installation of the god Śrī Jaya-Īśāna-Bhadreśvara in the year 913 (=991 A. D.) during the reign of king Vijaya-Śrī Harivarmadeva.

B. E. F. Vol. IV (pp. 113, 117, 933)
B. E. F. Vol. XV, No. 2, p. 49.

No. 52.

Pō Klauṅ Garai rock inscription of Parameśvaravarman I, Dated 972 Ś.

The inscription was edited by Finot (B. E. F., Vol. IX, p. 208) (cf. also B. E. F., Vol. XV, No. 2, pp. 39 ff.) (For localities cf. No. 53). It contains 9 lines of writing, of which about 5½ lines are in Sanskrit and the rest in Cham. The Sanskrit portion is written entirely in verse, and contains 4 stanzas, the metre being, vv. 1, 4, Anuṣṭubh; v. 2, Puṣpitāgrā, and v. 3, Śārdūlavikrīḍita.

The inscription relates how king Śrī Parameśvaravarmadeva suppressed the rebellion at Pāṇḍuraṅga, and records the erection of a Liṅga in 972 śaka (=1050 A. D.) by Śrī Devarāja general (Mahāsenāpati) and nephew of the king.

TEXT.

(a).

स्वस्ति ।

पक्षाद्रिनवभिर्भुक्ते शके लिङ्गमतिष्ठिपत् ।
नाम्ना श्री देवराजोऽसौ क्षत्रियो गुणकोविदः ॥

स जयति जितशत्रुवर्ग्ग आजावजितभुजविक्रम इन्द्रसूनुतुल्यः ।
पृथुयश-उपविष्टकम्बुराष्ट्रो दशदिशभयकृच्च चम्पराजपाली ॥

(b).

स्वस्ति ।

राजस् श्रीपरमेश्वरस्य महतः पुत्रोनुजाया जयी
त्यागी शीलगुणान्वितस्सुतनुमान् सस्वापतेयो महान् ।
शुद्धेन्दुद्युतिवद्यशोभिरनिशं प्रद्योतिताशो रणे
दाने शूरतरो रराज सततं श्रीदेवराजोद्धतम् ॥
कुचशैलगुहायुक्ते शककाले शिलात्मकं ।
लिङ्गं स्वल्पमपि स्वस्थं स्थापितन् तेन कीर्त्तये ॥

TRANSLATION.

(a).

Hail !

1. The Kṣatriya Devarāja, a connoisseur of merits, installed a *Linga* in the Śaka year denoted by '*pakṣa-adri-nava*' (972).

2. Victory unto the protector of Champā, who has vanquished the crowds of his enemies in battle; who is comparable to the son of Indra for the prowess of his unconquered arms: whose great glory has penetrated into the kingdom of Kambu (Cambodge), and who has protected the ten regions from fear.

(b).

Hail !

Devarāja was the son of the younger sister of the great (king) Śrī Parameśvara. He was victorious, liberal, endowed with virtue and talent, beautiful, wealthy and great; his glory, like pure moonlight, constantly illumined all the regions, and he always shone wonderfully as a mighty hero both in fight as well as in charity.

In the year of the Śakas denoted by '*kuca-śaila-guhā*' (972) a small but solid stone liṅga was installed by him for the sake of glory.

In the Śaka year 972 the pulyaṅ Śrī Devarāja Mahāsenāpati, nephew of the king Śrī Parameśvaravarmadeva, came to take this town of Pāṇḍuraṅga on behalf of (?) king Śrī Parameśvaravarmadeva. He had stones placed in various fortified enclosures, one by each man. And according to the number of soldiers....................he had them collected (?) ....For this reason all were for ever attached to Śrī Parameśvaravarmadeva. Then the men made a Śiva-Liṅga out of these stones and installed it for the sake of military glory in this world...........................for their soul in the other world.

No. 53.

Pō Klauṅ Garai rock inscription of Parameśvaravarman I, dated 972 Ś.

The inscription was discovered in 1901 by M. Parmentier and edited by M. Finot (B. E. F., Vol. III, p. 634 (No. VI) and pp. 643 ff.). Pō Klauṅ Garai is the name of one of the most beautiful ancient temples in the plain of Phanrang. The inscription is engraved on the three faces of a triangular pyramidal rock in front of this temple. The three faces have respectively five, seven and six lines of writing. The first four lines and a part of the fifth are written in Sanskrit, and the rest in Cham. The Sanskrit portion begins with '*Svasti*' and contains two verses.

The inscription refers to the king of Champā Parameśvaravarman Dharmarāja, whose fame as a conqueror spread to Kambudeśa (Cambodge), and records the installation of a Śivaliṅga by his Yuvarāja (heir-apparent) and commander-in-chief in 972 Śaka. (cf. B. E. F., Vol. XV, No. 2, p. 39).

Then follows the Cham text giving the detailed account of a revolt of the people of Phanrang against the king, and its suppression by the Yuvarāja. After suppressing the revolt the yuvarāja installed the Śivaliṅga and a column of victory.

TEXT.

स्वस्ति ।

नाम्ना श्री युवराजो यस्सेनाप्रभुरतिष्ठिपत् ।
लिङ्गमूर्व्याश्चिरङ्कीर्त्त्यै करण्णाद्र्यात्मशकाधिपे ॥
सकलजनमनोभिराम×(अ)न्द्रो
रणविदितोग्रयशोनिविष्टकम्बुदेशः ।
वरजनगदितोऽद्य दानपुण्ये
भुवि च विभात्यनिशं स चम्पदेशपाली ॥

TRANSLATION.

Hail !

The yuvarāja (by name ?), the commander of army, installed this *liṅga* in the world for eternal glory, in the year of the Śaka king denoted by '*Karṇṇa-adri-ātmā*' (972).

The protector of the kingdom of Champā—who charms the hearts of all people, whose great glory in battle has penetrated into the Kambu country (Cambodge), and who is even now praised by excellent men for his merit accruing from liberality;—constantly flourishes in this world.

Now the citizens of Panrāṅ,-wicked, vicious and stupid,-were always in revolt against all the sovereigns who reigned in the kingdom of Champā. Thus during the rule of Parameśvaravarmadeva Dharmarāja, the rebels proclaimed a native of the city as their king. As the king Parameśvaravarman was active and had numerous subjects, he sent troops in various batches and ordered his nephew the yuvarāja Mahāsenāpati to proceed with all his generals and conquer the city. All the troops of Panrāṅ came to fight. He pursued and crushed them all and they took shelter in mountains and caverns. But the yuvarāja who had a powerful army ordered his troops to pursue them in all directions. And these troops got hold of all the people of Panrāṅ with oxen, buffaloes, slaves and elephants, on behalf of king Parameśvaravarmadeva Dharmarāja. He........... the half of the people.................he ordered them to dwell there in order to re-establish the city. The other half he gave to temples, monasteries, religious buildings, *Sālās*, and hermitages for the sake of his own merit. Then the yuvarāja asked stones of the various troops and erected this *liṅga*. He also raised a column of victory. And on account of his piety to Śiva, when the people of this country saw the beauty and the marks of this *liṅga*........................they resolved to give up their revolts against the king of Champā who was always victorious.

No. 54.

Pō Klauṅ Garai rock inscription of Jaya Parameśvaravarman I, dated 972 Śaka.

The inscription was edited by M. Finot (B. E. F., Vol IX, p. 205). (For localities cf. No. 53). The inscription is engraved on two faces of the rock containing respectively seven and five lines. The first three lines contain a Sanskrit verse (metre—śārdūla vikrīḍita) and the rest is in Cham.

The inscription records that the king Śrī Parameśvaravarmadeva subdued rebellion in Pāṇḍuraṅga and erected a column of victory in 972 (=1050 A. D.).

TEXT.

स्वस्ति ।

श्रीमाञ्छ्री परमेश्वरो नरपतिर्नानाकलैकालयो

धर्म्मज्ञो वलवीर्य्यकीर्त्तिपरमः सन् सर्व्वभौमः कृती ।

जित्वा पापकपाण्डुरङ्गनृगणान् हस्ताद्रिरन्ध्रशके

सेनासाङ्ख्यकृतौ शिलाचयमिमं संथापयामास वै ॥

TRANSLATION.

(a).

Hail !

The illustrious king Śrī Parameśvara, the unique receptacle of various arts, possessing spiritual illumination, eminent in strength, valour and glory; successful as a universal ruler, having in the śaka year denoted by 'hasta-adri-randhra' (972), defeated the vicious people of Pāṇḍuraṅga, deposited here a collection of stones, corresponding to the number of soldiers.[1]

1. 'Senā-Sāṃkhya-Kṛtau' is an obscure expression but the sense is clear from the Cham portion translated below.

The people of Pāṇḍuraṅga were always stupid, of mischievous spirit, and evil-doers. For instance on several occasions they revolted against different kings of Champā down to the time of His Majesty Śrī Parameśvaravarmadeva who gave all the Barons of the country to the god Parameśvara (probably the country of Pāṇḍuraṅga had been placed under the suzerainty of a great monastery protected by the king). Nevertheless the people of Pāṇḍuraṅga were guilty of culpable acts. They set up different individuals one after another and proclaimed them kings of the country. Then His Majesty Śrī Parameśvaravarmadeva led troops for the conquest of the country and pursued and captured the people of Pāṇḍuraṅga who took shelter in the caves, forests, summits of mountains, and the border of forests.........

(b).

And the army captured them in the caves, in the narrow mountain passages and in the ravines—so that not one of them could escape. In the śaka year 972, on the 8th day of the bright fortnight of the 4th month, on Thursday, he made each person lay down a stone in various places, and by giving them to the army, he had a column of victory erected in this very place as a token of authority of His Majesty Śrī Parameśvaravarmadeva. And when this column of victory was completed, the people of Pāṇḍuraṅga, who had revolted, became, for ever, perfectly virtuous and loyal towards the king of Champā.

No. 55.

Po-Nagar Temple Inscription of Jaya Parameśvaravarman I, dated 972 Śaka.

The inscription was edited by M. Bergaigne (Corpus No. XXIX, p. 270). The inscription is engraved on the right door-pillar of the temple of Po-Nagar to the left. It contains thirteen lines of writing. The language is Sanskrit. There are three verses at the beginning followed by a prose text (metre being v. 1, Sragdharā; v. 2, Śārdūlavikrīḍita; v. 3, Anuṣṭubh).

The inscription records the donations of king Śrī Parameśvara to the 'divinity of Yapu-Nagara' *i. e.*, an image representing Śiva and his spouse Gaurī united in a single body. It is dated in 972 śaka (=1050 A. D.).

TEXT.

स्वस्ति ।

I. भूताभूतेशभूता भुवि भवविभवोद्भावभावात्मभावा
भावाभावास्वभावा भवभवकभवाभावभावैकभावा ।
भावाभावाग्रशक्तिः शशिमकुटतनोरर्धकाया सुकाया
काये कायेशकाया भगवति नमतो नो जयेव स्वसिद्ध्या ॥

II. सारासारविवेचनस्फुटमना मान्यो मनोनन्दनः
पापापापभयप्रियः प्रियकरः कीर्त्यर्ज्जनैकोद्यमः ।
लोकालोकिकलौ कलौ सतिसतस्त्रातुं भवद्भाविनो
भावोद्भावसुभावसद्गुणगणैर्धर्मं तनोत्येव यः ॥

III. वेलाद्रि नवमे द्मेशः श्रीद्धः श्रीपरमेश्वरः ।
स्वर्णविद्धघटन् तस्याः स्थापयेत् स्थानकस्थले ॥

इदन्तु पूजार्थमुत्तमं मकुटभूषणमेकं विचित्ररशनागुण एकः रूप्यमयभृङ्गार एकः मयूरच्छत्रमेकं पृथुरजतवितानमेकमेतत् सर्वं कलधौतमयैः सुकलशाष्टार्द्धवालभाजनपृथुभाजनैः साकन् तेनास्यै प्रहितमिति ॥

TRANSLATION.

I. "Thou art, O my goddess, the lord of what was and what was not; thou art, in real nature, the cause of the origin, continuity and development of this world; thou hast in thy nature both positive and negative aspects; thou art in thy very essence at one with whatever is in the world of God during its creation as well as in its dissolution; thou art the primordial energy of the existent and the non-existent; thou hast as body, half of that which has moon as its diadem (*i. e.* Mahādeva); thou art of beautiful appearance and form part of the body of the lord of embodied beings. May we triumph by our own success."—so saying the two (?) (donor and his wife) bow down.

II. He, whose intelligence is matured by the discrimination between what is real and substantial and what is not; who is worthy of regard; who is pleasing to the hearts of others; who loves those who are timid as to what is vice and what is not; who does good to others; who has acquisition of glory as the only object of his energy; who makes the law prevail in the world by means of many, inherently excellent, good qualities which have their origin in his own nature, in order to protect good persons, both born and unborn, in the Kali age when there is going on a struggle between the pious and the vicious.[1]

III. He, King Śrī Parameśvara, shining in his prosperity, has placed in her sanctury a vase inlaid with gold in the Śaka year denoted by 'velā-adri-nava' (972).

And he has given to that goddess for her worship: an excellent diadem, a variegated waist-band, a silver vase, an umbrella decorated with peacock feathers, a vast silver canopy, together with golden vases *viz.* excellent pitchers, and four small and big vases.

---

1. The text has 'lokālokiᴼ' but the 'i'kāra is unintelligible.

No. 56.

Lai-Cham Inscription of Jaya Parameśvara-varman I, dated 977 Śaka.

The inscription is engraved on a granite block in front of a cave, south of the village of Lai-Cham in the province of Khan-Hoa. It contains 2 lines of writing in Cham and records that in 977 Śaka (=1055 A. D.) during the reign of king Śrī Parameśvaravarmadeva, the cave was restored.

B. E. F., Vol. XV, No. 2, p. 42.

No. 57.

Phu-Qui Temple Inscription of Jaya Parameśvaravarman I, dated 977 Śaka.

The inscription was edited by G. Coedes (B. E. F., Vol. XII, No. 8, p. 16) (cf. also B. E. F., Vol. XV, No. 2, pp. 41 ff.). Phu-Qui is in Phanrang. The inscription contains 4 lines in Cham and is dated in the year 977 in the reign of king Śrī Parameśvaravarmadeva.

TRANSLATION.

In the Śaka year 977, His Majesty Śrī Parameśvaravarmadeva Īśvaramūrti, of the lineage of Uroja and king of kings (rājacakravartī) in the country of Champā, erected this Vihāra Rājakula. He decorated the house............and gave to it men, oxen, buffaloes, grains as well as all the vessels necessary for the worship of the gods. (These gifts are made) in perpetuity.

No. 58.

Po-Nagar Temple Inscription of Jaya Parameśvaravarman I.

It records the gift of king Śrī Jaya Parameśvaravarmadeva (I) to the goddess whose image was re-installed by him. The gift consisted of lands and 55 slaves of all nationalities such as the Cham, Khmer, Chinese and Siamese.

J. A. 1891 (I), p. 29.

No. 59.

Myson Pillar Inscription dated 978 Śaka.

The inscription was edited by M. Finot (B. E. F., Vol. IV, p. 943, No. XV). It is engraved on the two faces of a pillar each containing 22 lines of writing. The language is Cham. The inscription records the donations of the Yuvarāja Mahāsenāpati to the temple of Śrīśānabhadreśvara in the year 978 (=1056 A. D.).

TRANSLATION.

(a).

....................A number of temples; after which they were as beautiful as before. The Khmers, who were conquered by the Yuvarāja Mahāsenāpati when he took the town of Śambhupura, and whose sanctuaries were all destroyed by him, were given by him to the various temples of Śrīśānabhadreśvara. He made gifts to the temples, monasteries, *śālās* (houses of charity) and to all the temples *viz.*, temple of Śrīśānabhadreśvara (and others.....................). Being.................lākalpa (?) he celebrated the installation of *Lingas.* All the kings who have reigned in the kingdom of Champā came here. The kings knew that gifts made to these gods are a mode of purification and that the gods to whom these gifts are made, being present in their symbols (*cihna*), know the kings of Champā,..................who have installed these *lingas* in these temples. Being Senāpati (general)......................he installed these *lingas*. As the Yuvarāja Mahāsenāpati, who ....lākalpa (?) was firmly devoted to Dharma and Śiva, he installed these *lingas* at the same time as the kings who reigned in the kingdom of Champā had (formerly ?) installed them. The Yuvarāja embellished and enriched Śrīśānabhadreśvara; he increased the riches and the lands of the god; he acted with energy and resolution; the thought of the god Īśvaradevatā, otherwise known as Yogīśvara, was always present in his mind. By the force of effort and concentration of mind, he at last saw Īśvaradevatā by a mental perception which went as far as Śrīśānabhadreśvara. Then, without much effort on his part, Īśvaradevatā became entirely visible (pratyakṣa) to him. Then, as he was a man of the world, devoted to Śrīśānabhadreśvara.................knowing that the man enjoys prosperity in this world and in the other.

(*b*).

After that the Yuvarāja performed all kinds of good works and charitable acts. Then, knowing that the body and its pleasures are vain and transient, that it perishes and disappears, and that Śrīśānabhadreśvara is the supreme god in this world, the Yuvarāja erected this statue at the limit of the possessions (?) of Śrīśānabhadreśvara. Now in the Śaka year 978 the Yuvarāja Mahāsenāpati had erected this image of Liṅga and had given it the name of yu..............ralingeśvara. For the pious devotion towards the god Śiva and rendering prosperous the god Śrīśānabhadreśvara according to the vow of Yuvarāja Mahāsenāpati.................

And the Yuvarāja Mahāsenāpati has given a diadem, a vessel, a white umbrella, ornaments, a bracelet inlaid with precious stones, Brahmanical sacred thread, according to the needs of the god, and in pursuance of the order................ the men of the temple........................dancers, musicians, assistants, and all......................god Śrīśānabhadreśvara, and all................with the holy image of Liṅga.............. and he has given the domain of Svon Tralauṅ to different temples,......................again repairing the lands of Svon Tralauṅ..................he has established...................... various kinds of trees and...................................... god Śrīśānabhadreśvara as far as Siṅhapura, and he has ....the god Śrīśānabhadreśvara who lives..............

No. 60.

Po-Nagar Temple Inscription of Rudravarman III, dated 972 Śaka.

The inscription was edited by M. Bergaigne (Corpus No. XXX, p. 275).

The inscription is engraved on the left door-pillar of the temple of Po-Nagar to the left.

It contains 12 lines of writing in Sanskrit. It has two verses at the beginning, followed by a prose text (metre being v. 1, Sragdharā, v. 2, Śārdūlavikrīḍita).

The inscription records the donations of king Rudravarman who was born in the family of Parameśvara and the younger brother of Śrī Bhadravarmā. It is dated in the year 986.

TEXT.

स्वस्ति ।

I. भूतानां भूतभूत्यै भुवि धरणिभुजामात्मतेजोपि सर्व्वे
देशे देशे गुणानां प्रवितपति पृथग् धीन[1] मद्ध्योत्तमत्वात् ।
तेनैको रुद्रवर्मा रविरिव महता तेजसा यो ऽर्हतीद्धस्
तारातारािधनाथज्वलनमणिनिभास्सन्ति चान्येऽवनीशाः ॥

II. ज्येष्ठश्रीपरमेश्वरेश्वरकुलश्श्रीभद्रवर्म्मानुजः
सर्व्वं यः किल रुद्रवर्म्मनृपतिः खण्डत्रयं भाजनम् ।
रूप्यं राजतभाजनत्रयमिदं रैरञ्जितश्चान्तरे
सर्व्वं स्थूलदृढं रसाष्टविवरे सौऽस्यै ददौ भक्तये ॥

एतद् भारे संख्येये रक्तकलधौतं सप्तपणं सिततरकलधौतं त्रयोविंशतिकट्टिकामानं द्विपणोत्तरमिति । पुनरिदं ताम्बूलभाजनं जलदेवरूपं कलधौतकलधौतमयमेकं पञ्चकट्टिकामानमष्टपणोत्तरं कनकधूपाधारण मेकमेककट्टिकामानं द्विपणोत्तरं कम्बुजरजतभृङ्गारश्चैकः पञ्चकट्टिकामानो दशपणोत्तरः कनकछत्रं सप्तपणमानन्तेनास्यै प्रहितमुपभोगार्थमिति । अन्यस्तास्याः[2] स्थानविगमपादभूमिः शिलाभिः परिपूर्णाकृता तोरणश्चोपलनिचयेन यत्नतः कृतमिति ॥

TRANSLATION.

1. For the real prosperity of beings in this world, the splendour of the kings shines differently in different countries according as their qualities are inferior, average or superior. Thus Rudravarman alone is fit to be regarded as the Sun by means of his great splendour, while the other kings shine as the stars, the moon, the fire and the jewels.

---

1. Read 'धीन'.

2. Read 'अन्यच्चास्याः'.

2. The king Rudravarman, belonging to the noble and powerful family of Śrī Parameśvara, and younger brother of Śrī Bhadravarman, gave, out of devotion, in the year denoted by '**rasa-aṣṭa-vivara**' (986) a vessel in three pieces (?), silver coins and three silver vessels, all painted (?) in the interior and alike massive and solid.

Measured by weight, seven paṇas of gold, 23 kaṭṭikās and 2 paṇas of silver. Again, he has given for the enjoyment of the god, a golden vase of betel of the shape of the constellation 'Pūrvvāṣāḍhā', weighing 5 kaṭṭikās and 8 paṇas; a golden vase for burning incense weighing 1 kaṭṭikā and 2 paṇas; a silver vessel of Cambodge, weighing 5 kaṭṭikās and 10 paṇas; and a golden umbrella, weighing 7 paṇas. His pedestal[1] was paved with stones, and a gateway was carefully made with stones.

No. 61.

Myson Pillar Inscription of Harivarman II.

The inscription was edited by M. Finot (B. E. F., Vol. IV, p. 941, No. XIV). It is engraved on two faces of a pillar and contains 41 lines of writing. The language is Cham. It records the donations of king Harivarman and his younger brother Yuvarāja Mahāsenāpati to the temple of Śrīśānabhadreśvara.

TRANSLATION.

(a–b).

The enemy had entered into the kingdom of Champā and installed themselves as masters; having taken possession of all the royal property and the wealth of the gods; having pillaged the temples, the monasteries, the *sālās*; cells, her-

1. The quailities phrase '**sthāna-vigama**' is not quite clear.

mitages, villages and various edifices together with the horses, elephants, *padātis* (infantry ?), oxen, buffaloes, and the crops; having ravaged everything in the provinces of the kingdom of Champā; having plundered the temple of Śrīśānabhadreśvara and all that the kings of past times had granted as endowments to Śrīśānabhadreśvara; having taken all the riches of the god and carried away the men belonging to the temple, the dancers, musicians.................servants, together with the various properties of Śrīśānabhadreśvara; the temple remained empty and devoid of worship as the .... Then His Majesty Vijaya Śrī Harivarmadeva, yāṅ Devatāmūrti ascended the throne. He completely defeated the enemies, proceeded to the Nagara Champā, and restored the temple of Śrīśānabhadreśvara. He made......... and three grand festivals...........Śrī Harivarmadeva......... the god Śrīśānabhadreśvara according to the rules of the Maharṣis of old. He again gave eight.......................gold and silver ornaments and four different classes of royal insignia to Śrīśānabhadreśvara. And he re-established...... with all the crops destroyed................. The kingdom of Champā became prosperous as of old. Then Harivarman celebrated his coronation.............. His Majesty the king Utkṛṣṭarāja. After this Harivarman enjoyed a complete happiness and tasted royal felicities.

Now the pu lyaṅ Śrī Yuvarāja Mahāsenāpati, brother of Harivarman, skilful, endowed with talents, and possessing various qualifications, the commander-in-chief, watching both the friends and enemies of king Harivarman, noticed that the temple of the great god Śrīśānabhadreśvara was devastated. He restored it together with all the other temples with which kings of old endowed the god Śrīśānabhadreśvara, who rules over everything (?). He re-erected the temples, the chapels, the gateways and the different edifices in the domain of Śrīśānabhadreśvara and made them perfectly beautiful. He re-erected the temples in the various provinces of the kingdom of Champā. He gave all the necessary articles for the worship of the god with the servants of temples, dancers, musicians.................and all the worship as before. He re-established the sālās, the cells, and the hermitages in the various provinces of the kingdom of Champā............ He constructed the sālās, he constructed ....he gave...........to the different temples. He gave water and food to the different temples to last as long as eternity. But this is only briefly told. And.........the good work which the yuvarāja has made for...........in the temple of Śrī Vijaya Siṁheśvara.

No. 62.

Myson Stelae Inscription dated 1003.

The inscription was edited by M. Finot (B. E. F., Vol. IV, p. 933, No. XII) (For localities cf. No. 4). It is engraved on the four faces of a stelae containing respectively 25, 27, 27 and 28 lines. The first 20 lines (in the first face) are in Sanskrit. Tho rest is in Cham. The Sanskrit portion is written throughout in verse with the exception of 'Śrī svasti' at the commencement. The metres used are: vv. 1, 2, 4, 5, 6, Śārdūlavikrīḍita; vv. 3, 7, Sragdharā.

The inscription records the donations of king Harivarmā and is dated in 1003 (=1081 A. D.).

TEXT.

(a).

श्री स्वस्ति ।

I. जोषाजोषविजो ˘—˘ ˘ ˘— — — ज्वलींति स्थितो

— — —˘ ˘ चेष्टया विविधतां स्वां वक्तुकामो गते ।

लीणं साम्य ⏑—⏑— सुविदुषि स्वान्तेन तत्राक्षरं
सूक्ष्मात्तेन[1] परिक्षरन्ति तमपि — — नमद्ध्वं शिवम् ॥

II. प्राळेयेश्वरधर्मराजविदितो यो नारिकेळान्वियो
दायादङ् क्रमुकान्विये जनितवानासीन्नरेन्द्रानतं ।
तद्वत्सो हरिवर्मदेवनृपतिः क्ष्माभृद्व्रतस्थोरसि
चारुपादोषगणाग्रधान स कलौ चोर्व्यां पुपोष[2]क्षरः ॥

III. शास्त्रे शास्त्रेऽधिको वाक्पतिरिव हि रणे माधवो यो यथारं
सत्कान्तौ कामतुल्यो बहुमखसुविधाविन्द्ररूपोपमानः ।
ज्ञाने शंभूपमेयस्सरसिजजसमोऽनेकसर्गे विदग्धो
वाक्प्रीतौ सद्गुणौघेऽनुपमितसुमतिश्चम्पपस्सोऽधिकोभूः ॥

IV. तस्माच्छ्रीहरिवर्मभूपगुणधेस्सत्सूरयःशिल्पिनो
नानाज्ञानविदोपि नर्त्तकुशलस्सर्व्वायुधाभ्यासकाः ।
सर्वे सद्गुणिनो विदग्धपटवो गीतादयश्शूरका
नित्यन्नो स्वगुणं वदन्ति फणिनः कुर्वन्ति भीता यथा ॥

V. कामादीननिशं हृदि प्रतिदहद् सद्भिर्विवेकोदयैः
पाश्चाद् वैरिगणान् बलेन महतालं यद्मुखे नित्यशः ।
जित्वा योगविदग्धयोगपरमैस्सत्कर्मपुण्यैस्सदा
युक्तञ्छ्रीहरिवर्मदेवनृपतिः प्राश्नोति धीमद्धृदि ॥

VI. कोशं सुवर्णमयं मणीन्द्ररचितं प्रौढं प्रभालङ्कृतं
यद्वद् भास्करमेव भास्वरमिदं नाहर्निशन् सत्त्विषा ।
प्रेङ्खद्दलमरीचिराशिविमलं युक्तश्चतुर्भिर्मुखै-
र्भक्त्यादाद् हरिवर्मदेवनृपतिश्श्रीशानभद्रेश्वरे ॥

VII. वेलापर्यायधावज्ज्वलितजितनिशाकारतीक्ष्णांशुलक्ष्मीं
आशानामास्यदीपैरुदधिमणिमुखैः कालधौतात्मकोशं ।
कृत्वा पराद्ध्र्यधर्मी प्रगुणधिषणयादादरन् सर्वकोशैः
बाहुव्योमान्तरीक्षग्रहपतिलवनं यश्शिवेशानलिङ्गे ॥

---

1. Read क्षरा.
2. Read पुपोषा°.

TRANSLATION.

(a).

Hail !

I. ....Bow down to Śiva.

II. The king called Prāleyeśvara Dharmarāja of the family of Nārikela (cocoanut), who begat an heir, docile to him, in the family of Kramuka (betelnut), had a son king Harivarmadeva who, with a heart filled with devotion to royal duties, removed the multitude of defects of Champā, and even in this Kali age, prospered in the world without decay.

III. He, the protector of Champā, was versed in all the śāstras like Bṛhaspati; valorous in battle like Mādhava; beautiful like Kāma (Cupid); comparable to Indra in the number of sacrifices successfully performed; learned like Śambhu; and skilful in various creations like Brahmā. He excelled in respect of charming words, and the multitude of good qualities, and his excellent character was incomparable (to anything).

IV. The good scholars, the artists, men versed in different branches of learning, those who are skilful in dancing, those who know the use of all arms, all meritorious, wise and skilful persons, the musicians[1] and others, and valorous, persons, behaved like serpents smitten with fear, and did not speak out their own qualities in the presence of king Harivarmā, himself a repository of all good qualities.

V. Constantly burning the sensual and other passions in his heart by good promptings of conscience, and then

---

1. The original has 'गोतादृप:' which is unintelligible in the context but apparently means 'musician'.

utterly defeating every day the hosts of enemies by superior power,[1] the intelligent[2] king Śrī Harivarmadeva prospers by virtue of his meritorious deeds which attained their excellence as a result of his constant contact with persons proficient in *yoga*.

VI. King Harivarmadeva gave, out of devotion to Śrīśānabhadreśvara, a golden kośa decorated with best jewels, grand, resplendent and verily like the Sun—the latter, however, does not shine day and night—brilliant with the sparkling rays of the jewels and adorned with four faces.

VII. In course of time[3] having made a kośa of gold, more beautiful than the Sun and the Moon, with faces decorated by gems of the sea, as if they were lamps for the regions,—the king, endowed with sublime qualities, being guided by his superior intelligence, gave it like other kośas to Śiveśānaliṅga who had as sculptors 'the arms, sky, atmosphere and the moon' (*i. e.* which was made in the year 1002).

(Cham) The temple of Īśānabhadra had been devastated and taken................. The Yuvarāja ordered the people of Siṁhapura[4].......................to construct the temples, to build the houses, to make perpetual sacrifices, to re-erect the chapels and to re-construct the roads, all as before. He made.................without cessation. He gave the following

1. The word 'yadmukhe' is unintelligible. 'yat' may be explained as denoting the 'cause' and 'mukhe' may mean 'at first'. The word may be 'युध्+मुखः'.

2. The original has 'धीमन्' which should be 'धीमान्'.

3. The expression 'velāparyāyadhāvāl' is not quite clear to me.

4. It might also mean "The Yuvarāja named Siṁhapura."

goods *viz.* male and female servants, the śarīra (statue ?) of Maheśvara, and all other necessary articles, to the god Śrīśānabhadreśvara and made him as prosperous as before. His Highness applies himself....................body, words and heart.

(*b-d*).

Fortune ! There was a king called His Majesty Harivarmadeva, prince Thāñ..............yān Viṣṇumūrti, born in the betelnut (Kramuka) clan, an eminent race in the kingdom of Champā. He had the 32 signs as well as grace and beauty. He was fully endowed with all the qualities *viz.* the knowledge of 64 kalās (arts). He knew and practised the four expedients *viz.* conciliation (sāma), gifts (dāna), discord (bheda) and chastisement (daṇḍa). He possessed the capacity......................the intelligence, the capacity for all enterprises and the rules about what is good and bad. He maintained all the 18 titles of law and the uniformity (of procedure ?). He acted like visible Dharma in this world. He was powerful and merciful towards all the beings. He made pious works and gave gifts day and night without cessation. He was skilled in all the weapons and was heroic and energetic. He has dispersed the hostile troops in the field of battle as many as twelve times. He has cut off the heads of kings, generals, chiefs and other men in the field of battle....................nine times. He defeated the troops of Cambodge at Someśvara and captured the prince Śrī Nandanavarmadeva who commanded the army as Senāpati (commander-in-chief). And he has re-established the edifices and the city of Champā during the troublesome days of the war. And the city of Champā and all the edifices were enriched, as if by nature, and freshly decorated. And he enjoyed all the royal felicities. Knowing that the god Śrīśānabhadreśvara is the visible god Parameśvara in the world, and seeing Śrīśānabhadreśvara despoiled of all his possessions at the end of the war, he came to worship the god with a pious heart, and gave him all the booty taken at Someśvara and various objects *viz.* a golden kośa, decorated with four faces............. set with all kinds of jewels. And he has given.................an ornament. And he has given a diadem decorated with jewels, two necklaces, 4 *kamī*, 2 kalaśa (pitchers) of gold, 2 *vrah kalaśa* (pitchers ?) of gold, 8 *vrah kalaśa* of silver, 4 *suvauk*..........., 8 *suvauk* of silver, 8..............of silver, 8 *tapanah* of silver, 3 *tralāy* of silver, 2 *sanraun* of silver, 4 *paligah* of silver, 2 boxes of silver, 2 *von* of silver. one *mayur* (peacock ?) of gold, one *mayur* (peacock ?) of silver, one *harvai* of gold, one *harvai* of silver, 2 *tralāi*..........., one *paligah languv*, one *lusun* of sandalwood, one head of sandalwood. And he has given men of different kinds *viz*......................about a hundred male and female servants, oxen, buffaloes, elephants, and various kinds of goods to the god Śrīśānabhadreśvara, in śaka 1002.

And His Majesty Śrī Harivarmadeva, yāṅ Mādhava-mūrti....................... And he saw that the pu lyaṅ Śrī Rājadvāra, his eldest son, of illustrious race, had all the royal marks, complete with the Grahas (?), for governing the kingdom of Champā. Then he ordered virtuous persons to celebrate the coronation of pu lyaṅ Śrī Rājadvāra. They gave him the name of yāṅ po ku Śrī Jaya Indravarmadeva. Now, at the time when pu lyaṅ Rājadvāra took over the government of the kingdom, he was only a boy of nine years. Then the generals and all the soldiers.................to ....Śrī Harivarmadeva. ....The people offered the authority to his son........... Then he practised of his own accord spiritual exercises (dhyāna-yoga) and worship of Śiva. Constantly engaged in these spiritual exercises, he died in śaka 1103.[1] Then all the females of the household, the princesses, the various *mé lyaṅ* to the number of fourteen, followed him to death. Now.............. the bones remaining...................persons dead, in the sea ....Those who........ .....this destruction, faithful, affectionate, lived always doing good works for his sake.

Hail! There is a yuvarāja named Oṅ Dhanapati-Grāma. He went to Cambodge. The king of Cambodge welcomed him and gave him all kinds of goods. The yuvarāja lived at Cambodge. The king of Cambodge learnt that the town Malyaṅ had revolted. He ordered the yuvarāja to lead the troops of Cambodge and retake the town on his behalf......... all the...........Humā Padān joined the revolt........... The king of Cambodge commanded the yuvarāja to lead the troops of Cambodge, to take the town and to occupy it on behalf of the king of Cambodge. The king Sūryavarmadeva revolted against the king of Cambodge. The latter commanded the yuvarāja to lead the troops of Cambodge and capture the king. Then the putau Ājñā ku revolted. He conquered from Amarāvatī as far as Pidhyaṅ. The king of Cambodge commanded the yuvarāja to lead the troops of Cambodge and capture putau Ājñā po ku. He captured him and sent him to Cambodge according to the desire of the king. The king (of Cambodge, pleased at) the valour of yuvarāja, bestowed favours on him and gave him....................putra (the title of Rājaputra ?). Truly the men of Champā lived .... The yuvarāja Mahādharma..............knowing that the god Śrīśānabhadreśvara, who is a portion of god Parameśvara, grants favours and fulfilment of desires to people always devoted to the god...........

---

1. Read 1003.

No. 63.

Myson fragmentary Pillar Inscription of Paramabodhisatva dated 1003 Ś.

For localities cf. No. 4. It contains 19 lines in Sanskrit verse, but mostly illegible. It begins with an invocation to god Śrīśānabhadreśvara. Then it refers to king Harivarman who is said to have restored the old glory of Champā. The inscription then mentions a younger brother of the king apparently Pu lyaṅ yuvarāja Mahāsenāpati referred to in Nos. 59, 61 and 65 who ascended the throne in 1003 under the name Paramabodhisatva. The inscription further records that the yuvarāja installed an image of the god Śiva and granted gold, jewels, elephants, buffaloes, oxen, slaves and clothes to the God.

(B. E. F., Vol. IV, p. 940, No. XIII).

No. 64.

Po-Nagar Temple Inscription of Paramabodhisatva, dated 1006 Śaka.

We learn from this Cham inscription that Rudravarman was made prisoner and taken away from the kingdom, whereupon a long war of sixteen years followed, in course of which Śrī Paramabodhisatva became king and again reunited Champā. It records the donations made in 1006 (=1084 A. D.) to the goddess of Po-Nagar, the tutelary deity of the kingdom, by the king Śrī Paramabodhisatva, his sister (?) Garbha Lakṣmī and his eldest son Pulyaṅ Śrī Yuvarāja, prince vyu, for obtaining glory in this world and religious merit hereafter. The donations consisted, among other things, of elephants, a golden crown (mukuṭa), a necklace decorated with jewels and various other ornaments and utensils in gold and silver

The inscription incidentally states that during the dark days that followed the capture of the king, the people of Champā betook themselves to Panrang where a man set himself up as king and maintained himself as such for 16 years. But this man was imprisoned with his followers by Śrī Paramabodhisatva who spared their lives but confiscated their property.

J. A. 1891 (1) p. 33, No. 14.

No 65.

Myson stone slab inscription of Jaya Indravarman II dated 1010 Ś.

The inscription was edited by M. Finot (B. E. F., Vol. IV, p. 946, No. XVI). It is engraved on three faces of a sand-stone slab containing 92 lines of writing. The language is Cham.

The first part refers itself to the reign of Paramabodhisatva and the second is dated in 1010 Śaka during the reign of Jaya Indravarman, son of Harivarman. The inscription contains an interesting account of the political history of the time and records the donations of king Śrī Jaya Indravarmadeva to the god Bhadreśvara, in 1010 (=1088 A. D.).

TRANSLATION.

(a).

Fortune! There is (king) His Majesty Śrī Jaya Indravarmadeva, prince Vāk, son of His Majesty Śrī Harivarmadeva, prince Thāṅ.................. He reigned about a month. Then as Śrī Jaya Indravarmadeva was very young, did not know what was good or bad in the government of the kingdom and made everything contrary to the rules of government, Śrī Jaya Indravarmadeva with all the generals, Brāhmaṇs, astrologers, learned men, masters of ceremonies and the wives of Śrī Harivarmadeva, searched for a prince to govern the kingdom. Now they found that pu lyaṅ Śrī Yuvarāja Mahāsenāpati prince Pāñ, uncle of Śrī Jaya Indravarmadeva and younger brother of Śrī Harivarmadeva had all the marks of a Mahārāja, according to the canon, of 'rājacakravartin' and that he had the knowledge of the good and the bad, and possessed a sense of duty, liberality, truthfulness, and compassion towards all beings without any partiality, in the government. Śrī Jaya Indravarmadeva, nephew of pu lyaṅ Śrī Yuvarāja Mahāsenāpati, with the Brāhmaṇs, Kṣatriyas, Paṇḍits, astrologers, masters of ceremonies, with all the ladies, carrying one or more several precious objects (?) and the royal insignia went to pu lyaṅ Śrī Yuvarāja Mahāsenāpati and made him king. Śrī Paramabodhisatva ruled properly. And all the *senāpatis* Brāhmaṇs, Paṇḍits, astrologers, masters of ceremonies........ skilful................gave to Śrī Paramabodhisatva.............. And His Majesty Śrī Paramabodhisatva, possessed of great virtue, knew the supreme end...........all the people........... in times of distress; all the different kings................give according to the inferior, middle and superior quality. And Śrī Paramabodhisatva gave bounties to the *senāpatis* and to all the people of the country of Champā. And an uninterrupted bliss reigned as before. And Śrī Jaya Indravarmadeva prince Vāk, nephew of Śrī Paramabodhisatva........... riches, comfort and pleasure according to his will. And Śrī Paramabodhisatva governed the kingdom of Champā........ And Śrī Paramabodhisatva constantly practised Dharma with all his relations.

(b).

Fortune ! There is a king His Majesty Śrī Jaya Indravarmadeva, Paramarājādhirāja. His birth-place is the *lamvīn* of Champāpura. He belongs to an illustrious family pure on both the father's and mother's side. Śrī Jaya Indravarmadeva is possessed of 32 signs. He is endowed with grace, beauty, youth and ability. He is skilful, full of good qualities, possessed of innate courage, versed in all the arms, and of great strength. He always disperses the hostile troops. He knows the supreme truth and the absolute reality without egotism. He possesses the calm of heart, the compassion towards all the creatures, great liberality, patience and profound intelligence. He impartially pursued the three objects (*trivargga*), wealth (*artha*), virtue (*dharma*) and pleasure (*kāma*), without showing preference to any. He follows the four expedients *viz.* conciliation (*Sāma*), gifts (*dāna*), discord (*bheda*) and bribery (*upapradāna*) with respect to the enemies, the friends and the neutrals. He routed the six enemies *viz.* sensual passions (*kāma*), anger (*krodha*), covetousness (*lobha*), infatuation (*moha*), pride (*mada*) and malice (*mātsarya*). He knew the true import of the sixfold measures of the royal policy. (Ṣaḍguṇyābhiprāya)[1]. He followed the eighteen titles of law prescribed by Manu (Manumārgga)[2]. Even in the Kali age, he who is a Mahāpuruṣa enjoys the royal power with a unique quality (guṇa). Although Kali leads people to error and pride, he....................the spiritual exercises (yoga), the meditation (dhyāna), the concentration (samādhi), in

---

1. Finot takes it in the sense of 'Six good opinions' or 'six systems of philosophy.' But cf. Kautilya Arthaśāstra Book VII, Chap. I, entitled षाड्गुण्यसमुद्देशः.

2. Finot translates 'ways of men'.

view of the spiritual merit which results from good or bad done to others, and from proper and improper acts. He increased his glory..............both in this world and in the other. Śrī Jaya Indravarmadeva is full of these qualities and he enjoyed the royal power. And he knows that the body and its pleasures are ephemeral. He entirely relies upon efforts, spiritual exercises, meditation and concentration. He practises the virtue constantly and thoroughly.

Now this city of Champā was ruined and destroyed ....His Majesty Śrī Jaya Indravarmadeva yāṅ Devatāmūrti has reconstructed the town............completely ....till she was beautiful and prosperous as before. He has given a monastery to Śrī Indralokeśvara in the district (vijaya) of Tranul; he has given all the revenues to the god. And for all the various divinities, he has dedicated in their temples, gold and silver *kośa*, and faces and diadems of gold. He has given men, oxen, buffaloes, with all the utensils for the worship of these divinities. And all the temples of these divinities are prosperous, beautiful, and honoured as before. People of all the four castes Brāhmaṇs, Kṣatriyas, Vaiśyas and Śūdras are all happy.................. in the presence of His Majesty Śrī Jaya Indravarmadeva as the lotus and the water-lily in the presence of the Sun and the moon.

His Majesty Śrī Jaya Indravarmadeva, knowing that the god Bhadreśvara is the master of all things visible in the world has made a golden *kośa* of six faces, ornamented with serpents (*nāgas*) and decorated with coloured jewels fixed at sharp points in the diadem. And what is called Ūrddhvakośa is in magnificent gold, provided with a base (*ādhāra*) below, and the jewel Sūryakānti at the top of the diadem. The face turned to the east has a ruby,..............

at the top of the diadem, and the ornament *nāgarāja*. The faces turned to the north-east and the south-east have a sapphire in the eye of Nāga-rāja and at the top of the diadem. The face turned towards the south has a ruby...... at the top of the diadem. The face turned towards the west has a topaz at the top of the diadem. The face turned towards the north has a pearl (? *utturatna*). The golden kośa has 314 *thil* 9 *dram*..............of gold. The six faces with the diadems, the *nāgarāja* below, and the *ādhāra Ūrddhvamukha* weigh 136 *thil*; in all 450 thei 9 dram. In the year of the śaka king 1010.

No. 66.

Po Nagar Temple Inscription.

The inscription was edited by M. Bergaigne (Corpus No. XXXI, p. 279).

The inscription is engraved immediately below No. 60, and contains 7 lines of writing in Sanskrit verse, the metre being vv. 1–2, Vasantatilakā, v. 3, Indravajrā and v. 4, Upajāti.

The inscription does not contain any date or name of any king, but it is later than No. 60 and may be referred on palaeographic grounds to the reign of Jaya Indravarman II. Two of the verses are addressed to the divinity 'celebrated under the name of yāpu-nagara' and two others to another divinity called 'Śrī Maladākuṭhāra.'

TEXT.

स्वस्ति ।

I. पद्मोद्भवादिभिरमर्त्यगणैस्स्तुतो यो
देवी त्रिलोकजननी च तदीयदेवी ।

या ताञ्च याँपुनगर प्रथिताभिधानां
त्वामिष्टिदां शिवकरीं प्रणमे सुभक्त्या ॥

II. व्याप्नोति यो निखिलवस्त्वशुभं शुभं वा
नो लिप्यते रविरिवेद्धकला तदीया ।
देवोत्र याँपुनगर प्रथिताभिधाना
या सा नताभिमतदा मम शं कुरु त्वम् ॥

III. यो देवदेवर्षिसुरारिमौळौ
रत्नायमानाङ्घ्रिसरोजरेणुः ।
या देवि सा श्रीमलदाकुठारा-
ख्या शं हर त्वं मम तस्य भार्या ॥

IV. (देवो)प्यनाश्रित्य निमज्जनीशं
यं यानपात्रं भवसागरेऽस्मिन् ।
या देवि सा श्रीमलदाकुठारा-
ह्वया नमे त्वां किल तस्य पत्नीम् ॥

TRANSLATION.

Hail !

1. I bow with devotion to thee god, who is praised by Brahmā and other divine beings, and to his divine spouse, the mother of the three worlds, who is famous under the name yāँpunagara, who is auspicious and who grants all the desires.

2. Be propitious to me, thou, who penetrate into everything pure and impure, but no part of whom, like the sun, is affected thereby: and thou, his divine spouse, famous under the name Yāँpu Nagara, who art always beneficent and grant the desire of all who bow down to thee.

3. Bring me happiness, O goddess, who is called Śrī Maladākuṭhāra and who is the spouse of the god, the dust of whose lotus-like feet appears as jewels on the heads of gods, divine sages and the Asuras (demons).

4. I bow to thee, O goddess, called Śrī Maladākuṭhāra, the spouse of the god, who is like a vessel without which even the gods are drowned in this ocean of the world.

No. 67.

Huong-Quê stelae Inscription dated 1033 Ś.

The inscription, engraved on two faces of a stelae containing respectively 21 and 25 lines, was found at Huong-Quê to the west of Myson. It is written in Cham and records the donations of Pu lyaṅ Śrī Jaya Siṁha Varman to Śiva called Harinandaliṅgeśvara. It is dated in Śaka 1033 (=1111 A. D.). The number is expressed by the figure for 33 preceded by the symbol for 10 which was used thousands of years ago in the mainland of India.

B. E. F., Vol. XI, p. 13.

No. 68.

Myson stone Inscription of Harivarmadeva III, dated 1036 Śaka.

The inscription was edited by Finot (B. E. F., Vol. IV, p. 951, No. XVII). For localities (cf. No. 4). It is engraved on a block of sand-stone and contains 8 lines of writing in Cham. It records a donation made by king Śrī Jaya Harivarmadeva, nephew of king Śrī Jaya Indravarmadeva, to the god Śrīśānabhadreśvara in the year 1036 (=1114 A. D.).

TRANSLATION.

Hail! In the śaka year 1036, during the reign of His Majesty Śrī Harivarmadeva, nephew of His Majesty Śrī

Jaya Indravarmadeva......................seeing that the god Śrīśānabha..............His Majesty Śrī Harivarmadeva made one temple and then another temple. He built a palace for the god Śrīśānabhadreśvara and gave various articles of gold and silver: (details of gifts follow—but the names of most of the things are unintelligible).

No. 69.

Myson Pillar Inscription of Jaya Indravarman III, dated 1062 Śaka.

The inscription was edited by Finot (B. E. F., Vol. IV, p. 953, No. XVIII A). For localities (cf. No. 4). It is engraved on an octagonal pillar and contains 6 lines in Cham.

It resembles the Po-Nagar Temple inscription (No. 71) and describes the career of king Jaya Indravarman III.

TRANSLATION.

He was born in the śaka year 1028: he became Devarāja in 1051 and yuvarāja in 1055; he made gifts to god Saddharma (Buddhism ?) in 1060; he became king in 1061; he................of the solar race, in 1062................having erected the Śrīśānabhadreśvara.

He was king Uroja; he was.............the king Bhadravarman; he was Jaya Simhavarman........... He was thrice king up to the time of this king.. .... Then he was Indravarman.................... These were his four births as human beings.

No. 70.

Myson pedestal Inscription dated 1062 Śaka.

It records that prince Dav Veṇi Lakṣmī Sinyān, Rupaṅ Vijaya, son of Śrī Devarāja prince Sundaradeva gave slaves to the god Śrīśānabhadreśvara. The merit of the pious work belongs to his father (?). It is dated in Śaka 1062 (=1140 A. D.).

B. E. F., Vol. IV, p. 954–55, No. XIX.

No. 71.

Po-Nagar Temple Inscription of Jaya Indravarman III, dated 1065 Ś.

This cham inscription is engraved in three long lines on the outer wall of the temple to the right at Po-Nagar. It is too fragmentary to yield a complete sense. The following is a brief extract.

L. 1. "King Bhadra Varmā, again king Jaya Siṁha Varmā.........enemies expelled.........

L. 2. 1021[1] (date of) birth; 1051 (when he is) devarāja; 1055 (when he is) yuvarāja; 1060, he gave (or gave to) the god Saddharma; then in 1061 he is king; in 1062 he gave (or gave to) the god Śrīśāna (Śiva); in 1064 (he gave ?) the Śiva Liṅga and the Śrīśāna Viṣṇu.

L. 3. Long ago (?) about 1,780,500 (years ago ?) king Vicitra Sagara gave the Liṅga Kauṭhāra. The king gave the Śiva Liṅga in 1060. The king..............*sapakṣaḥ yuge*

1. Mistake for 1028 (cf. No. 69).

...............as far as the time of Jaya Indravarmā..............
again 1065, the other.

J. A. 1888 (1) p. 80, No 401.
J. A. 1891 (1) p. 36.

No. 72.

Myson Stelae Inscription of Jaya Harivarman I.

The inscription was edited by Finot (B. E. F., Vol. IV, p. 963, No. XXI). For localities (cf. No. 4). It is inscribed on the three faces of a stelae containing respectively 20, 21 and 9 lines. The language is Cham.

The inscription gives an interesting account of the career of king Jaya Harivarmadeva and records the erection of a temple and statues in honour of the god Śrīśānabhadreśvara.

TRANSLATION.

Hail! There is the king, His Majesty Śrī Jaya Harivarmadeva prince Śivānandana, son of His Majesty Śrī Parama-Brahmaloka, belonging to Brahma-Ksatriya caste, and the grandson of His Majesty Śrī Rudraloka.............. mūrti, the very eminent king. Jaya Harivarman is born of Paramasundarī Devī also known as the queen Jiñjyaṅ; his personal name was Ratnabhūmivijaya. He was a descendant of Śrī Paramabodhisatva, the supreme king: Jaya Harivarman is very beautiful and endowed with the complete 32 signs...........according to the Artha-purāṇaśāstra which has praised it beforehand. Jaya Harivarman is skilful and experienced in the knowledge of 64 *kalās, viz.*, the Grammar etc., up to the knowledge of the supreme truth. Jaya

Harivarman has great strength; he is skilful in the application of all the arms, heroic, and proud. He dispersed the hosts of enemies in all the battlefields. When Jaya Harivarman went to the southern country, the king of Cambodge commanded the general Śaṅkara, the foremost among his generals, to go with the troops of the district (Pramāṇa) of Sipakhyā and fight in the plain of Rājapura. Jaya Harivarman fought against general Śaṅkara, and all the other Cambodian generals with their troops. They died............ in the field of battle in the Pramāṇa of Thū.............. The king of Cambodge sent an army thousand times stronger than the previous one to fight in the plain of Vīrapura. Jaya Harivarman completely defeated the Cambodian troops .... The king of Cambodge consecrated as king the Kṣatriya prince Harideva, his brother-in-law, the younger brother of his first queen; and he commanded various generals to lead the Cambodian troops and protect the prince Harideva until he became king in the city of Vijaya. Jaya Harivarman returned to Vijaya. The two parties fought in the plain of Mahiśa. Jaya Harivarman destroyed the king with all his Cham and Cambodian generals and the Cham and Cambodian troops; they all perished........... Jaya Harivarman reigned as supreme king from this time.

The king of Cambodge learnt that the prince Harideva, his brother-in-law, had perished with all his troops and generals....................by the prowess of Jaya Harivarman. Then..............the neighbourhood of Vijaya.................... The king................the kings of Kirātas,...............the plain, the forest of south, the village of Slāy as far as the forest Vatta (?)....... ...fight. Jaya Harivarman defeated the army of the Kirātas. The Kirāta kings proclaimed his brother-in-law Vaṅśarāja, brother of his wife, as king in the city of Madhyamagrāma ....Jaya Harivarman led his army, defeated Vaṅśarāja, captured the Kirāṭa army, and defeated them all................. The king of Yavanas, learning that the king of Cambodge had created difficulties in the way of Jaya Harivarman......................proclaimed Vaṅśarāja, a citizen of Champā, as king; he gave him several Yavana generals together with hundred thousand valorous *Yavana* soldiers..............the plain of Dalvā and the plain ....fight. Then Jaya Harivarman conducted all the troops of Vijaya.............. The two parties were engaged in a terrible combat. Jaya Harivarman defeated Vaṅśarāja with all the................. Large number of *Yavana* troops lay dead on the field. Jaya Harivarman took booty and gave it to the temples of Sadāṅ and Son, and he gave the Cham servants..............Jaya Harivarman installed a *linga* on the Mahīśaparvata, the yāṅ Tdaḥ. He gave the northern Temple to his father Śrī Parama Brahmaloka. He gave to his mother, the queen Jiñjyaṅ, the temple................. He gave the statues to these *Śarīras*. Besides, formerly Jaya Harivarman made a vow to the god Śrīśānabhadreśvara to give him a temple on the Vugvan mount because Śrīśāna-bhadreśvara................. In conformity with that vow he has installed these statues on the mount Vugvan............. Śrīśānabhadreśvara.

No. 73.

Myson Pillar Inscription of Jaya Harivarman I.

The inscription was edited by M. Finot (B. E. F., Vol. IV, p. 966, No. XXII A). For localities (cf. No. 4). It is engraved on a pillar and contains 9 lines of writing, lines 1–5 being in Sanskrit, and lines 5-9 in Cham. The Sanskrit portion is written throughout in verse with the exception of the invocation at the beginning. There are altogether 4 verses, the metre being v. 1, Indravajrā; vv. 2, 4, Sragdharā; and v. 3, Upajāti.

The inscription records the donations of king Śrī Harivarmadeva to the temple of Śrīśānabhadreśvara.

TEXT.

स्वस्ति । राजेन्द्रपद्य.

I. यागेस्तिकानां[1] भविकघ्ययागो
याग भविभ्यो यदि दूरसंस्थः ।
अस्तीति मत्वेव जगत्समूह-
स्सर्वस्थितो यः प्रणमन्त्वदन्तम् ॥

II. प्राग्गौरीन्द्रैककाया नगपतितनया याद्वितीया द्वितीया
स्वाङ्गाद् भीमेन भिन्ना पुनरपि रतये शङ्करालिङ्गिताङ्गी ।
शश्वत् तद्रोषभीतेरिवजनितजगत्पार्वतीन्द्रेण सङ्गात्
देवी वै वन्धतामात्मवचनमनसा सा शिवानन्दवन्द्या ॥

III. श्रीशानभद्रेश्वरमन्दिरार्कम्
परैः पुरोरोजकृतं विशीर्णम् ।
पुनर्भवोहं स विनाशकांस्तान्
हत्वा रणे तस्य पुनः प्रचक्रे ॥

IV. श्रीमान् श्रीशानभद्रेश्वरममितमुदं स्थापयित्वाह्युरजो
नाकौकस्स्थापनस्यान्वयमुत स वुगवनभूधरस्याङ्कमूर्ध्वम्
कृत्वा चास्तङ्गतो भूः[2] पुनरहमपरो भावयित्वा विनष्टं
स्थानन्देवस्य तस्याभिमतरुचि वुगवन्स्थापितेशः पुरेष्ट्या ॥

---

1. Read 'यांगष्टिकानां'.

2. Read 'भूर'.

TRANSLATION.

1. Hail, the poetry of the king of kings.

Let all bow down to him, the destroyer, who embodied the entire world in himself, and permeated everything, as he thought that the performance of sacrifice will be difficult for the men of the world who desire it, should he remain far away from them.

2. At first, the daughter of the king of Mountains, who was the second (*i. e.* partner or spouse) of Śiva, and yet second to none (*i. e.* incomparable), had only one body with Gaurīndra (*i. e.* Śiva). Then she was separated by Bhīma (Śiva) from his body; but again she was embraced by Śaṅkara for pleasure Let the Lord of Pārvatī, who engendered this world by union with her, faithfully adore, from fear as it were, by his words, and in his mind, that goddess who is worthy of being adored with joy by Śiva (or object of adoration to Śivānanda, the name of king Harivarmā).

3. The temple of Śrīśānabhadreśvara, the Sun (*i. e.* the best) of the temples, formerly made by Uroja, was destroyed by the enemies. Having killed those destroyers in the battle I, an incarnation of Uroja, have built it again.

4. The illustrious Uroja, having installed Śrīśānabhadreśvara of unbounded joy, and having marked the high summit of the Vugvan mountain as the imperishable abode of the gods, disappeared. I, another Uroja, have restored the very beautiful temple of that god that was destroyed, and have installed Īśa on the mount Vugvan according to an old vow.

[Cham]. 'Seeing that the supreme god had been plundered with all his temples, and had suffered outrages in the hands of a powerful enemy, I, the king Śrī Harivarmadeva, prince Śivānandana, son of king Śrī Parama-Brahmaloka, have re-established the temple in its old beauty. And I have given all the necessary things to this god. And all the kings reigning in future in the kingdom of Champā who would be devoted to the god in mind and deed (lit. externally and internally) would surely enjoy his favour both in this world and in the next; therefore, I, the king Śrī Harivarmadeva, prince Śivānandana, have been pious towards the god and full of faith in all circumstances.

No. 74.

Myson Stelae Inscription of Jaya Harivarman I, dated 1079 Ś.

The inscription was edited by Finot (B. E. F., Vol. IV, p. 955, No. XX). For localities (cf. No. 4). It was engraved on the 3 faces of a stelae containing respectively 19, 24 and 25 lines. The first 41 lines are in Sanskrit and the rest is in Cham. The Sanskrit portion contains 34 verses and three prose pieces in addition to the word '*svasti*' at the beginning. The metres used are: A. vv. 1–3, 11, 15, Śloka; vv. 4–10, Indravajrā; v. 12, Vasantatilakā; vv. 13–14, Sragdharā.

B. vv. 1–7, Indravajrā; v. 8, Āryā; vv. 9–18, Śloka; v. 19, Upajāti.

The inscription records the donations of king Śrī Jaya Harivarmadeva to the god Śrī Harivarmeśvara.

TEXT.

(a).

स्वस्ति ॥

I. नमस्तस्मै शिवायास्तु यस्य नेत्राद्विनिर्गतः ।

वह्निस्स्मरस्य दाहाय दारुणाद्भुतकर्म्मणः ॥

II. चिय् शिवानन्दनो नाम ब्रह्मलोकस्य भूभृतः।
नै-जिङ्ग्यं-व्या-भजस्सुनुरासीद्राजा ˘—म्वरः ॥

III. विद्यामतिक्रियारूपवाक्चित्तैर्गणनेषु यः।
महतां भूभृतामादिस्तत्पितेव महीधरः ॥

IV. जातो यदन्तः क्षितिभृत्समूहः
स्वांशैरुरोजादिरहो यथेच्छं।
श्रान्तीच्छय[1]जोऽनुददौ स्ववीर्य्यं।
तेभ्यश्चतुर्भ्यः क्षितिपालनाय ॥

V. कीर्त्तिः परस्थानगतिस्वभावा
विद्या च वाग्भिर्बहुभिर्द्रुताभिः।
ते वल्लभे यस्य भुवेत्वलाया
अपक्षपातस्य कुतोप्यधीरे ॥

VI. एतावता यस्य व[चो]नुमेयं
सौन्दर्यमेकान्तशुभं प्रकर्षैः।
तद्भूप्रभृत्येव सदोपमानं
यूनस्सरूपस्य स यद् न कामः ॥

VII. कीर्त्तिः प्रिया यस्य महाप्रवीणा-
धीरा परस्थानगताधिकांदया।
परैर्भयाद्वा यशसोतिभीमाद्
गताच्च शक्या न तयैव लब्धुम् ॥

VIII. कान्त्या कजारेरजितस्य जेत्री
यत्कीर्त्तिरिद्धा यदुराजकीर्त्तिम्।
रामस्य कीर्त्तिश्च पुनर्जिगीषु
दिंक्षु स्थितेऽनु प्रतिदिक् प्रयाता ॥

IX. येनासिना वैरिवराङ्गवृन्दं
भिन्नं नभोव्यासमगान् महाजौ।
ग्रासस्य हेमाश्रयिणमुरूणां
इन्दोरिवारिर्बहुभिन्नमूर्द्धा ॥

---

1. Read °च्छया.

X. राज्यश्रियं यस्य बलार्णवस्य
कलिर्व्वली लोपयितुं न शक्तः ।
उत्पातभूतोपि मणिप्रदीपं
समीरसङ्घस्तरसा यथा वै ॥

XI. रती रतीन्द्ररिपुना[1] रतिर्दग्धे रतीश्वरे ।
यश्चेद् वीक्ष्यारतिन्नाप मतिप्रियोयमिति ध्रुवम् ॥

XII. भिन्नात्मणि[2] त्र्यवरजेन चतुर्व्विधाङ्के
प्रत्येकमल्पगुणके धनुरामभूते ।
भूतोच्युतस्स सकलाग्रवपुस्सलज्ज
एको य एकपरमेव गुणाकराणाम् ॥

XIII. यस्य श्रीभर्तृता श्रीपतिपटुतरसाज्ञापितास्येव शङ्कया
प्रत्येकं यद् भुवाभिर्व्विधुधरसुधियाम्भोजभूसर्व्वसृष्ट्या ।
वाचस्पत्यप्रवाचा सुगतसुकृपया चानुमेयैव सा यत्
सौन्दर्य्येणावगम्याच्युततनयमनोभूवपुस्सद्रुचा तु ॥

XIV. वा नाकन्नाथ कन्नोयमुपगमितवानित्यपत्यादयस्तत्
स्त्राणां सत्प्रशान्त्यास्थितवति ददतिस्मातिहर्षेण यस्मिन् ।
रैरत्नेभेन्द्रभृत्यप्रभृतिगणान् सत्कृतीर्यापयित्वा
युद्धे युद्धेऽरिराजान् विभुवपुषि विभोर्लोकमत्युप्रदोषा ॥

XV. यो भानु भानुना भानौ नृच्छिद्वद्विषताश्रितः ।
तमोमुखप्रवेशेऽग्रवीर्यो वीर्ये शुचौ शुचिः ॥

(b).

I. — — — — — — — — — — — कारकारी ।
इह — — — — — — — — — —गुणवृन्द ।

II. — — — — — — — — दशशीलर — — — ।
— — — — — चतुष्षष्टिकला अनून भर्त्ता ।

III. यदीयकीर्त्तिर्दश— ⌣ — —
— — ⌣ — — ⌣ ⌣ — ⌣ — णां ।

---

1. Read रिपुणा°.

2. Read °त्मनि.

वा रामकीर्त्तेर्न हि विष्णुमूर्त्ति-
र्देशोत्तमाङ्गस्य ˘ — ˘ वेति ॥

IV. शक्तिप्रशान्तप्रवरै ˘ — —
— — ˘ — — ˘ ˘ — प्रदाता ।
महीभृतां संपदमिच्छतां यो
वन्द्यश्च मान्यश्च सदा स्वराज्ये ॥

V. यदि स्म धावन्त्यनिशं सपत्नाः
समीक्ष्य नागा इव वैनतेयं ।
समित्सु शूरा अपि वीर्यवन्तो-
ऽप्यत्यन्तरौद्रा अपि यं बलाढ्यम् ॥

VI. शोभा यथा दिनकृता सरोजानां महौजसा ।
नानासंपन्मनुष्याणां ध्रुवं येन विभाव्यते ॥

VII. यथाश्रिताः परिचरान् मुच्यन्ते च प्रियप्रियम् ।
यमरेर्भूभृतश्शैशशिवं वा भवसागरात् ॥

यस्य भूधरस्य क्षितिपतिपतेः परसततविगतरतिनिरततर-
धरणिधरनिकरकरकृताञ्जलिपुटास्सरोरुहरागरत्नरागविर-
ञ्जितरुचिराङ्गुळिभूषणास्स तिशयकुलेशा यानि सकलधर-
णिवरनिकरगृहीतपूरणानि तदा तदाननमुदकभवारिमिव
सञ्छिन्स्य नाववोर्धिभवन्ति ॥

VIII. स स्थापयतिस्म सुरं श्रीजयहरिवर्मदेव इतिराजा ।
हरिवर्मेश्वरमधिकः कीर्त्या विलशैलखशशाङ्के ॥

एतेन पुराणार्थेन लक्षणेनैतद्गम्यते श्रीजयहरिवर्मदेवोयं स
उरोज एवेति ॥

IX. क्षत्रांशसुन्दरीजातो दीक्षितक्षितिभृत्सुतः ।
स्वग्रामहर्म्युरोङ्कस्थरत्नभूमिर्य ईश्वरः ॥

X. भ्राता तदनुजो नास्ति प्रधानोत्पत्तितो भुवि ।
प्रभुर्यस्सत्सुखं लेभे चम्पाया वृद्धिलक्षणम् ॥

XI. विहाय यस्स्वदेशं प्राक् परेषु सुखदुःखभाक् ।
देशेषु चिरकालेन चम्पेदां[1] पुनरागतः ॥

XII. यः प्राग् गुहेश्वरान् नद्यां गत्यागतिसमीपकं ।
प्रहृत्य राज्यभाग् याम्यां पार्थिवं मरणङ्गतम् ॥

XIII. पूर्व्वप्रतिज्ञया सैन्यं कम्वोश्च यवनस्य च ।
हत्वादौ यः पुनश्चक्रे शैवं तन्नाशितं गृहम् ॥

XIV. राज्यलीलामनुक्रम्य भजित्वा योऽनुकम्पया ।
काम्ववीयावनीं सेनां शक्त्यानुभवतिस्म च ॥

XV. पूर्व्वप्रतिज्ञया स्वाद्रौ पूर्व्वजन्मोपलक्षिते ।
वुग्वन्नामनि साध्यार्थं शिवं स्थापयतिस्म यः ॥

XVI. सर्व्वे देवा विवर्द्धन्ते तद्राज्ये सर्व्वसंपदा ।
लोकास्तथा सुवृष्ट्योर्व्वी चम्पा कृतयुगान्विता ॥

XVII. शिवानन्दनशब्दस्य हृष्टेनार्थाद्रिणा क्षितौ ।
उरोजो लोकवाच्यो यः पुराणार्थेन लक्षणी ॥

XVIII. चतुर्वारो ऽस्म्युरोजोऽभूः पुनर्भूर्नेति यद्यपि ।
मत्प्रतिज्ञासमृद्ध्यर्थं शिवस्यास्य पुनर्भवः ॥

XIX. श्रीशानभद्रेश्वरदेवदेवो
वुग्वन्प्रतिष्ठापितदेवदेवः ।
तथा तयोर्वृद्धिकर[2]स्स राजा
योंऽशो मम प्रार्थितशैवकीर्त्तेः ॥
इति पुराणार्थमुरोजलक्षणं जगतां वेदितव्यम् ॥

TRANSLATION.

(*a*).

Hail !

1. Homage to Śiva, the fire from whose eyes consumed the Cupid whose exploits were terrific and marvellous.

2. The prince Śivānandana, son of king Brahmaloka, husband of the queen Nai Jiññyan, was king.........

---

1. Read चम्पेडां. 2. Read °र्वृद्धिकर°.

3. From the point of view of knowledge, intelligence, work, beauty, eloquence and mental powers, the king is the foremost of kings, like his father.

4. In him the kings beginning with Uroja became incarnate in their parts, according to their own desire. Aja (god Brahmā), wishing for rest, gave his own prowess to those four kings for protecting the world.

5. Glory and knowledge, which are by nature liable to move from place to place by means of a multitude of rapid words (*i. e.* popular reports), are dearer unto this impartial king than the immovable earth, although they are inconstant in the case of all others.

6. His beauty, very auspicious through its excellence, could be inferred only from the statement that since his birth, he, not Kāma, is the standard of comparison for the beauty of youth.

7. Glory, although inconstant and desirous of moving to others' place, was his clever spouse for a long time. His enemies were unable to gain her, out of fear or out of regard for his terrible fame achieved in the past.[1]

8. Triumphant over the unconquered Moon[2] by his beauty, his shining glory went in all directions in order to surpass (lit. conquer) the glories of Rāma and Kṛṣṇa, firmly established in all directions.

9. The multitude of the heads of his enemies, cut off by his sword in a great battle and scattered in the sky, appeared like the scattered heads of Rāhu, the enemy of the

---

1. The word 'tayaiva' is inexplicable. It may be a mistake for 'tathaiva'. The words 'gatāt' and '°gatādhikāṅkṣyā' are also difficult to construe.

2. ब्जारि=ब्ज (जलज or शङ्ख)+अरि=Moon.

Moon, who is the morsel of food of the chief gods dwelling in the Meru.

10. Even the powerful Kali was unable to destroy the royal power of that ocean of strength, as the portentous whirlwind is unable to extinguish the light of a jewel-lamp.

11. The Cupid being destroyed by Śiva, Rati became devoid of pleasure; but she would not have become so if she had seen the king, for then she would have certainly thought "This is my beloved."

12. Dividing his essence, under the form of four Rāmas *viz.* Rāma and his three younger brothers, Viṣṇu had four bodies each endowed with inferior qualities. This king is however unique Viṣṇu with a complete body; he is modest and the foremost of men who are the repositories of qualities.

13. It appears as if the king, who is cleverer than the husband of Śrī, announced himself as the suitor for the hands of Śrī as everybody could infer from the following qualities of the king *viz.* the intelligence of Mahādeva, the creative power of Brahmā, the eloquence of Bṛhaspati, the mercy of Buddha, and the beauty of Cupid, the son of Viṣṇu.[1]

14. "To what heaven are you taking us, O Lord!" said the descendants of the Kṣatriyas when he, who has the form of Vibhu, gladly and with calm composure, made them gifts of wealth, jewels, lordly elephants, slaves and other rewards, after having, in each battle, despatched, by the power of his terrible arm, to the abode of Vibhu (*i. e.* killed), the enemy kings.[2]

---

1. The words 'पदुतरसा' and 'भुवाभिः' are not intelligible.
2. It is difficult to construe 'सद्रुक्तीः'.

15. The king resembles the sun in point of purity and power; both are foremost among the valorous ones, and shine with splendid lustre in piercing darkness; and while the king is resorted to by the chastened enemies (*Ucchiṣṭa-dviṣat*) the sun is resorted to by fire (*ucchiṣṭa-dviṣat* the destroyer of refuse of matter).

(*b*).

2. ....Sixty-four arts.

4. By the foremost among those who were overpowered by his prowess..............the kings who desire prosperity must respect and honour him in their kingdoms.

5. The enemies, heroic, valiant and very fierce though they are in battles, always fly away at the approach of that powerful king, like snakes before Garuḍa.

6. As the beauty of the lotus proceeds from the powerful sun, so the varied riches of the men verily proceed from that powerful king.

7. The kings who submit to and wait upon him, who is dear to his friends, are protected from enemy kings, as the Śaivas who take refuge in Śiva are delivered from the ocean of existence.

Even the best of noble lords, who were themselves waited upon with folded hands by hosts of cheerless enemy kings, and the fine ornaments of whose fingers were illumined by the splendour of the jewel called padmarāga, were struck dumb with astonishment by thinking of the beautiful moon-like face of the king and lord of the earth Harivarmā, and of the riches that were exacted by him from hosts of kings.

8. The king Harivarmā, possessed of supreme glory, installed the god Harivarmeśvara in the year denoted by 'vila-śaila-kha-Śāśāṅka' (1079).

Thus on the strength of the evidence of Purāṇārtha one can infer that 'The king Śrī Jaya Harivarmā is Uroja himself.'

9. Born of a beautiful woman in the Kṣatriya family, son of a consecrated king, he, the lord, was the most precious jewel of his village, as Kaustubha is on the breast of Hari.

10. He had no younger brother. Lord of the world by his high birth, he enjoyed pure happiness, a sign of the prosperity of Champā.

11. At first, having quitted his own country, he spent a long time in foreign lands amid joys and sorrows. Then he came back to Champā.

12. To the east of the temple of Guheśvara, on the river 'Yāmī' close to Gatyāgati,[1] he defeated and killed the king and took possession of the throne.

13. In accordance with his former vows he first destroyed the soldiers of Cambodge and Yavana, and then re-erected the temple of Śiva which they had destroyed.

14. Having obtained sovereignty, he took possession of the land of Kambu out of compassion and tested the strength of her army.

15. In conformity to a previous vow, he installed, for obtaining success, a Śiva on the mountain called Vugvan, which was his own, being marked in a previous birth.

1. Huber explains 'Gatyāgati' as 'where she (river Yāmī) approaches and moves away from the temple.' It is probably the name of a place.

16. Under his rule flourished all the gods, as well as the people, in abundant riches; the earth prospered in a fair share of rain, and the city of Champā did thrive as if the Golden Age come back to it.

17. Uroja is popularly accepted to be the same as Śivānandana and this is confirmed by Purāṇārtha, which is looked upon as a mine (lit. mountain) of useful information in this world.

18. Four times I have been incarnated as Uroja; lest I be not born again, I re-install this Śiva in fulfilment of the promise I made before.

19. The god of gods Śrīśānabhadreśvara, and the god of gods established on the Vugvan mountain,—both will be enriched by that king who is a portion of myself longing for the glory of a Śaiva.

Such is the Purāṇārtha, description of Uroja, which the world must know.

Here (is a list of) the plots of ground (sthāna) and the fields of the kingdom of Champā which the king Śrī Jaya Harivarmadeva gives to the god Śrī Harivarmeśvara (list follows).

No. 75.

Batau Tablaḥ Inscription of Jaya Hari-varman I, dated 1082 Ś.

This Sanskrit inscription is engraved on a granite boulder called Batau Tablaḥ which is lying in the fields near the village of Ram in the southern portion of the valley of Panrang. This superb monument contains 17 lines of writing in large and beautiful characters and gives an interesting account of the chief events of the reign of king Śrī Jaya Harivarmadeva, son of Śrī Jaya Rudravarmadeva, who belonged to Kṣatriya family on both his father's and mother's side. The events are arranged under different dates of the śaka era:

Ś. 1069—Śrī Jaya Rudravarman, an incarnation of Viṣṇu, died at Pāṇḍuraṅga, and the people of this town invited Harivarmā to be the king of Champā.

Ś. 1069—Large bodies of troops from Cambodge and Vijaya attacked the king at Chaklyaṅ (probably the Village of Chakling close to the findspot of this inscription).

Ś. 1070—Large bodies of troops from Cambodge and Vijaya attacked the king in the plain of Vīrapura at the field of Kayev. Fortunately, the king, possessed of heroism without comparison, defeated them in the twinkling of an eye.

Ś. 1071—King Harivarmā vanquished Harideva whom the king of Cambodge placed in charge of Champā, and defeated the troops of Cambodge and Vijaya in the plain of Mahī.

The king was consecrated to the throne with due ceremonials and defeated an Annamite army sent against him.

Ś. 1073—Some battles (details lost).

Ś. 1077—The troops of Pāṇḍuraṅga did some thing (details lost).

S. 1082—Some battles (details lost). The king made some donations to the god Jaya Hariliṅgeśvara.

J. A. 1888 (1) p. 83, No. 395.

J. A. 1891 (1) pp. 38 ff.

[The dates as originally read by Aymonier have been corrected by M. Finot (B. E. F., Vol. XV, No. 2, p. 50)].

No. 76.

Po-Nagar Temple Inscription of Jaya Harivarman I, dated 1082 Ś.

The Sanskrit portion was edited by Bergaigne (Corpus No. XXXII, p. 282) and the Cham portion by Aymonier (J. A. 1891, part I, p. 41). The date previously read as 1092, was corrected by Finot (B. E. F., Vol. XV, No. 2, p. 50, fn. 1).

The inscription is engraved on the right-hand door-pillar of the temple to the left at Po-Nagar. It contains 8 lines of writing, the first two and a part of the third being in Sanskrit and the rest in Cham. The Sanskrit portion consists of one verse in Vasanta-tilakā and is merely an invocation to the goddess of Yām̐pu Nagara. The Cham portion records the victory of king Śrī Jaya Harivarman, prince Śivānandana, son of king Śrī Jaya Rudravarman. The king is said to have triumphed over all his enemies, to wit: the Cambodgians, the Annamites, the people of Vijaya, Amarāvatī and all the countries of the north; the countries of the south and Pāṇḍuraṅga, the regions of the west and the Radê, the Mada and other barbarous tribes. The king being thus constantly victorious, made many gifts to the goddess of the kingdom in 1082 śaka (=1160 A. D.).

TEXT.

स्वस्ति ।

आसिन्धुभूतलपतित्वरसस्य लाभे
स्वर्गास्पदास्पदपतित्वरसस्य लाभम् ।
तस्मान् स याँपुनगराह्वयदेवतां प्राक
संसेवतेस्म सुधनेन नु तावतैनम् ॥

TRANSLATION.

After tasting the pleasures of sovereignty extending over the entire surface of the land as far as the sea, and looking forward to the pleasures of sovereignty over gods in heaven, he first of all honoured the goddess called Yāpunagara by giving her great riches.

No. 77.

47 Hoà-mi fragmentary rock Inscription of Jaya Harivarman I.

The inscription is engraved on a rock at Hoà-mi in the district of Quang-Nam. The inscription records the victories of Harivarman against the Khmers and the Annamites.

(J. A. 1896, part I, pp. 148-149).

No. 78.

44 Myson Temple Inscription.

This fragmentary inscription in Temple A, at Myson, records that it was restored by king Vijaya Śrī Harivarmadeva.

B. E. F., Vol. IV, p. 977, No. XXVI.

No. 79.

Myson Temple Inscription of Jaya Indravarman IV, dated 1085 Ś.

The inscription was edited by M. Finot (B. E. F., Vol. IV, p. 969, No. XXIII). For localities (cf. No. 4). It is engraved on a pillar in the temple and contains 19 lines.

The language is Sanskrit and the inscription is written throughout in verse. There are altogether six stanzas, the metre being vv. 1, 3–6, Indravajrā and v. 2, Vaṁśasthā.

The inscription records the donations of king Śrī Jaya Indravarman of Grāmapura to the god Śrīśānabhadreśvara in the year 1085 (=1163 A. D.).

TEXT.

I. पु चिय् अनाक् श्रीजय-इन्द्रवर्म्मा
प्रादादिदं ग्रामपुरप्रदेशः ।
वानाद्युखेन्द्राविव रत्नसानुं
श्रीशानभद्रेश्वर ईश्वरेशे ॥

II. सनीश्वरात्मा महदीश्वरीकृतो
हिरण्यगर्भो न स ईश्वरोऽधुना ।
हिरण्यगर्भीकृत वग्रतेदसे[1]
दशास्ततो येन स नु स्तुतस्सता ॥

III. नैवाशिषस्तत्सुधियानुशङ्क-
स्तस्मिन् स दातुं दशादिक्षु देवः ।
रत्नाकृतो भूभृति पञ्चवक्त्रः
पुनर्व्विभर्त्यद्य मुखानि पञ्च ॥

IV. दष्टैर्म्महास्यैर्वहुवाक् स शर्व्वस-
स्तुत्यात्म[2] यद्दत्तसुवर्णकोशः ।
तत्रैककान्त्यावचनो न्वलाभाद्
देयस्य दत्तेन समानकान्तेः ॥

V. दयाथ कीर्त्तिश्च गुणश्च यस्य
रूपञ्च वीर्यञ्च मुखानि पञ्च ।
एतानि वद्यद् युगपन् महेशे[3]
सत्कोशनं पञ्च विभर्त्ति वेदम्[4] ॥

---

1. Read उग्रतजसे.
2. Read स्तुत्यात्मा.
3. Read महेशः.
4. Read चेदम्.

VI. सत्कोशने तत्र परे सुवर्णे
करणैस्त्रिकरणां द्विवपुर्मणीन्द्रे ।
मुक्तासु धात्रीधरषट्समूहे
रूप्ये परोप्यम्बरशून्यकरणैः ॥

TRANSLATION.

1. Pu ciy Anāk Śrī Jaya Indravarmā, of Grāmapura, has given this, like a bejewelled peak, to the god of gods, Śrīśānabhadreśvara in the year denoted by 'arrow-eight-sky-moon' *i. e.* 1085.

2. That godly king being elevated to the position of over-lord, Brahmā (Hiranya-garbha) was no longer the lord of creation. The king then made himself such a *hiranya-garbha*[1] (*i. e.* one filled with gold) by means of his brilliant valour, and was on that account praised by the honest men.

3. The five-faced god was unable to give his blessings to the king in all the ten directions (on account of the wisdom of the great king ?); so for protecting the king he has again, to-day, put on five faces (thus making ten in total).

4. Śarvva, who is worthy of praise, has a great store of words, as is apparent from his (five) great and visible faces. But although presented with a golden kośa he remains dumb before its unique splendour, not having anything to give which equals in splendour the thing that was given to him.

5. In order to sing simultaneously the glories of the king's five-fold virtues *viz.* mercy, fame, merit, beauty and strength, Maheśa has assumed five faces as well as five kośas (coverings or vocabularies).[2]

---

1. Hence the contradiction.

2. 'Pañca satkośanam' is taken in a collective sense. The proper from would be 'satkosanapañcakam.'

6. 232 golden paṇas, 82precious stones, 67 groups of pearls, and 200 paṇas of silver have been given for the kośa.

No. 80.

Po-Nagar Temple inscription of Jaya Indravarman IV, dated 1089 Ś.

It records the donations to the goddess Bhagavatī Kauṭhāreśvarī made in 1089 Śaka (=1167 A. D.) by king Jaya Indravarmadeva (Grāmapura vijaya), the queens, Parameśvarī and Rayā, princess Bhāgyavatī, daughter of the king, princess Sumitrā, princess Sudakṣiṇā and Māṅ si ai Grāmapura vijaya. The donations consisted of various ornaments and utensils of gold and silver including a *mukuṭa* (crown) and a *kalaśa* (pitcher) in gold, sandal-wood etc. Part of these donations was made when the king went to conquer Cambodge.

J. A. 1891 (1) pp. 44–45.
B. E. F., Vol. XV, No. 2, p. 50.

No. 81.

Myson Stelae Inscription of Jaya Indravarman IV, dated 1092 Ś.

The inscription was edited by M. Finot (B. E. F., Vol. IV, p. 970, No. XXIV; also cf. B. E. F., Vol. XV, No. 2, p. 50). (For localities cf. No. 4): It is engraved on a single face of a stelae and contains 21 lines besides the invocation. The language is Cham.

The inscription records the donations of king Śrī Jaya Indravarman of Grāmapura vijaya to the god Srī‘ānabhadreśvara, and the installation of various images by the same king.

TRANSLATION.

Salutation to Śiva.

There is a king Śrī Jaya Indravarmadeva, belonging to a famous place known as Grāmapuravijaya. The king reigned at first for the good of the world. He possesses large army (pṛthuvala) and is proud of his heroism; he is skilful in the use of all arms; victorious over all enemies in battles; versed in all the śāstras, *viz.* Grammar, Astrology etc., and learned in all the philosophical doctrines *e. g.* the doctrine of Mahāyāna. He possesses exceptional beauty and charm; he is energetic in the protection of all creatures, and skilful in the application of the four means *viz.* conciliation, liberality, dissensions and chastisement. Versed in all the Dharmaśāstras, notably the Nāradīya and Bhārggavīya, he takes pleasure in Dharma, and makes gifts to all people.

The prince installed Buddha Lokeśvara, Jaya Indralokeśvara and Bhagavatī Srī Jaya Indreśvarī in the district of Buddhaloka, and Bhagavatī Śrī Indra-Gaurīśvarī in that of Śrī Vināyaka.

The Prince knowing that Śrīśānabhadreśvara, who is a portion of Śiva, always grants, in all the worlds, his favour to the pious men according to their desire, has given, at different times, all the riches and all the necessary articles to Śrīśānabhadreśvara, for the sake of increasing his merit.

In the first place he has given a golden kośa, weighing 137 *thil* with an alloy of 200 *thil* of silver, decorated with all the jewels, such as *dhūnī* and sapphire, in the śaka year 1085.

Then he has constructed an *antargṛha* with sandal-wood weighing 2 bhāra, 9 tul; the amount of silver applied in the decoration of this *antargṛha* weighed 1096 *thil* and the gold coating of the summit of the *antargṛha* weighed 26 *thei*. A *Cranāṅ* was constructed...............the four golden nāgas decorating the cranāṅ contained 30 *thei* (of gold) and 17 *thil* of silver. A *taṅgau* of silver.....................495 *thil* with a gem called Sūryakānti (?) at the top. All these have been given in śaka 1086.

Then, in śaka 1087 he has given a *sanrauṅ* of gold weighing 17 *thil*, a golden vessel weighing 24 *thei* with an alloy of 26 *thei* of silver; a golden pitcher of 8 *thei*; a *bak* of gold of 2 *thil*; a *srumvil* of gold of 45 *thei* with an alloy of 99 *thil* of silver...........a *nāgapattra* coated with golden plate (?).

Besides, in śaka 1089 he has given a *tralāy* of gold weighing 294 *thei*; a *hluk* of gold of 100 *thei*.

In śaka 1090 he has given large elephants, male and female slaves etc.

In śaka 1092 he has decorated the temple of Śrīśāna-bhadreśvara with 10 *bhāra* 3 *tul*, 5 kār 17 *thei* of silver; and he has applied 82 *thei* of gold for coating all the pinnacles of the temple with gold.

The king has given all these things, being wholly devoted, in mind, body and speech.

No. 82.

33 An Thuan stelae Inscription of Jaya Indravarman IV.

This Cham inscription, engraved on two faces of a stelae at An Thuan (cf. No. 83 below), contains 20 lines of writing. They record oaths of allegiance made by three dignitaries to the king Śrī Jaya Indravarmma Deva. The three dignitaries are named Taval Vīra Siṁha Oṅ Vayāk, Taval Śūrādhika Varma oṅ ja............and (Taval) Vikrānta Siṁha Oṅ Dhun. The oaths contain, among other promises, not fully intelligible, an undertaking to the effect, that the chiefs and their children will fight for their lord in case of war, as long as they live.

J. A. 1888 (1) p. 88, No. 424.

J. A. 1891 (1) p. 46, No. 424.

No. 83.

An Thuan Stelae Inscription of Jaya Indravarman IV.

The Sanskrit portion of the inscription was edited by M. Bergaigne (Corpus No. XXXIII, p. 286) and the Cham portion by Aymonier (J. A. 1891 [1] pp. 45-46).

The inscription is engraved on the two faces of a stelae found at An Thuan in the district of Binh Dinh. In addition to syllable om there are two lines in Sanskrit on one face and three lines in Cham on the other face. The Sanskrit portion contains a verse in Indravajrā. The text shows already the beginning of the effect of barbarian influence on Sanskrit.

The Sanskrit portion contains an invocation to Śiva. The Cham portion refers to the gifts of slaves and goods made by king Śrī Jaya Indravarmadeva of Grāmapura to the goddess of the kingdom (pu Nagara).

TEXT.

ओम्

स्वस्ति स्वभावप्रविभूति भूपो
स्वस्ति प्रभावप्रतिमे शिवोमे
स्वस्ति स्वजा[1] से[2] अवतान्तु ये ते
स्वस्तिष्ठदाशा[3]नृभिराश्रिते वः ॥

TRANSLATION.

Hail! magnificent is the king by nature! Hail! powerful are the images of Śiva and Umā; Hail! all my subjects and slaves, may you be protected by Śiva and Umā, whose protection is ever sought by mankind.

No. 84.

Myson Pillar Inscription dated 1125 Ś.

The inscription was edited by M. Finot (B. E. F., Vol. IV, p. 970, No. XXIV, B., C.). It was engraved on two faces of the same pillar which contains No. 81, and contains 38 lines of writing besides the invocation. The language is Cham.

The inscription consists of two parts. The first refers to king Sūryavarman, and the second to a yuvarāja named Managaḥña on Dhanapati. But the two parts are written consecutively and form one single narrative, *viz.*, the fight against Cambodge. The object of the inscription is to record the installation of an image of Śiva by the yuvarāja in śaka 1125 (=1203 A. D.).

---

1. Read 'प्रजा'.
2. Read 'मे'.
3. Read °दासा.

TRANSLATION.

Salutation to Śiva.

There is a king, Śrī Sūryavarmadeva, prince Śrī Vidyānandana, of Tumprauk-vijaya. The king practised the Mahāyāna dharma following the instructions of true knowledge. In his early youth, in the śaka year denoted by 'sea-sky-moon-moon' *i. e.* 1104, he went to Cambodge. The king of Cambodge ,seeing him possessed of all the 33 marks, received him favourably and taught him, like a prince, all the various branches of knowledge, and instructed him in various branches of military science. During his stay at Cambodge, a dependent town of Cambodge called Malyaṅ, inhabited by a multitude of bad men, revolted against the king of Cambodge. The latter seeing the prince well versed in arms, ordered him to lead the Cambodgian troops and take the town of Malyaṅ. He did all that the king of Cambodge desired. The latter, pleased at his valour, conferred on him the dignity of yuvarāja, and gave him all the pleasures and the good things which could be found in the kingdom of Cambodge.

In śaka 'two moon-moon-moon' (1112) the king Śrī Jaya Indravarmadeva oṅ Vatuv made war against the king of Cambodge. The latter sent the prince at the head of Cambodgian troops in order to take Vijaya and defeat the king Jaya Indravarman oṅ Vatuv. He captured the king and had him conducted to Cambodge by the Cambodgian troops. He proclaimed Sūrya Jayavarmadeva prince In, brother-in-law of the king of Cambodge, as king of the city of Vijaya. Then he returned and reigned at Rājapura in Panrāṅ. During his reign at Rājapura a number of pirates revolted against him. He fought with them, drove them back and defeated them all.

Śrī Sūryavarman, prince In, who had been proclaimed king in the kingdom of Vijaya, was driven away by prince Rasupati and returned to Cambodge. The prince Raṣupati reigned in the kingdom of Vijaya under the name of Śrī Jaya Indravarmadeva.

In śaka 'sea-moon-moon-moon' *i. e.* 1114, the king of Cambodge sent the Cambodgian generals with Śrī Jaya Indravarman oṅ Vatuv. He met the prince at Rājapura. The prince led the Cambodgian troops with Jaya Indravarman; he took Vijaya, defeated and killed Jaya Indravarman cei Rasupati and ruled over Vijaya. The same year Jaya Indravarman oṅ Vatuv fled from the Cambodgians and went to Amarāvatī. He revolted and raised troops in different districts at Amarāvatī, Ulik, Vvyar, Jriy and Traik. He went to take Vijaya. The prince led the troops and pursued (?) Jaya Indravarman oṅ Vatuv as far as Yāṅ Bharuv-Vijaya; he gave him battle, vanquished him, compelled him to fall back on Traik, and there captured him and put him to death. Henceforth the prince ruled without opposition.

In śaka 'five-moon-moon-moon' *i. e.* 1115, the Cambodgians..............the dwellings, took seven..............took eight.............. The prince fought with the Cambodgians and vanquished them.

In śaka 'six-moon-moon-moon' *i. e.* 1116, the king of Cambodge sent a large number of Cambodgian generals, with all sorts of arms. They came to fight with the prince. The latter fought at Jai Ramya-Vijaya and vanquished the generals of the Cambodgian army.............. After having fought with them, the prince marched to Amarāvatī. He re-erected all the houses; he constructed the house called Śrī Heruka-harmya; he made a kośa of gold; he gave to

Śrīśānabhadreśvara a ṣaḍmukha (six-faces) weighing 510 *thei*; he gave a golden *suvauk* weighing 5 *thil*; he gave a kanāp of Siṁhapura to Śrīśānabhadreśvara for the sake of acquiring merit both in this world and in the other.

I, yuvarâja, of illustrious birth, called Managahna oü Dhanapati, I..................rule (?) over Champā, and I am glorious. I have re-consecrated Śiva, who is Śrīśāna, and I worship him piously. I have given him riches and the slaves in śaka 1125 (the expression 'bhūtaḥ pakṣa 66 ka yaḥ' is unintelligible; bhūta-pakṣa denotes 25 and I therefore take the date as 1125; 66 is probably a misreading for 11. M. Finot takes the date doubtfully as 1166).

No 85.

Po-Nagar Temple inscription of Jaya Parameśvaravarman II, dated (?) 1148 Ś.

The inscription refers to king Śrī Jaya Parameśvaravarmadeva oṅ of Turai-Vijaya. It states that in 1112 Ś. (=1190 A. D.) there was a king of Cambodge named Vraḥ pāda Śrī Jayavarmadeva who conquered (?) the whole earth. He took the capital of Champā and carried away all the *liṅgas*. Then followed a war of 32 years. "He placed a Cambodgian general.............. In 1123 Ś. (=1201 A. D.) the king started..............took the name of pu pon pulyan Śrī yu.............. Then Cambodge and Champā.............. this king.................universal sovereignty. (The last line bears the date 1148 but whether the line is a part of this inscription has been doubted.)

J. A. 1891 (1) pp. 47-48, No. 409 B. 4.

No. 86.
Cho-dinh pillar Inscription of Śrī Jaya Parameśvaravarman II, dated 1148 Ś.

This Cham inscription, engraved on two faces of a pillar found at Cho-dinh, the market place of Phanrang, contains 41 lines of writing. The inscription is mutilated and a complete translation is not possible. It refers to king Jaya Parameśvaravarman in the last line and contains three dates 1129, 1142 and 1148 saka.

It refers to the war of 32 years which followed the conquest of Champā by the king of Cambodge (in 1112). In 1129 śaka (=1207 A. D.) the victorious Khmer king seems to have installed a yuvarāja at the head of the conquered territories. Then the Siamese and the Pukam (Pagan) came from Cambodge and a battle took place with the Annamites, apparently in the north of Champā. The Cambodgian generals led the troops which opposed the Annamites, and the loss on both sides was very great. In 1142 saka (=1220 A. D.) the Khmers evacuated Champā and (probably after having concluded peace in 1144 saka) the coronation of the Cham king Śrī Jaya Parameśvaravarman II took place in 1148 śaka (=1226 A. D.). Henceforth he reigned in peace, constructed palaces and temples at Śrī Vinaya and re-installed the images of gods.

The inscription on the second face records the donations made to the god (Liṅga) by the king. The donations consisted of utensils, lands and other things.

J. A. 1888 (1) p. 91, No. 383.
J. A. 1891 (1) pp. 50–52, No. 383.
B. E. F., Vol. III, p. 634, No. VIII.
B. E. F., Vol. XV, No. 2, p. 191.

No. 87.

Myson Temple Inscription dated 1152 Ś.

It records the donations of Kālāntakatha.................. nandana to the god Śrīśānabhadreśvara, consisting of gold, precious stones, female elephants copper utensils and slaves. It is dated in 1152 śaka (=1230 A. D.).

B. E. F. Vol. IV, p. 977, No. XXV B.

No. 88.

Po-Nagar Temple Inscription of Jaya Parameśvaravarman II, dated 1155 Ś.

This inscription appears to be a continuation of another (No. 85 ?). It begins thus: 'Again (punaḥ) in 1155 (=1233 A. D.) king Śrī Jaya Parameśvaravarmadeva made donations to the goddess Pu-Nagara and to the sacred image.' The concluding portion gives details of the donations consisting of lands and slaves. The slaves belonged to both the sexes and to various nationalities such as the Khmer, Cham, Chinese, and Siamese.

J. A. 1891 (1) pp. 48-49.

No. 89.

Cho-dinh Temple Inscription of Jaya Parameśvaravarman II, dated 1155 Ś.

This Sanskrit inscription was engraved on the door-front of a temple at Cho-Dinh, the market place of Phanrang. It records an order of the king Jaya Parameśvaravarman to his commander-in-chief Râmadeva to install an image of the god Svayam-utpanna. Reference is also made to donation of slaves, to wit, 7 Khmers, 11 Siamese, 1 Pukâm (Pagan) together with 1 elephant and 3 khmer (elephants ?). It is dated in 1155 śaka (=1233 A. D.).

J. A. 1888 (1) pp. 88–89, No. 382.
J. A. 1891 (1) pp. 49–50, No. 382.
B. E. F., Vol. III, p. 635 (No. X).

No. 90.

Myson Temple inscription of Jaya Parameśvaravarman II, dated 1156 Ś.

The inscription was edited by M. Finot (B. E. F., Vol. IV, p. 976, No. XXV A). (For localities cf. No. 4). It is engraved on a pillar inside the temple and contains 10 lines. The language is Cham.

The inscription records the religious foundations of the king Śrī Jaya Parameśvaravarmadeva and is dated in 1156 (=1234 A. D.).

TRANSLATION.

There is a king, His Majesty Śrī Jaya Parameśvaravarmadeva, oṅ Aṅśarāja, of Turai-Vijaya. During the disasters of the Cambodgian war which lasted for 32 years he was the sole king (Ekacchatra) in the kingdom of Champā. He re-installed all the *lingas* of the south *viz.* those of yāṅ Pu Nagara, and the *lingas* of the north *viz.* those of Śrī-śānabhadreśvara. He has given a silver *kośa* with a golden face, and the *koṣa* of Bhṛgu with all the utensils of gold and silver. Sumtotal: 100 thil of gold. In śaka 1156.

No. 91.

Lomngoeu stelae Inscription of Jaya Parameśvaravarman II.

This Cham inscription is engraved on a stelae found at Lomngoeu, at the mouth of the Phanrang river, where it served as the boundary stone between two villages.

The first four lines are the concluding portion of an inscription now lost, and refer to donations made to a temple *viz.* utensils, and Chinese, Siamese and Paganese slaves.

The remaining 11 lines record the donations of king Jaya Parameśvaravarman to the gods Śrī Campeśvara and Svayamutpanna. Among other things he improved the irrigation channels in the fields granted to these gods.

J. A. 1888 (1) p. 92, No. 392.
J. A. 1891 (1) pp. 52–53, No. 392.
B. E. F., Vol. III, p. 634, No. X.

No. 92.

Phanrang Pillar Inscription of Jaya Parameśvaravarman II.

This Cham inscription is engraved on two faces of a pillar at Phanrang. It records donations of king Parameśvaravarmadeva and Yuvarāja Nandabhadra to the gods Svayamutpanna and Jaya Artheśvara. The donations consist of lands, slaves, and silver etc.

(B. E. F., Vol. III, pp. 634, 646).

No. 93.

Kim Choua Inscription of Jaya Parameśvaravarman II.

The inscription is engraved on a stelae belonging to the temple of Kim Choua close to the citadel of Binh Dinh. It refers to the king Śrī Jaya Parameśvaravarmadeva (II) and contains the names of Buddhist divinities such as, Śrī Liṅgalokeśvara, Śrī Jina Parameśvara, Śrī Jinavṛddheśvarī, Śrī Jinalokeśvara, Śrī Saugatadeveśvara, Śrī Jinadevadevī.

J. A. 1888 (1) pp. 92–93, No. 411.

No. 94.

Myson Pillar Inscription of Jaya Indravarman V dated 1165 Ś.

The inscription was edited by M. Finot (B. E. F., Vol. IV, p. 953, No. XVIII C). It is engraved on the same pillar as No. 69 and contains 11 lines of writing in Cham. It records the pious donations of Jaya Indravarman V to the god Śrīśānabhadreśvara in 1165 śaka.

TRANSLATION.

Hail! There is a prince, king of kings, Jaya Indravarman, prince Harideva, of Sakan-Vijaya, grandson of His Majesty Jaya Harivarman, great king of kings, son of His Majesty Jaya Harivarman, great king of kings, younger brother of His Majesty Parameśvaravarman, the great king. He has all the thirty-three signs,..................youth, beauty, strength and pride of heroism.................he knows all the sciences...............he is versed in the philosophy of different schools. He is expert in all pleasures....................youth, but realising that the body and the pleasures of royalty are transitory................a famous glory in the world, and he restored it completely. And the king.................the god Śrīśānabhadreśvara who is the origin of the kingdom of Champā................objects to Śrīśānabhadreśvara, in śaka year..............inferior and middle, 'five-member-form-one' (pañcamāṅgaḥ rūpaikaḥ) *i. e.* 1165 (Finot reads the date as 1185).

No. 95.

Myson Pillar Inscription of Jaya Indravarman V.

The inscription was edited by M. Finot (B. E. F., Vol. IV, p. 966, No. XXII B). For localities (cf. No. 4). It is engraved on a pillar and contains 10 lines of writing. The language is Sanskrit and the inscription is written throughout in verse. There are altogether 10 stanzas but the last five are almost illegible. The metres used are vv. 1, 3, 5, Indravajrā; v. 2, Upajāti; v. 4, is mutilated and is either Indravajrā or Upajāti.

The inscription refers itself to the king Śrī Jaya Indravarman (V), son of Śrī Harivarmadeva, younger brother of Śrī Parameśvara and the grandson of Śrī Harivarmadeva.

TEXT.

I. तीच्णाङ्गसमनोदाधिमप्रमेयं
स्वस्योतिसूक्ष्मोपि कलां प्रकाश्य ।
संक्रीडते शक्तिभिरात्मशक्तौ
नैष्कल्यमृग्यस्स शिवो व — — ॥

II. आसीन्नृपश्श्री हरिवर्मदेव-
पौत्रोधिकश्श्री जयइन्द्रवर्मा ।
रराज च श्री हरिवर्मदेवा-
त्मजोनुजश्श्री परमेश्वरस्य ॥

III. विश्व ˘ — — ˘ ˘ भूतपूर्व्वं
भूभिर्भारिष्यन्त्ययमित्यवेत्य ।
बाल्ये गुरुस्सर्वचलाचला —
— — ˘ — — त्तयते स्वयं यम् ॥

IV. सौन्दर्यरूपो परलोप्त्र पूर्व्वान्
— — ˘ आमन्यत योधवीरान् ।
— — ˘ — — ˘ ˘ — त्रपा—
य दत्त शौर्यादिव पुष्प — — ॥

V. पञ्चल्यरूपापि पतिं विनाह्य
— — ˘ — — महिषी जह्वाति ।
बाल्यन्तु लक्ष्मीस्समवाप्य कान्तं
यं यत् पुराणं विजहाति बाल्यम् ॥

VI. — — — — — — विलासिनी कामजनेषु कामात् ॥

VII. एतावता स — — — ङ्गम् अनल्पपुण्यैः ॥

VIII. सदाहृताश्रीः कु — — — — स्य समाजहार ॥

IX. करदीकृतक्षितीशो जल — — —

X. दोर्म्मन्दराद्रिमन्थितासमित्समुद्रो नरो — — — —

TRANSLATION.

1. Adoration to Śiva, who sports in the limitless Mānasa lake with his own śaktis (wives) by means of his own prowess, thereby displaying his form, although he is resident of heaven, his body is imperceptible,[1] and he can be meditated upon as without any form.

2. There was the king Śrī Jaya Indravarmā, grandson

---

1. The meaning of the first line is a little obscure. The metre is also faulty.

of Śrī Harivarmmadeva, son of Śrī Harivarmmadeva and the younger brother of Śrī Parameśvara.

3-8. (Too mutilated to yield a satisfactory meaning; they apparently contain eulogy of the king).

9. ....who has made other kings tributary.

10. Who churned the ocean, which was the battle, by means of the Mandara mountain, which was his arm.

No. 96.

Phanrang Lintel Inscription dated 1166. Śaka.

This Cham inscription, engraved on a lintel at Phanrang, records that prince Paṅkaja Abhimanyudeva, governor of Pāṇḍuraṅga and commander-in-chief of king Jaya Parameśvaravarmadeva, came to Pāṇḍuraṅga by the order of the king in 1152 śaka, and gave in śaka 1166 various donations, including gold, silver and slaves, to the god Svayamutpanna.

(B. E. F., Vol. III, pp. 635, 648).

No. 97.

Po-Nagar Temple Inscription of princess Sūryyadevī dated 1178. Śaka.

The inscription refers to Pulyaṅ Ratnāvali, princess Sūryyadevī, daughter of king Jaya Indravarmadeva and queen Śrī Paramaratnastrī. She was united for ever, by ties of marriage, to a nobleman called Oṅ Rasu Nandana. The happy pair made various pious donations to the temple and installed an image of Bhagavati Mātṛliṅgeśvarī. In 1178 princess Ratnāvali gave various ornaments of gold and silver to the goddess Pu Nagara and prescribed regulations for the dancing girls employed in the service of the goddess.

J. A. 1891 (1) p. 53–4.

No. 98.

Po-Nagar Temple Inscription of Princess Sūryyadevī.

It records the gifts of Pulyaṅ Ratnāvalī princess Sūryyadevī of Manaḥ Vijaya to the goddess Bhagavatī Mātṛliṅgeśvarī. She also gave a sum of money for making a statue of the goddess Bhagavatī Kauṭhāreśvarī. The gifts consisted of various ornaments of gold and silver, slaves and a female elephant.

J. A. 1891 (1) p. 56, No. 408 B.

No. 99.

Po-Nagar Vase Inscription of Śakrānta dated 1179 Śaka.

The inscription is engraved on a copper vase found in the Temple of Po-Nagar. It records that the vase was given to the goddess Po-Nagara by the king Śakrānta belonging to Mandavijaya, in the year 1179 (=1257 A. D.). Śakrānta was probably an usurper.

B. E. F., Vol. VI, p. 291, f. n. (2).
J. A. 1906 (1) p. 518.
B. E. F., Vol. XV, No. 2, p. 192.

No. 100.

Bronze (?) Vase inscription of Jaya-Siṁhavarman II. dated 1181 Śaka.

A short Cham inscription engraved on the interior of a vase in possession of M. Neville. It records the pious gifts of Śrī Jaya Siṁhavarmadeva, prince Śrī Harideva, for the sake of merit in life hereafter. It is dated 1181 śaka (= 1259 A. D.).

J. A. 1888 (1) p. 96, No. 420.
J. A. 1891 (1) pp. 58-59.
B. E. F., Vol. XV, No. 2, p. 51.

No. 101.

Pilaster Inscription.

The origin of this inscription is unknown. It is engraved on the base of a pilaster and contains the name of Śrīśānabhadreśvara. The two last figures of the date are 81, and on palaeographical grounds it may be referred to 1181 śaka (=1259 A. D.) during the reign of Indravarman IV.

B. E. F., Vol. XV, No. 2, p. 19.

No. 102.

Choek yang stelae Inscription dated 1185 Śaka.

The Sanskrit portion was edited by Bergaigne (Corpus No. XXXV, p. 291) and the Cham portion translated by Aymonier (J. A. 1891, part 1, p. 55).

The inscription is engraved on a small stelae found in a cave on the Tchoek yang 'the divine mount' at the north-east of Panrang. It contains 6 lines of writing, three in Sanskrit and three in Cham, and a seventh line containing the figures 1185 denoting the date. The Sanskrit portion is in prose and merely contains an invocation to Śiva. The Cham text records that five dignitaries, sons of Sun (Sūryaputra) and belonging to Vīrapura, excavated the cave in śaka 1185 (=1263 A. D.).

TEXT.

L. 1. स्वस्ति जय सिद्धि

L. 2. श्रों नमश्शिवाय परमदानशर्व्वा-

L. 3. य ऊद्र्ध्वमूर्द्धने श्रह नमस्तु सदा ॥

TRANSLATION.

Hail, victory, success! Adoration to Śiva, to Śarvva, who makes the supreme gifts and who has his head erect. Oh, adoration always!

No. 103.

Kiem Ngoc (Binh Dinh) stelae Inscription dated 1187 (?) Śaka.

It contains an invocation to Buddha and refers to a king of Ksatriya family whose name is lost. It seems to contain a date 1187 but this is doubtful.

J. A. 1888 (1) p. 104, No. 423.
J. A. 1891 (1) p. 66, No. 423.

No. 104.

Batau Tablah Inscription of Jayasiṁha-varman II (Indravarman IV) Hari-deva dated 1188 Śaka.

This short inscription of four lines is engraved on a boulder called Batau-Tablah (cf. No. 75).

It records that king Indravarman, prince Śrī Harideva, bearing the name of Pulyaṅ Śrī Yuvarāja vlom (?) came to Panraṅ in 1171. Then having obtained the throne he took the royal name of Śrī Jaya Siṁhavarman and enjoyed himself at Panraṅ in 1179. Then having been formally consecrated to the throne he became the sovereign of the world, Indravarman, and enjoyed himself at Panrañ in 1188.

J A. 1888 (1) p. 967, No. 395.

J. A. 1891 (1) pp. 57–58.

B. E. F., Vol. XV, No. 2, p. 51.

No 105.

Po-Nagar Temple Inscription dated 1189 Śaka.

It records the gifts of princess Ratnāvalī (cf. Nos. 97, 98) to the goddess Pu-Nagara and to the goddess Mātṛi-Liṅgeśvarī in the year 1189 (=1267 A. D.). The gift consists of lands and slaves

J A. 1891 (1) p. 57, No. 408 C.

B. E. F., Vol. XV, No. 2, p. 51.

No. 106.

Phanrañ Lintel Inscription of Indra-varman IV. dated 1196, Śaka.

This Cham inscription engraved on a lintel at Phanrañ records the donations, consisting of a large elephant and six slaves, made to the god Svayamutpanna by the king Indra-varman IV in 1196 śaka (=1274 A. D.).

(B. E. F., Vol. III, pp. 635, 648).

B. E. F., Vol. XV, No. 2,. p. 51.

No. 107.

Yang Kur Inscription of Indravarman IV. dated 1200 Śaka.

This inscription in mixed Sanskrit and Cham is engraved on two faces of a stelae found at Yang kur (formerly called Pāṇḍuraṅga hill ?), quite close to that famous town. The inscription contains 23 lines of writing but very little can be deciphered. It begins with an invocation to Śiva and records that in 1200 (=1278 A. D.), in the reign of Indravarman, the noble queen Sūryalakṣmī installed the statue of the god Bhūmivijaya.

J. A. 1888 (1) p. 97, No. 389.
J. A. 1891 (1) p. 59, No. 389.
B. E. F., Vol. III, p. 635, No. XIV.

No. 108.

Po-Nagar Temple Inscription of Indravarman IV.

This Cham inscription is engraved on the left pillar of the outer gate of the temple to the right. The two faces of the pillar contain two different inscriptions. The earlier one containing four lines is illegible; only the word *Liṅga* can be made out with certainty. The later one contains six lines and records dedications of three infants to the god Śrī Indravarman Śivaliṅgeśvara, by king Indravarman, prince Śrī-Harideva of 'Śila vandha vijaya.' (The infants were probably condemned to slavery as a punishment to a person who spoke maliciously.)

J. A. 1888 (1) p. 98 No. 402.
J. A. 1891 (1) p. 59 No. 402 B.

No. 109.

Po-Nagar stelae Inscription of Indravarman IV.

The inscription is engraved on two faces of a stelae lying in the court-yard of the Po-Nagar Temple to the left. The inscription on the first face refers to king Indravarman and records gifts of lands to ling Bhagavati Kauṭhāreśvarī. The inscription on the other face refers to king Śrī Jaya Siṁha-Varman and king Indravarman and records the installation of Śiva liṅga and the God Śrīśānabhadreśvara.

J. A. 1888 (1) p. 103

J. A. 1891 (1) pp. 60-62.

No. 110.

Po sah fragmentary stelae Inscription of Jaya Siṁhavarman III dated 1228.

Po sah is close to the village of Chakling, in the south of the valley of Panrañ. The inscription is written on two faces of the stelae comprising respectively 22 and 9 lines. The language is Sanskrit but a good many words are lost and no complete text or translation is possible.

It records the career of prince Harijitātmaja, son of king Śrī Jayasiṁha Varman, the king of kings, and the queen Bhāskaradevī. The prince was born in 1196 (=1274 A. D.). In 1220 Śaka =(1298 A. D.) he received the epithet Taval Śurā Adhikavarman. In 1222 Śaka (=1300 A. D.) his father appointed him to govern a district extending from the river Vauk as far as Bhūmanā Vijaya. In 1223 śaka (=1301 A. D.) his father gave him the name of Pulyaṅ Uddhṛta Siṁhavarman. The prince was endowed with beauty and skill. He was a devotee of Śiva and respected his preceptor, father and mother. Knowing that the pleasures of this life are illusory like a dream he gave up a life of enjoyment and applied himself entirely to pious works such as digging tanks, building roads and making religious endowments, abstinence, meditation etc. In 1227 śaka (=1305 A. D.)[1] the king gave him the name Mahendra (?) Varman. In 1228 śaka he made donations of slaves etc. The inscription refers to two other queens of Jayasiṁhavarman viz. Parameśvarī, daughter of king Devādideva, and Tāpasi, the daughter of king of Yavadvīpa.

J. A. 1888 (1) p. 99, No. 398
J. A. 1891 (1) p. 62, No. 398
B. E. F. vol. III, p. 636, No. XVII.
Bulletin de la commission archaeologique de l' Indochine 1911, p. 13

Nos. 111-115.

Po Klong Gorai Inscriptions of Jayasiṁhavarman III.

These five inscriptions are engraved in a temple named Po-klong Gorai, the most beautiful ancient monument in the plain of Phanraṅ

No. 112, engraved on three faces of the stone, contains respectively 40, 41 and 42 lines. It begins with an invocation to Śiva and records the donations of slaves and lands

1. The date may be '1228'.

by the king Śrī Jayasiṁhavarmadeva to Jayasiṁhavarmaliṅgeśvara (i. e. Śiva-liṅga styled after the king).

The king's parentage is described in the following words. "Śrī Jayasiṁhavarmadeva pu (prince) ciy (master) Śrī Harijit Paramātmaja yāṅ poṅ ku (His divine Majesty) Indravarma Paramodbhava di (in) pu poṅ vyā (Her Majesty) Parameśvarī pu nai (princess) Gaurendralakṣmī paramapura." This expression is ambiguous and might mean that the king was son of Śrī Harijit. But it has been taken to mean on the analogy of Annamite expressions, that the king Jayasiṁhavarman (III), also called prince Harijit, was the son of king Indravarman and the queen Gaurendralakṣmī.

This preamble is followed by a detailed account of the fields and slaves granted to the temple which covers the rest of the inscription. Nos. 111, 113 and 115 also contain similar detailed account of lands and slaves. No. 114 is hardly legible and refers to the donation of a young beautiful lady (of the royal family).

It is interesting to note that among the names of slaves we have the female Rājaput, the boy Śivadit, the boy Aṅgāra, the boy Ṛddhi, and male Vāyudeva. There are also references to the nationalities of these slaves e.g. the female Javā (Malayan or Javanese) and the female Yvan (Annamite).

J. A. 1888 (1) pp. 101-103 Nos. 384-388.
J. A. 1891 (1) pp. 67-82.
B. E. F. Vol. III. p. 635-6 Nos. XV, XVI.

No. 116.

Tali Temple inscription of Jayasiṁhavarman III.

L. Finot refers to an inscription in a temple at Tali, a village in the district of Darlac. It is written in Cham and records the erection of a temple with a Mukhaliṅga under the name of Jaya Siṁhavarma-liṅgeśvara, by the king Jaya Simhavarman at the end of the thirteenth century.

B. E. F. Vol. IV.p. 534.

No. 117.

Binh Dinh Gate Inscription of Vīra Bhadravarman Dated 1323 Śaka.

The inscription was edited by M. Finot (B. E. F. Vol. XV, No. 2. p. 12). It is engraved on the plinth of the gate of the royal citadel of Binh Dinh. The language is Cham. There are 19 lines of writing.

The inscription records the donation of Vīra Bhadravarman in 1323 śaka (=1401 A. D.). It throws fresh light on the chronology of the last kings of Champā.

TRANSLATION.

Hail! There was a king of Bṛṣu family viz. His Majesty Śrī Jayasiṁhavarmadeva Śrī Harijātti Vīrasiṅha Champapūra who reigned full twelve years. Then his soul departed for the abode of Śiva in the land of Yāṅ....(Then) his son His Majesty Śrī Bṛṣu Viṣṇujātti Vīra Bhadravarmadeva reigned. As his father, mother and cousins were established in this country and had received in lease the uncultivated estates, he took the field at Luvuk which his royal father had cleared, consisting of 500 *Vījaih* of wood with the public serfs; a *gu̇ṇa* of silver, a silver kamaṇḍalu of 5 *thil*; a silver bottle of 1 *thil*; a silver case...of one *thil*; an elephant, two slaves; all these for being distributed as offerings......to the temple of Śrīśāna of this country—In śaka 1323 (=1401 A. D.)

No. 118.

Cheo-Reo Inscription of Viṣṇu-Jātti Vīra Bhadravarman dated 1331 Śaka.

This mutilated inscription, containing the date and name of the king, is engraved on a statue of Śiva, which originally belonged to the temple of Drang Lai, but is now placed in the temple of Yang Mum at Cheo-Reo in the Phu-yen district.

B. E. F., Vol. XV. No. 2, p. 13.

No. 119.

Cheo-Reo Inscription of Vīra Bhadravarman.

This mutilated inscription is engraved on a ruined stelae (For localities cf. No. 118). It contains the name of the king Śrī Bṛṣu Viṣṇujātti Vīra Bhadravarmadeva prince Nauk Glauṅ Vijaya.

B. E. F. Vol. XV, No. 2. p. 13.

No 120.

Phuoc-thinh (Dt. Phu-Yen) stelae Inscription dated 1333 Śaka.

Nothing but the date is legible.

B. E. F. Vol. XV, No. 2 p. 13, fn (4)

No. 121.

Bien Hoa Viṣṇu Image Inscription of Jayasiṁhavarman IV dated 1343 (?)

The inscription was noticed and partially read by Aymonier (J. A. 1891, part I pp. 84-85) but has since been properly edited by M. Cabaton (B. E. F. IV. pp. 687 ff).

The inscription is engraved on the pedestal of an image of Viṣṇu which was originally discovered near Bien-Hoa in French Cochin China. It contains 9 lines of writing. The language is Cham.

The inscription refers to a prince named Nauk Glauṅ Vijaya, son of king Śrī Jayasiṁha Varman (IV). The prince is said to have vanquished the Annamites (Yvan) and taken possession of a kingdom called Braḥ Kānda. He gained innumerable victories and returned to Champā in 1343 (?). He erected an image of Viṣṇu called Tribhuvanākrānta, with the booty he had taken from the Khmers (Kvir) and made donations to a number of liṅgas and gods.

The portion of the inscription containing the date is so much damaged that it has not been possible to arrive at a definite conclusion. M. Aymonier reads the date as "loka-aṣṭa-ardha-anala" = 1282 śaka; M. Cabaton reads the date as "loka-saṣṭārthānalaḥ' or 'loka aṣṭārthānalaḥ' = 1363 or 1383", while M. Finot reads the passage as "loka aṣṭārdhānalaḥ nrapaḥ = 1343 (nrapaḥ = nṛpaḥ = rājā = somaḥ = 1)". M. Finot's suggestion is generally accepted.

The image of viṣṇu on which the inscription is engraved has been described in B. E. F. Vol. I, p. 18. It shows the prevalence of Viṣṇu cult in Champā.

No. 122.

Nui Ben-Lang (Binh Dinh) stelae

Inscription of Indravarman

dated 1358 Śaka.

It records that there was a king Śrī Jaya Siṁhavarman of the Bṛsu family. His son reigned for 32 years, and then, after the royal consecration, took the name of Śrī Bṛsu Indravarman. It contains the date 1358 śaka (=1436 A. D.)

J. A. 1888 (1) p. 104 No. 413.
J. A. 1891 (1) p. 83-84 No. 413.

No. 123.

Ron Buddhist Inscription.

The inscription was edited by F. Huber (B. E. F. Vol. XI, p. 267). It is engraved on a stone lying in a field about two miles from Bac Ha in Quang Binh. It contains four lines of writing and records donations to a Buddhist Vihāra. The language is Sanskrit (the characters belong to about 9th or 10th century A. D.)

नमः तस्मै भगवते श्रीडामरेश्वराय तिल्वित-
क्षेत्रं पँरत्रेत्र त्रद्वः......देवमेतत् सर्व्वं मः
विहारद्रव्यं द्वीशतमानं पञ्चाशदधिकं श्री......
राजेन भक्तिमता दत्तमिति ये रक्षन्ति......
ये नाशयन्ति

Homage to the god Śrī Ḍāmareśvara. The fields of Tilvit, Păr, Tradvaḥ etc,—all these lands belonging to the monastery and containing 250 measures were given by the pious king Śrī.........Those who maintain.........Those who destroy

.........(Ḍāmareśvara, the chief of the Ḍāmaras, or *bhūtas* (goblins), is one of the numerous epithets which Avalokiteśvara has borrowed from Śiva.)

No. 124.

Phu-Luong fragmentary stelae Inscription.

Only the invocation 'Om namaś-Śivāya' 'Adoration to Śiva' has been deciphered. It probably belongs to the ninth century. (Phu-Luong is a few miles north of Hue in the district of Thua-thien).

J. A. 1898 part II p. 560

No. 125.

Dong-Duong Temple Inscription.

This short inscription of two lines refers to two fields. It may be referred on palaeographical grounds to a date earlier than the 11th century A. D. The inscription is of interest as it offers a *terminus ad quem* for the date of the temple of Dong-Duong (cf. No. 31)

B. E. F., Vol. IV. (112-113)

No. 126.

'Khânh Tho Dong' Buddhist Inscription.

The Buddhist formula 'Ye dharma' &c. is engraved on the back of a pedestal containing an image of Buddha. Khanh Tho Dong is in the district of Quang-Nam.

Parmentier-Inventaire descriftif des Monuments Chams Vol. I p. 244.

No. 127.

Ban Metruot Stone Inscription.

The Cham words 'pu vyā' meaning 'Her majesty the Queen', engraved on a grinding stone found close to the village of Ban Metruot about 18 miles to the north of Ban Methuot, chief town of the Laotian province of Darlak, indicates the extent of Cham influence in the savage country.

B. E. F., Vol. IV, p. 679.

No. 128.

Myson Pillar Inscription.

It is very fragmentary and refers to a 'rāja-paṇḍita-padya' or poem of a court poet. It is engraved on the same pillar on which No. 69 is inscribed.

B. E. F. Vol. IV. p. 953—954, No. XVIII B.

No. 129.

La-ṭho Silver plate Inscription.

It simply contains the words 'Śrī Vanāntareśvara', apparently the god to whom the plate was dedicated (La-ṭho is in the district of Quang-Nam)

B. E. F., Vol. XI, p. 471, No. 5

No. 130.

La-ṭho Silver jug Inscription.

It contains the following Sanskrit śloka.

वनान्तरेश्वरायास्मै श्रीमते दिव्यकीर्त्तये ।
चम्पापुरपतिः रौप्यं कलशं श्रद्धयात्मनः ॥

"I, the king of Champā (dedicate) this silver jug to the Majestic and glorious Vanāntareśvara with devotion."

B. E. F., Vol. XI. p. 472, No. 6.

Remarkable Books on Ancient India.

THE INDIAN COLONY OF SIAM.

BY

Prof. PHANINDRA NATH BOSE M.A., Prof. of History, Viswabharti, Santiniketan, together with a Foreward by Dr. P. C. Bagchi M. A., with 6 plates.

(Cloth Bound with gold letters.) 1927 Price Rs. 3-8-0.

"We in India are quite in dark as to the extent and greatness of that *Greater India* which had been established outside India by the brave and adventurous sons of India in the days of yore. In the present book, the author attempts to show how an Indian Colony had been established in Siam, and how even at the present day, the culture and civilisation of India survives in the kingdom of Siam."

CONTENTS

Sources of Siamese History—European travellers and writers of Siam—The colonisation of Siam—The Dynasty of Sukhothai—The kingdom of Ayuthia—The Dynasty of Bangkok—Monuments of Siam—Religion of Siam—Kingship in Siam—Literature in Siam—Appendix—Kings of Siam—Bibliography—An Indian Festival in Siam—Coronation of the Siamese king.

ANCIENT INDIAN TRIBES

BY

BIMALA CHURN Law M.A., B L., Ph. D. Sir Asutosh Mookerjee Gold Medalist, Calcutta University; Fellow, Royal

Historical Society: Corporate member of the American Oriental Society, Author, of Several works. With 5 plates.

(Cloth Bound with gold letters) Price Rs. 3-8-0.

"The present vol. deals with the five tribes, the Kasis, the Kosalas, the Assakas, the Magadhas, the Bhojas who played an important part in the history of Ancient India. The author has collected materials from the original works, Sanskrit, Pali, and Prakrit. Some scholars have dealt with the history of these tribes but the present treatment is quite different. The learned author has succeded in bringing together many new materials from Pali books and has presented the solid facts."

"Dr. B. C. Law's work on "Ancient Tribes of India" is marked by his well known qualities of thoroughness in the collection of material, and skill in its effective presentation. Historians of Indian politics, economics & society will find in it many valuable in the collection & evalvations of evidence" *Prof. A. B. Kieth M. A. Edinburgh.*

"It is most useful to have the widely scattered information thus gathered together in one volume." *Prof. E. J. Rapson, M. A., Cambridge.*

"Dr. B. C. Law's latest work entitled "Ancient Tribes of India" which constitutes a very valuable contribution to Indian History by filling up a gap in our knowledge of one of its important parts. Students of Indian History are indebted to Dr. Law for his researches in these untrodden fields which he had made his own, the history of those small states and peoples which made such important contribution to the general life and civilisation of India." *Dr. Radhakumud Mookerji, M. A., P. R. S., Ph. D. Lucknow.*

"......His information relates to the kings, their wars, their religions, educational, social and industrial life of the peoples and also geographical location & expansion. In some places the picture based on original records becomes very realisation',—*Bombay Chronical, 6-3 27.*

"...(Dr. Law) has maintained in this book on the spirit of original research. He has stopped with a careful collection and correct presentation of materials delineating the different aspects of life and history of the tribes he dealt with here but has refrained from building up doubtful theories and hypothosis from these" "*Forward 23-1-27.*"

PRINCIPLES OF INDIAN
Silpasastra.

Together With the Text of MAYASASTRA by Prof. PHANINDRA NATH BOSE, M. A. of Visvabharati University. Together with a foreword by Dr. JAMES, H. COUSINS, D. Lit. 1927.

(Cloth Bound with gold letters) Price Rs. 3-8-0.

OPINIONS

"Prof. Bose surveys the origin of Silpa (i.e., architecture, sculpture and painting), native text books on these arts, their principles and æsthetic standards, the materials and measurements of images, the beginnings of Hindu images, the traditional conventions as regards their postures, ornaments and decorations, general rules for building houses and temples and principles of painting with a brief list of the most important monuments of Indian Art, to which is added as an appendix the text of Mayaśāstra a sanskrit text on the proportions of images etc. The book on the whole is sound and will be useful as a general introduction to the study of the subject." "*Luzac's Book Review.*"

"Prof. Bose's chapters on the principles of Indian Art the Pratimalakshnam are very interesting. The main principles of Indian architecture, Sculpture and painting have all been dealt with in the later chapters, and every one interested in the History of Indian Art has a store of imformation in this little book" *"Journal of Mythic Society."*

"The author deserves grateful congratulations of all lovers of Ancient India for placing the Maya Sastra within their reach and for the first time attempting a systematic study of the principles of Indian painting and of collating them from ancient literature. The book is one which the reading public thinks to be long overdue and we are giad to see that some of the theories put forward by the author deserves a very special commendation." *"Mahabodhi Journal."*

"Prof. Bose's Principles of Indian Silpasastra is a most interesting presentation in concise form of the views of the mediaeval Silpasastrin's on the canons of sculpture and painting and ou architecture. Apart from its value as an introduction to the detailed study of those obscure and badly preserved works the Silpasastras it contains much that is valuable to all those concerned with Sanskrit literature in general, who will find in it satisfactory elucidation of many technical matters of which the lexica offer no ad equate account." *"Dr. A. B. Kieth M. A."*

THE PHILOSOPHY OF VAISNAVA RELIGION.

(With special reference to the Krishnite and Gaurangite Cults)

BY

Prof. GIRINDRA NARAYAN MALLIK M. A. B. L., of

Commilla Victoria College. (Copies Limited to 450 only for sale.)

(Cloth Bound with gold letters) 1927. Price Rs. 8-0-0

"In this treatise I have endeavoured to give a faithfull exposition of the principles of Vaisnava Philosophy, with special reference to the Bhagvata Cult and Gourangism. In the lines adopted to the method of western speculative thought." (Preface.)

Contents.

INTRODUCTION.

What do we understand by philosophy—Is there any necessity for a philosophy of Vaisnava Religion—The fundamental Doctrines common to the systems of Indian Philosophy—Topics for discussion in the present treatise—

BOOK I.

Sources of knowledge—Authoritativeness of the Vedas Supreme authoritativeness of Bhagavata—Importance popularity, and contents of Bhagavata.

BOOK II.

Problem of the Absolute—The concepts of Advaya Jñana Tattwa—The concept of Bhagavan-The concept of Brahman-The concept of Paramātma.

BOOK III.

The concept of Kṛṣṇa as the absolute—The principle of Radha—Meaning of Lila—Jiva or Individual soul—The doctrine of Maya—Relation between the Absolute (Bhagawan) and Individual soul (Jiva)—The Problem of Creation—The Cult of Guranga—

BOOK IV.

The Cult of Bhakti and the Summumbonum—Relation between the cult of Bhakti and other cults—Excellence of the

Bhakti Cult and Jiva's proneness thereto—Two stages of Bhakti—(a) injunctory (b) Raganuga or the flowing current of devotion. Summumbonum—different theories about it—The Highest Good or Summumbonum in the Vaisnava System—Definite character and content of Prema Bhakti—The Summumbonum—Place of morality in the system of Vaisnava Philosophy.

JAINA JATAKAS

or Lord Rishabh's Purvabhavas.

Being an ENGLISH TRANSLATION of Book I Canto I of Hemacandra's Trishashti-śalākā-purushacaritra, originally translated for the first time by Prof. Amulyacharan Vidyabhushana, revised and edited with notes, historical introduction, life of Sri Hemachandra, Jain cosmography etc. by Prof. Banarsi Das Jain M.A. Printed on best paper, cloth bound with gold letters. 1925. Rs. 4-8-0.

"The work, as its name implies, contains the history of sixty-three Salakapurushas or eminent persons, i.e., historical heroes of the Jain Religion. They are 24 Tirthankaras, 12 Cakravartins, 9 Vasudevas, 9 Baladevas, and 9, Prativasudevas."

The present part Jaina Jataka is not a narrative alone, but it also forms a good exposition of the tenets of Jaina Religion. Jaina Jatakas describes alone, what sort of food is acceptable to a Jain monk, advantages of practising virtues, four ways of practising virtues, the country of Uttara kuru, doctrines of the Carvaka or materialistic school and its refutation, the doctrines of momentariness or the Kashanika Vada of the Buddhists and its refutation, the doctrine of Maya and Advaitabada and its refutation. Ten grades of various class of gods, miseries of the world, Labdhis or Supernatural powers.

THE DATHAWAMSA

OR

A History of the Tooth-relic of the Buddha.

Original Pali text in Devanagri ch. edited and translated into English with notes, intro. etc., by Dr. Bimalacharan Law, Ph. D., M. A., B. L., Fellow of the Royal Historical Society translator and writer of many Buddhist Books, together with a foreward by Dr. William Stede, Ph. D., Joint-Editor, P.T.S. Dictionary. Printed on best ivory paper, cloth bound with gold letters. 1924. Price Rs. 4-0-0.

The Dathavamsa is an important contribution to the history of Pali-Buddhist Literature. It is an historical record of the incidents connected with the tooth-relic of the Buhdha. It is as important as the Mahavamsa and the Dipavamsa. The History of Ceylon would be incomplete without it. The work besides its historical value as an early document of the Ecclesia Buddhica, is remarkable because it shows us Pali as a Medium of Epic Poetry. Every Buddhist and Research Scholar ought to read this book once."

The Dathavamsa, one of the chronicles of Ceylon, has no· yet well attracted the attention of scholars. It ought to be widely read. It records the traditional history of the tooth-relic of the Buddha. In editing and translating this text Dr. Law has taken much pains and he has given valuable interpretation of all the important terms and passages occuring in the text. Dr. Law's translation is literal and impressive." *Mahabodhi Journal.*
